The Company and the Shogun

COLUMBIA STUDIES IN INTERNATIONAL AND GLOBAL HISTORY
Matthew Connelly and Adam McKeown, Series Editors

The idea of "globalization" has become a commonplace, but we lack good histories that can explain the transnational and global processes that have shaped the contemporary world. Columbia Studies in International and Global History will encourage serious scholarship on international and global history with an eye to explaining the origins of the contemporary era. Grounded in empirical research, the titles in the series will also transcend the usual area boundaries and will address questions of how history can help us understand contemporary problems, including poverty, inequality, power, political violence, and accountability beyond the nation-state.

Cemil Aydin, *The Politics of Anti-Westernism in Asia: Visions of World Order in Pan-Islamic and Pan-Asian Thought*

Adam M. McKeown, *Melancholy Order: Asian Migration and the Globalization of Borders*

Patrick Manning, *The African Diaspora: A History Through Culture*

James Rodger Fleming, *Fixing the Sky: The Checkered History of Weather and Climate Control*

Steven Bryan, *The Gold Standard at the Turn of the Twentieth Century: Rising Powers, Global Money, and the Age of Empire*

Heonik Kwon, *The Other Cold War*

Samuel Moyn and Andrew Sartori, eds., *Global Intellectual History*

The Company and the Shogun

THE DUTCH ENCOUNTER WITH TOKUGAWA JAPAN

Adam Clulow

Columbia University Press
New York

Columbia University Press
Publishers Since 1893
New York   Chichester, West Sussex
cup.columbia.edu
Copyright © 2014 Columbia University Press
Paperback edition, 2016
All rights reserved

Library of Congress Cataloging-in-Publication Data
Clulow, Adam.
The company and the shogun: The Dutch encounter with
Tokugawa Japan / Adam Clulow.
pages cm. —(Columbia studies in international and global history)
Includes bibliographical references and index.
ISBN 978-0-231-16428-3 (cloth : alk. paper)—ISBN 978-0-231-16429-0
(pbk. : alk. paper)—ISBN 978-0-231-53573-1 (e-book)
1. Nederlandsche Oost-Indische Compagnie—History. 2. Japan—Commerce—
Netherlands—History. 3. Netherlands—Commerce—Japan—History.
4. Japan—History—Tokugawa period, 1600–1868. I. Title.

HF483.E6C58   2014
382.09492'052—dc23   2013019450

Cover design by Julia Kishnirsky
Cover artwork: Merchant Ship of the Dutch East India Company, 1782.
Nagasaki School, published by Toshimaya. Hand-coloured woodblock
print. 65 x 58 cm. Courtesy of Bonhams Picture Library

CONTENTS

ACKNOWLEDGMENTS

In a decade since I first began work on this project, I have accumulated a number of scholarly and personal debts that I can never hope to repay. My career as a Japanese historian began, quite unexpectedly, when after completing my first degree in South Africa, I was awarded a *Monbukagakushō* scholarship to study in Japan. As the program had only just extended to South Africa, which had as yet no Japanese language programs, I traveled to Niigata University, my designated host institution, knowing no Japanese and without the slightest background in East Asian history. For these reasons, I am enormously grateful to all my teachers at Niigata University who enabled me first to find my footing and later to complete my master's degree. My thanks go especially to Yoshii Kenichi, who agreed to take on such a plainly underqualified student, and to Igor Saveliev, who was a constant source of support and encouragement, but also to Imura Tetsuo, Itō Rei, the inimitable Nakamura-*sensei*, Furamaya Tadao, and many others that I cannot name here.

This project first took tentative form during my doctoral studies at Columbia University, where I owe special thanks to my adviser, David Lurie, who took on a project very distant from his own work, but proved in every way the ideal academic mentor and who remains to this day my

viii ACKNOWLEDGMENTS

model for how to treat students. Carol Gluck, whose intellectual energy and organizational drive has been so central to the success of Columbia's Japanese history program, was equally supportive and I benefited as well from numerous discussions with Henry Smith, Greg Pflugfelder, and other Columbia faculty. Bob McCaughey sparked my interest in maritime history and, to my great benefit, drew first my research and later my teaching slowly out to sea. Lauren Benton, who generously agreed to serve on my dissertation committee, challenged me to think in new ways about legal history and her work and insights have shaped my research. I shared my time first at Columbia and later in Japan, with a group of scholars and friends who made the long hours of research and training an unexpected pleasure. Although I cannot name them all, I am especially grateful to Colin Jaundrill, Chelsea Foxwell, Reto Hofmann, Federico Marcon, Mathew Thompson, Ariel Fox, Steve Wills, Dennis Frost, Joy Kim, and Chad Diehl for their friendship and company.

Much of the research for this project was conducted at the Historiographical Institute at the University of Tokyo, to which I have returned on regular occasions. The field of Japanese-Dutch relations (*nichiran kankei*) relies on the tireless work of Matsui Yōko, Matsukata Fuyuko, and the staff of the Overseas Material Sections, who have taken on the onerous task of editing the diaries of the Dutch *opperhoofden* in Japan, and my research would not have been possible without everything they have done. They have also made each of my stays at the institute a pleasure and have generously made time to offer advice on a host of issues. It was my great privilege to work closely with Professor Matsukata on the translation of part of her pioneering monograph, and I learned more from this than I can say. At Tokyo University, Oka Mihoko, Yukitake Kazuhiro, Katō Eiichi, Haneda Masashi, Gonoi Takashi, Yamamoto Hirofumi, and the staff of the institute's library all helped me in a range of different ways while Ohashi Akiko, as she has done for so many visiting fellows, turned our shared office into far more than just a space for research. Nagazumi Yōko, the great historian of the Dutch in Japan, graciously agreed to meet with me and offered a range of insights into my work. I am also grateful to Igawa Kenji, who has helped me navigate the difficult terrain of seventeenth-century sources, and to Gotō Atsushi for his tireless assistance in fielding a seemingly endless sequence of translation-related queries.

My research was made possible by a Japan Foundation doctoral fellowship, which enabled me to spend a year in Japan. After I returned to the United States, the American Council of Learned Societies provided me with crucial writing time via a dissertation completion fellowship and subsequently an early career fellowship. A second fellowship from the Japan Foundation enabled me to return to Japan for three months in late 2009 to collect the last remaining sources for this project.

Over the years, I have made numerous visits to the Netherlands, where I received guidance and support from Cynthia Viallé, Willem Boot, Atsushi Ota, Femme Gaastra, and others. Special mention must be made of Leonard Blussé, the towering figure in my field, whose intellectual contribution and unrivaled production of source materials has transformed the way all of us do research. In all of our meetings, whether in Japan, the Netherlands, or the United States, he has pushed me to rethink my ideas while always inspiring me to go back to the archives with renewed enthusiasm. Although I was never part of the TANAP program, I have benefitted greatly from its reinvigoration of the field and from the steady stream of excellent monographs that it has produced. In the Netherlands my particular thanks must go to Nadia Kreeft, who visited the National Archives in The Hague numerous times on my behalf to scan and copy long lists of materials for this project, while also offering invaluable aid whenever I became stuck with a translation.

Monash University, which I joined in 2008, has provided an enormously collegial and highly supportive environment within which to complete research. All four of my heads of department, Barbara Caine, Mark Peel, Christina Twomey, and Al Thomson, generously allowed me time off teaching for research and writing while a very welcome sabbatical, coupled with generous research funding, in the second half of 2012 enabled the completion of this book. Bain Attwood worked tirelessly not only to safeguard my research time but also that of all junior scholars in the department. He took the time to read and offer tremendously valuable comments on the full draft of my manuscript as well. I thank all of my colleagues, many of whom have read chapters or listened to presentations related to this book, for their ongoing support, but especially Ernest Koh, Seamus O'Hanlon, Michael Hau, David Garrioch, Jane Drakard, Clare Monagle, and Susie Protschky. David Chandler, one of the preeminent historians of Southeast Asia, read the full manuscript and improved it greatly with his suggestions.

During my many years of research, I have discussed this work with a range of scholars who have all contributed valuable suggestions. These include Peter Shapinsky, who offered astute comments on my chapters on VOC privateering, Reinier Hesselink, Peter Borschberg, Martine van Ittersum, Ron Toby, Patrizia Carioti, Timon Screech, Stephen Turnbull, Kate Nakai, Robert Hellyer, Daphon Ho, Arano Yasunori and others. Jack Wills, who pioneered the study of VOC diplomacy, read drafts of some of my chapters and was always willing to share his encyclopedic knowledge of European expansion into Asia. I left each of our meetings with fresh insights and a long list of new sources to consider. The editors of *Japanese Studies*, the *Bulletin of Portuguese-Japanese Studies,* and *Itinerario* generously gave permission for those sections of this work that had previously been published in these journals to be included here.

I am especially grateful to Adam McKeown who steered this project through from rough idea to final publication. I first met Adam while I will still living in Japan in 2001 and was delighted to find he had subsequently moved to Columbia. I owe my interest in global history to him and my work has been shaped in more ways than I can list by his suggestions and insights. He encouraged me to think about placing this book in a global history series and shepherded it through the various stages. I also thank Anna Routon, my indefatigable editor at the press, Whitney Johnson and the two readers, who offered both astute comments and valuable correctives. Tonio Andrade, who waived his anonymity, produced page after page of helpful suggestions that greatly strengthened the final manuscript. As should be clear from the numerous references scattered throughout this study, his scholarship and especially his two superb books, on the company's colonization of Taiwan, and more recently on the military campaign that ended the Dutch presence on that island, have greatly influenced my own work while providing a template for the sort of history, engaging, provocative, but always grounded in meticulous research, that I aspire (if never with his measure of success) to write.

My wife Anna has lived with this project for year after year and has supported it in countless ways. My greatest thanks go to my parents, whose love, support, and encouragement have always sustained me. They endured as I, the youngest of their three sons, disappeared off to Japan, the United States, and then Australia for years on end, and have shown a remarkable willingness to hop on planes headed for the far-flung places that the life of an academic has taken me. This book would not have been possible without everything they had done for me, and I dedicate it to them.

ARCHIVAL SOURCES

The Dutch East India Company archives (*De archieven van de Verenigde Oostindische Compagnie*) are located in the National Archives in The Hague. Sources marked with VOC come from this archive and can be consulted using inventory 1.04.02. I have also relied heavily on the archive of the Dutch East India Company factory in Japan (*Archief van de Nederlandse Factorij in Japan te Hirado en te Deshima*), which is also located in the National Archives. Source marked with NFJ come from this archive and can be consulted using inventory 1.04.21. Unless otherwise indicated, all translations are my own. Whenever possible I have attempted to supply folio references or to indicate that a record is unfolioed. Dutch names from this period have multiple spellings. I have made use of the most common spelling in the main text, while maintaining the variations as they appear in the original documents in the notes.

Map 0.1. The Company's area of operations in Southeast and East Asia

Map 0.2. Tokugawa Japan

The Company and the Shogun

INTRODUCTION

TAMING THE DUTCH

In October 1627 a grand embassy arrived in Edo, the Tokugawa government's sprawling political capital. It had been sent by the Dutch East India Company, which was rapidly emerging as the most influential European enterprise in Asia. At the front of the procession borne high on the shoulders of six men in a special palanquin was Pieter Nuyts, recent graduate from Leiden University, extraordinary councilor of the Indies, and now special ambassador to the shogun of Japan. He was followed by an impressive retinue, almost three hundred strong, of Dutch soldiers, heavily armed samurai, liveried pages, translators, grooms, and dozens of servants. Carefully planned and enormously expensive, the 1627 embassy was intended to reflect the company's growing confidence, and it came equipped not only with a rich array of gifts but also a list of demands for the shogun.

Just over a month later, Nuyts prepared to flee Edo in the middle of the night, his embassy summarily rejected without ever seeing the shogun, his gifts brushed aside, his demands left unheard. This time no retinue gathered to accompany the ambassador on his journey. With no official permission to depart, Nuyts was only able to assemble a handful of bearers to carry his palanquin through the Edo's darkened streets.[1] Underway at last after hours of waiting, they made it only as far as the end of the road before they were halted by the cry of a local watchman. Startled by the command, the bearers abruptly dropped their burden and scattered, leaving the ambassador marooned in the middle of the street.

Nuyts's embassy may have been a particularly spectacular failure, but his more general experience was in no way unique. Indeed, many other European representatives in Asia found themselves in a similar position, isolated and shorn of any recognition of their status or authority. Individuals like Pieter Nuyts occupied a precarious position on the frontline of a global encounter between Europe and Asia that had commenced in 1497 when Vasco da Gama's small fleet opened up new trade routes to India. Over the next two hundred years these routes gradually lengthened until they encompassed the globe and thickened until they became reliable highways for long-distance commerce. After da Gama's pioneering voyage, tens of thousands of Europeans, first the Portuguese, but later the Spanish, Dutch, and English, moved into Asian waters. There they came into contact with a series of powerful states equipped with military, economic, and cultural resources far exceeding those wielded by the most dominant regimes in Europe. The result was scenes like that in Japan in 1627 as Europeans scrambled to find a place on the fringes of Asian orders.

This study examines one such encounter between Europeans and a powerful Asian state. It focuses on the interaction between the Dutch East India Company (Vereenigde Oost-Indische Compagnie or VOC), arguably the most formidable of all European overseas organizations active in Asia in the seventeenth century, and the Tokugawa regime, which maintained a tight grip over the Japanese archipelago for more than two hundred and fifty years. Through an analysis of key moments in this engagement, it aims to ask a series of questions about what is sometimes called the first age of globalization: What was the nature and extent of European power in early modern Asia? How did Europeans manage their encounters with Asian states like Tokugawa Japan and what place did they find in local political orders? Finally, how does an examination of the politics of encounter alter our understanding of what has traditionally been termed the "rise of Europe"?

THE GREAT DIVERGENCE

Da Gama was of course not the only mariner to venture forth in search of new lands in this period. Five years before his departure, another expedition dispatched by Portugal's more powerful neighbor, Spain, and placed under the command of Christopher Columbus, had left European shores in search of its own passage to India. Rather than converging on the subcontinent, these two fleets headed off in opposite directions, encountered disparate civilizations, and, in the end, set in motion two very different trajectories of European expansion. Unlike their counterparts in Asia, Europeans traveling west were able to conquer vast empires; subjugate people, cultures, and territory; and permanently transform the political and social landscape of the continents they discovered. Despite this striking divergence, a split that only widened over the subsequent centuries, the Columbian experience has escaped geographical boundaries to emerge as the dominant symbol of European expansion in the early modern period.

When he arrived back from his first voyage, Columbus reported that he had "discovered many islands, thickly peopled, of which I took possession in the name of our most illustrious Monarch."[2] His statement, with all its characteristic confidence, describes the key act of westward expansion, the ceremony of possession.[3] The first of Columbus's many such declarations took place on 12 October 1492 when, after a long voyage of thirty-three days, the admiral stepped onto the island of Guanahani carrying a royal flag. With his witnesses clustered around him and the distant bulk of his ships looming in the background, Columbus took "possession of the said island for the King and for the Queen . . . making the declarations that are required."[4] In the typically triumphalist depictions of this famous scene that still adorn many public buildings, the admiral is shown armed with a sword and banner claiming foreign lands on behalf of his Spanish masters as the indigenous population, both terrified and awed, huddles in the background offering no opposition.

Over the next decades, these ceremonies of possession were replicated again and again, laying the basis for an empire that stretched first along the coasts before pushing steadily inland. The rapid pace of European expansion is conventionally attributed to two key advantages that combined to push out the boundaries of influence and, in time, reorder the American continents. Historians have focused first on a fearsome set of technologies—iron weapons capable of slicing through cloth and flesh, firearms that could kill from a distance, and steel armor able to protect the wearer from harm—brought by Europeans and deployed with frightening effect.[5] In isolation these could be formidable, but together they proved almost unstoppable, capable of turning battles against far greater hosts. Just a few decades after the encounter on Guanahani, Hernán Cortés famously brought down the Aztec empire with a total force of just two thousand well-armed Spanish troops. His achievement was matched by a much smaller contingent of just 167 solders under the command of Francisco Pizarro that marched into Central America and, winning a series of victories along the way, overthrew the sprawling Incan state.[6] These tools of war were paired with a powerful sense of confidence that, scholars have argued, enabled Europeans to view the New World as a blank page onto which their desires and ambitions could be written.[7] This absolute belief in European superiority was buttressed, rather than undermined, by encounters with new civilizations, and it drove small, outnumbered groups of adventurers to lay claim to expansive tracts of land and declare war on powerful indigenous states.

In recent decades the triumphal narrative that once celebrated European explorers and settlers as pioneers of civilization has been largely silenced—at least in academic writing—and replaced with a new understanding of the destructive consequences of the Columbian experience. Yet, despite this shift, the basic outlines of the confident, conquering European remain largely unchanged.[8] While expansion westward, with its dramatic stories of conquest and subjugation, continues to occupy a central place in scholarship, considerably less attention has been paid to how Europeans fared in Asia and particularly to how they dealt with the states they found there. As a result, the familiar image of the European arriving on distant shores armed with technological advantages and an absolute belief in his own superiority is sometimes simply lifted from the American context and applied without much modification to Asia. In this way Columbus's shadow looms large over world history, undermining attempts to better understand the limits of European power in early modern Asia.[9]

Historians searching for evidence of European strength in Asia have turned to a familiar pairing. One group has argued that military technology, especially the gunned ship, transformed the politics of Asian seas, while a second has looked to cultural assumptions by suggesting that disparate encounters were underpinned by a basic confidence that enabled Europeans to silence their Asian interlocutors.[10] The latter is of course the logic of Edward Said's groundbreaking study of orientalism, which, though it focuses on a later period, has been projected back as historians, particularly those interested in establishing connections with modern empire, have reached across the historical divide to pull the politics of high imperialism into earlier centuries.[11] The rush of studies that have followed Said's pioneering work take the idea of the confident European secure in the knowledge of his own superiority as their most basic premise, while aiming simultaneously to unpick the internal logic of orientalist discourse. One figure to receive particular attention is Thomas Roe, an English ambassador sent to India in the seventeenth century, whose diaries provide evidence of what Jyotsna Singh calls the "colonizing imagination" that enabled Europeans to order the region and its people long before the age of territorial empire.[12]

When ideas about technology and cultural confidence merge, they create a notion readily visible in textbooks that 1500 represented a crucial historical moment when a confident, well-armed Europe surged ahead both in the New World and Asia, thereby creating the modern world. The idea of a European watershed finds one of its clearest expressions in a 1998 work by the eminent historian David Landes, *The Wealth and Poverty of Nations*.[13] For Landes, Columbus's and da Gama's voyages mark the onset of the modern age as Europeans, inheritors of a more vigorous culture, moved to confront and eventually overwhelm more static civilizations like Ming China, which "lacked range, focus, and above all, curiosity."[14] The theme of the work is one of inevitable European mastery organized around a single imperial time line.

But when we look more closely at the concrete details of the encounter between Europe and Asia, it becomes difficult to sustain any notion that 1500 marked a clear turning point. While there were occasional episodes of technological dominance and irresistible confidence, these cannot be strung together into a wider pattern of European power. This central fact has been recognized by a group of scholars who have argued against what Tonio Andrade, a leading representative of this revisionist approach, calls the "1492 Schema" of history that seeks to equate the voyages of exploration with the "rise of the west."[15] Working in a number of different fields, they have combined to batter away at this schema from a variety of angles.[16] Historians like Kenneth Swope, Peter Lorge, and Sun Laichen have argued against the excessive focus on European technological innovation by pointing to the existence of an Asian military revolution that paralleled developments in Europe.[17] Other scholars such as Leonard Blussé and Tonio Andrade himself have convincingly demonstrated the Asian roots of European success, showing how in places like Taiwan or Batavia a thin overlay of European structures served to conceal a far more substantial Asian base, while William Thompson and G. V. Scammell have focused on the key role played by local allies in facilitating European expansion.[18] They have been joined by a group of innovative economic historians who, contesting long-held views about comparative levels of development, have combined to mount a particularly vigorous attack on the "1492 Schema" with scholars such as Kenneth Pomeranz, R. Bin Wong, Andre Gunder Frank, and others arguing that the time line of European ascendancy should be pushed back beyond 1800.[19]

The result of such studies, of which only a handful has been mentioned here, has been to call into question any notion of a European watershed in the early modern period. Across the region the more common narrative was one of containment, as Europeans found that even the sharpest of weapons could be blunted or, as was the case in Japan, stripped away from them. In the absence of real leverage, they were forced to rely on negotiation, petition, and appeal to carve out what was at best a limited space for their operations within an extant political order. The protracted and often desperate scramble to secure a place in Asia had the added effect of undermining any illusion of superiority. In this way, European expansion in this period was characterized more by a sense of anxiety, which came to permeate a range of Asian interactions, than by confidence.

The key variable responsible for triggering an immediate divergence from the Columbian experience was the presence of Asian states, formidable political actors used to dealing with foreigners and fully capable of resisting their demands. From the moment of first contact, when his expedition arrived in the port of Calicut on the west coast of India in 1498, da Gama struggled to manage such encounters. Unable to bend the ruler of Calicut to his will, the Portuguese explorer was forced into the position of supplicant, appearing in court armed with diplomatic letters, rather than markers of possession, and eager to negotiate.[20] In the process, da Gama inaugurated a pattern that would be repeated as Europeans pushed deeper into Asia. Indeed, if the ceremony of possession stands at the heart of European expansion into the Americas, then its equivalent in Asia was the embassy dispatched to a local sovereign in order to bargain for concessions, and the sharp difference between the two acts highlights the divergent nature of the European experience.

While da Gama approached Calicut with considerable caution, its ruler was in fact a relatively minor potentate with no great influence, and within a few decades Europeans were thrust into contact with far more impressive states like Ming China, Mughal India, and Tokugawa Japan, which occupied central positions in an increasingly interconnected global economy. The size and power of such polities filled Europeans with trepidation. Writing about China, one author cautioned his readers that words alone could not convey the richness of the country: "I hereby give readers a necessary warning by which they can conjecture the greatness of the things of China, viz.—that whereas distant things often sound greater than they really are, this is clean contrary (because China is much more than it sounds). . . . This must be seen and not heard, because hearing it is nothing in comparison with seeing it."[21]

If we are to look for one representative to stand in for European expansion in early modern Asia, then we might find it in the unlikely figure of Jonathan Swift's intrepid mariner, Lemuel Gulliver, who made his debut in 1726.[22] Unlike other fictional castaways, most notably Robinson Crusoe, who carved out their own kingdoms, Gulliver runs into a succession of states and rulers.[23] In each case he is left impotent and uncertain, struggling to manage his encounter. In the kingdom of Lilliput, Swift's hero stumbles upon a realm populated by diminutive inhabitants less than one tenth his stature. Despite his size, Gulliver quickly discovers that he has no real influence. Rather than setting himself up as a godlike ruler, he is forced to render military service and to prostrate himself before the local monarch.[24]

On the island of Brobdingnag, Gulliver finds himself in a society of giants in which he is threatened by even the tiniest of the creatures. To survive, he becomes a royal plaything compelled to perform endlessly before the members of the court. Faced by the Houyhnhnms, a highly intelligent horselike species that he encounters in his final voyage, Gulliver loses all faith in the power of European civilization and resolves to abandon his homeland altogether. In each interaction Gulliver is isolated, stripped of the power that other explorers wield so confidently, and rendered desperately uncertain. In response, he is forced to adapt by declaring himself "most humble creature and vassal" in order to claim a position on the edges of more powerful societies.[25] In the end his transformation is so complete that he passes through civilizational barriers and emerges on the other side utterly changed. When compelled to leave his Houyhnhnm master, Gulliver kneels "to kiss his hoof" in a final act of submission to a superior society.[26]

Although of course fictional, the basic pattern of Gulliver's encounters would have been a familiar one for many European agents in Asia who found themselves similarly trapped in strange lands with no real power. Twin questions, one of interaction and one of adaptation, bring us to the heart of their experience. First, what was the nature of the encounter between European enterprises and Asian states? The goal here is not to answer the now dated call for autonomous history by writing Europeans out of the picture—although they were often marginal—but rather to document the precise nature of their engagements with the most important political units in Asia.[27] To do so requires a recognition of the often formidable tools brought by Europeans, but also an examination of how these were actually deployed on the ground.

In the decades since scholars first started to reassess the nature of the European presence in Asia, two models capable of providing a broad framework within which to consider interaction have emerged. Both emphasize the limited nature of European incursions into Asia, but they do so in very different ways. Arguing against notions of a unitary "Vasco da Gama epoch" of European hegemony stretching from the moment of first arrival in 1498 to the onset of decolonization in 1945, Holden Furber famously described the early modern period as an "age of partnership" in which close bonds developed between Europeans and their Asian interlocutors.[28] For Furber, this long time span was characterized more by cooperation "than by assertions of power and hostility."[29] The result was to treat Europe's push into Asia as an extended and relatively conflict-free learning process during which both sides drew gradually closer to each other. Furber's approach, with its emphasis on mutual accommodation, lends itself naturally to a *longue durée* style of analysis that considers interaction across multiple decades or even centuries rather than years. One of the more recent of many successor studies to adopt this framework examines the Dutch presence in Siam across the period from 1604 to 1765.[30] Although individual episodes are treated as important milestones, the overall emphasis is on the steady accretion of knowledge over time, a process that was only broken by the advent of industrial imperialism in the early nineteenth century.

While recognizing its importance in changing the terms of the historical debate, some scholars have criticized Furber's work for offering an overly rosy view of relations characterized by mutual understanding and shared structures.[31] In 1990, Sanjay Subrahmanyam challenged this notion of an extended partnership by highlighting the underlying violence of the period and the incessant conflicts that took place between Europeans and Asian rulers, officials, or merchants. His work described the period more darkly as an "age of contained conflict" in which there were "numerous trials of strength, mutual probings for chinks in the armour, and repeated localized conflicts."[32] Unlike the sweeping studies that make use of the "age of partnership" framework, this model proves best suited to a different kind of analysis oriented around highly detailed accounts of individual conflicts.[33] Although the focus is on the breakdown of relations, Subrahmanyam's notion of a period marked by regular clashes incorporates a kind of learning process, but a far more violent one in which accommodation was reached more often because the weaker side retreated than because the two parties met in the middle. In this way these conflicts can be seen as something more than anomalous moments when otherwise functional arrangements broke down. To the contrary, such skirmishes were, in many cases, directly responsible for creating a system capable of regulating relations between European enterprises and Asian states. They were, in other words, productive, functioning to set the rules for subsequent interactions.

The emphasis on conflict and its productive capacity leads in turn to a second question about the nature of the European response and particularly to a focus on adaptation. Like Gulliver, Europeans in Asia were compelled to shift position, make concessions, or, at times, wholly reinvent themselves to secure a place on the fringes of powerful local states. This process of adjustment and accommodation was central to the European experience in early modern Asia, but a focus on it runs against one of the most well-established conventions in Asian history, that is, the overwhelming emphasis on understanding how Asian states either adapted to claim a place in a Western-dominated world order in the nineteenth century or succumbed to a colonial embrace. And yet, however important, this later period was, in the final assessment, relatively brief. The result of work by Pomeranz and other economic historians has been to show that Asian states were far more powerful for far longer than previously imagined and to reveal the temporal limitations of European dominance. Indeed, it has become increasingly apparent that the default setting for the bulk of recorded history, aside from a clearly bracketed phase in which the tools of industrial imperialism allowed unprecedented expansion, was one in which Asia was paramount.[34] If this is the case, it becomes all the more important to move away from Eurocentric or Americentric versions of history to understand exactly how Europeans adapted to find a place in Asian-dominated political orders. This study aims to contribute to this wider program by considering the Dutch encounter with Japan.

THE COMPANY AND THE SHOGUN

The first VOC ships appeared in Japan in 1609, just as a newly established regime, usually labeled by modern scholars as the Tokugawa Bakufu, was in the process of consolidating its hold over the archipelago. Emerging after a long period of endemic conflict, the system of government crafted by Tokugawa Ieyasu (1543–1616), the last of Japan's three great unifiers, welded a central administration to over two hundred semi-independent domainal lords (daimyo) who were permitted to retain significant autonomy, including the right to maintain their own armies and collect taxes.[35] Refined by Ieyasu's son (Hidetada, 1579–1632) and grandson (Iemitsu, 1604–1651), the Bakufu would, after weathering a period of initial turmoil, remain in place until the second half of the nineteenth century.

As they landed on Japanese soil for the first time, the Dutch found, in stark contrast to nearby China, a government willing, even eager, to engage with them and prepared to allow their representatives access to its political and commercial centers. The subsequent relationship between company and shogun proved remarkably durable, continuing virtually uninterrupted until the VOC collapsed under the weight of its debts in 1795.[36] From 1609 onward, the Dutch operated a permanently staffed base in Japan, first in the domain of Hirado on the northwestern tip of Kyushu and later on the small island of Deshima in Nagasaki harbor.

Although both iterations of the Japan factory, the contemporary term for a trading post, were situated on the western edges of the archipelago in Kyushu, VOC envoys traveled to Edo almost every year, often staying in the city for a number of months before receiving permission to depart. During these visits the Dutch came into regular contact with the shogun as well as the extended apparatus of the Tokugawa state.

Despite its astonishing longevity, the Tokugawa/VOC relationship has, especially in recent years, received comparatively little attention from scholars. This can be partly explained by developments within Tokugawa historiography and is the result of past attempts to over-emphasize the importance of European influence on early modern Japan. In his much-reprinted work, *The Christian Century in Japan, 1549–1650*, Charles Boxer argued that the introduction of Christianity in the sixteenth century by European missionaries had a transformative effect on the country, leading Japanese authorities, who were increasingly fearful of the subversive power of the new religion, to cut off contact with the outside world through the promulgation of the famous maritime restriction edicts of the 1630s.[37] Boxer's study placed Europe at the center of Tokugawa foreign relations and assumed that the near total closure of ties with European overseas enterprises initiated a period of Japanese isolation. This view was decisively challenged in the 1980s by two scholars, Ronald Toby and Arano Yasunori, who demonstrated that Japan remained closely engaged with states in Asia, most notably Korea and the Ryukyu kingdom, long after the advent of Tokugawa maritime restrictions.[38] While their work was remarkably successful in putting Japan back into Asia and proving that links with Europe were not the sum total of foreign policy, an added consequence of Toby and Arano's intervention has been an understandable turn away from a focus on Europeans in Japan.

Those studies that do exist have, with some important exceptions such as work by Reinier Hesselink and Matsukata Fuyoko, traditionally adopted one of two perspectives.[39] The first, particularly favored by Japanese scholars, is a narrow focus on trade. The approach is typified by Ryūto Shimada's work, *The Intra-Asian Trade in Japanese Copper by the Dutch East India Company During the Eighteenth Century*, which, like many recent studies of the VOC more generally, treats it as a purely commercial organization and seeks to understand the nature of Dutch trading networks. The second, perhaps best described as the comprehensive approach, aims to provide a general overview of the company's position in Japan. The most important work in this vein is by the pioneering historian of the Dutch in Japan, Nagazumi Yōko, who separates out the Hirado period (1609–1641) to provide a reasonable focus for a broad-brush analysis that includes discussion of trade, politics, daily life, and a host of other issues.[40] While studies based on these two approaches make an invaluable contribution to understanding the Dutch presence in Japan, neither gets to the central question of the relationship between the company and the Tokugawa regime.

This study seeks to adopt a different approach. Its starting point is to look again at the nature of the organization itself. Although the use of the label *company* to describe the Vereenigde Oost-Indische Compagnie is ubiquitous (and will be employed throughout this study), this apparently straightforward term can in fact be highly misleading. The VOC, which has been called the world's first multinational, did have certain features that made it look much like a modern company, but it also possessed sovereign powers to which even the most formidable Fortune 500 behemoth could never lay claim.[41] Because of this, it can, following Jurrien van Goor, best be described as a hybrid organization that successfully combined the attributes of both corporation and state.[42]

This composite nature can be traced directly back to the company's foundational document, the 1602 charter, and particularly to a single article. Buried among a sequence of dry clauses stipulating the organization's complicated business structure can be found article 35, which gave the VOC sovereign rights of the kind more conventionally monopolized by the state. It stated: "East of the Cape of Good Hope but also in and beyond the straits of Magellan, those of the aforementioned Company shall be allowed to enter into agreements and contracts with princes and potentates in the name of the States-General of the United Netherlands. They may also build fortresses and strongholds, appoint governors, armed forces, officers of justice and officers of other necessary services in order to preserve these places and maintain them in good order."[43] Pulled apart, article 35 described three wide-ranging powers: the right to conduct direct diplomacy with any ruler it might encounter, the right to maintain (and of course deploy) military forces, and the right to seize control of territory (by building fortresses and strongholds). This potent trinity formed the organization's birthright, and, from the moment its first ships appeared in Asian waters, the company made full use thereof.

Of the three powers listed here, there can be no question as to which were most frequently used. Leonard Blussé, the great historian of the VOC, has suggested that the company's entire strategy in Asia hinged on two tools, diplomacy and violence. He describes the shift back and forth between "*schenkagie* (the pursuit of favourable trading conditions through gifts and diplomacy)" and "*conqueste* (the conquest of land or the exaction of favourable trade conditions through the medium of violence)" that came to characterize the organization's operations.[44] Armed with letters and gifts, the leaders of the first Dutch expeditions sought to open direct ties with sovereigns across the region and use these to secure access to diplomatic networks. Although treaties had to be submitted to the States-General, the Dutch parliament, for approval, the great distances separating Europe and Asia meant that the company had what amounted to a free hand to engage in independent diplomacy. Running in parallel with this diplomatic push was an equally vigorous military one. Created by a state that was itself in the midst of a seemingly endless war, the VOC was deeply implicated in violence from the beginning. Dutch fleets attacked Iberian trading networks in Asia, targeted key strongholds like Manila and Melaka, and engaged in wide-scale privateering. Determined to gain access to the most profitable trading networks, the company was equally prepared to turn its guns against local rivals, firing on shipping belonging to Asian states when officials, denied access to markets, made common cause with their enemies or were seen to have violated perceived contractual rights. In addition to the rights to engage in diplomacy and violence, the VOC also claimed via article 35 the authority to build forts, appoint governors, create legal structures, and establish the full apparatus of government. This was in effect a blank check to establish colonies and it was cashed in places like Amboina, Java, Banda, and Taiwan, where the company acquired its first territorial holdings.

Historians of the VOC sometimes describe a process in which an essentially commercial organization was drawn reluctantly into empire building and gradually transformed in the process.[45] While it is true that the company never possessed a grand design for empire, it was also never just a conglomerate of merchants eager to buy cheaply and sell dearly. A study of the letters written by senior personnel based in

Asia gives little sense that they thought of their employer as a limited organization that should concentrate its attentions purely on trade and avoid other entanglements. Instead, they saw it as a composite body with a route to profit that ran most directly through the expansion of Dutch power in Asia.[46] Although they have perhaps been cited too many times in too many different contexts, the words of Jan Pieterszoon Coen, an early governor-general, remain indicative of the wider attitudes displayed by officials on the frontier: "the Indies trade has to be pursued and maintained under the protection of one's own arms and . . . the weapons must be financed through the profits so earned by trade. In short, trade without war or war without trade cannot be maintained."[47] Rather than a reluctant actor led down a strange route by an uncertain political environment in Asia, the company was, from the beginning, as much a political and military creature as it was an economic one.[48]

It was a feature clearly recognized by its competitors, who saw this as the most important characteristic of the Dutch model for expansion and something that required emulation if they wished to achieve the same measure of success. One of the most revealing assessments of the Dutch template came from the pen of the great seventeenth-century observer of the United Provinces, William Temple:

> The last, I shall mention, is, the mighty advance they have made towards engrossing the whole commerce of the East-Indies, by their successes against the Portuguese, and by their many wars and victories against the natives, whereby they have forced them to treaties of commerce, exclusive to all other nations, and to the admission of Forts to be built upon straits and passes, that command the entrances into the traffic of such places. This has been [achieved] . . . by the conduct and application of the East-India company, who have managed it like a commonwealth, rather than a trade, and thereby raised a State in the Indies, governed indeed by the orders of the company, but otherwise appearing to those nations like a Sovereign State, making war and peace with their greatest Kings, and able to bring to sea forty or fifty men of war, and thirty thousand men at land, by the modestest computations.[49]

We should be careful, therefore, of dismissing the company's use of its sovereign powers as a peripheral activity incidental to the more important business of trade. Instead, the rights granted in article 35 were integral to the Dutch push into Asia.

Officials belonging to Asian states never read the 1602 charter, but they confronted an organization determined to make full use of its provisions. In the seventeenth century the company arrived in dozens of states ranging from tiny port polities to massive empires with clear ideas about its rights and a determination to use its full panoply of powers to achieve its desired ends. The result was often conflict, as local officials pushed back against an aggressive interloper that seemed to have no obvious place in existing diplomatic, political, or commercial circuits.

Such a pattern is immediately evident in Japan where the company arrived with ambitious plans to secure Tokugawa diplomatic recognition (in order to improve its negotiating position), gain control over key trading routes, evict its rivals (most notably the Portuguese), and establish itself as the preeminent maritime power in East Asia. In discussions with Bakufu officials, company agents asserted—after a temporary interlude in which they reached back to Europe for diplomatic legitimacy— the governor-general's rights to dispatch embassies directly to Edo, insisted that they could wage war in the shogun's waters against Japan's most important trading partners, and claimed part of the island of Taiwan for themselves while denying access to Japanese merchants who had sailed there for years. To realize these ambitions, the company was ready to deploy its own weapons, most notably a powerful fleet, but also a versatile language of legal rationalization that was supplied in part by famous scholars such as Hugo Grotius.[50]

Such tactics turned the company into an unruly presence in an increasingly orderly Tokugawa world and brought it into repeated conflict with Japanese authorities. The resultant clashes over diplomacy, violence, and sovereignty, the three powers granted by article 35 of the charter, provide the subject of this book. Like Subrahmanyam, I see this period as an "age of contained conflict" in which interaction was defined not by a relatively harmonious partnership but by a sequence of clashes. Tunneling down through the available sources (both Dutch and Japanese), my aim is to provide detailed case studies of these individual conflicts. In this way the book eschews a more comprehensive approach in favor of a focus on a series of key moments. It is not, in other words, a history of the Dutch in Japan or indeed of VOC trade, which has been covered in considerable detail by a number of different scholars, but rather an analysis of how the company's nature as a hybrid organization played out in the archipelago.[51]

Focusing on these conflicts allows a pivot away from the well-known story of Dutch moderation in Japan. The standard analysis of the Dutch highlights their role as enterprising Protestant merchants interested exclusively in trade and who pursued, in Grant Goodman's words, a "steady and moderate policy" that enabled them—in contrast to their Portuguese rivals who were more concerned with saving souls—to avoid unnecessary clashes with the Japanese regime.[52] In fact a closer look at the first half of the seventeenth century shows that the Dutch in Japan veered precariously from confrontation to confrontation. Whereas VOC records tend to present the Bakufu as a tyrannical regime that persisted in making unreasonable demands, many of the problems that the organization encountered were to a large extent of its own creation, and they stemmed not from shogunal whims but from the company's policies. Far from the meek merchants they are sometimes imagined as, the Dutch were, particularly in the early years of the Japan factory, a violent and disruptive presence in Tokugawa Japan.

In addition to documenting the individual disputes that emerged as a result of the company's insistence on its sovereign prerogatives, I seek to demonstrate that they enduringly shaped the nature of the Dutch presence in Japan. When their first ships appeared in Japanese harbors in 1609, the Dutch did not immediately slot into a fixed position within the Tokugawa order. Rather a final settlement only began to emerge after a series of contained conflicts that prompted the company to abandon its usual prerogatives and remake itself in order to meet Tokugawa expectations. Within the confines of these confrontations, the terms of the relationship between the Bakufu and the VOC first took shape and were subsequently set into what would become their permanent form. As such, these clashes were, to return to an earlier point, essentially productive, although the result was not a mutual convergence on the middle but rather a series of retreats by the weaker party and a shift to new ground.

In each case, the same basic pattern is evident, with initial claims about the company's rights to diplomacy, violence, and sovereignty triggering a sequence of conflicts that were only resolved by VOC withdrawals, concessions, or outright surrender. This is a story of how the Dutch were defeated by an unstable diplomatic narrative that failed to convince Bakufu officials of the governor-general's legitimacy and his right to dispatch embassies; of how they found the use of their most reliable tools, including maritime violence, first curtailed then largely prohibited; and of how they struggled to explain and defend colonial possessions in the shadow of powerful Asian states. The result was that the Dutch were compelled over time to abandon their claims to sovereign powers and to refashion themselves—from subjects of a fictive king to loyal vassals of the shogun, from aggressive pirates to meek merchants, and from insistent defenders of colonial sovereignty to legal subjects of the Tokugawa state. By the end of this process of adaptation, the VOC had assumed a very different form in Japan.

While, in line with Subrahmanyam's model, the broad framework of incessant conflict fits the pattern in other parts of Asia, the situation in Japan was distinct in that these conflicts were almost uniformly resolved in one side's favor. Unlike European relations with other Asian states, there was not much give and take here, with the company discovering again and again how little bargaining power it had in Japan. Rather than mastering Tokugawa Japan, the Dutch were, to put it simply, mastered by it. Not surprisingly, the experience was an unsettling one in which technological advantages were nullified, a legal language that seemed so powerful on paper rendered mute, and the confidence of even the most aggressive of VOC officials profoundly shaken.

To gain some sense of the end result of this process, we can turn back to Gulliver, who alongside his fictional destinations visited one real country. Landing in the port of Shimonoseki on Japan's main island, Gulliver decides "to disguise my country, and call myself an Hollander, because . . . the Dutch were the only Europeans permitted to enter into that kingdom."[53] Travelling to Edo, he observes the Dutch engaged in the *fumi-e*, a ritual trampling of a crucifix required of the shogun's subjects. Rather than being forced into this act of Christian denial by a ruthless despot, they are willing participants, eager to hide any trace of their faith in order to win the shogun's favor. Bound, as Gulliver was himself in past encounters, to a foreign monarch, they compete to prove their allegiance through conspicuous shows of devotion.

Swift was of course describing a fictional encounter, but his account of the Dutch situation in Japan was rooted in historical fact. The exact materials that he read in preparation for this section of the novel remains a matter of debate, but there are some grounds to believe that the author may have been familiar with Engelbert's Kaempfer's *History of Japan*, which finally appeared in print in England in 1727.[54] A German physician who worked in Nagasaki for two years from 1690 to 1692, Kaempfer produced one of the most detailed and widely read accounts of the Dutch situation in Japan. Highly critical of his former employers, Kaempfer condemned them as being too ready to bow to the wishes of a heathen ruler. Perhaps the best-known part of the work is his description of the audience given by the shogun to the head (*opperhoofd*) of the Japan factory:

> As soon as the captain appeared, someone shouted in an exaggeratedly loud voice "oranda kapitan" [Holland captain] to prompt him to step forward and pay his respects. Thereupon he crawled forward on his hands and knees between the place where the presents had been lined up and the high seat of his majesty as far as they motioned him. Crouching on his knees, he bent his head to the floor and then, like a lobster, crawled back in this very same position, without one word being exchanged. This short, miserable procedure is all that there is to this famous audience.[55]

Unable to raise their heads, the Dutch cannot get a clear view of the shogun, who sits at the opposite end of a massive hall, and must crawl away without even sighting the object of their devotion.

While observers like Swift or Kaempfer tended to fixate on the most humiliating details of the *fumi-e* or the shogunal audience, these were only the most visible symbols of the wider relationship. In Japan, the VOC was constrained within a framework of control that was as complete as any wrapped around a European overseas enterprise in Asia. There the Tokugawa regime succeeded in fencing in the company, constraining its activities and transforming it into an obedient servant that was willing to supply the shogun with military service and a steady flow of intelligence concerning events across the world. By the 1630s the company had, in its representative's own words, become "a faithful vassal" of the Tokugawa state, with one governor-general declaring, in a particularly hyperbolic flourish, that he and his subordinates stood ready "to act in the service of the shogun and to preserve the Japanese realm with our last drop of blood."[56]

Language on its own can, of course, be deceptive, and we would be right to be cautious about this kind of overblown rhetoric, which should be familiar to any historian of European expansion more generally. In most cases it served simply to hide a power grab beneath a cloak of local legitimacy. In India, for example, Robert Clive made use of similar rhetoric, when, after his victory at Buxar in 1765, he claimed a position for the English company as the loyal vassal of the Mughal emperor.[57] Despite these and other proclamations, privileges and power flowed to the English, including the great prize of revenue rights to a number of rich Indian provinces, which rescued Clive's employers from dire financial straits. In this case, words about service and vassalage concealed the hollowing out of a once powerful Asian state until it was little more than a brittle shell. In Japan, however, this rhetoric of European subordination functioned quite differently. Here, it was the company and not the Tokugawa state that found itself hollowed out as it was stripped of its ability to act and forced to accept a circumscribed position within the Japanese order. In addition to making declarations of loyalty, the VOC was compelled to actually discharge its duties as vassal, sometimes in extremely disconcerting ways. The most dramatic example of this came in 1638 when the company volunteered to serve the shogun by turning its guns against Christian rebels holed up in a ruined fortress at Shimabara.

This process of containment had important consequences for the VOC, which was never in a position to claim the dominant commercial position it had once sought, but also for Japan itself.[58] The terms of the relationship enabled the Tokugawa state to draw selectively on technology, information, and goods without accepting any of the more damaging side effects that generally accompanied European incursions into Asia. The VOC factory was never Japan's only window to the world, but it provided an important conduit into the archipelago and one that the company, in its role as loyal vassal, had little choice but to facilitate, even after its own profits dried up. At the same time, the implications of the settlement rippled out more widely, particularly after the translation and publication of Kaempfer's description of the Dutch position in Japan. Robert Markley notes that Japan "provoked a crisis in seventeenth and eighteenth-century historiography because the defeat of Christianity and the ongoing abjection of the Dutch on Deshima mocked the values and assumptions of Eurocentric ideology."[59] For the readers of Kaempfer's history and other accounts like it, the Dutch position in Japan was a stark reminder of the ongoing power of Asian states and the inability of Europeans to control the terms of international engagements.

While the idea that the Dutch East India Company occupied a particularly weak position in Japan is in no way controversial, and indeed has been well documented both by contemporary writers like Kaempfer as well as by modern scholars, the goal of this study is to show how and why the Dutch ended up where they did in Tokugawa Japan. To do this, it is divided into three parts focused on conflicts over diplomacy, violence, and sovereignty. Although these overlap chronologically, they have been separated out in order to reveal individual time lines. Part 1 begins with the first diplomatic letter sent to Japan by Victor Sprinckel in 1608 and concludes by looking at the company's involvement in the Shimabara uprising. By following diplomacy across this period, it traces the full trajectory of interaction and the series of different guises assumed by Dutch representatives in Japan. Part 2 examines privateering campaigns stretching from 1609, when the VOC first arrived in Japan, to 1665, when it agreed to call off its operations against Chinese shipping sailing to the archipelago. The focus is on the company's largely failed attempt across more than half a century to make use of its superior naval power in the waters around Japan. Part 3 investigates a dispute over sovereignty that commenced in 1624, when the company planted its flag on Tayouan, and closed in the 1630s, after it agreed to hand over the former governor of that colony to Bakufu jurisdiction.

CIVILIZATION AND SOCIALIZATION

In Japanese history the image of the heavily armed Western gunboat arriving in local waters carrying a list of demands is a potent one. The appearance of Perry's fleet of black ships in Edo bay in 1853, an event uniformly regarded as a pivotal turning point in Japanese history, triggered a process of massive change, as Meiji leaders worked to reshape the country by overhauling its social, economic, and legal structures. The goal of this massive upheaval was to bring Japan up to the standard of a "civilized nation," as defined by Western powers, so that it could join the family of nations as an equal member. In the words of one Meiji politician, Japan must "consider carefully the rights and duties . . . [that being a civilized nation] entails. Civilized nations uphold certain right (*tsūgi*);

to do so is a requirement for acceptance to their ranks."[60] In this way, Perry's ships initiated a process of forced socialization in which Japan was compelled to accommodate itself to an existing political order that it possessed little power to change.[61] As part of this process, its leaders embraced new norms about how the country should behave on the global stage as well as an unfamiliar vocabulary of international law.

While veritable rivers of ink have been spilt describing Japan's transformation in order to claim a place in international orders, there was another process of socialization involving the West and Japan that has not received even a fraction of this attention. Although it would be a mistake to minimize the importance of the Meiji moment, it was in fact born out of a fairly short span of European dominance in the nineteenth and early twentieth centuries. For a far longer period the dynamic was reversed, with Asia occupying a position at the center. Because of this, when an earlier fleet of foreign warships appeared in Japanese harbors in the seventeenth century, it received a very different reception from that afforded to Perry. While the arrival of this first generation of black ships also triggered a process of socialization, it was one in which Europeans were forced to adapt in order to claim a place in a political order that they could do little to alter. To find an accommodation with Tokugawa Japan, Dutch East India Company officials were compelled to accept a set of new rules for proper conduct, as well as a new political vocabulary, and to abandon established practices. In the end, they, like the leaders of Meiji Japan, found a secure place in a foreign order, but discovered that it came at a significant cost.

1
Diplomacy

CHAPTER ONE

ROYAL LETTERS FROM THE REPUBLIC

I have come here . . . because of the command
of the King of Holland.

—Admiral Cornelis Matelieff de Jonge, 1607

In 1609 two ships belonging to the Dutch East India Company arrived in Hirado in western Japan. After dropping anchor in the port's narrow harbor, the leaders of the expedition prepared to dispatch a small group of representatives to seek an audience with Tokugawa Ieyasu, the founder of a military government then approaching the anniversary of its first decade in power. Some accounts of the Dutch in Japan reference a letter from Prince Maurits, a high-ranking Dutch aristocrat, but its purpose and why a delegation belonging to an independent mercantile company based in a republic would have transported such a document to Japan is left unexplained, making it seem little more than a historical footnote.[1] According to most descriptions of what happened next, the Dutch, private merchants interested only in trade and without any particular diplomatic pretensions, were well received by a friendly shogun who swiftly granted all their requests.[2] In this way the moment of first contact is typically presented as an uncomplicated interaction, an easy meeting of minds between the shogun and the company's men that, despite the fact the VOC was an unfamiliar interloper into Asian politics, required little mediation or additional explanation.

This tendency to gloss over European diplomatic activity as an essentially straightforward process of negotiation is not limited to Japan. After their ships dropped anchor, whether in tiny port polities or on the maritime fringes of powerful states, commanders from da Gama onward invariably sought access to the highest authority in the land by dispatching embassies armed with official letters and bearing gifts. From the beginning, therefore, the embassy was a fundamental instrument for expansion, but while historians have long been interested in the ways in which Europeans broke into Asian commercial networks, there are far fewer studies detailing the nature of their diplomatic engagements. The result has been that, even after the pioneering work of scholars like Jack Wills, we know considerably less about the challenges faced by European ambassadors than we do about the struggles of European merchants to master the difficult trading environment they found in Asia.[3]

While some ambassadors were extremely successful, the complexity of the diplomatic circuits into which they demanded access—networks that could be just as intricate, incomprehensible, and resistant to penetration as any commercial system—should not be underestimated. An examination of the documents produced by ambassadors reveals that the process of diplomatic engagement with Asian states was a far trickier affair than it sometimes appears and one that routinely generated problems for European enterprises. In the same way as European merchants found they had nothing to sell, European ambassadors frequently discovered they were ill-prepared to participate in the business of diplomacy in Asia. Staffed with poorly qualified personnel, equipped with inappropriate gifts or problematic documents, and armed with unrealistic aims, many embassies struggled to make headway. There was, to put it more plainly, nothing straightforward about diplomacy, particularly in the initial phase of interaction when Europeans attempted to establish a presence in Asia.

In recent years this point has been well illustrated by scholars such as Richmond Barbour who have analyzed the trials and tribulations faced by early English diplomats in India.[4] One of the more persistent difficulties illuminated by such research concerns the various ways in which ambassadors attached to the English East India Company struggled to persuade anyone that their monarch, the putative figurehead for the organization's diplomatic efforts, should be viewed as something more than, to quote one Mughal official, a "pettie prince" deserving of little respect in the grand courts that dominated the region.[5]

Such studies raise an obvious question as to the fate of their VOC counterparts. The fact that the Dutch emerged from a republic has prompted some scholars to suggest that the VOC and its forerunner organizations enjoyed a unique advantage that enabled their representatives to maneuver easily in their negotiations with Asian states. In her study of the company's activities in India, Ann Radwan argues that the Dutch were distinctly fortunate as the nature of their home state meant that they were not called upon to constantly defend a distant monarch's honor.[6] While there were certainly some circumstances in which this may have been the case, there is also plenty of evidence to suggest that the republican background was often more handicap than advantage.

As the employees of a company of merchants led by merchants, VOC officials struggled to explain what exactly they represented and why a private organization was so determined to gain entrance into diplomatic circuits that were conventionally monopolized by states. To further complicate the matter, the company could not simply look toward Europe to borrow legitimacy from the sovereign there. Occupying an uncertain position within Europe itself, the Dutch Republic was a political experiment ruled by an unruly parliament and lacking a monarch, the one readily translatable figure that could be inserted into diplomatic negotiations. The combination of these facts meant that while all Europeans struggled to navigate diplomatic circuits, the Dutch, precisely because of the nature of their home state, faced a particularly thorny problem when it came to crafting an acceptable narrative for consumption in courts across Asia. Their way round this problem brings us back to the 1609 delegation and to the letter it carried from Prince Maurits.

When this small group of envoys traveled to meet with the shogun, they did so not as private merchants seeking entry into a category that came to be known by Tokugawa officials as *tsūsho*, or commercial relations, but as ambassadors who claimed to represent the "king of Holland," a fictive sovereign built around a carefully blurred vision of Prince Maurits.[7] The introduction of this figure offered a kind of royal disguise that could be draped over the company's activities, thereby obscuring the unfamiliar nature of the organization, while also smoothing the way for diplomatic interaction by boosting the status of Dutch envoys and providing them with a ready framework for exchange. It had the added effect of postponing any clash over the company's diplomatic ambitions, which were effectively concealed from view until a later period when, as detailed in the next chapter, the VOC chose to engage with the shogun without the mediation of a royal figurehead. The aim of this chapter is to put the "king of Holland" back into the story of the Dutch encounter with the Tokugawa Bakufu by looking at what VOC representatives actually said (or wrote) and by assuming that such statements carried weight. When envoys explained that they came from the "king of Holland," this was not an accident of translation or a kind of diplomatic garnish loosely sprinkled over something more substantial. Instead, as the Tokugawa records make clear, it provided both structure and logic to the first phase of negotiations between the company and the shogun.

EUROPEAN AMBASSADORS IN ASIA

The European enterprises that moved into Asia in the sixteenth and seventeenth centuries all struggled to find the right keys to unlock the varied diplomatic circuits they encountered across the region. When Vasco da Gama arrived in Calicut in 1498, he immediately dispatched a missive to the local ruler "informing him that an ambassador had arrived from the king of Portugal with letters."[8] Taking on the identity of royal representative, he presented himself as a kingly proxy charged by the sovereign to make contact with potentates in Asia. Although da Gama was prone to exaggerations about Portuguese power, this representation of himself and his role was rooted in fact. As was the case with Columbus's voyage, his expedition had been authorized and bankrolled by a crown eager to secure the riches of Asian trade. Unlike the mercantile companies that eclipsed it in the seventeenth century, the Estado da India, the primary vehicle for Portuguese expansion into Asia, was a centrally controlled enterprise. Because of this, every Portuguese subject who ventured east "did so in the service of the Crown," although most sought to supplement their salaries by engaging in private trade on their own account.[9]

After the first meeting in Calicut, dozens of Portuguese ambassadors fanned out across Asia in a burst of activity that took them, in the space of just a few decades, from the shores of India to the Chinese court. Like their famous predecessor, these envoys relied on the distant presence of the king in Europe to provide both legitimacy for their missions and a framework for exchange. Delegations traveled under royal banners, carried documents marked with the king's seal, and presented portraits of the monarch.[10] The outlines of the subsequent offer also remained largely consistent. In 1498 da Gama had explained that "he had been instructed to say by word of mouth that . . . [the king of Portugal] desired to be . . . [the ruler of Calicut's] friend and brother."[11] In subsequent negotiations with a range of sovereigns, ambassadors consistently offered the king's "friendship" (*amizade*) and "brotherhood" (*irmandade*) in return for political alliances and trading concessions.[12] Both concepts were freighted with meaning; brotherhood "signified an imaginary blood relationship with spiritual overtones," a way to make connections across cultures by establishing a league of sympathetic monarchs joined together for a common purpose, while friendship came with its own set of mutual obligations.[13] In this way the notion of a personal connection between monarchs, something possible across great distances and without any requirement for face-to-face contact, provided an organizing structure for exchange and a coherent logic for subsequent interactions.

Although it offered a valuable framework for communication, the reliance on the king as the key to diplomatic exchange created its own complications. The most common problem lay in persuading anyone to take the Portuguese sovereign seriously. Ambassadors struggled to reconcile their grand claims about the power of their overlord and the desirability of his friendship with the humble and at times desperately shoddy appearance of their embassies. The chasm between claim and appearance was laid bare as early as 1498 when the king of Calicut noted that da Gama "had told him that he came from a very rich kingdom, and yet had brought him nothing."[14] Using royal brotherhood as an instrument for cross-cultural interaction could also backfire when it was introduced to sovereigns like the emperor of China who, presiding over a hierarchical system of relations that ascended through assorted levels of barbarians to the center of civilization in the imperial capital, was prone to reject any notion of equivalence with a minor potentate in Europe.

But, for all these problems, the Portuguese presentation did have the great merit of simplicity. In contrast, the English merchants that started to appear in Asian port cities in the seventeenth century arrived in the service of a far more complex sponsor. Like its Dutch counterpart, the English East India Company was a private mercantile corporation organized, bankrolled, and populated by merchants, who operated independently of the state. Its agents were thus, to use George Masselman's phrase, "in the employ of anonymous capital" rather than a monarch.[15] How then to represent an autonomous organization controlled by a governing body made up of more than twenty individuals?[16] The obvious solution, adopted swiftly and without apparent dispute, was to paper over the organization's independent character by borrowing legitimacy from the crown. As they fitted out their first vessels for an expedition to Asia, the organizing committee resolved to solicit letters "from the Queen, to the princes and potentates in India, this being held to be the most obvious expedient for insuring a favorable reception."[17] The reasoning was clear: if the Company's employees did not actually represent the English crown, in this case Queen Elizabeth, they could at least graft the monarch's name and prestige onto their endeavors, thereby gaining access where it would otherwise be denied.[18]

When James Lancaster, the commander of this first expedition, arrived in Aceh, a powerful maritime kingdom located on the northern tip of Sumatra that would also welcome ambassadors from the "king of Holland," in 1602, he made full use of his letters from the queen, quickly assuming the role of ambassador and relying on a logic of royal contact to explain his presence. Brought before the sultan, he "made his obeysance after the manner of the country, declaring that hee was sent from the most mightie Queene of England to congratulate with his highnesse and treat with him concerning a peace and amitie with his Maiestie."[19] The letter itself, addressed from "Elizabeth by the Grace of God, Queene of England, France, and Ireland. . . . To the great and mightie King of Achem, &c. in the Island of Sumatra, our loving Brother," began with an immediate invocation of brotherhood between sovereigns.[20] It went on to offer the "friendship and league" between equivalent rulers as a framework for relations between the Acehnese and the English company's merchants. These ties of amity, once accepted, were to produce a defined set of privileges for Elizabeth's subjects in Asia and hence to engineer an advantageous trading position.[21]

As it had in the Portuguese case, the reliance on a monarch gave clear benefits while also creating a separate set of not insubstantial problems.

The crown was at best a fair weather friend, often eager to help but occasionally working actively against the company's interests by allowing rival merchants into its area of operations.[22] More significantly, overlaying a thin covering of royal prestige onto a private commercial enterprise could sometimes hurt more than it helped, engendering a palpable sense of uncertainty and confusion that could undermine diplomatic missions.[23] Royal letters were occasionally handed to hastily conscripted merchants who were poorly equipped to play the part of royal ambassador. When one Mr. Edwards, an unfortunate figure described by his compatriots as a "mecannycal fellowe," assumed the "title and state of an ambassador" to India in 1614, the result was disastrous.[24] After he behaved "himselfe not as beseeminge an ambassador, especiallye sente from soe worthye and greate a prince as the Kinge of England," he was "kicked and spurned by the [Mughal] King's porters out of the courte-gates, to the unrecoverable disgrace of our Kinge and nation."[25]

Although there were failures along the way, the introduction of the monarch provided, particularly in the first phase of contact, a vital enabling mechanism for English representatives in Asia. More than simply raising the status of individual envoys, it offered both a structure and a language for exchange. Like their English counterparts, Dutch ambassadors in Asia were also employees of an independent mercantile organization, but their republican background meant that they lacked a monarch capable of being drafted immediately into service as an obvious figurehead.

THE DUTCH PROBLEM

The Dutch Republic, also known as the United Provinces, was born in the midst of a bitter struggle with the armies of Habsburg Spain.[26] Commencing in 1568 when a number of provinces in the northern Netherlands revolted against Phillip II (r. 1556–98), the conflict continued unbroken, except for a truce between 1609 and 1621, for the next eighty years until 1648. Over the course of the long struggle with Spain, the leaders of the rebellious provinces constructed a new apparatus of government that endured until the outbreak of the French Revolution. Despite its remarkable longevity, the republic's political form was not the product of a deliberate and overarching plan conceived by resolute democrats. Instead it cohered piece by piece after the gradual elimination of possible alternatives.[27]

The political system that emerged out of the revolt was highly decentralized, as each province sought collective security without surrendering individual entitlements. In the words of William Temple, the resultant system was "a confederacy of Seven Sovereign Provinces, united together for their common and mutual defense, but without any dependence one upon the other."[28] The central organ of government, the States-General, consisted of representatives of each of the provincial parliaments or states. Since each province received one vote, the system should in theory have guaranteed equality, but the body was traditionally dominated by Holland, the largest and wealthiest of the seven. While it had control over declarations of war and peace as well as matters related to defense and international diplomacy, the States-General had limited rights over the individual provinces as well as the cities and towns therein, which retained a measure of autonomy.[29]

Although they represented an emerging power, Dutch envoys confronted three interrelated issues when they sought access to diplomatic circuits both in Europe as well as in Asia.[30] First, the United Provinces not only lacked a monarch but was, as its critics delighted in pointing out, in an ongoing state of revolt against its former king. Second, it possessed as its sovereign authority a diverse body, the States-General, that had few obvious counterparts in international politics.[31] Finally, the republic occupied a precarious position within Europe where it remained locked in a desperate war with a powerful foe. The combination of these issues ensured that it was widely regarded, particularly before the signing of the 1609 truce, as a diplomatic outsider, a rebel state whose representatives should not be accorded the same treatment as full ambassadors.[32]

The question as to how best to represent such a state in Asia came to the fore in 1595, some seven years before the formation of the Dutch East India Company, when Cornelis de Houtman led a small fleet into the Indian Ocean. His expedition had been dispatched by the Far Lands Company (Compagnie Van Verre), one of a number of such organizations created by eager merchants in the United Provinces to break into Asian markets. Known collectively as the precompanies (voorcompagnieën), these enterprises combined to dispatch fifteen expeditions with a total of sixty-five vessels to Asia.[33] Although some were comparatively successful, bringing in rich cargos and amply rewarded their investors, the precompanies did not survive for long. As the new century opened, the Dutch state moved to rein in unrestricted competition by convening a conference that brought together the directors of the rival companies. The eventual product after months of hard-fought negotiations was the Dutch East India Company, which was formed by merging six of the precompanies.

Before they disappeared, organizations like the Far Lands Company succeeded in establishing an enduring pattern for diplomatic exchange that was subsequently picked up and expanded by the VOC. When de Houtman stepped ashore in the bustling port of Banten in western Java in 1596, he assumed the identity of ambassador and proceeded to open diplomatic ties with the local sovereign.[34] The precise nature of his presentation hinged on a decision made months earlier by the expedition's backers to reach beyond the fractious States-General to a separate, quasi-kingly, and hence, in diplomatic terms, far more familiar, figure for legitimacy. The individual in question was Prince Maurits, the republic's *Stadhouder* and a key figure in the early history of the United Provinces, who would come to play a vital role in the first phase of Dutch expansion into Asia.

The office of Stadhouder was a remnant left over from an earlier period of Habsburg control during which its holders had functioned as local proxies for the monarch. Having sworn an oath of loyalty to the king, they functioned in his place but were not royal figures themselves. When sovereignty was transferred from Philip II to the provinces via the act of violent rebellion, the office of Stadhouder did not, as might have been expected, simply fade from the scene. Instead, it remained in place and was in fact gradually strengthened, although its holders were transformed from royal proxies into servants of the States-General.[35] In principle, each of the provincial states chose their own Stadhouder, but several provinces conventionally elected the same individual, and the office came to be largely monopolized by the minor princely family of Orange-Nassau.[36] In 1595 when de Houtman arrived in Banten, it was held by Prince Maurits (1567–1625) who had succeeded to the position after the assassination of his famous father, Willem de Zwijger, in 1584.

The formal powers attached to the office of Stadhouder related principally to military matters and, in his position as commander of the republic's armies, Maurits took charge of the war against Spain, leading Dutch forces to victory in a string of important engagements.[37] Over time, however, the Stadhouder's influence came to extend far beyond the battlefield into the very heart of Dutch politics.[38] As the most prominent aristocrat in the republic and one of the few unifying symbols around which a sense of national identity could coalesce, the Stadhouder enjoyed tremendous prestige and an increasingly central role in government. In the last years of his life, for example, Maurits managed to oust his long-serving domestic rival, Johan van Oldenbarnevelt to emerge as the dominant political force in the United Provinces. But, for all their power, these were not kings. Instead the Stadhouders remained trapped throughout the seventeenth century in an ambiguous position in the shadow of republican institutions. Even in those periods in which they were ascendant, the Stadhouders were compelled to cooperate with the States-General and to work through consensus rather than imposing policy by fiat. Indeed, the office itself was not even a permanent fixture in the Dutch political landscape, lying empty for a long stretch in the middle of the century when the States-General asserted its primacy.[39]

Although he never traveled outside Europe, Maurits's name and image appeared again and again wherever the Dutch companies, first the *voorcompagnieën* and later the VOC, were active.[40] Ambassadors carried letters signed by the Stadhouder, presented gifts from him, signed treaties in his name, and generally offered Maurits up as a symbolic presence standing behind their activities in Asia. In itself, his central place in diplomatic negotiations is not particularly surprising for the Stadhouder functioned in a similar capacity in Europe, where the States-General recognized that a "a kind of 'royal personage' was necessary when dealing with Europe's monarchs, in order to ensure communication between equals."[41] But in Asia this role was considerably magnified for he appeared here, albeit always in symbolic form, both much earlier and in a more prominent position.[42] The leeway afforded to Dutch representatives by the great distances between Europe and Asia served to inflate the status of this figure, who tended, in a range of diplomatic negotiations, either to displace the States-General or to assume a new and far grander identity as monarch.[43] In discussions with Asian rulers and officials Maurits was routinely identified either by his proper title but with the States-General discreetly pushed to the side, or presented, as was the case in Japan, more directly as the "king of Holland."[44] He appears in the latter guise in one version of the very first agreement signed by Dutch representatives in Asia, a treaty between de Houtman and officials in Banten, which includes a reference to the "king of Holland."[45]

The ability to describe Maurits in this way was aided by the fact that he looked the part, allowing less a wholesale refashioning than a simple blurring around the edges to present the Stadhouder as a convincing monarch. Sovereign figures in their own right, albeit over the tiny French principality of Orange, Maurits and his successors stood at the center of a court that steadily increased in size and opulence during the seventeenth century.[46] In typical portraits, some of which were actually transported to Asia, he appears in an imperious pose surrounded by the characteristic symbols of kingship. In one famous image by Michiel Jansz. van Mierevelt, Maurits stands dressed in a brilliant suit of gilded armor that had been given to him by the state, a general's baton grasped in his right hand and a lavishly plumed helmet sitting on a pedestal to the side.[47]

One way to understand the appearance of a figure like the "king of Holland" in diplomatic negotiations is as an improvised response forced on reluctant Dutch envoys by a lack of understanding on the part of their Asian interlocutors.[48] Given the fact that the United Provinces did possess a remarkably complex system of government that defied easy characterization (while also lacking any obvious parallel in early modern Asia), there is clearly some truth to this explanation, but it ignores the fact that Dutch representatives made a deliberate decision to introduce a royal figurehead into negotiations so as to boost their standing. Put another way, ambassadors referenced this figure not simply because they had to but rather because they wanted to.

This becomes clear if we examine the timing of the Stadhouder's introduction into Asia. He did not surface in diplomatic negotiations after a long struggle in which hardy republicans attempted again and again to explain the nature of their state before, thwarted one too many times by local ignorance, simply giving up. Rather, the backers of the first expeditions to Asia procured documents from the prince of Orange before a single ship had set sail, that is to say months or even years before the moment of actual contact. When they departed Europe, de Houtman and three other officers took with them general letters known as patents from Maurits that were subsequently presented to officials in Banten in order to initiate relations and "make a firm alliance of peace and union."[49] In this way the decision to push the Stadhouder forward

Figure 1.1. Portrait of Maurits, prince of Orange, ca. 1613–15. Michiel Jansz. van Mierevelt. *Courtesy of the Collection Rijksmuseum, Amsterdam*

represented a premeditated attempt to make use of this figure in order to initiate exchange.

The introduction of a royal figurehead offered significant advantages when it came to breaking into local diplomatic circuits. The precompanies' strategy in Asia—and this applied even more so to the VOC—depended on gaining a direct pathway into the court in order to conclude treaties, make alliances, and secure concessions. Because of this, when Dutch representatives landed in a new territory, their first goal was always to, if we quote one early source, "speak to the king."[50] The problem was, however, that private groups of merchants had little standing across the region, and many rulers were inclined to follow the Chinese maxim that only monarchs should be involved in diplomacy (*renqing wu waijiao*).[51] If Dutch envoys were dismissed as traders that should concern themselves simply with their own profits and not intrude into diplomacy, then it undermined any chance of securing their desired outcome. By linking themselves to a kingly figure, de Houtman and others like him were transformed from merchants into royal ambassadors and a clear path was opened up into the court. As was the case for English representatives, the injection of a sovereign into negotiations had the additional advantage of giving Dutch envoys a ready structure for exchange that was oriented around personal connections between powerful individuals. This facilitated the opening of relations with a range of different states while also providing a mechanism to extract concessions via reference to the ongoing friendship between the Stadhouder and his Asian counterparts.

Given these benefits, it is not surprising that Maurits's distant presence loomed large over the first phase of Dutch expansion. In the two decades after de Houtman arrived in Banten, the Stadhouder made a symbolic appearance in diverse states across Asia. In response, a range of local rulers dispatched their own letters and, in some cases, their own embassies back to the "king of Holland."[52] In one exchange, the ruler of Ternate, a small clove-producing sultanate, presented his greetings from the "possessor of the clove trees, in the land above the winds" to "the exalted king of Holland in the land below the winds."[53] On the Malay Peninsula, the sultan of Johor, who had welcomed the Dutch as valuable allies against the Portuguese, persistently referred to the Stadhouder as "our brother" and invoked a logic of martial fellowship, of two kings united against a common enemy and pledged to support each other.[54]

Similar language was used by the ruler of Pegu in Burma when he wrote to "my brother in arms, the powerful King of Holland."[55]

One of the most enduring relationships was established with the kingdom of Ayutthaya in Siam, where successive rulers embraced the connection with the Stadhouder by parading letters from their distant correspondent through the capital. In fact, so interested were the Ayutthayan monarchs in this link that king Ekatotsarot (r. 1605–10) dispatched his own embassy to the "king of Holland" in 1606. Arriving in the United Provinces after a long voyage, the envoys from Siam offered a royal letter "inscribed on beaten gold" to Maurits "whom they always called the King of Holland."[56] To ensure the continuation of the relationship, the company subsequently presented at least four separate letters and a range of gifts from the Stadhouder to Siam.[57]

Maurits's prominent role in diplomatic negotiations is perhaps most strikingly visible in the records kept by the company's competitors. English merchants, who operated in close proximity to the Dutch, protested that their rivals "doe not spare to bragge very much of their King, meaning Grave [Count] Maurice, whom they call in all these parts at every word Raja Hollanda [the Raj of Holland]."[58] News of this style of presentation eventually traveled back to England where James I summoned a Dutch delegation to berate them that your "people over there represent everywhere your Prince of Orange as a great King and Lord, and hold me up as a little kinglet, as if I stood under him, thus misleading the barbarian kings."[59]

Eager to secure an advantage over their competitors, English merchants pointedly reminded Asian officials that the United Provinces was a minor political anomaly bearing no comparison to the great kingdoms of Europe.[60] When a Dutch representative in Japan "began to extoll their kinge of Holland to be the greatest king in Christendom & one that held all the others under," his English counterpart announced to the assembled audience that he "needed not to lie soe loude, for that they hadd no king at all in Holland but were governed by a conte [count], or rather they governed him."[61] In Banten, where de Houtman had first produced letters from the "king of Holland," English agents made a great show of celebrating their monarch's coronation day by dressing up with "Scarfes of white and red Taffata" and decorating their lodge with "a Flagge with the red Crosse through the middle." When a large crowd had gathered before the gaudily adorned structure, they announced that, while they were the subjects of a powerful sovereign, the Hollanders "had no King, but their Land was ruled by Governors."[62]

While letters from the Stadhouder provided a valuable tool for ambassadors, they were no guarantee of success. Like Mr. Edwards, the "mecannycal fellowe" whose disastrous embassy was spurned by Mughal officials, some Dutch representatives proved poorly suited to the role. In 1603, for example, Sebald van de Weerd, a Dutch vice admiral charged with establishing an alliance with the king of Kandy, managed to so enrage his hosts that he was ultimately murdered.[63] The more common problem, however, stemmed less from such abject performances than from a general lack of resources. Many of the missions that cohered around these documents were so hurriedly improvised and badly equipped that they undermined the very basis of the company's presentation. This was the case in Japan where the Dutch stumbled toward their opening encounter with the shogun armed with inadequate tools.

FINDING JAPAN

First contact between Japan and the Dutch was made not by the VOC but by one of the *voorcompagnieën* that preceded it into Asia and it took place in particularly inauspicious circumstances. In 1598 a group of merchants from the city of Rotterdam assembled a small fleet for an expedition to Asia.[64] Consisting of five vessels, the splendidly named *Hoop* (Hope), *Liefde* (Love), *Geloof* (Faith), *Trouwe* (Fidelity), and the *Blijde Boodschap* (Good Tidings), the fleet was placed under the command of Jacques Mahu and Simon de Cordes, who were tasked to take a westerly route through the Straits of Magellan and on into the Pacific. From the beginning, the progress of the expedition was handicapped by a series of setbacks prompted by poor leadership and bad weather. Just two ships, *Liefde* and *Hoop*, managed to rendezvous successfully in the Pacific after traversing the notoriously dangerous straits. In April 1600 the *Liefde*, having lost its sister ship on the way, reached the island of Kyushu in Japan. By this time the vessel and its crew were in a terrible state. Of the original contingent of over a hundred mariners, only twenty-four men survived, and many of these were close to death. As such, contact with Japan was made by a group that looked far closer to shipwrecked sailors than the members of an organized expedition, and indeed the *Liefde* itself was later destroyed, leaving the survivors effectively marooned on the archipelago.

The Dutch had arrived in Japan at a crucial juncture, just six months before the decisive battle of Sekigahara that brought the Tokugawa regime to power. As one of the few officers in reasonable health, William Adams, the *Liefde*'s English pilot and the subject of much subsequent fascination, was dispatched to meet with Tokugawa Ieyasu. Brought before the future shogun in May 1600, he was questioned about the origins and purpose of the expedition as well as wider political conditions in Europe.[65] But while there was clearly considerable interest in this new European group, there was also, given the state of the *Liefde*'s crew and the as yet minimal Dutch presence in Asia, no obvious mechanism to bring about further contact. As a result, the survivors, who lacked the means to leave the archipelago, settled into an extended residence in Japan. Their subsequent fortunes were mixed. Two members of the crew, Jan Joosten van Lodenstein and William Adams, rose to some prominence by serving as occasional advisers to the shogun, although they were never as influential as they would later claim.[66] Others like Melchior van Santvoort, the *Liefde*'s former clerk, took advantage of a boom in Japanese trade to establish themselves as independent merchants.

In 1605 word reached Japan that the Dutch East India Company, which had been established just three years earlier, had opened a trading base in the port of Patani on the Malay Peninsula. In response, a group of *Liefde* survivors petitioned the Bakufu successfully for permission to make contact with their countrymen. Responsibility for the subsequent expedition fell to Jacob Quaeckernaeck, the *Liefde*'s former skipper, and the always enterprising Melchior van Santvoort. With no ship of their own, they were compelled to seek passage aboard a vessel provided and equipped by the lords of Hirado domain, who hoped to lure rich Dutch trading vessels to their territory.[67] Before he departed, Bakufu officials issued Quaeckernaeck with a document described in Dutch sources as "letters of charter."[68] Although it was later interpreted as a special dispensation for trade and hence clear evidence of shogunal favor, this assumption, as many others that would follow it, rested on an overly optimistic appraisal of an unexceptional document. Instead of handing over a raft of valuable concessions, the "letters of charter" seem to have been little more than a basic travel pass. A second document issued to Dutch merchants a year later and presumably almost identical in content authorized its holders to use any port in the Japanese archipelago and guaranteed they would not be harmed or mistreated.[69]

After a reasonably quick voyage, Quaeckernaeck and van Santvoort reached Patani in December 1605 where they discovered a small Dutch factory. Although the reunion with their countrymen was doubtless welcome, the factory lacked the necessary resources to dispatch its own mission to make contact with the shogun. As a result, van Santvoort, who clearly had no interest in resuming life as a lowly clerk, opted to return to Japan to continue his flourishing business there, leaving Quaeckernaeck to wait for the arrival of the next VOC fleet. Eventually in July 1606, the former skipper received word that Dutch warships under the command of Cornelis Matelieff de Jonge, by coincidence his cousin, were laying siege to the Portuguese-controlled port of Melaka located on the opposite side of the peninsula. Journeying overland, Quaeckernaeck reached the fleet a month later and handed over the letters of charter to Matelieff. Having survived so much, he died shortly thereafter, shot through the head by a Portuguese musket.

Back in the United Provinces, the company's directors, the so-called Heeren 17 (Gentlemen 17), who knew nothing of these developments, commenced their own preparations to open relations with Japan. In keeping with well-established practices, they turned to the Stadhouder, resolving in February 1606 to request a letter from Maurits for the "king of Japan."[70] Carried to Asia aboard a fleet commanded by Paulus van Caarden, this document was later transferred to another expedition before resurfacing in Japan in 1609. While it was still in transit, however, Victor Sprinckel, the newly installed *opperhoofd* of the factory in Patani, decided that some attempt should be made to establish contact with the Tokugawa regime and assure it that the company was indeed planning to send an expedition to Japan. His chosen tool to do this was a letter to the shogun that was to be carried to the archipelago by Melchior van Santvoort, who was now trading regularly with Patani, and once there handed over to William Adams for delivery to the shogun.

As the first official document sent by a VOC representative to the Tokugawa Bakufu and the first to reference the "king of Holland," Sprinckel's letter, which is dated February 1608, is of obvious importance but it also stands out as an example of diplomatic improvisation. The company's favored instrument for opening relations with Asian states was an actual letter from the prince of Orange, but with no way to get hold of this most basic of diplomatic props, Sprinckel was compelled to make things up as he went along. In so doing, he set the tone for the subsequent phase of interaction, which was characterized by hastily written documents and jury-rigged embassies. The opening phrases of his letter, which also marked Maurits's first appearance in Japan, were telling. In the absence of a missive from the Stadhouder, Sprinckel opted instead to wrap himself in a shroud of royal legitimacy while skirting around a variety of difficult questions. He began by pushing the sovereign to the fore, explaining, in a neat mix of invented and actual titles, that he was writing "in the name of our King (*onsen Coninck*) and Princely Excellence, duke maurijtius of Nassau."[71] In this way Sprinckel immediately assumed a role as royal proxy, a loyal servant tasked by his master to make contact on his behalf.

Having established these credentials, he proceeded to recite a brief history of contact:

> Your Majesty shall know that on 2 December 1605 Jacob Quaecker-naeck and Melchior van Santvoort arrived . . . and we learnt from them of the success of the permission that Your Majesty granted for the profit of His Princely Excellency and our Netherlanders of Holland and Zeeland. From the strength of Your Majesty's letters, which the aforementioned Quaeckernaeck handed to Admiral Cornelis Matelief de Jonge before his death and which we hope will have arrived within nine months from that day in Holland, and will be delivered into the hands of His Princely Excellence [Maurits], we cannot thank Your Majesty enough (in the name of our Princely Excellence).

The account was carefully designed to emphasize the possibility of a direct connection between shogun and king. Ieyasu's letter would, Sprinckel suggested, have by now arrived in the United Provinces and, more particularly, in Maurits's own hands. In this way a simple travel pass morphed into a direct communication dispatched from the shogun to his Dutch counterpart. Once the Stadhouder had received a message from his brother monarch, he would of course respond with his own document, thereby opening the way for formal relations to be initiated.

Although hampered by the absence of a document from the Stadhouder, Sprinckel managed to maneuver himself into a position as royal proxy, but his grand claims to speak for the crown created their own dilemma. If the letter was to be sent in the name of the "king of Holland," then it should be accompanied by a suitably rich array of gifts. The problem was of course that the author, marooned in a remote factory and with no access to the sort of prestige goods used by other Dutch ambassadors, possessed nothing of real value to send along with his letter. The predictable result was further contortions, with Sprinckel explaining that the objects dispatched with his letter should not be seen "as gifts but should be accepted by way of congratulations, that is not considering the present but the will behind the deed."[72] Although the exact distinction between gifts and congratulatory offerings is far from obvious, it is clear that Sprinckel believed it had to be made in order to draw a line between the "king of Holland" and what was a particularly unimpressive collection of items consisting of crystal goblets, glassware, and cloth worth just 112 guilders. If something had to presented, it must not, he took pains to ensure, tarnish the Stadhouder's name.

The letter closed by assuring the shogun that Dutch vessels would arrive in Japan within the next three years. In fact, a small expedition would reach the archipelago long before this self-appointed deadline, but, as was the case when Sprinckel sat down to pen his 1608 missive, it was largely unprepared for the task at hand.

THE FIRST EMBASSY

In 1607, Pieter Verhoeff departed Europe with a fleet of thirteen ships, two of which would eventually reach Japan and establish a permanent VOC presence there. When he arrived in Banten, Verhoeff received word that the Portuguese were in the process of preparing the great cargo ship that sailed annually between Macao and Nagasaki. Eager to capture such a valuable prize, he dispatched a message to two of his ships, the *Vereenichde Leeuw met Pylen* and the *Griffoen*, that were lying off the coast of Johor with instructions to "seize the ship that will come from Macao to Japan, which we are certain and well aware is very richly laden."[73] Only if they failed in this task were they to sail onto Japan and, once there, open relations with the shogun.

Before setting off in pursuit of the Macao carrack (*kraak*), as it is usually referred to in VOC sources, the *Vereenichde Leeuw met Pylen* and the

Griffoen stopped off in Patani, where they "took on some silk, pepper and lead so that if we were not able to seize the carrack, we could show evidence that we desired to trade and establish a factory [in Japan]."[74] The hasty stopover, very much in keeping with the improvised nature of the first phase of contact, was designed to prove the company's credentials as a legitimate merchant enterprise and give some substance to its promises of future trade. This made it yet another disguise, serving in this case to conceal the fact that the VOC was far more interested in these early years in the rich prize represented by Portuguese shipping than in the long-term prospects of trade with Japan.

Despite their best efforts, the *Vereenichde Leeuw met Pylen* and the *Griffoen* were unable to capture the carrack, which beat them by two days to Japan. Having failed in their primary aim, they proceeded on to Kyushu in an attempt to carry out Verhoeff's additional instructions. Arriving in the port of Hirado, the same entrepôt from which Quaeckernaeck had departed in 1605, they were warmly welcomed by local officials eager to attract another group of foreign merchants to the domain. Like all the company's expeditions, however, this one had no intention of negotiating with minor functionaries on the periphery. Instead, the ships' council quickly resolved to dispatch an embassy into the interior to conclude "a treaty of free trade and commerce with his Imperial Majesty [the shogun]."[75] In so doing, the company's representatives, following the expectations set out in the organization's charter, pushed aggressively into diplomatic circuits and a space conventionally occupied within Japan by state ambassadors.

But this was, of course, easier said than done. Because it was more the result of accident than deliberate design, the 1609 mission was singularly ill-equipped to play the part. Indeed, when compared to the other diplomatic delegations, such as those from Korea or the Ryukyu kingdom, that arrived in Japan in this period or even to equivalent Dutch missions sent to other parts of Asia, it looked at best a pale shadow of a conventional mission. Embassies typically consisted of four interlocking elements, ambassador, procession, gift, and state letter. While the company's mission to Japan included all four of these, not all were particularly convincing. Standing at the center of any diplomatic mission in this period was the ambassador. As the personal representative of the sovereign, it was his task to ensure that the honor of the home state was maintained at all times. On a more practical level, such envoys were also called upon to participate in the lavish ceremonies and cultural exchanges that formed part of these missions. Because it was so demanding, the assignment was often entrusted to a senior bureaucrat or a high-ranking aristocrat. The embassies from the Ryukyu kingdom that arrived throughout the Tokugawa period were, for example, traditionally led by a prince, usually the son of the ruling monarch, while Korean embassies, which could include as many as three separate ambassadors, were placed under the charge of senior officials.[76] The contrast with the Dutch embassy is obvious. As ambassadors, the ships' council appointed two low-ranking merchants, Abraham van den Broek and Nicolaes Puyck, who were temporarily drafted into service as diplomats. Both were unexceptional, to the extent that they barely feature in the company's vast archives, and boasted no special qualifications for, or experience of, diplomacy.[77]

The embassies that traversed Japan in the first decade of the seventeenth century usually included large processions of support staff whose passage through the archipelago combined to turn them into lavish spectacles. A typical cortege from Korea, one of which had arrived in 1607, numbered around four hundred and could include translators, copyists, literary officials, artists, doctors, musicians, conductors, military officers, horsemen, swordsmen, drummers, signalers, ship captains, maritime pilots, guides, stable masters, trumpeters, messengers, servants, sailors, and butchers.[78] In contrast, the company mustered a cast of just five, the two ambassadors, Melchior van Santvoort who acted as interpreter, and two unnamed assistants. Even compared to equivalent Dutch missions to Asian courts, the procession did not match up. When he came ashore in Banten in 1596, Cornelis de Houtman arrived with eight officers clad in satin and velvet, twelve boatswains, a trumpeter, and a servant carrying a ceremonial parasol of the kind traditionally reserved for nobility.[79] A later ambassador to the Kandyan kingdom in what is now Sri Lanka included in his procession three trumpeters and two flag bearers, one tasked with carrying the prince of Orange's banner out in front while the second dragged the Spanish flag on the ground behind him.[80]

The third element, gifts, was a further problem. In keeping with their large size, Korean and Ryukyuan embassies often brought very substantial offerings to Japan, but even if the focus is narrowed just to the Dutch, the 1609 mission still falls short.[81] Other embassies were careful to transport sumptuous items directly connected with the Stadhouder that could serve as concrete signifiers of his status and friendship. A 1601 mission dispatched to the sultan of Aceh carried a thousand gold coins, specially gilded weapons, and a set of mirrors "as a token of my [Maurits's] wish to maintain friendship with Your Majesty."[82] On different occasions, the ruler of Siam received a suit of armor, some pistols, a shield, a halberd, and, most impressively, a "gold imperial crown" garnished with pearls.[83] Perhaps the most striking gift was the portrait, one of which was presented by Dutch ambassadors to the king of Kandy. Carefully chosen to buttress the notion of the Stadhouder as an equivalent monarch, it depicted Maurits "mounted on horseback in full armor in form and size of horse and person as he was painted at the battle of Flanders."[84]

Since the 1609 embassy to Japan was so hastily assembled, it brought no such gifts from the Stadhouder and indeed almost no items capable of serving as acceptable offerings. When it met to consider what to offer the shogun and his officials, the ships' council concluded that "there is nothing in these vessels that can be used for gifts although these are essential."[85] The solution was further improvisation and a short shopping trip to a nearby port. Although embassies traditionally brought items from their home states, the council decided it was necessary to dispatch one of its members with "two hundred reals of eight to purchase second or third hand in Nagasaki some silk which would be useful to honor some of the nobles here."[86] The chosen emporium, Nagasaki, was conveniently located less than a hundred miles to the south and, as the principal trading hub for Portuguese merchants in Japan, offered a reliable supply of luxury goods. In the end, the actual gifts presented to the shogun consisted of an odd assortment of objects, including 2 cases of raw silk, 130 bars of lead, 2 gold goblets, and some ivory. As a result, the council, clearly unimpressed by the offerings, was compelled to add vague promises of future riches by pledging "that his Majesty would receive better contentment from ships in the future."[87]

Problems with the ambassadors, their procession and the company's gifts combined to make the last element of the 1609 embassy, the letter from the Stadhouder, all the more important. Indeed, it provided—far more than the ambassadors themselves—a focal point for the entire enterprise, and it is telling that Dutch sources described the rationale for the embassy in terms of this document. Its purpose became simply to "show [*vertoonen*] the letter of His Princely Excellence to His Imperial

Majesty [the shogun]" and to hope that this would be enough to secure appropriate recognition.[88] In this way, Puyck and van den Broek, despite their status as ambassadors, retreated almost into the background while the letter, clearly the centerpiece of the entire enterprise, pushed to the fore. Although no copy of the document in question survives, it is possible to obtain some sense of the likely contents by examining other letters sent out by the Stadhouder to Asia. These, particularly when intended (as was the case here) for a generic sovereign whom the Dutch had yet to make contact with, returned again and again to the same basic themes.

Text aside, such missives were impressive visual objects that were designed to convey authority even if the recipient was unable to comprehend the written contents. Like the letters sent by English monarchs to Asia, they incorporated elaborate calligraphy, impressive seals, and gorgeously decorated borders.[89] One document included Maurits's titles written in gold ink, the outsized letters stretching boldly across the top and framed by a striking band of red velvet at the bottom.[90] The text of another was hemmed in on three sides by thick bands of gold that created an arresting combination of gleaming color, black ink, and creamy paper.[91] Indeed, so important was physical appearance that one VOC official encouraged his superiors to make sure that the Stadhouder used as many seals as possible in order to provide the best effect.[92]

Letters from the Stadhouder conventionally opened with an offer of "friendship" (vriendschap) to his remote correspondent.[93] The proposition assumed the existence of a network spanning vast distances in which equivalent figures possessed of a similar authority corresponded with each other on an essentially equal basis.[94] The presence of this imagined community of sovereigns enabled the Stadhouder to reach across thousand of miles, as well as a yawning divide of language and culture, to communicate directly with a diverse array of "emperors, dukes, lords and governors."[95] Although the connection was a personal one, to be made and sustained through the exchange of individual letters, it carried with it far-ranging implications; the acceptance of Maurits's friendship—or brotherhood, as it sometimes appears in these letters—came tied to a set of specific obligations.[96] In this way friendship became another commodity, as important as any material object, that could be exchanged between sovereigns and used to establish a basis for trade.

Once he had acquiesced to this offer of friendship, the brother monarch was to respond by presenting his support to Dutch merchants in

Asia, in effect granting them favorable commercial and legal concessions. This is summed up in one document issued by Maurits:

> The people of these our provinces are greatly inclined towards
> trade, and are ready to visit islands, provinces and people how-
> ever remote and to conduct trade with them. And it seems good
> to encourage their natural desires and to have thereby occasion
> to make accords with the residents of those [distant] lands and to
> have mutual and firm friendship. . . . We pray and seek therefore
> that generally and especially in any lands, harbors and beaches that
> our admiral with his ships and goods anchors, you will not only
> receive and welcome them, but also offer them all possible support
> and guide them in all ways to the wished, successful end of their
> honorable and praiseworthy enterprise. I promise and assure with
> our most sacred promises and assurances, that if some of their
> ships or subjects come to these our provinces, we will thankfully
> show them our gratitude for this help and will repay them with all
> possible help and service.[97]

It was not to be a one-way street, and the letter was careful to emphasize
that all concessions were to be entirely reciprocal. Thus the Stadhouder
promised that if any vessels or traders attached to his correspondent's
country arrived in the United Provinces, they would receive precisely
the same set of privileges. It was an appealing and apparently straightforward logic of royal kinship—I will grant your subjects the right to
trade freely in my lands if you do the same for my subjects—but it was
also illusory. As Stadhouder, Maurits did not have the authority to make
such a commitment and, in any case, there was no expectation that
Asian merchants would make their way to the United Provinces. Rather,
exchange was to flow in one direction, allowing Dutch merchants to
demand extensive trading rights as a direct consequence of this personal relationship with their sovereign while yielding nothing in return.

Just as these letters simplified politics by reducing a complicated
landscape crowded with diverse states with little in common into a network of equal sovereigns, so did they work to manage the Dutch East
India Company's difficult profile. Documents from the Stadhouder
smoothed out the complexities involved in the Dutch push into Asia
and replaced these with a simpler vision consisting of two parts, ruler

and subject. The company was a new kind of organization in Asia, a hybrid enterprise armed with a set of sovereign powers that operated independently of the state, but one struggles to find any reference to this in such documents.[98] Rather, they acted to throw a royal cloak over Dutch activities in Asia, concealing the newness of the organization behind a familiar facade. The Dutch were, in Maurits's own words, simply "my subjects" (mijne ondersaten), and their presence in Asia could be understood in this way.[99]

The result was to transform men like Puyck and van den Broek from corporate employees acting in the service of their shareholders into royal subjects intent only on discharging their duties. In this way VOC diplomatic exchange was reduced, at least from a Japanese point of view, to a far more familiar equation. No different from the ambassadors from Korea, the Ryukyu kingdom, or any one of a number of states, the Dutch were rendered just another group of envoys sent by their sovereign to open ties on his behalf and fully capable, therefore, of slotting into existing diplomatic categories.

Armed with their letter from the Stadhouder, Puyck and van den Broek departed Hirado on 27 July.[100] Traveling by boat through the busy shipping lanes of the Inland Sea, they reached the commercial metropolis of Osaka a week later. Here they received their first sign that they would be treated as an official state embassy when they were provided with free transport and access to a system of post-horses.[101] On 13 August the group arrived in Sunpu, the small town in modern Shizuoka prefecture where the retired shogun had established his court. Once there, the pace of interaction rapidly sped up. The ambassadors' first meeting was with two of the shogun's most senior advisers, Gotō Shōzaburō and Honda Masazumi, who welcomed the delegation and promised to secure it an audience.[102] They proved good to their word and on the next day the ambassadors were brought directly before Tokugawa Ieyasu himself.

Two important descriptions of this crucial first meeting between VOC envoys and the shogun survive, one in the company's archives and another in Japanese sources. According to Dutch sources, Puyck and van den Broek were summoned "into the castle. [There], they presented the shogun with some gifts of raw silk and lead. They also handed over the letter of his princely excellency and presented our requests. His Majesty was very pleased and promised to grant us our wishes and offer free trade."[103] Ikoku nikki, a record of Bakufu diplomatic activity compiled by the Zen monk Konchiin Sūden, provides a second account of the embassy's reception: "On the 11th day of the 7th month, in the central keep, Honda Masazumi announced that a letter had come from Holland. We could not understand the language of this country and hence it has been translated by interpreters. The letter indicated that they wish to send ships and thus asked for permission for their vessels to enter our harbors and to come and go. They presented two gold cups, 350 kin of silk, 3000 pieces of lead, and 2 pieces of ivory."[104]

The descriptions, though short, are revealing. Both show, first of all, a marked passivity on the part of Tokugawa officials who made no attempt to subject their Dutch guests to the kind of rigorous interrogation we might have expected about the nature and form of their delegation. The absence of cross-examination sets these particular ambassadors apart from the more general experience of European diplomatic missions to Asia, many of which struggled with a variant of the same question put to da Gama by the king of Calicut: why had a delegation that claimed to come "from a very rich kingdom . . . brought him nothing."[105] In Puyck and van den Broek's case the disconnect between appearance and claim was far more glaring than usual, yet despite this fact no questions were asked about the ambassadors' credentials, the nature of their gifts, or why a powerful monarch like the "king of Holland" had dispatched such poorly equipped representatives. This willingness to accept the ambassadors' presentation without further interrogation becomes even more intriguing when it is set against the fate of later Dutch ambassadors to Japan, such as the ones discussed in chapter 2, who were grilled relentlessly about their origins, backers, and purpose. Why then were Tokugawa officials so willing to sign off on the embassy without question or query?

Although they could not know it, Puyck and van den Broek had arrived at a uniquely receptive moment for diplomatic engagement, and it was this fact that more than anything else assured them a trouble-free stay in Sunpu. In 1600, when Tokugawa Ieyasu seized power, Japan was a diplomatic outcast. Hideyoshi's invasion of Korea had cut ties with other states, turning Japan into an international pariah stripped of access to traditional diplomatic circuits in East Asia. In response, Ieyasu initiated an active campaign designed to reestablish Japan's position as a diplomatic center in its own right. Arano Yasunori calls this period the "Tokugawa international debut," and it was marked by a frenetic burst of diplomatic exchange.[106] Between 1601 and

1614 Bakufu officials dispatched a total of seventy-six official letters, forty-eight of which came directly from the shogun, to twelve different states. These included neighboring polities like China and Korea, but also a diverse range of new diplomatic partners such as Patani, Cochinchina, Cambodia, Champa, Siam, England, the Philippines, and the United Provinces. The table below reflects this period of intense diplomatic activity, which rapidly slowed after Ieyasu's death in 1616 before coming to a virtual stop:[107]

Table 1.1 Tokugawa Diplomatic Letters

Period	All diplomatic letters	Personal letters from the shogun	Average per year (all letters)
1601–1614	76	48	5.4
1615–1633	34	5	1.8
1633–1643	15	2	1.5

From an average of more than five each year while Ieyasu was alive, the rate of outgoing letters dropped to just below 2 and then to 1.5. Even more dramatically, the number of personal letters from the shogun plummeted from close to 50 to just 7 over the period from 1615 to 1643.

As it reached out to states in Southeast Asia and Europe, the regime also moved to extend an enthusiastic welcome to any embassy prepared to make the long trip to Japan. The result was a kind of "no questions asked" diplomacy in which any interrogation of qualification or credential was suppressed. While Ieyasu was alive, no embassy was turned away and no letter left unanswered, even if it came from a state that Japan had never engaged with before or from a ruler with limited standing in regional politics.[108] The tone of this period stands in stark contrast to what was to follow. Once its newly constituted diplomatic networks were in place, the Tokugawa regime under Hidetada and Iemitsu came to apply a far more rigorous set of standards to its international partners. Incoming letters that failed to meet Tokugawa conventions were rejected out of hand while embassies dispatched by rulers with unsettled claims to legitimacy were stopped at Japan's borders and sent back without an answer.[109] In this way the reception accorded to Puyck and van den Broek stemmed largely from timing, related to a highly specific and relatively short-lived phase of Tokugawa diplomatic practice, and had little to do with the ambassadors themselves.

Both the Dutch and Japanese descriptions of the ambassadors' audience with the shogun highlight the importance of the Stadhouder's distant presence, with Suden's description focusing entirely on the letter from Holland while foregoing any mention of the envoys themselves. Like Sprinckel a year earlier, Puyck and van den Broek seem to have presented Maurits directly as the king or, more precisely, the "sovereign of Holland." That he was understood in this way is clear from the return letter presented by the shogun a few days after the initial audience:

> The sovereign of Japan (*Nihon kokushu*) Minamoto Ieyasu replies to the sovereign of Holland (*Oranda kokushu*). Your Highness, your letter has come from far away, but when I view it I feel as if I am close to you. I am very pleased with the presents you have given me. I have heard that your country has dispatched many warships, generals, officers and men to foreign countries. Some of them have arrived in Matsura province [Hirado] in my country in order to open friendly relations. This is also my wish. If both our countries have the same desires, though separated by a thousand miles of ocean, they may by yearly communications become not dissimilar. In my country, we correct those without order and bring them to order. If merchants come from your country, they will be able to reside in safety. If you send several people, we will allow them to construct a trading post on our land. Your ships may use any harbor. I believe our relations will become even friendlier.[110]

If the Stadhouder's correspondence was premised on the notion of a royal network spanning continents, the letter from the shogun picked up on the theme by suggesting the existence of two parallel kingdoms and two sovereigns of roughly commensurate status. This was reflected both in the address from the "sovereign of Japan" to the "sovereign of Holland" as well as in the use of the term *Your Highness* (*denka*), a title reserved for communication between kings, to refer to the Stadhouder. Analyzing letters exchanged with the king of Korea, which also made use of the same term, Ron Toby writes that it served to place the two rulers "on exactly the same hierarchical plane . . . expressing equal status and mutual respect."[111]

In the process of translation, the Dutch version of this document was lengthened and its basic content augmented with a number of embellishments:

> I, emperor and king of Japan, send my greetings to the king of Holland (*Coninck van Hollant*) who has contacted me from such far lands. I am very pleased with the letter and the offering of Your Majesty's friendship. I wish our lands lay closer to each other so that we may maintain and increase our newly commenced friendship. I imagine in my mind to see Your Majesty although you are unknown to me, and Your Majesty's affection stretches to me, through Your Majesty's liberalness in awarding me with gifts. . . . I am partly ashamed that the subjects of Your Majesty, whose name and renown is known throughout the entire world through his manly deeds, should come from such a far land to such an unfitting land as this to seek me and to present your friendship. I have not deserved this. But considering that your affection has been the cause thereof, I could not but entertain your subjects with friendliness and grant their requests. . . . I will maintain and defend them as my own subjects.[112]

At first glance, the letter, whether in the original Japanese or the Dutch translation, seems particularly friendly, but when compared with dozens of similar documents dispatched from Japan in this period it becomes clear that it consisted largely of unremarkable diplomatic boilerplate.[113] In October 1606, three years before Puyck and van de Broek appeared, Ieyasu initiated contact with the kingdom of Siam by sending a letter with some familiar phrases: "Minamoto Ieyasu of Japan respectfully says to Your Highness (*denka*) the sovereign of Siam: In the matter of making alliances and exchanges, even if distances are not great between two countries, if they are not friendly then it is as if they are a thousand miles away. However, even if the countries are not near, if they have communication then they are like neighbors."[114] The contents of a subsequent missive, dispatched to Siam in 1610, closely match those of the letter issued to the Stadhouder one year earlier:

Minamoto Ieyasu of Japan respectfully says to Your Highness the sovereign of Siam. Even if lands are separated by a thousand miles of mountains and sea, if there is friendship, they are close. This summer a merchant ship arrived with a letter from your honored country. Although I did not move a foot, I felt I could see your honored face, and I was very happy. . . . If trade and merchants ships come between your honored country and my country every year, both our countries will be peaceful and our people will be prosperous.[115]

Although, viewed in this context, the letter to Maurits seems less favorable, it was precisely this uniformity, the lack of a distinct response and the inclusion instead of a uniform set of phrases issued to any one of a number of kings, that signaled the achievement of the company's goal. In his document the shogun treated the Dutch, the employees of a mercantile organization with no standing in traditional diplomatic circuits, just like any other representatives of a distant monarch. In so doing, he accepted Maurits's identity as the "sovereign of Holland" and Puyck and van den Broek's role as royal ambassadors dispatched by their ruler to open friendly relations. The result was to slot both the United Provinces and its envoys in Japan into an existing framework. Exactly as it was intended, the presence of the "king of Holland" smoothed out the company's rough edges by providing the Dutch with a straightforward identity and an easy structure for exchange oriented around the friendship of two sovereigns.

On 22 August, less than ten days after their initial arrival in Sunpu, Puyck and van den Broek departed with the letter from the shogun and permission to conduct "free trade in any place we desired in his lands, to build a house [factory] as big or as small as we wanted, and permission to bring merchandize and to sell it at our own prices."[116] Although the ambassadors (and their superiors) viewed these concessions as an unprecedented set of privileges skillfully drawn from a favorable shogun by Dutch expertise, they sprang, like the letter issued to Maurits, from a stock template that was extended to other groups of foreign merchants.[117] The king of Siam was, for example, assured that "the commanders of your vessels as may visit us from year to year shall have accorded to them every kind of gracious treatment."[118] In much the same way, the Bakufu informed Spanish representatives that when "trade ships from your country come to our coasts, they will receive a hearty welcome . . . [and] will be given full privileges to enter any port, bay, or waterway in our country. They may engage in trade wherever they like."[119]

THE STADHOUDER REPLIES

Since the shogun had written directly to the Stadhouder, it was imperative that company officials, who were eager to use this opening cycle of correspondence to secure further concessions, obtain a formal response as quickly as possible. The great distances involved between Japan and Maurits's home in Europe made this, however, a difficult task. Indeed, one of the most significant problems brought about by the continued reliance on the Stadhouder was the slow pace it enforced on diplomatic transactions. In most cases it took at least two years—and sometimes considerably longer—to secure a return response from the United Provinces. Such delays were part of the reason why the company moved later to shift its diplomatic strategy away from Europe to focus on Batavia, but in the meantime it fell to VOC agents in Japan and particularly the newly appointed *opperhoofd* of the Hirado trading post, Jacques Specx, to urge his superiors to further speed. Chafing at the enforced delay, he asked the Heeren 17 in November 1610 to assure a regular supply of letters from Maurits: "Your Honours should not neglect [to] send with each voyage of the ships coming this way a patent [letter] of his Princely Excellency to his Imperial Majesty [the shogun], [which] should be [executed] in the most splendid manner with seals and decorated in other ways where possible. This greatly pleases his Majesty and makes him feel more honored than any other thing."[120]

Despite such pleas, it was not until 1612 that a new document from the Stadhouder reached Japan. Once there, it was immediately carried back to the shogun's court for presentation.[121] Dated 18 December 1610, the letter began with a long list of Maurits's titles, although these were converted in the Japanese translation into the same formulation used earlier, *Oranda kokushu* or the sovereign of Holland. Intended to cement his newly established bonds with the shogun, Maurits's missive returned to the twin themes of friendship and reciprocity:

> To the all powerful emperor and king of Japan, salute. I have received Your Imperial Majesty's letter with great esteem. I am delighted to learn that it has pleased Your Imperial Majesty to take the Hollanders, my subjects, with such friendship into your great, well-known and famous realm. You have allowed them permission to traffic and trade in all places, lands and islands in Your Imperial Majesty's territory and you have taken them under Your Imperial Majesty's protection. This makes me very happy. I thank Your Majesty greatly for this good deed. I wish well, with Your Imperial Majesty, that your lands lay closer to my territory, so that Your Imperial Majesty's subjects could visit the same [my lands], because then I could better show my pleasure in thanking Your Majesty for the favor that you have shown my subjects. But now because of the great distance between our lands this cannot happen, and so I hope that there will be further occasion in time for me to prove my great affection for our recently commenced friendship.

Saluting their "recently commenced friendship," Maurits expressed his hope that he might be able to demonstrate his "great affection" for his Japanese counterpart in the future. This personal bond was to flow downward, providing space for Dutch East India Company merchants, described here simply as "my subjects" (*mijne ondersaten*), to operate in Japan. In this way, permission "to traffic and trade in all places, lands and islands in Your Majesty's territory" arose naturally out of the connection between shogun and Stadhouder. Once again, there was a notable absence of any reference to the company, the organization that had actually brought Dutch merchants to Japan. The result was to reduce a complex set of interactions to a direct link between powerful individuals, prompting Maurits to express his happiness and personal thanks to the shogun for extending such favors to his subjects. Going one step further, he requested that Ieyasu offer his "help and favor in trade with Korea," thereby securing additional concessions for "my subjects [who] look for trade in all lands and places with friendship and sincerity." Their friendship was, it seemed, thus to extend beyond Japan's borders to open up a pathway into another East Asian market.

As in other letters, the Stadhouder gestured to a logic of reciprocal privileges, but clearly, given the shogun's own insistence, in the Dutch translation of the document presented to Puyck and van den Broek, on the great distances lying between their lands, it was not possible simply to repeat his standard promise that Japanese merchants in Europe could count on the same privileges extended to Dutch traders in Asia. Instead, he opted for the middle ground, arguing that reciprocal sentiments did in fact exist, even if the practical circumstances were not conducive to an actual exchange. If, by a fortuitous turn of event, some Tokugawa subjects succeeded in reaching the United Provinces, they would automatically receive the same protections and favors, with only distance standing in the way of this happening.

In the last part of the letter the Stadhouder turned his attention to the company's enemies by unleashing a ferocious attack on the Portuguese and Spanish. If the sovereigns of Holland and Japan were equivalent figures tied by friendship, then they could also be defined in opposition to an illegitimate actor, the king of Spain. The result was to draw the shogun closer by establishing a sense of shared identity, of two rulers unified in resistance against a sinister third presence.[122] The particular charges deployed here mirrored the accusations made in anti-Spanish propaganda in Europe, which painted the Iberian monarch as a dark figure consumed by megalomaniacal obsessions.[123] Driven by an insatiable lust for power, the king of Spain was unable to coexist peacefully with other countries, but sought always to undermine and eventually to dominate. Presented in the form of benign advice from one friend to another, Maurits offered a dire warning, cautioning Ieyasu to guard against Spain's desire for "monarchy over the whole world." The charge had the additional benefit of undermining the Portuguese and the Jesuits, who were both firmly established in Japan. Linking these groups together with the "Castilians," Maurits denounced their "cunning and deceit," which extended beyond unfair practices and constant lies to a vast conspiracy designed to overthrow the shogun. Aided by their Portuguese allies, the Jesuits planned, the letter explained, to seize control of the shogun's realm by using their converts to bring Japan to "division, partisanship and eventually to civil war."[124]

In this way the December 1610 letter arrived in Japan attached to high expectations, that an already promising link with the shogun could be expanded and used to secure new privileges for Dutch merchants in

East Asia. Ieyasu's response proved, however, deeply disappointing, taking the form of an extremely short and quite obviously formulaic letter that made no attempt to reply to the specifics of Maurits's requests. Addressed again to the "sovereign of Holland," it noted simply that "your letter has come from far away. I have reread it many times. . . . If your ships continue to come and go, then although we are separated by thousands of miles, it is as if we are one family."[125] Even to the most optimistic of observers, it was clear that this was little more than a stock diplomatic response. Hendrik Brouwer, who made the trip to Sunpu, complained that, even after all the effort expended on arranging the delivery of the Stadhouder's document, it had produced nothing more than a polite response and no opportunity to "discuss anything special."[126] The only bright spot came in the shogun's decision to present the "sovereign of Holland" with two swords and a magnificent suit of armor.

The obvious conclusion, and the one immediately reached by VOC agents, was that further letters from the Stadhouder would not produce significant gains; hence there was little reason to waste time and money on procuring additional documents. As a result, the company elected to close off its cycle of diplomatic engagement with the shogun and to focus its attention elsewhere. Rather than arranging new embassies, Dutch agents in Japan relied from 1612 onward on informal delegations, which were able to travel to the shogun's headquarters without special credentials or fanfare, when they wished to make contact with the regime. The result was a long lapse in official contact between the company and the shogun that was only broken in 1627 when VOC leaders determined that an emerging crisis in Taiwan merited the dispatch of a formal embassy. By the time it moved to send a new mission to Japan, the company had, however, flung off its royal disguise and asserted its own rights to engage directly with governments across Asia without mediation by the Stadhouder. The result was a sustained conflict over VOC diplomatic prerogatives that came to paralyze relations with Japan.

CHAPTER TWO

THE LORD OF BATAVIA

Our Lord General . . . is of such a status that he sends ambassadors to the principal kings of China, Siam, Aceh and Patani; to the emperors of Java and Persia; [and] to the Great Mughal.

—Ambassador Pieter Nuyts, 1627

On 1 January 1624, two ambassadors from China arrived in Batavia, the Dutch East India Company's new Asian headquarters. This dramatic event, unprecedented in the short history of Dutch settlement there, provided the opening entry of the voluminous Batavia *Dagregister*, the daily account of operations that forms a vital source for historians working on this period.[1] The pair had been dispatched by the governor of Fujian province to discuss recent developments on the Penghu Islands, a small chain in the Taiwan straits that Dutch forces had occupied two years earlier. Accompanied by four elephants hurriedly drafted in by local officials to add a touch of grandeur, the ambassadors' procession wound its way through the city before ending its journey at Batavia Castle, the squat, heavily armed fortress that the company had erected to guard its most important territorial possession in Asia. Passing through two lines of soldiers arrayed in front of the gate, they were led into the sweltering confines of the stronghold. Waiting for them in a central chamber was "His Excellency the General," the highest-ranking Dutch official in Asia and the new face of VOC diplomacy in the region.

The arrival of the embassy from China and others like it marks an important shift in the nature of VOC diplomatic practice—one that would not only alter the way it did business in Asia but would also have far-reaching consequences for the company's relationship with the Tokugawa regime. With the conquest of Jayakarta in 1619, the VOC claimed a firm foothold on Asian soil, putting down deep roots that would only be dislodged centuries later. As the city expanded and grew, the organization's diplomatic strategy began to adjust accordingly, shifting away from its prior reliance on the distant figure of the Stadhouder to a new focus on the governor-general and Batavia Castle as the fulcrum for diplomatic activity. In the decades that followed the mission from Fujian, these officials welcomed dozens of ambassadors into the audience hall located deep inside the fortress. This stream of incoming delegations was matched by a steady flow of embassies, carrying letters issued by the governor-general and bearing no trace of the "king of Holland," out of the castle to a range of Asian states.

One such mission, sent to Japan in 1627 and placed under the command of Pieter Nuyts, forms the subject of this chapter.[2] In contrast to its humble predecessor that had arrived in Sunpu eighteen years earlier, Nuyts's embassy was a carefully planned affair, led by a genuine member of the VOC elite and equipped with a rich array of gifts. And yet, despite its extensive preparation and the tens of thousands of guilders that were poured into it, the embassy was an abject failure. That such a well-planned mission would fail where Puyck and van den Broek's jury-rigged effort had succeeded seems so obviously contradictory that it demands an explanation.

When it came time to account for what had happened, the ambassador, eager to escape personal punishment for the debacle, happily offered up a list of villains that included incompetent interpreters, ignorant Bakufu officials, treacherous allies, and determined enemies intent on pushing the Dutch out of Japan.[3] But as more and more details emerged from Japan, his superiors concluded that Nuyts himself was the primary culprit. He had, they railed, been too arrogant, too intolerant, and, above all, too inflexible in his dealings with the Japanese, needlessly aggravating problems when a better diplomat could have quieted the Bakufu's concerns while steering the embassy to successful completion. While he fully deserves much of the criticism directed his way—indeed Nuyts emerges as a strikingly unsympathetic figure—this focus on a single individual leaves out an important part of the story of what went wrong in Edo.[4] Perhaps more important, it tends to flatten out the problems inherent in this interaction and to assume that any disagreements could have been settled if the ambassador had simply adopted a suitably humble attitude, presented the right gift, or used the right words. This was never the case. Although he was clearly a poor choice, Nuyts struggled with larger structural issues beyond his control.

By the time he arrived in Japan, the company, shrugging off the royal disguise (detailed in the previous chapter), was in the process of asserting its own right to engage directly with Asian rulers without mediation from the Stadhouder. When Tokugawa officials discovered that his delegation came from Batavia and not the "king of Holland," it triggered a crisis that defied easy resolution. Over the next weeks Nuyts's mission became trapped in an uncertain space between two distinct diplomatic narratives, unable to prove its connection to the "king of Holland," but also incapable of showing that the governor-general was a legitimate actor in his own right. To assume that it failed because of one inept individual is, therefore, to overlook a basic point, that the embassy was not an infinitely malleable tool that could be shaped to European wishes by skillful ambassadors. Rather, diplomatic missions had to conform to a logic mandated by Asian officials, and not all embassies, irrespective of the personal qualities of their chief representatives, were able to pass such a test. In this way there was, to return to an earlier point, nothing straightforward about diplomacy.

While few diplomatic encounters were quite as fraught as Nuyts's embassy, which ran into a perfect storm of problems, his broader experience as a European ambassador in Asia was not exceptional. During such missions, European conceptions about the proper order of international relations and the rights of diplomatic envoys collided with political realities in Asia. The result was often an overriding sense of anxiety as ambassadors struggled to manage their encounters. This was famously the case with another highly qualified envoy, Thomas Roe, who was sent by the English East India Company to negotiate with the Mughal emperor in 1615. Although he enjoyed more success, Roe's experience, closely documented in his lengthy diary, often mirrored that of his Dutch counterpart.[5] Both ambassadors tried at every turn to compel respect for mission and master, often by using similar tactics and a shared reliance on theatrical display, but both found themselves constantly on the defensive. For Nuyts, the embassy became a terrible "labyrinth" from which he could see no exit; for Roe it transformed into a "Camp of Confusion" that resisted all his attempts to impose order.[6]

BATAVIA AS DIPLOMATIC CAPITAL

In many ways the gradual move away from a previous dependence on the Stadhouder as a diplomatic mediator was the inevitable product of the company's development and its transformation from an unfamiliar interloper into a formidable power with its own territorial base in Asia. However, the precise nature of the strategy that emerged to replace it can be traced back to two momentous developments, the creation of the office of governor-general in 1609 and the conquest of Jayakarta a decade later, that combined to lay the basis for a new diplomatic capital in Asia. In the first years after the company's formation in 1602, the Heeren 17, a body based in the United Provinces, constituted the organization's sole permanent command structure. The regular fleets that departed from Europe were placed under the control of an admiral who was commissioned to lead his ships to Asia and, once there, to take command of the company's operations. But his tenure only extended until such time as a new fleet and a new admiral arrived, creating a sequence of temporary appointments. Although this did, at least in theory, guarantee a clear chain of command, the reality was a highly decentralized system in which fleets operated independently of each other and with minimal coordination. The result was that individual commanders clashed, promises were broken, and the company's efforts were hampered by disorganization.

As the area of operations expanded and as more and more ships arrived in Asia, it became clear that these arrangements could not be sustained, and in 1609 the Heeren 17 elected to overhaul this system. Their ambitious solution was to create a separate office, the governor-general (*Gouveneur-Generaal*), that was to be based permanently in Asia and to take control of all operations there. The decision pushed the VOC onto a different path from its English rival, which continued to rely on a model organized around individual fleets, and brought it more in line with the Portuguese system with its central authority in Goa.[7] To fill the new office, the Heeren 17 selected Pieter Both, an experienced merchant who had traveled to Asia on one of the precompany voyages. He was instructed to assume control over all VOC activities in Asia and to bring them back onto a firm footing.[8]

In addition to creating a centralized office, the directors recognized that they needed to establish a permanent headquarters in Asia from which the company's affairs could be directed. The proposed rendezvous, as it appears in VOC documents, needed to posses a good natural harbor in which an ever growing fleet could be refitted, a strategic location preferably at the confluence of major trade routes, and room for expansion, ideally because the territory had already come under the company's sovereignty or because it fell under the control of a weak political authority willing to grant substantial concessions. The choice eventually settled on Jayakarta, a port city located near Banten that was under the control of a minor prince. In 1610 agreement was reached to allow the company to set up operations there, but relations gradually deteriorated; within a decade there was open war. By the time the dust had settled, the prince had been deposed and his dominion claimed as VOC territory.

The establishment of Batavia permanently altered the trajectory of the company's development by creating a sovereign space in which it could operate unhampered by external authority.[9] Over the next decades, the limits of its authority gradually swelled outward from the tight constrictions of these original boundaries until the company controlled large swathes of Java. The conquest of Jayakarta had the added consequence of creating a rival center of power within the organization itself. From the beginning, the slow pace of communication between Europe and Asia gave the governors-general considerable freedom to operate independently. If so inclined, Batavia could simply ignore or selectively interpret directives by pointing to changed circumstances. The more ambitious governors-general were content to take matters more fully into their hands and to present the directors with a fait accompli. Antonio van Diemen, who held the office from 1636 to 1645, informed his superiors that "we have said and we confirm with this that we *must be trusted with the matters of the Indies,* and therefore cannot wait for orders if we are to do the Company's service."[10] Another governor-general put it even more directly when he noted that "the Gentlemen in the fatherland make the decisions there that they consider the best, but we do it here according to our own good judgment."[11] The result was that these officials became an increasingly dominant force within the organization while the Heeren 17 were reduced to a more reactive role.[12]

Figure 2.1. The Castle of Batavia, ca. 1656–58. Andries Beeckman. *Courtesy of the Collection Rijksmuseum, Amsterdam*

As the company's internal politics evolved, its diplomatic strategy began to shift away from Europe. The new focus on Batavia was in part a pragmatic response to the rapid expansion in the organization's activities and reach. By the 1620s the company was engaged in ongoing negotiations with a range of emperors, kings, sultans, and other rulers across Asia. The sheer volume of diplomatic traffic meant that it could no longer afford to wait for documents from the Stadhouder's palace, which could, as had been the case in Japan, take years to obtain. At the same time, some within the company began to suspect that a reliance on a figure in Europe for endorsement undermined the governor-general's own position. As it expanded within Asia, the organization was increasingly obsessed with its own reputation, viewing it as a vital instrument needed to lure allies closer to Batavia while keeping rivals in check.[13] A strong governor-general capable of commanding respect from the "feigned friends and declared enemies" that surrounded Batavia was crucial to the organization's survival, and persistent references to a more senior figure in Europe could only undermine his hard-won status.[14] Addressing this point directly, one official commented that his superiors should no longer procure letters from the Stadhouder as "the respect for the governor-general is markedly lessened (to the company's disadvantage)."[15]

The shift from Holland to Batavia could not have happened, however, without a transformation in the nature of the governor-general's office. Its first incumbents were comparatively modest figures poorly suited for any role as diplomatic figureheads. Unlike the Portuguese viceroys in Goa, the governors-general were not aristocrats, and many came from extremely humble backgrounds, ascending gradually from the lowest rungs to positions of power via decades of service.[16] Some, like Antonio van Diemen, who had fled the United Provinces under an assumed name to avoid legal proceedings, had more colorful pasts. Once they arrived in Asia, the first governors-general, possessing none of the kingly accoutrements of local potentates, struggled to distinguish themselves as anything more than chief merchants. It is not surprising, therefore, that many nearby rulers dismissed the office as lacking the necessary status to engage in diplomacy. One sultan summed up a more general attitude when he proclaimed that sending an embassy to meet with the governor-general "would be in conflict with his honor. If prince Mauritius [Maurits] was here, he would send [an envoy] to him as to a brother, but he would not stoop to [send an embassy] to the general, who was just the overseer of merchants."[17] Indeed, it was for this reason that the company continued to rely on letters from the Stadhouder for several years after Both's initial appointment in 1609.

Changing this perception required time. After the conquest of Jayakarta, the VOC set about constructing a new city on the ruins of the old settlement.[18] Over the next decades, laborers straightened rivers, dug canals, and erected rows of gabled houses, transforming the city from a backwater into a booming colonial metropolis that became known as the "queen of the East."[19] Like Batavia itself, the office of governor-general was remade and all trace of the humble chief merchant erased. By the time the first detailed reports written by foreign travelers to Batavia emerged around the middle of the seventeenth century, the governor-general had become an increasingly imperious figure who had more in common with local rulers than any "overseer of merchants."[20] Whenever he ventured out, the governor-general traveled in a special carriage of state pulled by six horses and accompanied by a troop of horsemen as well as a bodyguard of richly clad halberdiers. Jean-Baptiste Tavernier,

Figure 2.2. Governor-General Pieter Both, Unknown artists, ca. 1750–80. *Courtesy of the Collection Rijksmuseum, Amsterdam*

a French traveler who provided one of the earliest descriptions of Batavia by an outsider, commented that there was "no Cavalry in Europe so well clad or mounted as his; the Horsemen all upon Persian or Arabian Steeds. Nor is his Foot Guard less sumptuous: His Halberdiers wear their yellow Satten Doublets, Scarlet Breeches lac'd with Silver Lace, and their Silk Stockins."[21]

The overall effect was unmistakably regal. He "displays," one author summarized, "absolutely the pomp and state of a distinguished sovereign. Not only does he reside in an impressive palace, but his entire state, train and government is kingly."[22] Another noted that the governor-general was "provided with no less Pomp and State than the Princes of Europe,"[23] while a third explained simply that the incumbent was known as "the Raya de Jaccatra of the Hollanders, that is the king of Jaccatra."[24] Much like a king, the key episodes of the governor-general's life—his accession, birthdays, and funeral—were all celebrated with carefully staged events that brought the city to a standstill.[25] The assumption of office took place in front of large crowds who were compelled to swear an "oath of faithfulness" to the incoming incumbent.[26] The conclusion of the ceremony was marked by volleys of musket and cannon fire, after which the city's leading figures made their way to the castle to offer personal congratulations.

Christopher Fryke, a soldier enlisted in the company's army, provided a description of the equally lavish birthday celebrations:

It being the General's Birth-Day . . . all the Burghers and Freemen were in Arms, and drew up before the General's Lodgings in the Castle, where after the Discharge of all the Cannon about the Castle and City, they saluted his Excellency with several Vollies of Shot. Each Nation then came in a distinct Body with Presents to the General; as first, the Chineses, Siamers, Japonneses, Macassars, Amboineses, Bandaneses, &c. and even the Javians, who are not permitted to set a foot in the Castle on any other time, were then let in. . . . These Presents are Magnificent. . . . Besides this, all the Streets were full of Lights, Bonefires, and Fireworks.[27]

The greatest pomp was reserved, however, for the funeral of those governors-general who died in office. These could be enormously expensive affairs, in one case costing over 13,000 rijksdaalders, a huge sum that included 267 gold and silver medals that were specially struck for the occasion.[28] The climax of such ceremonies involved a long cortege formed of hundreds of citizens, employees, musicians, local dignitaries, and foreign ambassadors that wound its way through the streets of Batavia accompanied by volley after volley of cannon fire.[29] At its center, and in a manner befitting any monarch, walked a solemn procession of officials carrying the deceased's regalia, including his helmet, sword, tunic, gloves, and spurs.

The detailed codification of rules and rituals, the carefully choreographed and often enormously expensive ceremonies used to celebrate major events, and the deliberate fencing off of certain privileges suggest a program that extended far beyond individual whims. While it is clear that many incumbents delighted in such regal trappings, the wholescale refashioning of the office undertaken in this period was clearly motivated by a desire to boost the governor-general's status for political reasons.[30] This fact was recognized by contemporary observers, including Tavernier, who noted that to "maintain their Authority and Commerce in the *Indies*, [the company] believes it to be to their advantage, that the General . . . should keep up the Port of a Prince."[31]

A governor-general capable of keeping the "Port of a Prince" provided a natural focus for diplomacy, and foreign embassies such as the 1609 mission from Siam that had once made the long trip to Europe to meet with the Stadhouder were gradually redirected to Batavia. In their complexity and rigid insistence on proper protocol, the rituals developed in this city to accommodate diplomatic envoys rivaled those of any royal court with precise requirements detailed in VOC records for each stage, participant, and action.[32] When they arrived, visiting ambassadors were brought ashore in specially decorated vessels while the guns of the assembled fleet boomed overhead. Once on firm ground, they were greeted by a group of high-ranking officials and taken to lodgings specially constructed for "Ambassadors and Envoys of Princes or Foreign states."[33]

On the day of the audience, a "carriage of state" (*caros van staat*) guarded by a contingent of company troops transported the ambassadors to Batavia Castle, the key ceremonial space for diplomatic interaction.[34] Guy Tachard, a Jesuit visitor to Batavia in the late seventeenth century, noted that the "Citadel hath four Bastions faced and mounted with a great number of brass Guns. There is a good Garison kept in it, not only to hold it out against *Indians* and *Europeans*, and to succour the other Places in case of necessity ; but also to shew the Greatness and Power of the Company to Ambassadors and Princes, who come thither from all Places of the *Indies*."[35] When they reached the stronghold, the envoys handed over their diplomatic letters to a splendidly attired halberdier who placed the documents on a silver or gold platter covered in satin and held under a yellow "parasol of state."[36]

These documents, hundreds of which are recorded in the Batavia *Dagregister*, reflect the emergence of the governor-general as a diplomatic actor in his own right, another kingly figure in a crowded political landscape. A 1648 missive sent from the ruler of the same state that had once dismissed the governor-general as a merchant of little consequence addressed him as lord "over all lands, castles, ships, yachts and Netherlanders below the winds and powerful in his rule on land as well as on sea."[37] In 1664 the occupant of the "kingly throne of Jambi" in Java wrote to "to the Governor-General . . . that sits upon the throne of power in the city of Batavia and rules the nation of Holland in [the lands] above and below the winds."[38] In 1691 the ruler of Abyssinia addressed his correspondence to the "most honorable Sultan of Sultans of the Hollanders and the great king of kings of the land Batavia," while a letter from the sovereign of Tonkin was directed simply to the "king of Batavia."[39] Other rulers opted to refer to the governor-general in more intimate terms as father or grandfather.[40]

Alongside the incoming embassies that confirmed Batavia's role as an increasingly important diplomatic hub, there was an equally active flow of traffic out of the city. After the conquest of Jayakarta, dozens of embassies equipped with letters and gifts from the governor-general appeared in capitals across Asia. The most impressive of these traveled to regional powers like Mughal India or Safavid Persia and included elaborate processions that made carefully choreographed entrances into capital cities led by splendidly attired ambassadors.[41] They did so carrying letters from the governor-general, which increasingly replaced documents from the Stadhouder as the standard instrument for VOC diplomatic exchange.[42] The broad trend was thus away from the "king of Holland" template toward a new model oriented around an increasingly regal governor-general who stood confidently at the center of an expansive web of diplomatic links.[43] The moment of transition as Batavia pushed to the fore was not, however, always smooth and a handful of rulers, particularly those that had exchanged a series of documents with the Prince of Orange, protested his retreat from the scene.

In Siam, where the Ayutthayan monarchs had treated the arrival of letters from the Stadhouder as an opportunity to stage lavish spectacles designed to buttress the crown's authority, the company encountered sustained resistance to its attempt to close down contact with the "king of Holland." Eventually in 1639, after frequent inquiries about the prospect of future letters from the prince of Orange, the governor-general requested that the king of Siam correspond directly with him and abandon any attempt to communicate with the Stadhouder.[44] The next year, Batavia procured a letter from Maurits's successor, Frederik Hendrik, asking for a halt to their correspondence.[45] By way of justification, the prince pointed to the great distances separating Siam and the Netherlands, while explaining that the governor-general, the designated overlord of the Dutch in Asia and the possessor himself of sovereign powers, should handle all diplomatic matters. After considerable back and forth, officials in Siam finally consented to this new arrangement and agreed to redirect letters and embassies to Batavia. The situation was quite different in Japan where the diplomatic shift away from Holland prompted outrage.

A NEW EMBASSY TO JAPAN

In 1627, more than a decade after its last embassy had arrived in Japan, the company resolved to send a new delegation to the shogun's court. Momentum for such a mission had been building for a number of years, partly in response to a series of restrictions that had been placed on the Dutch by Ieyasu's successor, Tokugawa Hidetada. But, while there was considerable enthusiasm in some parts of the organization, not everyone was convinced a new embassy would achieve its designated aims. In particular, Cornelis van Neijenroode, *opperhoofd* of the Japan factory from 1623 to 1632, protested that such a mission would consume significant resources without generating positive results for the company. In a perceptive assessment of what was in fact a sizable divergence between VOC and Tokugawa expectations about diplomacy, he argued that any ambassador would only be able to see the shogun once or twice and would be prohibited from addressing him directly. In Japan, van

Neijenroode explained, an ambassador was "nothing more than a letter bearer," tasked with handing over official documents and participating in accompanying ceremonies, but lacking any ability to break through Tokugawa protocol to negotiate directly with the shogun and secure new concessions.[46] As such, any attempt to use an embassy to open up a new space for dialogue was destined to fail and, rather than lavishing limited funds on such an enterprise, the company would be better served by continuing to rely on the informal delegations, which had traveled intermittently to Edo in the years since the Stadhouder's last letter, if it wanted to make contact with the shogun.

The catalyst that finally triggered the dispatch of an embassy came not in the form of another restriction on VOC trade in Japan but rather from events on the island of Taiwan. In 1624, the VOC had established a colony, its first in East Asia, on the bay of Tayouan near the modern city of Tainan. When the company moved to exclude Japanese traders who had been using that part of the island for a number of years prior to its arrival, it encountered immediate resistance. The subsequent fight back was spearheaded by Suetsugu Heizō, a Nagasaki merchant and official who refused to relinquish his lucrative trading rights with Tayouan.[47] When news of the conflict between Heizō's agents and the Dutch prompted outrage in Japan, Batavia determined that something needed to be done to make sure that it did not poison relations with the Tokugawa regime.

The chosen solution, quickly settled on by the incumbent governor-general, Pieter de Carpentier (in office 1623–27), was an embassy. The decision reflected a more general view within the organization of such missions as a vital policy instrument. By providing a mechanism to place a high-ranking Dutch official armed with all the necessary documents and gifts in an Asian capital for a prolonged period of time, the embassy represented a versatile tool capable of being used to resolve a wide range of problems. As such, it was repeatedly pressed into service whenever Batavia confronted significant obstacles. In keeping with this, the embassy to Japan was assigned two important aims.[48] It was first of all to reestablish formal contact between the shogun and the company that had lapsed since the arrival of the last official mission with Maurits's letter in 1612. The appearance in Edo of an impressive ambassador armed with precious gifts would, it was hoped, be enough to secure the shogun's good will and improve the company's position in Japan. The second aim concerned Tayouan. The embassy was dispatched to provide an explanation for the company's conduct there and, by so doing, to counteract the complaints brought by Suetsugu Heizō and other Japanese merchants. If this discussion proceeded favorably, the ambassador was to petition the shogun to halt Japanese trade with Tayouan by suspending the issue of maritime passes to that destination. In this way, by negotiating directly with the regime, the mission was designed to advance the company's interests on several fronts, thereby strengthening its position in Japan.

For such an important undertaking, it was crucial to select the right ambassador. The days of simply nominating whoever was closest at hand—a policy that had resulted in Puyck and van den Broek's appointment as unlikely ambassadors—were long behind the company, which had become more discerning in its choice of representatives in the intervening years. The appointment had to be senior enough to impress the shogun while also possessing the initiative and wherewithal to drive negotiations forward. Fortunately for de Carpentier, a vessel had just arrived from Europe carrying with it an apparently ideal candidate. The fortuitous arrival was Pieter Nuyts, a talented scholar with great ambitions. Born to a prosperous merchant family in Middleburg in 1598, Nuyts had entered Leiden University at just fifteen.[49] After graduating with a doctorate in philosophy in 1620, he took up a position in his father's business and married soon after. The steady rhythms of the textile trade seems to have held little appeal, however, and in 1626, at the age of twenty-eight, Nuyts entered the company's service. Like so many of its employees, he was determined to use his time in Asia to secure both fortune and status. He had, in his own words, "not come out . . . to eat hay" but to make money and to do so as quickly as possible using any means at his disposal.[50]

Nuyts's timing was especially good; he had applied to join the company at a time when its administrators were eager to replace the rough adventurers that had initially flocked to Asia with a new generation of educated men better suited to employment in an increasingly prosperous organization. Although lacking any experience of trade outside of Europe, Nuyts was, with the backing of the Zeeland chamber, immediately promoted to the high rank of extraordinary councilor of the Indies. He departed for Asia aboard the *Gulden Zeepaert* in May 1626 accompanied by his young son, Laurens, who was to meet a tragic end in Japan.

After a voyage of eleven months that included an unplanned detour to the west coast of Australia, Nuyts arrived in Batavia in April 1627, where he was selected to take on two important roles. He was charged first to travel Japan as ambassador and, once this task has been successfully accomplished, to take up the equally critical position of governor of the Tayouan colony.[51] To aid him in the first task, Pieter Muijser, a seasoned merchant who had traveled to Edo before, was appointed deputy ambassador. Although he was the more experienced of the pair, Muijser seems to have retreated into the background, ceding control of the embassy to the far pushier Nuyts.

With the decision as to ambassadors settled, officials in Batavia moved to equip the mission with the familiar elements of a formal embassy: letters, a suitable retinue, and gifts. Of most importance were two documents prepared for Hidetada and his son Iemitsu. By 1627, Hidetada had officially retired as shogun, but he retained a considerable measure of power, and there was no question that the first missive, addressed to the "old emperor," was the more significant. At first reading, this document appears entirely uncontroversial, a straightforward greeting filled with appropriately humble phrases and punctuated by the occasional obsequious flourish:

We recognize and are extremely grateful for the great friendship and favor that the Dutch nation has enjoyed for so many years through Your Majesty's special kindness in the lands of Japan. We could not therefore neglect to reverently and honorably thank Your Majesty. . . . In order to convey our sentiments we have expressly dispatched our envoy, the Honorable Mr Nuyts, and one of our closest councilors, P. Muyser, to present our letter with all due respect to Your Majesty and to reverently seek that your kindness and affection for the Dutch nation shall continue. . . . As confirmation of our thanks and as evidence of our friendship . . . we present you with two metal cannon from Holland, powder, cannon balls and other accessories as well as some small gifts. Our envoy will present these to Your Majesty and we hope that you will be pleased to accept them. Further, please faithfully credit and trust all matters that our envoys will further explain to Your Majesty. [Signed, your obedient servant, the Honorable General Pieter de Carpentier in the] Castle of Batavia, May 10, 1627.[52]

To understand why such an inoffensive letter became an immediate source of contention in Edo requires us to look beyond its bland phrasing to consider the writer's unstated assumptions. Although couched in modest terms that positioned the governor-general as a supplicant eager to retain the shogun's favor so that his subordinates could operate in Japan, de Carpentier's letter was, at the same time, a confident assertion of the office's rights.

When it first made contact with Tokugawa Ieyasu, the company had deliberately sought out letters from the Stadhouder to supply an appropriate basis for diplomacy. The result was to bind its representatives to a figure presented, and certainly understood, in Japan as the "king of Holland." In contrast, de Carpentier's letter, written in a period in which the company was turning away from this older model of interaction, made no mention of its former figurehead. Instead, the "king of Holland" was mysteriously erased, supplanted instead by a new sovereign who wrote to the shogun from his headquarters in Batavia offering friendship. Even though the letter made no grand claims about the governor-general's influence or power, it was nonetheless premised on a basic assumption: that de Carpentier should be seen as an independent political actor fully entitled to dispatch ambassadors and hence to take up his place, without any reference to an external authority, in Japanese diplomatic circuits alongside more conventional sovereigns. Because this was self-evident, the letter made no attempt to explain exactly who the "Honorable General" was or to provide a justification for his role. Instead, diplomacy was presented as a natural extension of his office, a sovereign prerogative that could and should simply be accepted as a given. This was of course the company's official position, clearly outlined in article 35 of its charter, which had handed the organization (and hence its chief official in Asia) the right to engage with foreign princes and potentates without reliance on a separate figure. But, as Nuyts would soon discover, just because a right had been granted in Europe did not mean that it was automatically recognized on the other side of the world where diplomacy came with its own set of rules.

One additional assumption buried within the letter should also be mentioned. At the end of the document, de Carpentier asked the shogun to "faithfully credit and trust all matters that our envoys will further explain." As Bakufu officials later pointed out, this short clause effectively empowered the ambassador to hold talks directly with the shogun. Rather than functioning simply as a letter bearer, Nuyts traveled to Edo, therefore, as an active negotiator charged to speak on behalf of Batavia by opening a direct dialogue with the shogun, or at least his closest advisers, in order to advance the company's interests across a broad range of issues. This result was yet another hidden pitfall primed to claim the ambassadors once they arrived in Edo.

Whereas Puyck and van den Broek had been forced to cobble their embassy together with whatever could be found at hand, Nuyts's mission was to lack for nothing. By 1627 the company, keenly aware that its embassies needed to look the part, was prepared to invest significant funds in providing all the trappings of a sovereign delegation. As ambassador, Nuyts was provided with a personal retinue of four servants clad in livery, two bodyguards, and two secretaries. The final procession, as detailed in his instructions, was to consist of thirty-four participants including a similar escort for his deputy Muijser, two merchants from the Japan factory, four translators and assistants, six Japanese servants, and three black slaves.[53] In contrast to their predecessors' odd assortment of presents, the ambassadors were provided with a lavish array of gifts.[54] The key offering was a set of four heavy cannon brought all the way from Europe and designed to satisfy a long-standing Tokugawa interest in European artillery, one area in which the Dutch held an undisputed lead over the Japanese. In addition, the company planned to present the shogun with large quantities of sandalwood and silk as well as a selection of more exotic items that included Persian rugs, Spanish wine, Chinese garments, and European firearms. To further smooth the embassy's progress, officials in Batavia drew up a list of important Bakufu officials who were to be presented with gifts of their own.

All these preparations meant that by the time the embassy departed, it had been carefully equipped with every possible tool that Batavia could provide. Given how much more impressive it was than the company's early efforts in Japan, there seemed every reason to believe that the mission would achieve its aims, initiating a shift in Bakufu policy toward Tayouan and securing a general improvement in the Dutch position in Japan.

THE AMBASSADORS ARRIVE

Departing Batavia in June 1627, Nuyts headed first to Tayouan to inspect the company's settlement there before continuing on to Japan. On the morning of 1 August, his ship sailed into the harbor at Hirado decorated with a special set of oversized banners and flags.[55] The ostentatious gesture provides the first suggestion as to how Nuyts conceived of his own role and highlights the obsessive concern with display that became the hallmark of his embassy. Although earning him the later opprobrium of his superiors, who condemned it as a product of a character defect, and hence fitting neatly into the story emphasizing Nuyts personal failings, it was a preoccupation that he shared with other European ambassadors in Asia, many of whom adopted notably similar tactics.[56]

All embassies are a kind of diplomatic theater, but this particular group of envoys was especially dependent on, to use Richmond Barbour's words, the "language of spectacle" to make their case.[57] Operating in distant lands and armed with distinctly limited tools, European ambassadors in Asia fell naturally into a role as central players in an elaborate pantomime designed to prove their quality and the authority of the sponsor. The result was to ensure that each stage of their embassies became a performance, invariably starring the ambassador in a leading part, to be arranged in such a way as to demonstrate that this was someone and something worth taking seriously. In India Thomas Roe, perhaps the most famous of the early ambassadors, sought every opportunity to use display to prove his elevated position and thus uphold the "honor and dignity" of his royal master.[58] In this way the key moments of his embassy became opportunities for theatrical demonstration, each one meticulously arranged to show that he was "an Ambassador from a Mightie King."[59] Like Roe, Nuyts embraced the role of actor, using every occasion to map out his status through gesture or display. For him, the preservation of the "honor and reputation of our embassy" was of paramount concern requiring careful shelter from slights and enhancement through spectacle.[60] When viewed in this light, his tactics seem less the product of individual failings than of the precarious position that European ambassadors occupied in early modern Asia.

For envoys like Nuyts or Roe, the moment of transfer from ship to shore provided the first stage on which to mark out their authority and required, for this reason, special care. The act itself was fraught with

meaning.[61] If the wooden walls of the ship were a prison to be endured
for months or even years on end, they also offered a comforting space,
a floating site of European jurisdiction where the ambassador's authority was unquestioned and internal hierarchies secure. If the ship was
safe, the land could hold any number of perils. In making the transition
to solid ground, ambassadors were forced to subject their persons to
the vagaries of their Asian hosts, to rules they could not control and
to conditions they held no mastery over. Because of this, the moment
of transfer needed to set the right tone for the subsequent embassy.
A successful disembarkation could firmly establish the ambassador's
authority, making it clear that he was no ordinary traveler and ensuring
special treatment in the future. If the embassy started badly, however, it
might continue that way, dooming the mission before it was even properly underway.

Eager to get things just right, envoys were prepared to wait aboard
their ship for days until the proper conditions for landing could be guaranteed. In India, Thomas Roe made landfall only after he had arranged
for a magnificent, carefully choreographed landing complete with a
"Court of Guard, and the shippes in their best Equipage giuing me their
ordinance as I passed ; with his trumpetts and Musique ahead my boate
in the best manner."[62] Despite these preparations, his grand procession
faltered when local officials, in accordance with well-established procedures, insisted on searching the ambassador and his retinue. Protesting
that he was the "Ambassador of a Mightie and free Prince" who could
never submit to such indignities, Roe was compelled to retreat back to
the boats until a new arrangement could be worked out.[63]

In Japan, Nuyts followed a similar pattern. Like Roe, the ambassador was determined to show that the status of his office merited special treatment. All ships arriving in Hirado were required to wait in the
harbor for inspection by local officials before disembarking their crews
and passengers. Seeing this as an unacceptable affront, the ambassador insisted that he be allowed to disembark immediately, informing
officials arriving to conduct the inspection that the quality of his office
meant that such rules could not apply to him. Such "insolent authority"
could not, Nuyts insisted, be tolerated, for it would undermine the very
basis of his embassy.[64] When his protests failed to elicit the requisite
exemption, he decided to take matters into his own hands by landing on
his own initiative without submitting to a search. If officials in Hirado

could not grasp the distinction between a formal envoy and an ordinary Dutch merchant, then it must be demonstrated to them by action.

That these comedies of manners played out with such earnestness over seemingly trivial issues speaks to the importance of display. The same concern drove Nuyts's subsequent preparations in Hirado. Whereas Batavia's initial plans had called for a thirty-four-member suite, once in Japan the ambassador opted to increase this figure to seventy. Eager to make an even bigger splash, he sought out a group of trumpeters capable of marking the progress of the embassy with appropriate fanfare.[65] As transport for the procession, Nuyts insisted that officials in Hirado, already antagonized by his earlier conduct, loan him the domain's flagship, a splendid fifty-six-oar galley the daimyo maintained for his personal use.[66] When they refused, he complained bitterly that the embassy was being treated in a belittling manner with no sign of the appropriate level of respect.[67]

On 15 August the embassy departed Hirado, reaching the port city of Shimonoseki five days later. Contrary winds kept the party stuck in the port for a week, allowing Nuyts to make use of the enforced delay to arrange for a Japanese translation of the letters from the governor-general.[68] The decision to translate these documents while in transit raises the obvious question as to why this crucial task had not been done in Hirado, where assistance could be sought both from the staff of the Japan factory and members of the ruling Matsura family. In later accounts sent to his superiors, van Neijenroode, the opperhoofd, wrote furiously about the seemingly cavalier way in which the process of translation had been treated. Lamenting Nuyts's rushed job, he contrasted it with the procedures followed for earlier letters from the Stadhouder, which had been carefully translated in consultation with Japanese officials before being checked and rechecked.[69] Still more infuriating, Nuyts had not even seen fit to show the original documents to van Neijenroode, who had direct experience dealing with the Bakufu. Instead, he seems to have been determined to jealously guard access to these letters, secreting them away until the triumphal moment of presentation. The result was an essentially literal translation that made little attempt to reshape the letter for its intended audience.

Once the winds had turned, the embassy was able to proceed again and reached Osaka on 1 September. Leaving their vessels, they applied for permission from Bakufu authorities to continue on to Edo by land.

Just over two weeks later, word reached the group that they were authorized to proceed and could make use of the regime's transportation and accommodation network.[70] In addition to providing a welcome endorsement of the delegation's status as an official embassy, the news initiated a dramatic enlargement of the ambassador's retinue, which, augmented by dozens of samurai, grooms, and palanquin bearers, blew out to 240 men.[71] From Osaka, Nuyts and his men proceeded along the Tōkaidō thoroughfare, the great eastern coastal route that bound the economic and political capitals of Japan. Their newly conferred status allowing rapid travel along the bustling tree-lined highway, they entered the western boundaries of Edo proper on 1 October.

For once even Nuyts appears to have been content with the honor accorded to the embassy as it made its way into the sprawling city.[72] Accompanied by officials belonging to Hirado domain, the procession moved slowly through streets that had been specially cleaned for the occasion and strewn with sand. Like other embassies arriving in Edo in this period, it drew huge crowds. To facilitate uninterrupted passage, Tokugawa authorities had cordoned off the route by closing the connecting streets so the ambassadors could pass without a crush of onlookers. In the spaces between these intersections, thousands of spectators, eager to catch a glimpse of the exotic visitors, had gathered, sitting, according to the embassy diary, in "great numbers in perfect and still order to see us passing."[73] Nuyts's natural tendency to demand a greater show of respect quickly resurfaced, however, when the procession reached its designated accommodation near the center of the city. Like other foreign envoys, they were housed in a Buddhist temple, which had been temporarily requisitioned for the purpose.[74] In the absence of other appropriate structures, temples were considered the natural site for hosting large processions of diplomats, far more suitable than the alternative, which would require the Bakufu to displace a daimyo from his residence. Predictably, Nuyts did not see it this way, and, after insisting that their accommodation was not appropriate to "lodge such persons," he agreed to relent only when informed that the shogun had specifically mandated the arrangement.[75]

Once he had settled in, Nuyts had his first opportunity to meet with Matsura Takanobu (1591–1637), the daimyo of Hirado and the designated broker between the Dutch and the Bakufu. The master of a territory heavily dependent on the income from foreign trade, Takanobu was the company's most consistent, if also most self-interested, ally in Japan.[76] But he was also the most exposed if the Dutch ran into problems, and, when the embassy's prospects for success dimmed, the daimyo moved to actively distance himself from Nuyts by joining in the chorus of condemnation. During these early meetings, however, when a favorable outcome seemed assured, the ambassador recorded his trust in this "friend of the [Dutch] nation" and promised his full cooperation with anything Takanobu might suggest.[77]

On 3 October a small group of senior Bakufu officials requested to see the ambassador's official letters so they could approve them before the formal presentation in Edo Castle. Later that day, a message came back informing Nuyts that the documents appeared broadly acceptable, but that they did require some modification. The problems seemed relatively minor, stemming from questions of translation, and could, at least according to Matsura Takanobu, be easily remedied by changing a few words. Even better, an influential Tokugawa official, Itami Yasukatsu, had volunteered to work with the ambassador to adjust the letters to "Japanese style" so that they could be delivered to the shogun without delay.[78] That night heavy rain fell, drenching the city and cascading off the tiled roof of the temple. The next morning, as the rain continued, Nuyts dispatched his deputy, Pieter Muijser, to the meeting with Itami in the lord of Hirado's walled compound.

Expecting a friendly discussion, Muijser was subjected instead to an extended interrogation that had been prompted by growing Bakufu concerns over the precise nature of the embassy. The questioning was led by Itami Yasukatsu, but also present were two monks, described in the diary as "Japanese papen," who sat quietly recording all of Muijser's answers for later submission to Edo Castle.[79] For the deputy ambassador, the attendance of these silent scribes was clearly unsettling, and an almost palpable sense of anxiety pervades the pages of the diary whenever they are mentioned. These were "sly and cunning people" who could not be trusted, dangerous individuals who threatened the success of the embassy.[80] As the employee of an organization obsessed with record keeping—to the extent that it created one of the great archives of the early modern world—Muijser must have been used to the presence of scribes, raising the obvious question as to why he felt such evident unease.

For Europeans traveling into the New World, writing formed one part of a potent suite of technologies that included gunpowder and steel.

At home, propagandists of empire rejoiced in what one author dubbed the "literall advantage" conferred on them by the ability to write and keep records. If speech separated man from beast, writing divided different kinds of societies, giving advantage to some. As Samuel Purchas noted, "God hath added herein a further grace, that as men by the former exceed Beasts, so hereby one man may excell another; and amongst Men, some are accounted Civill, and more Sociable and religious, by the Use of letters and of Writing, which others wanting are esteemed Brutish, Savage, Barbarous."[81] With their means of record limited to speech, the peoples of the New World remained trapped, he explained, forever in the present. In contrast, Europeans, because of their access to writing, gained a kind of immortality, a link to the great "Patriarkes, Prophets, Apostles, Fathers, Philosophers, [or] Historians" that enabled them to transcend the relentlessly ticking clock of life and which set them apart from the barbarians they had discovered in the Americas.[82]

Europeans moving into Asia encountered highly literate societies in which writing served many different purposes. In the Tokugawa Bakufu the Dutch found a regime served by a steadily expanding bureaucracy whose rule was underpinned by the unceasing accumulation of written materials. In the face of such cultures, any notion of "literall advantage" slipped away, taking with it some of the characteristic confidence exhibited by Europeans in the New World. The hushed sound of brush on paper as the two monks "wrote everything down before we had even finished speaking," reminded Muijser that both sides were keeping records.[83] While European promoters of expansion in the New World could rejoice at the lack of an indigenous past, their counterparts in Asia contended with a recorded history over which they had no control. It was, in this moment, all too clear to Muijser that the fate of the embassy hinged not on Dutch but on Japanese writing. Indeed, it was the looming presence of past VOC delegations preserved in the Bakufu's own diplomatic records that doomed the embassy to failure. Despite their attempts to bluff their way out of trouble, the ambassadors found they could not escape the documentary evidence left over from the company's earlier embassies to Japan. As Itami's two scribes took down the twists and turns of Muijser's hastily improvised explanations, they had only to look to their own records to expose a string of damning contradictions.

Already unnerved, Muijser's composure was soon shattered. The interview commenced with a simple question: "where has Nuyts actually come from?" The deputy ambassador replied that he "has come from Java via Tayouan and has now arrived in Edo."[84] A second question followed quickly. Had Nuyts "been sent to the emperor [shogun] of Japan from the king in Holland or from Batavia?" Attempting somehow to steer a middle path between two distinct alternatives, Muijser replied that Nuyts "has come from Holland to the Indies to aid in government. He was sent as ambassador with another qualified person to the emperor [shogun] of Japan from the governor-general in Batavia to thank His Majesty for the friendship we have received and to ask that it continues in the future." His answer, rapidly communicated to Edo Castle, exposed the fact that the ambassadors had come from Batavia and hence lacked any connection with the "king of Holland." The result was to rip away the diplomatic scaffolding laboriously assembled by earlier envoys and to throw the framework for interaction between the company and the shogun into doubt.

Turning to the charged question of documents, Itami pushed for further detail. "Were the letters," he wanted to know, "written and signed in Holland or in Batavia?" The pressure mounting, Muijser moved to assert the governor-general's position as a monarch in his own right. The documents were, he stated, not from Holland, but had been "written and signed by the king of the Indies in Batavia (*Connick in Indien op Batavia*)." If the letters and the ambassadors came from Batavia, what about the gifts they had brought with them? Once again, Muijser sought a middle road by explaining that, whereas the "cannon and most of the other gifts were brought from Holland," at least some of the offerings did indeed come from Batavia.

Returning to the question of political sponsors, Itami asked what links existed between the "king of Batavia," a figure unfamiliar to the Japanese, the "king of Holland," and the ambassador himself? Were they all part of one royal dynasty tied by a single bloodline? Opting this time for a clear falsehood rather than a blurring of title and position, Muijser replied that the "king of Batavia and the king of Holland were blood relations. As a result they corresponded frequently with each other. The ambassador was an important man, a councilor of the Indies and not inferior in lineage to the king." The origins of the embassy firmly established, Itami pressed Muijser as to its real purpose. Initially reluctant to admit that they had any ambition beyond expressing gratitude to the shogun, the deputy ambassador eventually conceded that Nuyts was really here to talk about events on the company's colony of Tayouan.

With that the long interrogation came to an end, giving Muijser his first chance to recover from the relentless barrage of questions. The experience had been disturbingly close to a trial, with questions raining down one after another, all "asked in such an impertinent way and with such authority as if we were common criminals."[85] However one looked at it, it was clear that the ground had shifted under the ambassadors' feet and that the fate of the mission, which had seemed so assured just a few days earlier, hung now in the balance. In the days after Muijser's interview, Matsura Takanobu, who had been charged by the Bakufu to get to the bottom of these unexpected developments, interrogated the two ambassadors on multiple occasions. Since the central fact that they had not been sent by the "king of Holland" was now abundantly clear, attention turned to the figure of the governor-general. Bakufu officials wished to know who he was and whether the office was in fact suitably "qualified to send an ambassador to the shogun."[86] The task of answering these questions and hence of proving that the embassy merited official recognition fell to Nuyts.[87]

EDO AS LABYRINTH

Although inflected by the company's particular characteristics, the essential problem was the same one faced by so many European ambassadors in early modern Asia. Unable to dictate terms, individuals like Thomas Roe, Pieter Nuyts, or any one of a string of equivalent figures were compelled to find a way to fit within existing diplomatic norms. But, when they tried to do so, they often found that their missions failed to match up to even the most basic of local expectations. Nuyts's situation was made more difficult by the fact that Tokugawa diplomatic practice had become increasingly rigid in the intervening years since the company had first made contact. Whereas Puyck and van den Broek had arrived at an especially receptive moment for diplomatic engagement, Nuyts was far less fortunate in his timing. Since the death of the first shogun, the regime had become steadily more inflexible, permitting less and less room for any deviation from its prescribed norms about proper diplomacy. Only recognized sovereigns who used the right kind of diplomatic language were permitted to correspond with the shogun, and any lapse in protocol could trigger immediate rejection of missive or mission.

In 1627, for example, the same year that Nuyts arrived in Edo, Bakufu officials dismissed a letter from Cochinchina, an emerging state in Southeast Asia that had exchanged numerous missives with Tokugawa Ieyasu, as "too discourteous . . . [to] be communicated to the shogun."[88] Formal embassies, even if they came from a powerful polity with a long history of contact with Japan, could also suffer the same treatment if there was any question about the ruler's broader legitimacy. This was the fate of a series of missions sent from the king of Siam in 1634, 1635–36, 1653, and 1655–56 that were all turned back after questions were raised about the manner in which he had seized power from his royal predecessor.[89] The tenor of the Bakufu's response to these embassies was revealing with one official noting that "in view of the fact that Siam is a country of injustice where a traitor killed the King and usurped the Kingdom, the Shogun did not accept the letter."[90]

The incessant questioning pulled Nuyts into a labyrinth, a confusing maze in which each turn required yet another defense of the embassy's claims. For an ambassador obsessed with his own prestige, it was almost too much to bear, and he lamented the constant attack on his authority.[91] The seemingly endless rounds of interrogation centered on three key assertions that were either disputed or dismissed out of hand by Tokugawa authorities. First, the ambassador maintained that the governor-general was a sovereign ruler in his own right. As the "absolute lord over our lands in the Indies," he wielded the same powers as a more conventional head of state and should be treated as such.[92] In making the argument, Nuyts showed no hesitation in adopting the language of kingship, which had already been used by Muijser, by describing the general as "our king" and the king of the Dutch Indies.[93] In case there was any doubt about what he meant, he made the direct link to the Japanese system by arguing that the Dutch looked at the governor-general in the same way as Tokugawa subjects viewed the shogun.[94] Aware that he had to justify the switch from the Stadhouder to Batavia, Nuyts explained that the king of the Indies and the king of Holland were, in political terms, virtually identical figures who shared the same "potency and strength."[95] Since this was the case, and if one added in the fact that they were in constant correspondence, the result was that it did not really matter whether it was the ruler of Holland or Batavia who had actually dispatched the embassy to Japan. In this way, there was, Nuyts asserted, no contradiction between his mission and the claims made by earlier delegations.

Although Nuyts piled claim after claim about the governor-general's position, one on top of another, the flood of questions did not abate. Like other European ambassadors, he struggled to provide evidence to support his grander statements about the strength of his master and thereby to give weight to his assertions. The daily frustrations he encountered stand in stark contrast to one of the few seventeenth-century imaginings of VOC diplomacy, a painting by Jan Baptist Weenix that shows an ambassador, Johan van Twist, on his way to meet with the sultan of Bijapur.[96] In it the Dutch envoy is depicted on horseback riding alongside local officials with a powerful VOC fleet looming in the background. Although he is in India to seek help, the ambassador appears in every way the dominant figure, able to control negotiations by pointing to the massed array of ships, cannon smoke billowing from their gun ports, to support his assertions. In fact, this image bears little connection to the realities of most embassies. Isolated in Edo, Nuyts could not summon witnesses or point to an assembled fleet to confirm Batavia's power. Instead, the only tactic left available to him was to offer up claim after unsupported claim and to hope that the right combination would convince his listeners of the governor-general's status.

With no ability to substantiate his declarations, he was reduced to vague threats, complaining ceaselessly about the lack of respect and warning that "if these reach the ears of our lord he will take it badly."[97] A similar fate befell Thomas Roe in India. In his commission Roe had been instructed to awe his Mughal interlocutors by describing the English king's "power and strength at Sea, which giveth us not onelie reputacion and auority amongst the Greatest Princes of Christendome, but Maketh us even a Terrour to all other Nations."[98] But once at court he found himself unable to substantiate his claims about English authority and was, like his Dutch counterpart, compelled to rely on bluff and bluster.[99] The result was a precarious situation in which representatives like Roe and Nuyts could, all too easily, start to appear, according to the damning critique leveled at the VOC envoy by one Japanese observer, "more like swindlers (*bedriegers*) than ambassadors."[100]

While Nuyts's inability to back up his assertions was problem enough, the situation deteriorated further when the Bakufu began to assemble its own evidence. Its first exhibit was the governor-general's letter to the shogun. If diplomatic missives were key instruments in the European push into Asia, they were also, as Miles Ogborn has shown in his analysis

Figure 2.3. Johan van Twist as ambassador to the Sultan of Bijapur, ca. 1645–60. Jan Baptist Weenix. Courtesy of the Collection Rijksmuseum, Amsterdam

of English letters, inherently fraught. Just as ambassadors "delivered poor presents, and often delivered them badly, so they brought poor letters."[101] Often clumsily prepared or shoddily translated, such documents could, once relinquished to local officials, swiftly transform from substandard examples of diplomatic correspondence into genuinely perilous objects. This was the case with the missive that Nuyts carried from the governor-general. Intended as a key prop capable of buttressing his authority, it became instead a millstone around the ambassadors' neck, dragging the embassy farther and farther down.

The problem, aside from the obvious lack of reference to the Stadhouder, centered on the most innocuous of lines, the valediction "your obedient servant" that appeared, as in so many Dutch documents of the period, at the end of the letter. In the Japanese translation, this was rendered as *miuchi no mono*, a term usually used to describe low-ranking vassals or retainers. Because of this it was immediately seized upon by Tokugawa officials as evidence that the governor-general was not the powerful sovereign described by the ambassadors. If he was truly a kinglike figure, why did the lord of Batavia insist on using such "humble and submissive (*ootmoedige*)" language that not only violated Japanese diplomatic conventions but also bore no resemblance to the "style of a sovereign lord?" In response, Nuyts explained that the valediction was simply an "ordinary Dutch custom," a inconsequential courtesy without any real meaning that should simply be ignored.[102] The explanation did not, however, placate Bakufu officials, who would return to this particular phrase weeks later when they met to discuss the fate of the embassy.

The image of the trial in which the ambassadors stood in the dock as common criminals took on a more ominous meaning as the Bakufu started to call its own witnesses. If the Dutch Republic was a remote presence able to be easily manipulated by VOC representatives who could mold their presentation of its political arrangements to their benefit, Batavia, located on the edges of Japanese trading circuits, was a different matter altogether. Although they tried to present it in the best possible light, the Dutch held no monopoly over information within Japan about the city or its administrators. Instead, Bakufu officials could call on several groups, including Kyushu-based merchants who traded in the region around the company's headquarters, Japanese mariners and mercenaries who had been hired by the Dutch to make up their labor shortage, and members of the Chinese community in Japan with direct knowledge of Batavia. On 7 October Nuyts received word that Edo Castle was searching for individuals who had traveled to Southeast Asia and possessed some first-hand knowledge of the city and its chief official. Although we do not know all the details, the subsequent search seems to have turned up a sailor who, having served aboard a VOC ship, was able to confirm that the governor-general was more official than sovereign.[103]

When confronted with this testimony, which came from a period before the development of the lavish ceremonies described in the earlier part of this chapter, the ambassador responded that such an uninformed witness clearly had no real knowledge of Batavia. If he had truly appeared before the governor-general, there would be no question as to that office's status or authority. Despite these protests, the combination of the letter and such accounts led Bakufu officials inexorably to one conclusion, that the governor-general could not be "an absolute and potent lord but must be a vassal or servant of the prince or king in Holland."[104] If Nuyts had compared de Carpentier to the shogun, they had a far less flattering figure in mind; The governor-general was, the ambassadors were informed, more like the governor of Nagasaki, a subordinate official with limited authority and certainly no claim to sovereign status.

The second set of assertions put forward by the ambassadors concerned the governor-general's place in established diplomatic orders. In an effort to convince Bakufu officials of his mission's essential legitimacy, Nuyts insisted that since Batavia occupied a well-defined position in international orders there was no basis to question the governor-general's right to dispatch embassies or letters directly to the shogun. Far from being the unruly upstart that Tokugawa officials seemed to imagine, Batavia was already integrated into a global diplomatic network: "Our Lord General [the governor-general]. . . sends ambassadors to the principal kings of China, Siam, Aceh and Patani; to the emperors of Java and Persia; to the Great Mughal (who is one of the most powerful lords in the world); and to many other potentates. And in none of these cases was his authority or absolute strength ever questioned in any way. But in all cases the ambassadors were accepted as if they had come from a sovereign prince."[105] If such a diverse list of states, including the great superpowers of Asian politics, had not objected to the arrival of an embassy from Batavia, what right did the shogun have to protest? On a later occasion the ambassador returned to the same point, but with a different set of partners. "The Lord General's ambassadors were," he suggested "accepted by all the kings and princes around [Japan], namely by those of China, Siam, Aceh, Patani, Moluccas, Amboina, Banda, as well as many others," and always honored appropriately.[106]

The claim attempted to turn the tables by suggesting that it was not the company that was in violation of accepted protocol but rather the Bakufu, which had failed to grasp the nature of the wider diplomatic landscape. It was an argument made equally forcefully by other European envoys who used similar assertions about an established diplomatic order to lend credence to their claims for recognition. In India Roe explained that his interpretation of proper diplomatic practice derived not simply from "the customs of England, but [from] the consent of all the world."[107] Once again, however, the difficulty lay in providing proof and ambassadors quickly veered into fiction to strengthen their case. Compelling as Nuyts's long list of diplomatic partners appears at first, it does not stand up to scrutiny, including tiny islands like Amboina or the Banda archipelago, where the company's success depended on bullying local leaders into submission, but also China, which remained beyond the reach of VOC diplomats. Indeed, no embassy from Batavia had made it into the Chinese interior, and it would be a number of decades, long after the collapse of the Ming regime, before an official mission from the governor-general finally arrived in Beijing.[108]

The third and final group of assertions centered on the role of the ambassador. Like other European envoys in this period, Nuyts arrived with a clear set of expectations about the proper nature of diplomacy. Chief among these was the ambassador's right to not only represent the person of his master, in this case the governor-general, but also to engage directly in negotiations with foreign rulers on his behalf. The view reflected what was in fact standard VOC policy. The company used embassies for highly specific purposes, to win concessions, negotiate treaties, or resolve issues of particular concern through face to face talks with the sovereign and his court. The most successful ambassadors returned home with treaties precisely laying out their employer's rights and privileges in foreign territories. This essentially utilitarian approach to diplomacy reflected the nature of the organization and its overriding concern with balance sheets. For de Carpentier and other governors-general, the embassy was, above all else, an investment designed to achieve returns far exceeding its related expenditures. The sizable debit represented by each diplomatic mission had, therefore, to be matched by a larger gain somewhere else on the ledger. In the case of Nuyts's mission, it had been dispatched in the hope that it would conjure up absolute control over trade between Taiwan and Japan, an economic prize worth many times the anticipated costs of the embassy.

The Bakufu possessed a very different view of the ambassador's role. Once again it was the letter, or more particularly the clause empowering Nuyts as negotiator, that exposed the divergence. Such language was, the Dutch were informed, appropriate to "petitioners," but not to ambassadors, and had no place at the shogun's court.[109] After a sustained burst of improvisation under the first shogun, Tokugawa diplomatic practice had by 1627 settled into a fixed, largely ritualized pattern. The arrival of foreign embassies, the key event in the diplomatic calendar, became an occasion for the confirmation of an existing order rather than an opportunity to push policy out in new directions through dialogue. In this way, as Ron Toby's study of Tokugawa diplomacy has so persuasively shown, delegations came to serve as the centerpiece of carefully stage-managed pageants designed to project an idealized vision of international politics centered on the shogun. They provided, in his words, an opportunity to "create the illusion of an East Asian world order that was Japanese in design and Japanese in focus."[110]

This goal left little room for the idea of the ambassador as negotiator and no space for direct talks with the court. Envoys to Edo were not expected to bring with them a list of demands, or even a set of issues to be discussed directly with the Tokugawa shogun, but rather to act out their role in a prearranged drama and depart without troubling the basis of the Bakufu's order.[111] This view of diplomacy was perfectly summed up at the time by one Japanese official who explained that "envoys or ambassadors . . . were people who had been sent from their lord or prince to the shogun to pay him homage, wish him well and nothing else. In contrast, people who came with presents trying to seek something were entirely different. Their presents were given in order to obtain something and not out of true reverence for the emperor [shogun]."[112] While there was some room for negotiation, it was to be done in the margins of the embassy with a designated groups of intermediaries, rather than in the halls of Edo Castle.[113]

For Nuyts, there was no credible distinction between petitioner and ambassador, with the two roles overlapping so fundamentally that they could not be separated out. As before, he turned to international norms to support his argument by explaining that the "law and nature of ambassadors were common not only to Holland but also France, England, Spain, Italy, Germany and even to the Great Turk as well as other princes and potentates."[114] Like other envoys, he had been sent to give presents and letters to the shogun and his advisers, but also to discuss matters of mutual concern. If the shogun did not want to grant his requests, then he could simply refuse and send the ambassadors home. In fact, the assessment missed the point almost completely. Rather than being concerned with how best to respond to the company's requests, the Bakufu had rejected the premise of the ambassador as petitioner. If the Dutch wanted to discuss specific issues, they could do so with officials attached to Hirado domain, the designated mediator for communications between the company and Edo, but no direct dialogue with the shogun would take place during the embassy. To reinforce the message, Matsura Takanobu asked Nuyts to sign a document pledging that he would not attempt to present any demands to the shogun if an audience was in fact eventually granted. Instead he was, the daimyo insisted, to content himself with handing over his letters and thanking the shogun "for the great generosity he has shown to our nation."[115]

After a week of questioning, the ambassadors were worn out. Their interwoven claims about the governor-general's power, his place in an international diplomatic order, and the proper rights of ambassadors had been systematically picked apart by relentless interrogation. Increasingly Nuyts, his grand entrance into the city a distant memory, retreated to sullen expressions of disgust while lamenting that he had not been sent to explain the nature and form of his government to the Japanese. As his despair swelled, so did the need to assign blame elsewhere. Suspicion fell first on the Japanese interpreters. Either they were incompetent, unable to properly convey even the simplest of concepts, or they were treacherous, intentionally distorting statements in order to sabotage the embassy. Any trust in the daimyo of Hirado quickly receded as well; he was not, the ambassador concluded, "our friend or at least he does not have the authority to bring our affairs to a good outcome."[116]

As their trust in putative allies diminished, fear about their enemies' baleful influence surged. The ambassadors increasingly traced all their problems back to Suetsugu Heizō, the Nagasaki merchant/official intent on keeping open Japan's trading links with Tayouan. He had, they imagined, orchestrated a vast conspiracy stretching all the way up to the highest levels of the Bakufu. As the shadowy puppet master pulling the strings behind the scenes, he was responsible for the embassy's misfortunes. All this was aggravated, the ambassadors maintained, by the flawed character of the Japanese. Japan's inhabitants were, Nuyts maintained, chronic liars who sought constantly to defraud. Condensing his feelings into an overarching equation of deceit, he insisted that any visitor to the archipelago could only trust one person in ten, and even he lied 90 percent of the time.[117] The constant deceit and obstinate rigidity of the Japanese allowed no room for negotiation or even the application of reason, and it meant that the ambassadors were stuck in an endless loop, repeating the same assertions to a people incapable of understanding them.[118]

REJECTION AND BLAME

The embassy dragged on for another three weeks in this poisonous climate. Each day conditions seemed to deteriorate a little further, until the ambassadors were reduced to the role of captives, unable to leave their lodgings without special permission.[119] Finally, on 5 November, Bakufu officials summoned the Dutch envoys to deliver their final verdict. This time, a junior merchant, Francois Caron, was dispatched to the meeting in place of the exhausted ambassadors. The news was not good. Doi Toshikatsu, a senior adviser to the shogun, announced that the embassy had been officially rejected because the governor-general was nothing more than a subordinate of the "king of Holland" and hence clearly not qualified to send a diplomatic mission to the shogun:

> They understood that Pieter de Carpentier was a servant or a servant of a servant of our king in Holland. They had learnt this from the humble ending of the letters, and particularly the phrase "your obedient servant" which can only be interpreted as having been written by a minor flunky. . . . They had, moreover, never heard of Java or Batavia and ships from either place had never come to Japan. . . . They had discussed this matter in detail and were forced to conclude that we are not ambassadors from our king in Holland. Therefore they cannot receive us and we should now depart.[120]

The description can be matched with the Japanese record of the meeting, which appears in *Ikoku nikki*:

> A letter has been presented from Holland and was [initially] mediated by the Matsura of Hizen. The letter was written by a vassal of Java. It was written in kana and kanji. Java is a county of the same status as Holland. Because the Dutch do not know letters [are illiterate in Japanese], they have made those from Java write the letter. . . . We have never heard of a letter coming from Java or its vassals. There were many strange parts [in this document]. As to the words "miuchi no mono," the envoy explained that he understood this phrase meant vassal in Japan. In any case the letter was discourteous, and even for a robber country [like Holland] we have never heard of something like this.[121]

Both accounts emphasized the multiple issues that had plagued the embassy since it arrived in Edo. First, the delegation clearly did not, as admitted by its own participants, originate with the "king of Holland." Second, the Bakufu had never heard of Batavia or Java, and, third, it was unwilling to accept a diplomatic letter from a low-ranking official like de Carpentier. Both descriptions specifically mentioned the letter's valediction, which was used as irrefutable evidence of the governor-general's low status. *Miuchi no mono* the Japanese rendition of "your obedient servant," belonged to the language of vassals rather than sovereigns and had no place in official diplomatic correspondence.

While the signs had not been good, the Bakufu's rejection was unexpectedly comprehensive, and it meant that, far from securing new privileges from the shogun, the ambassadors had not even made it within the walls of Edo Castle. Considering the scale of the failure and the costs involved, someone had to take the blame, but Nuyts was determined that it would not be him. Despite his best efforts, however, officials in Batavia, after dismissing a long list of the ambassador's preferred scapegoats, eventually concluded that he should be held personally responsible for the debacle.[122] Although Nuyts, who emerges in the record as an impetuous, confrontational, and excessively intolerant individual, was undoubtedly a poor candidate to head a diplomatic mission, he cannot be held entirely accountable for what happened. His own failings as ambassador do not change the consistent nature of Bakufu objections, which remained unchanged after the initial meeting with Itami Yasukatsu on 4 October. In a subsequent interview the daimyo of Hirado gave a succinct explanation of what had gone wrong: "It was understood that you were an ambassador who had come directly out of Holland and therefore you were received with honor. However when it was found that you came from Java or Jaccatra or Batavia from a king or a general that was not known, then the emperor [shogun] would not receive you or speak with you."[123]

The 1627 mission collapsed, therefore, because it possessed no connection with the "king of Holland" and because, having determined this fact, Bakufu officials refused to recognize the governor-general's right to engage in diplomacy. Neither issue had much to do with Nuyts's own conduct, although he certainly did not help the situation, and even the most skillful of diplomats would have struggled to reconcile the basic contradiction at the center of the embassy. Having accepted missions and letters from the "king of Holland" in 1609 and 1612, the Bakufu refused in 1627 to endorse the company's clumsy sleight of hand—its attempt to substitute one sovereign with another without preparing the ground for the transfer. In effect, the Japanese regime, which could simply reference its own diplomatic archives for proof of past assertions about Dutch power structures, did nothing more than hold the company's representatives to their own statements about the Stadhouder and demand that they remain consistent.

While it took the ambassadors by surprise, the clash between the shogun and the company had in fact been brewing quietly for some time. The diplomatic camouflage provided by the presence of the Stadhouder was never intended to be permanent, and it was only a matter of time before the company, and its chief official in Asia, asserted their rights to engage in independent diplomacy without reaching back to the United Provinces. When this finally happened in 1627, the result was an immediate conflict over diplomatic rights that left Nuyts, who lacked any means to impose the company's terms on negotiations by compelling recognition, scrambling to defend his superior's position. The Bakufu's eventual response, so clearly summed up by Doi Toshikatsu, was to dismiss the governor-general as a lowly official who had no place in the business of diplomacy.[124] The result was to throw the company's diplomatic strategy in Japan into disarray. In the end, the fate of his mission was a stark reminder that, for all its ambitions, a hybrid enterprise like the company had no assurances of success when it attempted to force its way into Asian diplomatic circuits that possessed their own rules and expectations. Diplomacy was, as Nuyts could readily testify, difficult, and it was all too easy for even the best prepared of ambassadors to become, like him, just another "swindler" trapped with an unhelpful piece of paper thousands of miles from home.

CHAPTER THREE

THE SHOGUN'S LOYAL VASSALS

We are ready to act in service of his majesty as his faithful vassals
and to preserve the Japanese realm with our last drop of blood.

—Governor-General Antonio van Diemen, 1642

Two famous scenes serve to represent the Dutch position in Japan as
it stabilized after the collapse of Nuyts's embassy in 1627. The first, a
familiar image reproduced in dozens of accounts, has at its center the
opperhoofd, prostrate on the floor of Edo Castle's expansive audience
chamber. Gifts stacked neatly to the side, he offers annual greetings
from the *Oranda kapitan,* or "Holland captain," to an indifferent shogun
sitting in shadows at the opposite end of the hall. The second, also a sta-
ple of accounts of the Dutch in Japan, took place hundreds of miles away
from the Bakufu's center of power in a remote part of Kyushu. In 1638,
a VOC ship, the *Rijp,* dropped anchor near Hara Castle in Shimabara
domain. Inside the walls of this dilapidated but still formidable fortress,
the Dutch crew found tens of thousands of rebels, many of them Christians, that were locked in conflict with the Tokugawa regime. The *Rijp*
had not, however, arrived to help. Instead, the ship's gunners opened
fire, lobbing hundreds of shells into the rebel encampment and killing
or injuring dozens of defenders.

Both of these familiar scenes appear in Kaempfer's account of the
Dutch in Japan as the product of a top-down process, humiliating measures that "this heathen court [the Bakufu] had no qualms in inflicting

upon" an unwilling company.[1] While the Dutch seem to slip naturally into this role as passive victims, the assessment strips away their own agency in crafting the framework that ultimately gave birth to such moments. Once the automatic assumption of Bakufu culpability is dropped, it becomes clear that both scenes stemmed in fact from a deliberate shift in VOC policy toward Japan that emerged as a result of the failure of Nuyts's embassy. Beginning in the early 1630s, the company crafted a new diplomatic strategy that saw its agents in Japan repackaged not as representatives of the "king of Holland" or a sovereign lord of Batavia but as loyal vassals of the Tokugawa shogun. Repeating again and again that they aspired only to be dutiful vassals who stood ready to present their service, Dutch representatives crafted a distinctive rhetoric of subordination that came to underpin their interactions with the shogun. The result was a remarkably durable, although conspicuously unequal, framework for interaction that remained in place until the nineteenth century.

In contrast to Nuyts's spectacular failure, the company's diplomatic record in Japan after 1627 was far more successful, with accommodation replacing conflict as the central theme. Yet this story of adaptation, in which VOC agents pivoted to secure a place in the Tokugawa order, came at a cost. The move into the new category of subsovereign vassal stripped away the diplomatic rights that Nuyts had so vociferously defended and denied the company access to one of its most reliable policy instruments. At the same time, the reconfigured presentation came with its own requirements. Rather than simply consenting to Dutch protestations about their role as loyal vassals, the Bakufu gave concrete form to these when it required the opperhoofd to participate in the same ceremonies mandated of the shogun's other subordinates. The result was the annual court visit, or *hofreis,* that paired rhetorical claims with a heavy ceremonial requirement. When the opperhoofd pressed his head to the floor of the castle's audience chamber, he did so not as an ambassador—indeed there were no more official VOC embassies to Japan after 1627—but as a loyal vassal required like other vassals in the Tokugawa system to perform his part in a relentless theater of submission.[2]

Even more worryingly, the company's new presentation morphed into an occasional requirement for actual service. To their very real discomfort, VOC agents discovered that hyperbolic declarations were not always enough and they were expected to discharge their obligations as dutiful subordinates by providing ships and men for service against the Bakufu's enemies. The result was to give weight to something that had started off as little more than a flattering lie, a glossy trick designed to satisfy an otherwise intractable regime. As the decades wore on and words were wrapped together with ceremony and service, it became increasingly unclear who was actually tricking whom or where performance ended and reality began.

That the company was prepared to use such rhetoric in dealing with an Asian ruler is not in itself particularly noteworthy. European enterprises in Asia frequently made use of terms of like *vassal* or *loyal servant* to hide their activities behind a cloak of political legitimacy supplied by the putative overlord. This was famously the case in India, where English representatives employed the language of dutiful service to conceal what was in fact a massive expansion of their area of influence and a further hollowing out of Mughal structures. In Japan, on the other hand, the rhetoric of subordination functioned quite differently. Rather than providing room to maneuver, it hardened, creating walls that penned in the company and limited its actions.

This chapter explores the origins, development, and implications of the idea of the Dutch as the shogun's vassals.[3] It aims to show how VOC agents crafted the initial outlines of a new settlement with the shogun as well as to consider the ways in which its central logic gradually evolved until it slipped from their hands to gain an unexpected substance. It does this by tracing the thread of an idea from its first appearance in 1630 running through the hofreis to the Shimabara uprising and beyond, attempting in the process to show how disparate events in the history of the VOC presence in Japan can be linked together to form one coherent story.

LANGUAGE AND RHETORIC

In the months after the failure of Nuyts's embassy, the question of diplomacy was temporarily pushed to one side by a conflict that erupted between Japanese merchants and Dutch authorities on Taiwan. While company officials worked to resolve this crisis, which will be treated in chapter 6, they struggled with a second question: how best to reconstitute diplomatic ties once the impasse had been removed. Although it was abundantly clear that the shogun would not receive ambassadors from Batavia, there was no consensus as to how to move forward. For Jan Pieterszoon Coen, who had taken over from Pieter de Carpentier as governor-general, the solution was obvious: the company must resuscitate its older model for diplomacy and should do so as soon as possible. Having disappeared, mysteriously erased from the 1627 letter to the shogun, the Stadhouder was, Coen decided, due for an unexpected return.

With this goal in mind, he wrote to the current incumbent, Frederik Hendrik, to request a letter for the Japanese ruler. Such a document would, Coen believed, "remove all disturbances," effectively resetting the clock and allowing the company to pick up where it had left off before Nuyts's unfortunate embassy.[4] The governor-general was not the only one to reach this conclusion. Having struggled for weeks to explain Batavia's authority, Nuyts himself had also decided that a letter from the "king of Holland" held the key to diplomatic interaction with Japan.[5] A return to a model of negotiation built around the Stadhouder offered an obvious advantage. While Bakufu officials were adamant that they would not accept an embassy from Batavia, the door remained firmly open for a new delegation carrying appropriate letters from the "king of Holland." But for all this, it was also a significant step backward for the company. The entire thrust of VOC diplomacy in this period was, as detailed in the previous chapter, away from a reliance on the Stadhouder toward a focus on Batavia Castle, which had become increasingly well-established as a fulcrum for diplomatic activity.

While Coen was eager to secure a letter as soon as possible, one of the problems with relying on a distant figure in Europe for diplomatic legitimation stemmed from the long delays it imposed on any interactions and before a document from Frederik Hendrik could arrive in Batavia, the governor-general died in office, leaving his successor to inherit the problem. By chance, the position fell to an old Japan hand, Jacques Specx, who had served as the first opperhoofd of the Hirado factory and was unquestionably the most experienced of the company's employees when it came to dealing with the Tokugawa regime. An unpopular choice with the Heeren 17, who, clearly believing he was not the right man for the job, moved swiftly to end his tenure, Specx succeeded in engineering two significant policy shifts that reoriented Dutch relations with Japan before he was replaced by his employer's preferred candidate, Hendrik Brouwer, in 1633. The first resolved the ongoing crisis over Taiwan while the second put in place a new diplomatic strategy for dealing with the Bakufu. Instead of following Coen's plan and waiting for the letter from Frederik Hendrik, Specx decided that the company must adapt itself to new circumstances. Rather than going backward to reclaim a role as the subjects of the "king of Holland" or persisting with attempts to secure Tokugawa recognition for Batavia, he carved out a third path that pushed the Dutch into a new diplomatic category within Japan.

The first formulation of Specx's presentation came in two letters sent from Batavia to Edo in 1630.[6] Deliberately omitting any reference to an external authority, he informed the Bakufu that "the Netherlanders shall display such faithful service to his Majesty [the shogun] in all matters just as his Majesty expects from the Japanese that are his own vassals (*haere Majt eigen vassalen*)."[7] Although it seems at first a throwaway line of no great significance, this statement was in fact to reshape the nature of the relationship between the company and the shogun. After 1630 the notion of the Dutch as vassals gradually seeped down until it became a standard theme that was repeated by VOC agents in Japan, Specx's successors as governors-general, and even by Tokugawa officials. While the precise formulation could vary, the underlying logic remained essentially consistent. At different times company agents explained that that wished "to be like vassals of His Majesty [the shogun]," that they were "and shall remain faithful vassals of the Japanese realm," and that they should be treated "as faithful vassals of His Majesty."[8] Phrased initially in relatively bland terms, the presentation gradually became more hyperbolic, until it reached a crescendo in 1642 when one governor-general proclaimed in a letter to Edo that he and his subordinates were willing to spill "their last drop of blood in service of His Majesty and preservation of the Japanese realm."[9]

The claim was also picked up by the company's Japanese allies including the Matsura family, who made sure that it was continually referenced during the company's interactions with the Bakufu. In one particularly important episode, Matsura Takanobu personally intervened to alter documents from Batavia to support the reconfigured presentation. In 1633 Specx's successor, Hendrik Brouwer, had dispatched a letter to senior Bakufu officials in Edo thanking them for reopening trade.[10] Although there was nothing particularly controversial about the contents of the document, it failed to make any mention of the Dutch as vassals, and, when he received the letter, Takanobu elected to rewrite it to match Specx's presentation. The revised document left no doubt as to the place of the Dutch in Japan, asking the shogun to "please hold the Hollanders as His Majesty's own people (*eijgen volck te houden*) and order us in his service. If you recognize us as such, we will always be grateful because we wish to serve his majesty until death."[11]

Sitting at the top of what was once labeled a feudal structure, the Tokugawa shogun had of course many subordinates that might be called vassals. Who then was Specx, an official with considerable experience of Japan, referring to when he described the Dutch as the equivalent of the regime's *eigen vassalen*? Some sense of this is provided in two extant Japanese translations of VOC letters to the Bakufu. The first of these is a translation of Specx's original 1630 document while the second comes from 1642 when governor-general Antonio van Diemen wrote to Edo.[12] In these documents, which were prepared by translators working for the company, the word *fudai* (譜代) appears as the most common designation for the suggested relationship. Referring to vassals or servants that stood in hereditary subordination to another family or group and who were defined by their record of loyal service, the term had by this period acquired a strong connection to one particular group within the Tokugawa order: the fudai daimyo.

Under the settlement crafted by Ieyasu, all daimyo swore an oath of loyalty to the shogun and were, at least in theory, loyal vassals, but the strength and reliability of their devotion varied enormously. On the outer end of the scale were the *tozama* or outside lords, who had only recognized Tokugawa authority either during or after the battle of Sekigahara in 1600. This group included domains like Satsuma that had a decidedly antagonistic relationship with the regime. In contrast, the fudai lords were hereditary vassals who had been allied to the Tokugawa family in the years prior to its ascension to power.[13] Tied by sturdy bonds to the government, the group formed a crucial buttress to the state, staffing Edo's expanding bureaucracy and providing the shogun with administrative muscle. In return, the fudai lords, many of whom possessed very limited income from land holdings, relied on the stipends provided by these offices to survive. The result was a system of mutual dependence that ensured their commitment to the ongoing survival of the government.[14]

While it is impossible to say for certain that the use of the term *fudai* by the Dutch was deliberate, it matches too closely to be dismissed out of hand. These lords were the exemplary loyal vassals within the Tokugawa system and an obvious point of reference for a presentation that emphasized ongoing devotion to the regime. Even if we cannot be sure about this link, it is abundantly clear, however, that the comparison was not with low-ranking retainers but with a more elevated category of vassal, the daimyo, and it is no coincidence that the Dutch were subsequently drawn into the same ceremonial requirement enforced on these lords.

To support their claims, VOC officials from Specx onward worked, in much the same way as the daimyo themselves, to construct a genealogy of service capable of tying them directly to Ieyasu, the center of an expanding Tokugawa cult. As the first VOC ships had arrived in Japan in 1609, nine years after the crucial battle at Sekigahara, it was not possible to attach the company to this momentous victory, but it could claim a connection, albeit a very limited one, to the second great campaign of the Tokugawa period, the siege of the massive fortress at Osaka that had commenced in 1614. During this crucial campaign, Ieyasu's forces eliminated Hideyoshi's son, Toyotomi Hideyori (1593–1615), as an alternative source of legitimacy, thereby ensuring the security of the regime. In his 1630 letter Specx noted that the Dutch had dutifully "served His Majesty Ongosio-sama [Ieyasu] in the war at Osaka with as many cannon and constables [gunners] as they had in Hirado."[15]

While the claim looked good on paper, the details were much murkier. Like many groups in Japan, the Dutch had a far more ambiguous relationship with Hideyoshi's young heir than their later presentation suggested. When he first arrived in Japan as opperhoofd, Specx had attempted to play both sides of the fence by presenting gifts not only to Ieyasu but also to Osaka Castle in case Toyotomi loyalists prevailed.[16] When war broke out, VOC merchants supplied Bakufu forces with military provisions, but they did so at a price, hoping to profit off the increased demand for military items.[17] The story of the constable was even less laudable. In September 1615, some months after the siege had concluded, the Bakufu requested a master gunner "for the service of His Imperial Majesty."[18] The one qualified candidate, Claes Gerritsen, was needed aboard his ship, and the governing council in Hirado was not prepared to commit such a useful employee to the shogun's service.

Their preferred nominee, a drink-prone master gunner called Frans Andriessen, proved a disaster and was recalled in disgrace, leaving the shogun's request unfulfilled.[19] Although not particularly convincing at first, the genealogy of service looked much better after the Shimabara revolt in 1637 when VOC agents were able to tie themselves to two of the three great conflicts of the Tokugawa period by arguing that "we [had] served His Majesty Ongosio Samma [Ieyasu] in the war of Osaka and the currently ruling emperor [shogun], may he long reign, against the rebels and papists of Amakusa and Arima [Shimabara]."[20]

After 1630, notions of the Dutch as vassals were also mobilized to provide a structure for communication with the Bakufu. In this way company agents articulated complaints in the language of an aggrieved vassal and justified new requests by pointing to a long record of faithful service. When confronted with the possibility of new restrictions, their immediate response was to present themselves as wronged subordinates with an unblemished record of service who had been unfairly subjected to doubt through no fault of their own. Any hint of suspicion was met with an exaggerated sense of anguish: "It distresses us to learn what feelings the high authorities have to the Hollanders, especially as we are faithful vassals of His Majesty [the shogun], that are ready to risk our lives and goods [in his service], which we trust will be understood and recognized by His Majesty."[21] A 1642 letter went even further, lamenting that the Dutch simply could not understand the shogun's new restrictions because they had "always tried to serve the Japanese realm with humble dutifulness as faithful vassals." So hurtful were these unwarranted suspicions that it was preferable to leave Japan than to be doubted by the shogun "as our faithfulness and sincerity . . . are as bright as the midday sun."[22]

Such protestations meant little, however, if they fell on deaf ears in Edo or, worse still, produced the sort of interrogation that Nuyts and Muijser had been subjected to in 1627. But, whereas Tokugawa officials decisively rejected the ambassadors' claims about the governor-general, they proved far more receptive to the presentation of the Dutch as vassals. Thus senior Bakufu representatives, the same officials who had dismissed de Carpentier's letter to the shogun out of hand, showed no hesitation in responding to documents that presented the Dutch as loyal subordinates, accepting the parameters of the new vision apparently without dissent.[23] In the process they brushed aside past statements by

VOC representatives in favor of the new consensus: If the Dutch wished to present themselves as vassals defined only by their connection to the shogun, the regime, which had its own interests in keeping its relationship with the company functioning, was quite clearly ready to consent, and there was no parallel to the relentless barrage of questions detailed in Nuyts's diary.

This said, it would be a mistake to confuse consent with belief, and it is doubtful that any Tokugawa officials were genuinely convinced of the essential truth of these claims, particularly when they took the form of hyperbolic assertions about the willingness of Dutch representatives to shed their last drop of blood in service of the shogun. Rather the Bakufu displayed a clear willingness to accept these ideas as a framework for dealing with the company and organizing relations with its agents in Japan. Indeed, as will be discussed later, the regime was more concerned with maintaining the external appearance of devotion than with resolving the contradictions hidden behind the presentation of the Dutch as vassals.

What did it mean for VOC agents, who had once compared the governor-general to a sovereign king, to claim a place as the shogun's vassals? At its heart, Specx's strategy hinged on a basic denial of foreignness. In staking out a role as loyal subordinates, he argued that the Dutch no longer wished to be counted as outsiders but desired instead to take up a position alongside the shogun's other subjects as "faithful vassals of His Majesty and not foreigners."[24] The result was to pull Dutch agents in Japan into a domestic political landscape and shrink the boundaries of their world to one circumscribed by the shogun's authority. Prior to his intervention, VOC agents had always claimed to represent a sovereign authority located outside Japan and had used this connection to assert their rights to negotiate with the shogun in the same way as the representatives of a more conventional state. Starting off as the Stadhouder, this external authority had by 1627 become the governor-general who wrote to Edo from his stronghold in Batavia.

Although such claims provided a way into diplomatic circuits, they also set a high bar for interaction, requiring Japanese officials to recognize the authority of castle Batavia as a starting point for engagement. Specx's new presentation effectively removed any such requirement, for, to function smoothly, it required the shogun simply to consent to Dutch assertions that they were loyal vassals. In this way VOC agents became defined not by a connection to an external sponsor but rather to the shogun himself, thereby erasing the question—who exactly do you represent?—that had so plagued their past diplomatic efforts. The revised framework simplified the company's role in Japan by taking it out of the business of official diplomacy. Whereas Nuyts had struggled to stake out a place for the organization within the Tokugawa diplomatic order alongside other sovereign actors, Specx opted simply to retreat to a new subsovereign category. Since they were tethered to a domestic overlord, vassals had no need to write diplomatic letters, to send embassies, or to prove their right to correspond directly with the shogun.

Although the decision to claim a role as vassals removed a series of hurdles, it also marked a retreat from rights the company took for granted in other parts of Asia. By 1630, when the idea of the Dutch as vassals was first aired, Batavia had been transformed into a diplomatic hub that stood at the center of an increasingly expansive web of international relations. Even if he was prone to exaggeration, Nuyts's basic assertion that the governor-general was "of such a status that he sends ambassadors to the principal kings of China, Siam, Aceh and Patani; to the emperors of Java and Persia; to the Great Mughal" was grounded in fact.[25] Taking on a role as vassals signaled an implicit abandonment of these diplomatic prerogatives. Rather than trying to convince the Japanese of the governor-general's capacity to send embassies, Specx resolved instead to shelter in the shadow of the shogun and abandon any claim for Dutch representatives to be treated in the same way as those of a more conventional state. It was not to prove a temporary withdrawal. After 1630 the company dispatched no further official embassies to Japan. There was thus no equivalent in Japan to the splendid VOC delegations sent from Batavia to India, Persia, and other powerful states across Asia.[26]

The scale of the concession was significant. For all its costs, and even though there was always a potential for failure, the embassy remained a vital policy tool for the VOC in Asia. For close to two centuries, formal diplomatic missions dispatched from Batavia with documents, gifts, and a clear set of aims remained the one weapon called into action whenever the company faced a crisis, hoped to secure a significant concession or simply wanted something from an Asian ruler. It was for this reason that de Carpentier had dispatched Nuyts in the first place, in order to defuse the escalating crisis over Tayouan, and why it continued to rely on such delegations whenever a serious problem arose. That Specx was prepared to take such a step—and his successors to confirm it—was a measure of the company's desperation and a frank acknowledgement of the difficulty its representatives faced in securing sovereign recognition in Japan. Rather than, as Nuyts had done, endlessly protesting about the governor-general's diplomatic rights, the company's representatives chose to adapt by shifting course to secure an ongoing framework for exchange with the shogun. In this way, for all its success in stabilizing relations with Edo, the decision to abandon Batavia's diplomatic prerogatives represented a significant retreat, the first in a number, from the trinity of powers laid out in the company's 1602 charter.

Given the nature of the concession, it is not surprising that some VOC officials toyed occasionally with the idea of getting back into the embassy business, but these plans were swiftly quashed.[27] Strikingly, even when Bakufu officials specifically requested a new mission, the Dutch pulled back. To jump briefly ahead, this was the case after the Breskens incident, which has been superbly documented by Reinier Hesselink in his important 2002 book. In 1643 ten Dutch sailors were arrested after landing unexpectedly in the port of Nanbu in northern Japan. After they agreed to free these prisoners, Bakufu officials demanded that the Dutch arrange an embassy from Holland to thank the regime for its generosity.[28] Hesselink suggests, and he is surely correct, that the request came directly from the shogun himself and was prompted by a desire to parade a lavish embassy from the "king of Holland" through his capital.

Setting aside the fact that they believed the original arrest of their employees had been illegal, the request presented VOC officials with a problem. If the shogun wanted an embassy, one had to be provided, but what sort of delegation could possibly be sent?

By 1646, when the embassy was requested, the company was no longer prepared to make use of the "king of Holland" model of diplomacy, which had been abandoned across its area of operations. It was also, given its experience with Nuyts's embassy, not willing to send a formal mission from Batavia equipped with letters and gifts from the governor-general. Confronted with this dilemma, it opted for a bizarre delegation headed by a dying ambassador who was dispatched with the expectation that he would succumb to his illness before he reached Japan, thereby muddying the waters enough to prevent any backlash when the embassy failed to meet Bakufu expectations. This so confused Tokugawa officials that they eventually concluded that although the surviving members of the embassy must be recognized in some way they could not possibly appear before the shogun and abandoned any further talk of an embassy from Holland. The result was to confirm the conclusion that Specx had reached years earlier, that there was no acceptable route back into the embassy business for the Dutch in Japan.

In the early 1630s, to return to the period under discussion, Bakufu officials displayed far more interest in securing a workable framework for interaction with the Dutch than in encouraging any thoughts of a new embassy. Because of this, they were quick to accept VOC documents organized around the notion of the Dutch as vassals and made no objections even to the company's more florid claims. In fact, the Bakufu did more than simply tolerate this idea. Rather, it added a heavy ceremonial requirement to the company's rhetoric, giving an unexpected weight to the idea first introduced by Specx and creating the conditions for the notion of the Dutch as domestic vassals to take on a life of its own within Japan

THE HOFREIS

In April 1634, the staff of the Japan factory learned that they were now expected to travel to Edo every year to pay homage to the shogun.[29] Although it came with little fanfare, this announcement marked the beginning of one of the most enduring ceremonial requirements for Europeans in Asia, the hofreis or the annual visit to court, that would continue essentially uninterrupted from 1634 to 1850. Described in hundreds of accounts, the hofreis, and particularly its ceremonial climax in which the opperhoofd pressed his face to the floor in front of the shogun, has become such a familiar feature of descriptions of the VOC presence in Japan that the exact reasons for its introduction have become blurred.[30] The result has been that while most scholars agree that the hofreis proper commenced in 1634, there is no clear consensus as to what prompted its development and why the visit to the court took on the form it did.[31] If we look more closely at the nature of these visits, however, it becomes clear that the hofreis was, in many ways, a direct response to the rhetoric of subordination; it served, quite simply, to place the company's representatives in Japan in the role they had claimed for themselves. Because of this, its genesis lay in the shift in VOC diplomatic strategy that had taken place in 1630.

In 1634, when the Bakufu mandated annual journeys to Edo, two alternatives existed that were capable of providing a model for the opperhoofd's visit to the court. The first was arranged around the state embassy. Although it included the first Dutch missions to Japan, this template was most closely associated with delegations from Korea and the Ryukyu kingdom that continued to arrive across the long expanse of the Tokugawa period. The embassy model incorporated four distinct features that were present regardless of where the delegation originated. The first of these related to timing. Embassies were not regular events. Instead, their arrival was triggered by special occasions such as the accession of a new shogun, making them extremely sporadic. Over a period of more than two centuries, only twelve delegations arrived in Japan from Korea, and even the more numerous missions from the Ryukyu kingdom just reached twenty.[32]

Second, embassies merited official support from the central regime. As soon as they set foot on Japanese soil, embassy processions, which often consisted of hundreds of participants, received financial backing, sometimes at a ruinous cost both to the Bakufu and the unfortunate domains that lay on their route through the archipelago.[33] Third, embassies arrived in Edo as the representatives of an external power. Although ambassadors could be influential figures in their own right, their primary role was to act as proxies for the sovereign, with the result that their most important responsibility was the delivery of the diplomatic letters they carried.[34] Fourth, once in Edo, embassies were incorporated into impressive ceremonies that climaxed with the presentation of official greetings in the castle's audience chamber.[35] While these were designed to demonstrate the shogun's position at the center of a Japanocentric order, they nonetheless accorded the ambassador, as the representative of an external power, considerable status.

Tellingly, the Dutch hofreis incorporated none of these features. Instead, it drew on a different template that had been crafted for the shogun's domestic vassals and which was coming to final development at the exact moment when annual visits to court became a requirement for the opperhoofd. After the Bakufu seized power in 1600, it became an unwritten expectation for daimyo to make regular journeys to its headquarters, and by the time of Ieyasu's death in 1615 many of these lords were frequent guests at the shogun's court.[36] While this ensured periodic visits to Edo, the system was flexible as it hinged largely on the timetables of individual domains. This changed in 1635, just one year after the Dutch hofreis commenced, when the Bakufu issued an edict instructing the daimyo to "serve in turns [kōtai] at Edo. They shall proceed hither [sankin] every year in summer during the course of the fourth month."[37] The order marked the beginning of the famous alternate attendance or *sankin kōtai* system, which turned the daimyo visit from a voluntary act into a fixed obligation.

Although it also culminated in an audience with the shogun, the daimyo visit, as one would expect for a system organized for domestic subordinates, looked nothing like the model developed for embassies. It was, first of all, fixed according to a rigid schedule that saw most lords make annual visits to Edo.[38] Since all costs were borne by the domain, the arrangement effectively required individual daimyo to turn over a significant portion of their income funds to a repetitive cycle of travel. Once in Edo, these lords participated in ceremonies designed to hammer home a straightforward message of Bakufu dominance and domainal submission. In this way the sankin kōtai system provided a potent symbol of a much larger program in which, to use Eiko Ikegami's description, the Bakufu "compelled the daimyo (who had originally held equal status) to accept a hierarchically structured relationship between them, with the shogun as the master and the daimyo as subordinate vassals."[39]

The link between the Dutch hofreis and the sankin kōtai system was obvious to company employees, who instinctively made the comparison. Engelbert Kaempfer, a participant in two visits to the court, noted that: "all daimyo and shomyo, that is, all greater and lesser territorial lords, appear annually at the shogun's court. They pay homage by offering their respects and presenting gifts: while the greatest of them—one could call them princes or petty kings—call on the shogun personally, the lesser are received by an assembly of councilors. This custom is also enforced upon the servants of our illustrious Dutch company."[40] While Kaempfer was an astute observer of Japanese customs, it was a natural conclusion to reach with each stage of the hofreis closely matching its daimyo equivalent and incorporating a comparable dynamic of authority and submission. This fact becomes immediately clear when the two are set alongside each other. To illustrate this point it is possible to select almost at random, since the hofreis possessed a remarkable uniformity over its more than two centuries of operation, but as one representative example we can focus on Zacharias Wagenaer's 1657 visit to the shogun's court.[41] Until he was caught up at the end of his stay in Edo in the devastating Meireki fires, Wagenaer's experience was utterly unexceptional, following a well-worn path that was in turn duplicated by dozens of his successors.

Wagenaer arrived in Nagasaki in August 1656 to take up his post as head of the Japan factory. Once the official handover had taken place in November, he began preparations for his trip to Edo, which formed the most pressing duty for any new opperhoofd. Unlike embassies, which required a special cue, the hofreis was a legal requirement that could not be ignored, substantially delayed, or significantly altered. It was thus a built-in function of the ongoing relationship between the company and the shogun. Like the daimyo, the various heads of the Japan factory were required to travel to Edo at regular intervals, but their timetable was in fact more onerous than that enforced on the majority of domainal lords. The classic sankin kōtai timetable saw most daimyo spend every alternate year in Edo while only a select group of minor fudai lords, who ruled over domains located close to the shogun's headquarters were required to undertake annual journeys. Despite the distances involved between Edo and their base in Kyushu, the Dutch were instructed to make the journey to the shogun's court every year, receiving exemptions only in the most extraordinary of circumstances.[42]

After making all the necessary arrangements, Wagenaer left Nagasaki on 18 January 1657 or the fourth day of the twelfth month in the second year of Meireki. The timing of his departure was important. As was the case with daimyo visits to court, the precise schedule of the hofreis evolved over time to become increasingly rigid. When it commenced in 1634, the Dutch were advised to arrive before the end of the Japanese year so they could be granted an audience in the first month of the Japanese calendar.[43] During the 1640s, audiences generally took place earlier in the eleventh or twelfth month, but by the time Wagenaer left Nagasaki they had been pushed back to the original schedule, usually occurring on the fifteenth or twenty-eighth day of the first month.[44] The timing allowed some flexibility, permitting the opperhoofd to choose when he wanted to leave, with the condition, of course, that he appeared in Edo at the right time. This leeway was erased, however, in 1660, when Bakufu mandated the fifteenth day of the first month as the required date for departure from Nagasaki.[45] The decision brought the hofreis into line with daimyo conventions, prompting Kaempfer to note that just "as the shogun gives every prince and vassal in the empire a day on which he has to set out and begin his annual journey to court, so the Dutch too are assigned a day for their departure. This is the fifteenth or the sixteenth day of the Japanese first month, which corresponds to February in our calendar."[46]

Leaving Nagasaki, Wagenaer traveled by sea to Osaka before proceeding on land to Edo.[47] Whereas state ambassadors could count on the Bakufu's support to defray any costs, the opperhoofd was required to pay for all expenses as he made his way through Japan. These were considerable. In Osaka, Wagenaer made arrangements to hire 85 bearers and 46 horses to transport his group to the shogun's capital.[48] To these expenses were added the costs for accommodation (both on the road and in Edo), food, and miscellaneous items such as tea and tobacco.[49] Once everything was included, the total for Wagenaer's hofreis came to the large sum of 15,893 guilders.[50] Given that a similar expenditure was required each year, it constituted an onerous burden on the factory, which was compelled to pay out regardless of the season's trading profits. This said, the daimyo, who could not draw on the vast financial resources of a multinational organization to subsidize their journey to court, suffered far more from the requirement. For many of these lords, the expenses associated with the sankin kōtai system consumed a large percentage of their available income, draining away resources and requiring the accumulation of huge debts.[51]

After a relatively quick journey, Wagenaer reached Edo on 16 February 1657, just in time to notice smoke rising from the eastern side of the vast metropolis.[52] The next day he discovered that the audience had been set for 27 February or the fifteenth day of the first month. Although this was Wagenaer's first experience of the hofreis, he would have known what to expect from his predecessors who had participated in almost identical ceremonies in the years since 1634. While it took a similar form to the daimyo audience, the ritual climax of the hofreis also marked out the opperhoofd's unique status in the Tokugawa system. In Edo, low-ranking daimyo such as the lords of Hirado domain took part in mass audiences during which they prostrated themselves in a ritualized performance of submission before a shogun who was often partially obscured from view in a raised part of the audience chamber.[53] With no opportunity for deviation, the daimyo—powerful individuals in their own right—were reduced to the role of mute participants compelled to

Figure 3.1. The Dutch procession to Edo. Courtesy of the British Library, Sloane Manuscript 3060, folio 501

follow a script they had no power to alter. In contrast, the opperhoofd received the rare privilege of an individual audience, but this had more to do with his ambiguous position in the Tokugawa order than it was indicative of a particularly high status.

Although it often required weeks of waiting, the actual audience lasted just a few seconds. In his diary Wagenaer provided a description of the ceremony, noting that "I pressed my face down, whereupon immediately I heard a loud cry 'Holland Captain.' With that the song and the ceremony came to an end."[54] A more detailed account was provided by one of his predecessors who made the trip to Edo three years earlier:

I was suddenly summoned [after a two to three hour wait] to present myself before the Japanese monarch. I followed stiffly behind Sickingo [Inoue Masashige] and Quiemon [Kiemon Masanobu] through a covered passage and then went at a pace as the old commissioner called out occasionally, "Hurry, hurry." We went round the outside of the palace and turned two corners, passing by a large hall with many lords and came to where our gifts had been placed. There I was instructed to bow down with my face to the planks (I

did not even step onto the mats). Right across the hall the councilors and the shogun were standing and Ando Okiosamma [Andō
Shigenaga] loudly called out "Holland Captain." If I was to say that
I had seen this powerful lord more than I had heard, my heart
would contradict it.[55]

During the audience, the shogun stood in the furthest recesses of
the audience hall, partially concealed from the opperhoofd by distance
and lighting. The arrangement served to open up the maximum possible
space between overlord and supplicant, who were positioned at opposite ends of the massive chamber. Determined to catch a better glimpse
of the object of devotion, Wagenaer contravened instructions by deliberately raising his head as he stood up and managed in this way to make
out a shadowy figure "standing in a dark place" across the expanse of
the hall.[56]

As was the case across the duration of the hofreis, the Dutch representative was announced simply as *Oranda kapitan* or the "Holland Captain." The designation was a telling one, for, in contrast to the embassy
equivalent, it omitted any reference to an external figure standing
outside Japan. The result was to define Wagenaer's position within a
domestic political order that was bounded by the shogun's authority.
Rather than a proxy of some greater power, he was announced simply
as the captain of a small piece of territory within the shogun's realm.
The label was particularly appropriate after 1641 when the factory was
moved from Hirado to the tiny man-made island of Deshima in Nagasaki harbor, which formed a self-contained Dutch enclave under the
control of the opperhoofd. There, on a tiny speck of land measuring just
1.31 hectares or just over three acres, the "Holland Captain" presided
over a kind of domain, complete with its own laws and administration,
albeit one shrunk to a miniature scale.

Although the location of the audience is traditionally identified as
the *ōhiroma* or great hall, the exact placement of the ceremony could be
more complicated than this. A key ceremonial space within the castle, the
ōhiroma was divided into six separate sections, access to which was reg-
ulated according to a strict hierarchy. Thus, for example, a low-ranking
daimyo might offer reverence from one of the lesser sections of the
hall, while a more senior lord could occupy a more elevated space.[57] The
opperhoofd was, however, frequently pushed outside the walls of the

Figure 3.2. Kaempfer's audience with shogun. This image shows a second, more informal meeting that took place after the official audience with the opperhoofd. Nonetheless it provides a good sense of the scale and layout of the great hall. As can be seen here, the Dutch were in this case given access to the hall itself. Courtesy of the British Library, Sloane Manuscript 3060, folio 514

ōhiroma itself to the verandah (*ochien*) that encircled it. This was the case with Wagenaer whose "gifts were," according to *Tsūkō ichiran*, "laid out on the verandah of the great hall and Hollanders made their greetings [from there]."[58] Gabriel Happart, who traveled to Edo three years earlier, noted that he was not allowed to step onto the mats of the great hall but had to press his face to the wooden planks of the verandah.[59]

The choice of this section, a liminal space both part and not part of the main audience hall, perfectly encapsulated the nature of the opperhoofd's position. Simultaneously a daimyo and not, he was marooned on the peripheries of the great hall, a participant in the same ceremonies as the shogun's vassals but without consistent access to the space used by his domestic counterparts.[60] At times the Dutch were pushed back even one step further to the uncomfortable edges of the ōhiroma. When Wagenaer returned for a second audience in 1659, he offered his greetings on an outer walkway that ran round the side of the verandah.[61] The contrast with foreign ambassadors, who were permitted access to a far more prestigious section of the hall, is obvious, while there was, as Ron Toby

Figure 3.3. Audience hall with presents for the shogun. Courtesy of the British Library, Sloane Manuscript 3060, folio 512

notes, an additional divide in terminology. Whereas embassies were received "in audience" (*inken* or *nyūetsu*), the Dutch and their gifts were, in a further marker of their distinct status, simply "viewed" (*goran*).[62]

During the audience the opperhoofd pressed his head to the floor alongside the company's offerings for the year. In Dutch records these are described as *schenkagie*, or gifts, a generic designation that gives little sense as to what the items actually meant in this context. Japanese sources are clearer, routinely describing these items as "tribute" (*nyūkō* or *kenjō butsu*).[63] Rather than embassy gifts presented as a token of friendship from one sovereign to another, these were ritual items offered from vassal to suzerain. In this way they parallel the offerings made by the daimyo who were also required to give tribute, usually known as *sanpu kenjō*, when they arrived in Edo.[64] Since bonds of fealty were meant to be reciprocal, the shogun responded with his own gifts in the form of seasonal clothing, or *jifuku*, that were presented to the opperhoofd at the conclusion of his stay in Edo. According to a later account from 1664: "He [the Nagasaki *bugyō*, Shimada Kyūtarō Toshiki] indicated three large present trays that lay a little way away from me. On each of these were ten dresses (*rocken*). He said that these were the return gifts of his majesty, which must be accepted and taken away. After giving my thanks, I crawled over to the middle tray of the three and lying down with my face on the ground placed the sleeve of one of the aforementioned dresses against my head."[65] For the Dutch, such objects, which possessed little or no commercial value outside of Japan, were frustrating as they offered no way to recoup the expenses involved in the hofreis but, as the description makes clear, they recognized the heavy symbolic weight of the transaction and acted accordingly. Once again, the parallel was with the daimyo, who received similar items when they headed back to their domains.[66]

While the audience represented the climax of the hofreis, it did not signal the end of the opperhoofd's stay in Edo, and there was one further reminder of his role as ersatz vassal. Throughout the 1640s, Bakufu officials periodically issued the Dutch factory with instructions to avoid contact with the Portuguese and to make sure that no Japan-bound ships carried missionaries or Christian paraphernalia. In 1659 this practice was transformed into a formal set of written orders that were issued to the opperhoofd at the conclusion of his stay in Edo. During his second stint in Japan, Wagenaer was called back to the castle ten days after his initial audience and brought again to the verandah where he had prostrated himself before the shogun. There he was presented with a set of orders that were read out by a court functionary in the presence of four senior Bakufu officials.[67] The exact content of these orders varied over time, gradually gaining new clauses until they eventually assumed a settled six-part form in 1673. Of these six parts, which were continually issued to VOC representatives across the long history of the hofreis, two stand out in particular.[68]

First, the Bakufu prohibited the Dutch from having any dealings, whether political, commercial, or diplomatic, with the Portuguese, who had been expelled from Japan in 1639. To help police the provision, the regime ordered the company to supply it with a list of possible contact points where the Dutch might encounter the Portuguese so it could investigate any rumor of correspondence between the two nations. Second, and arguably more important, the opperhoofd was ordered to report any news about Catholic expansion into new territories or planned voyages to Japan. This requirement translated over time into a formal intelligence report that was delivered annually to Bakufu officials in Nagasaki. At first focused on the Iberian powers, these documents, which came to be known as the *Oranda fūsetsugaki* or "reports of rumors from the Dutch," became steadily more expansive until the company was required, in the words of one opperhoofd, to provide "general news, including reports of wars, peace, battles, victories, successions, the death of kings, and other such things, [which] is presented and written down by the interpreters."[69] Starved of information from other sources, the regime came to rely on these reports as a vital conduit for intelligence, and their focus was adjusted according to the Bakufu's own preoccupations, shifting from a seventeenth-century obsession with Catholicism to a nineteenth-century concern with the rising tide of Western imperialism.[70] As such, the *Oranda fūsetsugaki* formed a concrete and highly visible emblem of the company's ongoing service that was offered up year after year without respite.

The regime's six-part orders, another item that had no place in an embassy, further reinforced the link with the daimyo, who like the opperhoofd returned from Edo with instructions from the shogun. The annual reading out of these orders provided yet another occasion for the company's representative to act out his designated role as loyal subordinate. During the ceremony he was required to wait in respectful silence by kneeling with his face turned downward and, once it was completed, he was then to respond with an enthusiastic affirmation of loyalty.[71] One opperhoofd declared that "we would obey the instructions of the emperor [shogun] and would always try to serve the Japanese realm," while a second explained that "the emperor, the councilors, and the whole of Japan could be certain of our loyalty to the realm."[72]

In these ways the hofreis, which drew on daimyo practices, treated the Dutch as domestic vassals tied directly to the shogun. Because of this, it would be a mistake to dismiss the connection between what Specx and other VOC representatives were saying about their place in Japan and the reconfigured form of the court visit as coincidence. Rather, the inception of hofreis was inextricably bound up with the company's post-1630 strategy, which deliberately positioned its employees in this role. But, if it stemmed originally from a VOC policy, the hofreis was also a new development that pushed the Dutch down an unfamiliar road. The initial formulations of the rhetoric of subordination were comparatively loose and lacked any real detail. Even more importantly, they were conspicuously devoid of any real obligation beyond the need to repeat vague declarations of loyalty. When it mandated an annual visit to Edo that ran in parallel with sankin kōtai conventions, the Bakufu gave the idea of the Dutch as domestic vassals physical form by providing the opperhoofd with a fixed script that he was required to follow. The result was to add a heavy ceremonial burden to what had previously been little more than a convenient fiction designed to smooth over potential difficulties with the regime.

All of this raises some obvious questions. How could the Dutch be so palpably foreign, the subject of wondrous accounts in Tokugawa period literature, and yet assume a role as domestic vassals? If their primary connection was with the shogun, what about the Dutch "king" in Holland or the governor-general in Batavia, both of whom Bakufu officials continued to refer periodically to?[73] Finally, how could the opperhoofd act (and be treated) like a daimyo if his domain extended to just a handful of Dutch employees who made up the factory's permanent staff? To understand how this string of obvious contradictions could be tolerated requires a brief examination of the nature of the Tokugawa regime, which displayed a surprising capacity to accommodate such paradoxes.

The Tokugawa Bakufu has always resisted easy characterization. At its heart lay a basic contradiction between the existence of a central government that claimed dominion over the archipelago and dozens of semi-autonomous domains, which retained considerable financial, military, and legal power. Indeed, it is precisely because of this basic paradox that historians sometimes make use of oxymoronic designations to define the regime. Edwin Reischauer, for example, famously described the Tokugawa state as an example of that rarest of political oddities, "centralized feudalism," a regime that was never properly centralized nor fully feudal.[74] Recent studies have shown that these contradictions extended beyond the basic structure of the regime to the way it operated from day to day. Of most relevance to this discussion is Luke Roberts's groundbreaking work, published in 2012, which focuses on the Bakufu's interactions with the domains.[75] Although the daimyo appear in Tokugawa sources as undifferentiated and perfectly regimented servants of the regime, their relationship with the Bakufu incorporated a mass of contradictions. Thus, as Roberts has shown, one daimyo might be both dead and alive in order to facilitate a successful adoption, while another might supply false or misleading information about the condition of his domain "with the full complicity of Tokugawa officials," who supposedly prized accurate intelligence on precisely these questions.[76]

For Roberts, this willingness to tolerate seemingly obvious contradictions stems from a crucial but largely neglected distinction between two key concepts, *uchi*, the (often) hidden inside, and *omote*, the outside facade presented to the world, that were integral to the functioning of the Tokugawa state. The Bakufu's governing dynamic relied on keeping these two categories separate, allowing the domains considerable autonomy within their own spaces of operation as long they preserved the outward illusion of perfect subservience. This translated into a preoccupation with performance; Roberts writes that the "ability to command performance of duty—in the thespian sense when actual performance of duty might be lacking—was a crucial tool of Tokugawa power that effectively worked toward preserving the peace in the realm."[77] Because of this, the regime was prepared to tolerate a range of otherwise disruptive behaviors within the domain's interior spaces as long as they were hidden behind an unblemished performance of subservience.

On the other side of the equation, the daimyo were able to adopt multiple identities that changed according to situation and audience. In Roberts' words, "the identity and subjectivity of actors changed radically, depending upon whether they were operating in an *omote* space or an *uchi* space, and reveals that the character of political units themselves were likewise expressed differently according to *omote* and *uchi*."[78] By recognizing that one language was used within the domains while a second quite different set of terms and ideas could appear in documents exchanged between the regime and the daimyo, Roberts is able to reconcile the apparently conflicting identities of Tokugawa period domains, which sometimes appear as independent political units, that is, states or countries in their own right, while also seeming, when viewed from a different perspective, nothing more than subordinate components of the Tokugawa system and subsovereign parts of the national polity.[79]

The distance between a daimyo who might be simultaneously both living and dead or a domain with a dual political status and the opperhoofd's unusual place in Tokugawa Japan is not as far as it may appear at first. Indeed it is precisely the same distinction Roberts describes, a division between an inside or *uchi* identity and the outside or *omote* facade, that enabled the company's rhetoric of subordination to function. The opperhoofd's actual status and whatever he did or said within the walls of the Japan factory were less important than the conduct of the company's representatives in Edo and their willingness to stage a perfect performance of subservience. And it was in this sphere that, after the commencement of the hofreis in 1634, the Dutch proved consistently reliable. In contrast with Nuyts's and his botched embassy, *opperhoofden* like Zacharias Wagenaer became adept at following the script that was provided for them by the regime. If, as Roberts maintains, the "key demands of the Tokugawa were for everyone to hold up a front of compliance and respect and to see that disorder did not erupt into the outside of their realms," then the company's representatives had by this point learned to excel in precisely this department.[80]

This sense of dependable performance was reflected in Tokugawa sources recording Dutch visits to the court after 1634.[81] In these brief accounts, the Dutch are depicted as devoted and predictable servants, arriving in Edo at the right time, performing the appropriate ceremonies, and leaving when they were told to do so. Although the entry for each year is slightly different, they follow the same basic pattern: The Hollanders (*ranjin* or *orandajin*) arrive in the castle with their tribute (*nyūkō*), which is subsequently viewed (*goran*) either by the shogun or senior officials (if he is not available), and the audience concludes.[82] From the regime's point of view, the *omote* illusion of perfect subservience was thus preserved, leaving the opperhoofd free, as his domainal counterparts were, to maintain a different *uchi* identity as long as it did not breach the surface and disrupt relations with the Bakufu.

Maintaining this illusion, however, required considerable effort for the company and its representatives. When the hofreis commenced in 1634, its first participants expressed no particular distaste for the new arrangement. To the contrary, the initiation of regular court visits was welcomed by the Dutch as the clearest sign that relations with the shogun had finally begun to stabilize after years of difficulty. But this sense of satisfaction gradually faded as the years dragged on without any loosening of the requirement. By the 1650s, when Zacharias Wagenaer completed his two visits to the court, the hofreis, with its exaggerated marks of subordination and unrelenting time line, had become increasingly unpalatable, wearing down its primary participants, whose resentment bubbled to the surface of their diaries. In 1654 one opperhoofd lamented that "this is what we usually call the audience before the Japanese Majesty. It would be better to call it reverence (or better still) submissive performance, abject humiliation or another kind of vile homage [*homagie*]."[83] But as much as they protested in internal documents, Dutch agents in Japan recognized that they possessed no power to alter the form of the ceremony or the requirement for annual performance.

At first glance, the sheer durability of the hofreis is difficult to grasp. It remained an annual requirement for over 150 years, until 1790, during which time the Dutch made a total of 167 visits to the court.[84] In 1790 the Bakufu finally reformed the system, but only by shifting the hofreis from its annual basis to once every 5 years, leaving the form of the ceremony unchanged. As a result, the last hofreis only took place in 1850, just 3 years before Perry's fleet arrived in Edo bay. As such, it outlasted the Dutch Republic and the company itself, which collapsed at the end of the eighteenth century. Across this period the nature of the ceremony remained remarkably consistent. Despite the momentous political changes that had occurred in the intervening years since its creation, the nineteenth-century hofreis would have been immediately familiar to individuals like Wagenaer.

This is clear from the account of one opperhoofd, Hendrik Doeff, who made four visits to court in 1804, 1806, 1810, and 1814. Like his seventeenth-century predecessors, Doeff departed Nagasaki on a fixed day, traveled along a familiar route to Edo, and once there participated in an unchanged ritual, although he was at least given access to the ōhiroma itself:

> Through a wooden gallery, I was escorted to the *hall with the hundred mats*. . . . I went alone with the governor of Nagasaki into the audience hall where I found the presents at my left hand side. . . . I paid my respects in the same manner as all the princes of the realm do, whereupon one member of the government council introduced me by calling out: Oranda kapitan. After this, the governor of Nagasaki who stood a few feet behind me pulled at my cloak to indicate that the audience was over. The whole ceremony took at most one whole minute.[85]

Tellingly, Doeff also made the link with the daimyo, noting that he paid his respects "in the same manner as all the princes [daimyo] of the realm."[86] Returning to the castle a few days after the audience, he received the Bakufu's standard six-part set of orders, including outdated warnings about contact with the Catholic powers. In this way, and though separated by a significant span of time from the original presentation of the Dutch as domestic vassals, a nineteenth-century opperhoofd was compelled to act out the role that had first been outlined in Specx's letter so many years earlier. Once claimed, the role could not be, Doeff's experience makes clear, easily discarded.

FROM WORD TO DEED

While the hofreis gave physical form to the company's rhetoric of subordination, it was not the only instance in which VOC agents were called
upon to pair their words with deeds, and eight years after Specx's letter
the Dutch found themselves unexpectedly involved in military operations against the shogun's enemies. The company's participation in the
campaign to put down the Shimabara uprising, a domestic rebellion
with a significant Christian element that commenced in 1637, has long
attracted controversy. For (usually non-Dutch) critics, the willingness of
the company to assault fellow believers in the service of a foreign potentate was unforgivable. Kaempfer, a German by birth, lamented the company's involvement as despicable while a later American writer described
it "an act . . . too clearly proved to admit of denial, and too wicked and
infamous to allow of palliation."[87] In contrast, Dutch writers, including
a number who worked in the Japan factory, have vigorously protested
the tendency of "ignorant foreigners . . . [to] put this matter in the most
despicable light" by arguing that the VOC opperhoofd was called upon
simply to lend assistance against domestic insurgents.[88]

This back and forth between accusation and defense brings us no
closer to explaining why the company was involved in the first place. One
explanation put forward by modern scholars suggests that the Dutch
were the victims of a test engineered by Bakufu officials to make sure
they could be completely trusted.[89] If the Dutch were prepared to turn
their guns against fellow believers, they could, so the reasoning went,
be relied upon to fully submit to the shogun's anti-Christian prohibitions. But this explanation, though certainly neat, relies on an assumption that Bakufu officials, in the middle of putting down the first major
challenge to the regime's authority in decades, paused to orchestrate a
test of loyalty for a minor foreign group. The theory becomes even less
convincing when it is traced back to its origins, a comment supposedly
made by a Bakufu commander that was later reported second or third
hand to the Dutch.[90]

To understand the factors that propelled the company's involvement
in the uprising requires first a damping down of some of the associated
rhetoric.[91] When separated out from some of the more knee-jerk accusations of Dutch wickedness, the facts of the case are not as shocking as
some writers make them seem. While Shimabara was in part a Christian

uprising, it was also a Catholic one, sparked by decades of Jesuit prose-lytizing in Kyushu. By 1638, when the company opened fire on the rebel encampment, it had been engaged in a vicious war against Portugal and Spain, the Catholic powers in Asia, and their local allies for almost four decades. Back in Europe, its home state, the Dutch Republic had been fighting for survival against Spanish incursions for considerably lon-ger. The Dutch crew that manned the vessel dispatched to Shimabara were thus no strangers to violence directed against Catholic targets, and there was no special immunity conferred on the rebels by their Chris-tian faith.

And yet it is nonetheless surprising that the company, an organi-zation that consistently refused to devote resources to nonessential military campaigns, was willing to commit ships and men to the sup-pression of a domestic revolt that offered no direct benefit to its bot-tom line while consuming valuable resources and disrupting its trading schedule.[92] The precise way in which the commitment materialized also demands explanation. Rather than being trapped by a Bakufu test, the Dutch volunteered to act, and they did so by citing their responsibilities as the shogun's loyal vassals. At the same time, the interactions between VOC agents and the Bakufu officials tasked with the suppression of the revolt were coated with a thick layer of the kind of rhetoric first introduced by Specx in 1630. All of this suggests that a direct line can be drawn from events at Shimabara to the shift in diplomatic strategy described in this chapter. Indeed, the ways in which the organization responded to the uprising provides some of the clearest evidence yet as to how central the notion of a lord-vassal relationship had become to the company's interactions with the shogun.

The ease with which talk about loyal service could morph into a com-mitment to actual action first became clear some months before the opening salvos were fired at Shimabara. In the second half of 1637, offi-cials in Nagasaki began to hint with increasing boldness that the Dutch should volunteer for an ambitious scheme to attack the Spanish colonial city of Manila.[93] The proposed assault was intended as punishment for the sinking of a Japanese ship carrying a Bakufu-issued trading pass by a Spanish fleet years earlier in 1628.[94] It followed on from a earlier attempt to attack Manila, which had been organized in the immediate aftermath of the incident but had failed when Matsukura Shigemasa, the daimyo placed in charge of scouting out the city's defenses, died leaving no obvious replacement.[95] In 1637, however, the plan was resurrected by officials in Nagasaki who saw an opportunity to curry favor with their superiors in Edo by presenting a low-cost way to take revenge on the Spanish through the pairing of Japanese military might with Dutch maritime technology. It was rendered still more attractive by its promise to permanently shut down the missionary pipeline from Manila, which had become an increasing source of concern for Tokugawa officials.

In September 1637 the two Nagasaki governors (*bugyō*), Baba Saburōzaemon Toshishige (in office 1636–52) and Sakakibara Hida-no-kami Motonao (in office 1634–38) learned from some captured Dominican friars that the colonial government in Manila was planning to send a steady flow of missionaries into Japan.[96] They responded to the threat by maneuvering to pull the Dutch into a proposed campaign against Manila. On 30 October the bugyō made their opening gambit when they asked the opperhoofd why the Dutch allowed "Manila to remain unmolested." If the city was attacked and destroyed, it would, they explained, greatly please the shogun.[97] The implication was clear: as faithful servants of the regime, the Dutch should anticipate the shogun's wishes and volunteer their services for a campaign against his enemies. While the company was, of course, at war with the Spanish, the governors' plan carried with it huge risks. Since its establishment in 1571, Manila had become one of the best-defended European enclaves in Asia, fortified with thick walls mounted with heavy cannon and manned by a large garrison.[98] A failed offensive could devastate the company's fleet, causing large numbers of casualties and permanently disrupting its trading activities. Keenly aware of these perils, the opperhoofd resisted the bugyō's suggestions by explaining that the Dutch were more merchants than soldiers and lacked the resources necessary to mount such a campaign.

The next day the lobbying campaign was renewed by a subordinate official, the Nagasaki magistrate (*daikan*), who explained that he had prepared a petition for the Dutch to sign and submit in their name to Edo. Framed in the language of the loyal vassal eager to serve his master, the document volunteered the company's ships, men, and ordinance for the campaign in unambiguous terms:

Recently, we [the Dutch] have understood that the people of Manila are breaking the emperor's [shogun's] prohibitions and are sending priests, who are forbidden in Japan. As a result, they are viewed as criminals (*misdadigen*) by Your Honors. If the high Authorities decide to destroy this place, the Hollanders, who bring a good number of ships to Japan every year, are always ready, in time or opportunity, to present our ships and cannon for your service. We ask that Your Honors trust and believe that we are, in all matters without exception, ready to serve Japan. For this reason, we are presenting this to Your Honors.[99]

The document was rife with potential dangers. Once put into writing and dispatched to Edo, the promise to provide military support could not be retracted, with the result that the petition amounted to a contract pledging Batavia's men and ships if the regime decided to revive the planned attack against Manila.

Unwilling to make such an open-ended commitment, the factory's representative demurred by explaining that such an important matter had to go up the chain of command to the governor-general before it could be approved. Clearly expecting such an answer, the magistrate demanded that the company make good on its promises: "How cowardly. What are you saying? I do not wish [to know] of your ways and surely you do not wish that the regents [bugyō] hear this answer. You should rightly say 'O happy time that we have wished for so long. Now we can show his majesty [the shogun] that we are ready to serve Japan.' I want to tell you the results of what will happen if you refuse. First, you will be thought of as unwilling liars as you always say that you are ready to serve Japan with all your might."[100] Going on, he explained that he had always told his superiors that the Dutch were trustworthy and stood ready to serve the shogun with their "strength, ships and ordinance, indeed so faithfully and furiously as one of the lords of his Majesty's own land." If, having already promised so much, they were now to refuse service, their claims would "be known to be a lie"[101]

Although they came from the mouth of a Japanese official, the remarks almost perfectly parroted the sentiments voiced by VOC representatives, and they provide some sense of how widely the idea of the Dutch as vassals had spread. But, while repetition reinforced the company's own presentation in useful ways, it also indicated how little control the Dutch in Japan retained over its central logic. By 1637, as the *daikan*'s comments make clear, the ideas first introduced by VOC agents could no longer be restrained and the company's rhetoric had become accessible to a range of groups with their own interests. By simply recit- ing VOC declarations of loyalty, the magistrate offered a script for the Dutch to follow, demanding, as was the case in the hofreis, that they act out the role they had claimed for themselves.

In the factory the governing council convened to discuss the petition. Its members quickly recognized the precariousness of their situation, caught between the risks of having their claims exposed and the danger of military participation. The petition could not simply be dismissed, for doing so would amount to an admission that past protestations about their willingness to serve had been a sham. This would cause, the members of the council lamented, the Dutch to be regarded as "liars and unwilling people" because they had offered "our assistance and service to Japan many times before this."[102] On the other hand, the council was understandably reluctant to make an open-ended pledge to commit the company's "naval might of ships and weapons to the service of Japan." With neither prospect particularly appealing, the final decision was in favor of giving in. Concluding that it was more dangerous to contradict promises already made than to offer support, the council resolved to volunteer six vessels, four ships, and two yachts for the attack.[103]

Before any steps could be taken to realize the Manila plan, events in Shimabara intervened to turn the Bakufu's attention to domestic issues. On 17 December, word reached Hirado "that the residents or the peasants of the territory of Arima have rebelled and are fighting against their lord."[104] The revolt had been prompted by rising discontent with the high taxes ordered by the local daimyo, but the wider area was a tinderbox ready to spark into flames, and the uprising quickly spread to Amakusa Island where hundreds of villagers took up arms. As it grew, the rebellion began to draw on support from hidden Christians eager to escape Tokugawa persecution. In Hirado the Dutch received word that villagers were burning shrines and temples, erecting in their place churches adorned with images of Jesus and Mary.[105] Poorly armed and badly supplied, the rebels quickly ran into resistance and, after suffering a series of setbacks, elected to make their stand in Hara Castle, an aban- doned fortress in Shimabara domain. Surrounded on three sides by the sea and guarded by thick walls, the fortress was, even in its crumbling state, a formidable stronghold, and there thirty thousand men, women, and children gathered to await the inevitable response from Edo.

The rebellion shocked the Tokugawa regime, which found itself faced by a challenge to its authority from an unexpected quarter. It responded by dispatching Itakura Shigemasa at the head of a large force to crush the uprising and restore order. Moving as fast as it could, the army reached Kyushu around the middle of January 1638.[106] Given the recent discussion over the Manila campaign and the immediacy of the threat to Tokugawa authority, the opperhoofd, Nicolaes Couckebacker, was left with little choice but to immediately offer his support. In a letter dated 17 January he did so in unequivocal terms. Adopting the by now well-worn language of the faithful vassal, he assured Itakura that "if you need anything, that is within our capabilities, please command as we are always ready to serve faithfully."[107] The result was to volunteer the company for service in the campaign while making it clear (without any prompting from Tokugawa officials) that the Dutch were prepared to play their designated role as loyal subordinates.

It did not take long for the first request to arrive. On 27 January, the Nagasaki magistrate wrote to Couckebacker asking him to send a large quantity of gunpowder to supply the Bakufu forces gathering near Hara Castle.[108] Having dispatched six barrels of gunpowder, Couckebacker decided on 5 February to make another offer of service, this time to the Nagasaki bugyō, who was stationed with the main force of Bakufu troops: "With respect, we send Your Honors this letter. . . . We have prepared a supply of cannon and shot in case your Honors deem it necessary. We shall supply it whenever Your Honors order. . . . If there is anything without exception that the Hollanders are capable of serving Your Honors in, please command us."[109] The offer prompted another request with Couckebacker receiving instructions on 10 February to send additional gunpowder as well as five large cannon to Shimabara. Writing back to the Nagasaki magistrate, he boasted that he had dispatched the most powerful guns at his disposal for service in the shogun's campaign.[110]

While this exchange was going on, Itakura's campaign stumbled from one setback to another. Two assaults succeeded only in producing large numbers of casualties without making any inroads into the rebel fortification. Unhappy with the progress of the campaign, Edo decided to replace Itakura with two new generals, Matsudaira Nobutsuna and Toda Ujikane. By the time they arrived, Itakura was dead, killed in a third—and equally fruitless—assault launched on 14 February. Recognizing that a frontal attack was unlikely to succeed, Matsudaira and Toda opted instead for a prolonged siege. It was at this point that the Dutch were called upon to redeem their promises, and on 19 February the opperhoofd was instructed to send all available "ships and cannon" for service in the siege.[111] The order pulled the company from the margins, where it had been content to provide material support, and required it to participate directly in the campaign. Although the opperhoofd had no desire to disrupt the factory's trading plans by sending off his few available vessels for an unspecified period of service, demands couched in the language of loyal service could not be easily refused. But if this was the case, the potential damage could at least be reduced, and, acting quickly, Couckebacker instructed one of the pair of VOC ships anchored in Japanese harbors to sail out of sight of land. With that done, he departed for Hara Castle aboard the second vessel, the *Rijp*, on 21 February to take personal charge of the expedition.

Four days later the opperhoofd held his first meeting with Matsudaira, Toda, and the two Nagasaki bugyō. Contrary to what we might expect, there was no sign in these discussions of any sense that the arrival of a VOC vessel for service in a Bakufu operation was at all strange. Instead, mirroring the company's own rhetoric, these officials described the *Rijp*'s arrival as the natural extension of past promises, explaining that the Dutch "have been saying for more than three years that they wish to serve His Majesty and the land of Japan with their ships, cannon and men. They have repeatedly wished for this opportunity and now they have shown [their service]."[112] The result was to naturalize the appearance of the *Rijp* and to render the Dutch just another contingent of vassals arriving to discharge their stated responsibilities to their distant master. Indeed, the connection was made explicit by Bakufu commanders, who noted that the Dutch had "presented their service as was done by the other lords."[113] There was, in other words, nothing exceptional about the company's involvement in a domestic campaign; it was simply the logical outcome of the regime's wider muster of its vassals.

The *Rijp* and its crew were put quickly to work. Over the next two weeks, Dutch gunners fired over four hundred shots into Hara Castle from ship-mounted guns, and a battery assembled on shore.[114] Although it is difficult to assess the precise impact of the company's contribution, Bakufu officials were insistent that they were satisfied with the scale of the damage, and a defector from Hara Castle reported that there were

"5, 10 or 15 casualties, either dead or injured" in the encampment every day.[115] Despite the fact that the rebels had no means of returning fire, there were still casualties on the VOC side. On 11 March an exploding cannon killed a mason called Gillis, who had been servicing one of the *Rijp*'s guns. When they learned of his death, Bakufu commanders promised Couckebacker that the shogun would be informed of the sacrifice, and the company was later presented with a small sum in recompense for the loss.[116] The next day the steady routine of bombardment was halted when Couckebacker received permission for the *Rijp* to depart. Still playing the part of the dutiful vassal, he offered to remain at his post until the conflict was brought to a final end, but was assured that the company's services were no longer required as the siege works had moved so close to the fortress that it was no longer safe to continue the bombardment. As he made preparations to leave, Couckebacker was told that the Dutch had performed a valuable service and that their involvement had been reported to the shogun "daily in the coming and going post."[117] Exactly a month later, Bakufu forces finally broke into the castle, massacring the surviving rebels and ending the revolt.

Although they had very different outcomes, the same thread ran through the planned campaign against Manila and the company's participation in Shimabara. In both cases VOC agents found themselves penned in by past rhetoric and forced to play a role as dutiful subordinates eager to serve. Given the fact that less than a decade had elapsed since Specx's 1630 letter, which first articulated the notion of the Dutch as vassals, and the company's involvement in military operations against the shogun's foes, it is striking how quickly this idea had evolved. By the time the *Rijp* appeared off Hara Castle, the notion of the Dutch as vassals had become unexpectedly concrete, requiring action to be matched with words and leaving the opperhoofd with little capacity to resist. After Shimabara, Bakufu officials gradually lost interest in grand plans for expeditions against Manila or other foreign targets, but the assumption that the Dutch would continue to offer military service alongside the shogun's other vassals remained in place.[118] Given that there were no further wars or other conflicts to which VOC ships or sailors could be lent, this took the form, as previously indicated, of the *Oranda fūsetsugaki*, the yearly intelligence reports that became the company's most important military service across the long duration of the Tokugawa period.

"FLOWER OF THE EMPIRE, DEFENDER OF THE COUNTRY"

That these ideas of loyal service gathered weight over time, steadily becoming stronger and stronger, sets the company's experience in Japan apart from that of other European overseas enterprises in Asia. It was not uncommon for European representatives to drape themselves beneath a cloak of indigenous sovereignty by claiming to be vassals of powerful Asian rulers, but the rhetoric was essentially temporary, lasting just long enough to provide a space for the realignment of relations. This was the case in the company's interaction with Mataram, a powerful kingdom on Java, where such language was also used.[119] The VOC sparred perennially with Mataram until 1646 when it concluded a settlement that deliberately positioned the Dutch as vassals. In the final document, the governor-general promised to send tribute in the form of rare gifts to Mataram and to aid its ruler if he "comes into war with any of his enemies."[120] But while the framework held for a number of years, it was always more about providing breathing room than requiring an ongoing commitment, and over time Batavia was able to use its support for rival claimants to the throne to transform itself from a vassal into the dominant political force within the kingdom.[121] By the end of the process the former subordinate had assumed political power while the putative overlord was forced into a new role as the company's client state.

A more famous example comes from India where the English East India Company initially pledged allegiance to the Mughal emperor. In the early part of the eighteenth century, English agents dispatched petitions to the court phrased in the distinctive language of the loyal servant. One 1712 letter from the chief administrator in Bengal, John Russell, provides a flavor of this correspondence: "The Supplication of John Russell, who is as the Minutest Grain of Sand, and whose forehead is the tip of his footstool, who is Absolute Monarch and Prop of the Universe. . . . We Englishmen having Traded hitherto in Bengall, Orixa and Beharr Custome free (Except in Suratt), are Your Majesties most Obedient Slaves, always intent upon your commands."[122] But as Mughal power diminished and English influence grew, any notion of Indian sovereignty became little more than a convenient fiction that could be manipulated at will to advance English interests. It was against this backdrop that the famous campaigns of the 1750s and 1760s, which led ultimately to the creation of the British Raj, were waged. Rather than acting for their own profit, English agents declared that they were fighting to uphold the authority of their distant lord, thereby reconfiguring expansionist campaigns as defensive actions designed to preserve the overarching framework of Mughal sovereignty.

Such claims allowed Robert Clive, the great protagonist of English empire in Asia, to argue, at least initially, that he had acted simply to preserve "the power of the Great Mogul."[123] In the capital a largely powerless emperor was forced to adopt the same language, framing the grant of revenue rights to three provinces, Bengal, Bihar, and Orissa, after the Battle of Buxar in 1765, as a reward for loyal service. Thus the company was praised as "the high and mighty, the noblest of exalted nobles, the chief of illustrious warriors, our faithful servants and sincere well-wishers, worthy of our royal favours," while Clive received the title "Flower of the empire; defender of the country; the brave; firm in war."[124] In this case exaggerated rhetoric about submission and service concealed a dynamic in which the primary benefits, either political legitimacy or economic concessions, flowed back to the European partner. When such fictions no longer suited their purposes, the curtain was drawn back and the reality of relations exposed.[125]

In Japan such claims functioned quite differently. There the rhetoric of subordination did not conceal a gradual expansion of European power or any tilting of the relationship in favor of the supposed vassal. Equally important, instead of dissipating once it had outlived its value to the company, the idea of the Dutch as vassals in fact gained weight. As the Tokugawa period wore on and hofreis followed hofreis, it became increasingly difficult to separate out performance from reality and to determine whether the Dutch were simply playing a role or if they had indeed become loyal servants of the Tokugawa state. Official compilations from the Tokugawa period give little sense of ambiguity in this regard, revealing the Dutch as dutiful vassals, loyally discharging—with only the rarest of exceptions—their allocated responsibilities within the parameters of the Tokugawa order.

Perhaps the most revealing source in this regard is *Tsūkō ichiran*, a nineteenth-century documentary compendium of Bakufu foreign relations. The text of this sprawling account is divided into a series of chapters detailing Tokugawa relations with a range of foreign groups. These are further broken down into a number of categories—correspondence, visits to Japan, points of dispute, etc.—that are largely standard across the compilation. While the chapter devoted to the Dutch includes these conventional categories, it has one additional section that is not duplicated in any other part of the lengthy text. As such, it serves to set the Dutch apart from all other foreign groups with which the Bakufu maintained relations. Entitled simply *hōko,* or service, it describes the company's performance of its obligations year after year to successive shoguns.[126] The section takes in hundreds of years of loyal service, including the Shimabara uprising and dozens of intelligence reports, the *Oranda fūsetsugaki,* that are included as concrete proof of Dutch devotion. The overall effect is to blur any line between performance and reality. If the Dutch had started off by simply pretending to be loyal vassals eager to dupe a Japanese audience for their own benefit, they had come to play the role so well and for so long that they had in effect surrendered any alternate identity in Japan. From the Bakufu's perspective, they had indeed become dutiful subordinates, loyal vassals that could be relied upon to provide service alongside their domestic counterparts. Thus a disguise, thrown on hastily in the 1630s, had become permanent, clinging tighter and tighter until it could no longer be removed.

In this way the conflict over diplomacy gave rise to a new framework for interaction as the Dutch transformed themselves in order to claim a secure place in the Tokugawa order. However one looks at it, the scale of the VOC's diplomatic adaptation was significant. Within the space of a few decades, the company's representatives in Japan had switched from a role as agents of a Dutch king to ambassadors of an imperious governor-general in Batavia before finally settling into one as loyal vassals of the shogun. In that process the organization retreated from its own claims, most notably as they related to the governor-general's status, but also from the sovereign powers laid out in article 35 of its charter. A similar process took place on the seas around Japan, where VOC captains discovered that their rights to wage war were also subject to Tokugawa restrictions.

2
Violence

CHAPTER FOUR

THE VIOLENT SEA

The Christians [are] Lions of the Sea . . . [and] God has allotted
that Unstable Element for their Rule.

—Emperor Aurangzeb, as reported by John Fryer, 1698

To show our teeth or to use violence [in Japan] is completely
impossible, unless we want to leave this land and never come again.

— Consideration of the Present State of the Company's Trade in Japan, 1707

If diplomacy provided a difficult stage on which Europeans were compelled to engage with complex orders armed with inadequate tools, the ocean was surely the quintessential space for European dominance in the early modern world.[1] Unlike the labyrinthine capitals through which Nuyts and other ambassadors struggled to chart a course, the sea was reassuringly open and accessible to influence. It was also an arena over which Europeans held an unmistakable advantage. The overseas enterprises that began to push into Asian waters in the sixteenth and seventeenth centuries were maritime organizations specifically geared toward seaborne warfare, and they brought with them a formidable technological combination of heavy guns and robust ship design. It is not surprising then that European overseas enterprises were, from the beginning, heavily dependent on the use of maritime force to establish a presence in Asia.[2] This was the case with the Portuguese, who pioneered such tactics by relying on superior naval power to seize control of cities and trade routes, but also with later competitors like the Dutch East India Company, which similarly embraced the ship's cannon as a vital policy instrument.

There can be no doubting the potency of European maritime technology. Indeed, the history of the push into Asian waters is punctuated with accounts of engagements in which ships from Europe were able to inflict overwhelming defeats on much larger fleets assembled to oppose them.[3] Such encounters have prompted historians like Carlo Cipolla and Geoffrey Parker to place maritime technology at the center of a wider story about the "rise of Europe." For Parker, the gunned vessel, the product of a unique military revolution not matched elsewhere in the world, permitted Europeans to sweep aside possible rivals and achieve mastery over Asian waters in the early modern period.[4] There was, he argues, "a revolution in naval warfare . . . in early modern Europe, which was no less important than that by land, for it opened the way to the exercise of European hegemony over most of the world's oceans for much of the early modern period."[5] In this view, 1500 represents a moment when control over the oceans flipped to Europeans even as they struggled to establish a presence on land.

Such assertions have prompted a group of revisionist historians to look again at the traditional story of European maritime technology by examining how a select group of Asian states or organizations were able to mount a successful challenge to European dominance on the ocean. One of the most interesting recent studies in this vein is by Giancarlo Casale who argues for the existence of an Ottoman Age of Exploration that parallels European developments.[6] Other historians like Sanjay Subrahmanyam or Tonio Andrade have pointed to the Ya'rubi Dynasty of Oman or the Zheng maritime network, which will be discussed in the next chapter, as formidable competitors able to field powerful maritime forces more than capable of holding their own against European fleets.[7]

A second approach to the question of European advantage seeks to shift the debate away from technology and its focus on the specifics of ship design or the efficiency of cannon fire to consider the political and legal contexts in which these operated. As such, it calls into question the assumption that European maritime firepower was a constant that could be readily deployed whenever needed. As recent conflicts in Iraq or Afghanistan tells us, even the most potent technological advantage requires the presence of specific conditions in order to be used effectively. In early modern Asia these prerequisites were only rarely met and there was a significant gap between potential and actual application. For every instance of a successful campaign, there are numerous other examples in which the capacity to make effective use of superior technology was partially curtailed, largely contained or entirely suppressed.

One starting point to think through why this happened is with images of the sea. In thinking about the ocean in early modern Asia, we are accustomed to two kinds of representations. Seventeenth-century maps produced in Europe show the sea as a largely empty space cut only by identical grids and unmarked by distinctive features.[8] While they offer a better sense of maritime activity, modern maps showing the European presence in Asia can also be misleading, featuring bold arrows confidently sweeping across empty waters marking trade routes and the flow of commodities. Noticeably absent from either of these representations is any sign of political or legal influence exerted over the ocean by the Asian states that cluster on the shoreline. This image ties in neatly with notions put forward by the famous seventeenth-century Dutch scholar Hugo Grotius of the maritime world as a uniquely open space free to all mariners and governed by the principles of natural law rather than by the regulations of any one state.[9] One revealing 1633 cover piece of his celebrated work on the free seas shows a European vessel traversing the ocean under the banner of natural law unimpeded by the pronouncements of any territorial ruler.[10]

In fact, the seas were far more complex than any of these images suggest. In her groundbreaking study of sovereignty in the early modern world, Lauren Benton argues that even "as freedom of the seas developed as a legal doctrine, Europeans recognized that ocean space was crisscrossed by corridors of imperial control."[11] In her view, the oceans were marked by shifting zones of law and jurisdiction, which turned them into a judicial patchwork filled with "jurisdictional tangles" that required decoding.[12] Although Benton's focus is primarily on European law, some of these tangles can be traced back to Asian rulers, officials and administrators, whose influence contributed to turning the early modern ocean into "variegated spaces transected by law."[13]

If this assertion seems less than self-evident, it is in part because the famously dismissive remarks made by one Indian ruler, who commented that "wars by sea are merchants affair and of no concern to the prestige of kings," are sometimes taken as reflective of a more general view held by Asian elites toward the ocean.[14] If one accepts this as a representative outlook, it follows that the rulers of powerful territorial states like Mughal India largely ignored maritime developments, essentially ceding control to Europeans over an arena in which they had little interest. These comments do not, however, tell the whole story, and even the most land-centric of regimes could, if sufficiently pushed, intervene in that "Unstable Element," the maritime realm.[15] In most cases they did so not in the most visible way by assembling fleets of their own but rather by the selective use of legal markers, which, when combined with a willingness to punish violations by exacting retribution on European assets or personnel on land, served to limit the use of maritime force.

In a perceptive analysis, Ashin das Gupta has called this dynamic, in which the ability of European fleets to seize ships belonging to or at least claiming ties with Asian states was constrained by a fear of reprisals on the ground, the "balance of blackmail . . . between land and sea."[16] The result was a finely tuned, constantly shifting equilibrium between the power of European ships and the constraining influence of land-based legal structures that offered, in many cases, a far surer and more economical way for Asian states to exert influence over the ocean without the vast expenditure and technological challenges involved in maintaining a fleet. Although it was often done in a jerky, inconsistent, or essentially improvised manner, this drawing of jurisdictional lines limited, arguably more than any other factor, the power of the gunned vessel on Asian seas. To understand the world in which European overseas enterprises operated, we need to overlay a second chart marking the legal patchwork described by Benton over maps showing the ocean as an empty space. Only when this is done can we obtain a sense of the limited spaces in which technological advantage could be deployed and thereby erase any notion of unchallenged European maritime hegemony.

The tension between European technology and Asian law sits at the heart of these two chapters, which examine the intersection between the Dutch East India Company, maritime violence, and the Tokugawa Bakufu. When it was chartered in 1602, the VOC was given the right to recruit military forces, and by the time it arrived in Japan seven years later it possessed arguably the best ships and certainly the largest concentration of maritime firepower in East Asian waters. The power of the company's fleets was augmented by an elastic legal framework that could be wrapped around even the most aggressive and hastily improvised campaign. To justify their use of force, VOC administrators reached into a well-equipped legal toolbox stocked by writers like Grotius himself, who rose to prominence as a defender of Dutch activities in Asia. In this way the company's operations were invariably represented—and understood within the organization—as legal privateering and never as illicit piracy, as justified force and never as unnecessary violence, as legitimate action in pursuit of higher goals and never simply as a base scrabbling for plunder.[17] The combination of these factors meant that the VOC made frequent use of violence, particularly during its first decades in Asia.[18] Indeed, to the description of the company as the "largest, best-capitalized privateering enterprise in the world" can be added the fact that it was also, as clearly demonstrated by Peter Borschberg's recent work, the most active, launching repeated campaigns against European rivals and local competitors.[19] This has led a range of scholars to argue that the use of force was, from the beginning, "a necessary and integrated part of the market strategy of the VOC."[20]

In the Tokugawa Bakufu the company encountered a state with very limited maritime resources, one that seemed at times, particularly after the promulgation of the famous "closed country" edicts of the 1630s, to possess an actively hostile attitude to the ocean. Indeed W. J. Boot is not wrong when he suggests that the Bakufu, despite the fact that it ruled over a chain of islands, defined itself in some ways "as a landlocked, agrarian empire."[21] And yet, for all these facts, it was the company that found itself strikingly powerless on the seas around Japan. The explanation for this surprising development lies not in the existence of a Bakufu navy—for there was during most of the period under discussion no force worthy of such a name—but in the nature of the regime's legal markers.[22] Once in Japan, the VOC became entangled within a Tokugawa legal order in which its freedom to act against its three primary competitors—Japan-based merchants, the Portuguese, and Chinese traders—was significantly constrained. The result was first to limit and then to almost completely suppress the company's use of what was always the sharpest weapon in its arsenal and to frustrate an organization that had once seemed set to dominate the seas around Japan.

For all its success, the Bakufu never set out to contain maritime violence and possessed no blueprint to do so. Its most effective tool was a system of maritime passes known as shuinjō, but this was created for a different set of reasons that had nothing to do with European maritime predation. In the case of Portuguese and Chinese shipping, which Tokugawa policies gradually pushed beyond the company's reach, the Bakufu's response was improvised, spasmodic, and always reactive. It was driven not by the center but by individual protests filed by aggrieved merchants either at the shogun's court in Edo or, in later periods, the governor's office in Nagasaki. As complaints flowed into these two cities, they were transformed into spaces for international arbitration as Bakufu officials convened improvised courts of maritime adjudication to consider disputes that had taken place hundreds or sometimes even thousands of miles away. The eventual result of these cases was the expansion of Bakufu legal markers, which, spread over a period of several decades, pushed out from the decks of individual ships to a band around the archipelago before finally encompassing corridors stretching deep into the ocean. Each stage of this process signaled the further limitation of the company's ability to act, more than once spiking its guns at those moments when it was most determined to use force. Because of this, an examination of the Bakufu's response to VOC privateering in Japan provides some of the best evidence of how legal webs could ensnare even the most formidable of European overseas enterprises.

MARITIME PASSES

While the European gunboat anchored off a foreign port and prepared to attack local shipping until it had secured a shift in government policy is traditionally associated with the nineteenth century, it made a regular appearance in early modern Asia.[23] For the Dutch, gunboat diplomacy was a familiar policy instrument, and the earliest expeditions to Asia made repeated use of force in order to pressure local political elites into action. Indeed, the first encounter between a *voorcompagnieën* expedition and an Asian ruler, the sultan of Banten, ended in a spasm of violence, with Dutch ships "blockading the harbor and firing our ordinance, defying the town with as much spitefulness and rude behavior as we could muster."[24] Similar tactics were used by VOC captains after the formation of the organization in 1602. In general, the application of violence served one of two purposes, to gain access to domestic markets by prying open port cities or as a powerful bargaining chip to improve trading conditions once relations had been opened, but there are plenty of instances in which its precise logic was more difficult to determine.[25]

The targets for such tactics ranged from tiny port polities to massive empires. In 1622, for example, the company famously declared war on

China. Frustrated by a series of failed attempts to gain access to the Chinese market, VOC administrators decided that a swift campaign offered the best chance of bringing Ming officials to the negotiating table. As a mark of how easily justification could be found for violent action, they argued that Chinese recalcitrance and the general unwillingness of Ming officials to open their ports to foreign commerce represented a clear violation of the natural law of free trade. The admiral of the VOC fleet was directed "to declare open war on the Chinese, and to do all possible damage to them, without sparing junks, place or people."[26] The muted tone of the orders, phrased in the calm, almost technical language preferred by Batavia, disguised what was in fact an ambitious assault on the most formidable state in the region. The result was an extended campaign that targeted vulnerable Chinese shipping and coastal communities but failed to secure the company's desired goal.

In those parts of Asia where trade had successfully been opened, the company continued to rely on the use of force to cut through difficult problems and enhance its commercial prospects. In 1648, for example, the VOC launched an aggressive campaign against Indian shipping attached to the Mughal port of Surat.[27] The operation was the result of a complex backstory that commenced in 1641 after the VOC captured the key Portuguese port of Melaka. As part of its campaign to direct shipping through its new possession, which sat astride key sea routes, the VOC ordered merchants coming from Surat to sail directly to Melaka without calling at ports on the Malay Peninsula and in northern Sumatra where they were able to acquire goods without paying tolls. Since the policy threatened to damage trade in Surat, it was vigorously resisted by local merchants and officials. At first both sides attempted to pressure each other into backing down, but the dispute soon turned violent when a group of assailants attacked the VOC factory in Surat, injuring a number of employees and seizing a large quantity of goods.[28] Although it was not clear who had ordered the attack, the governor-general in Batavia decided, with some justification, that Mughal officials must have at least condoned it and determined that the organization should seek "redress with weapons."[29] A privateering campaign promised to kill two birds with one stone, gaining compensation for the attack on the factory while forcing Mughal authorities to ensure that shipping from Surat complied with the company's new policies.

In July 1648, a fleet under the command of Arent Barentszoon was dispatched to the Indian coast with instructions to capture any vessels coming to Surat from the Red Sea and to hold them until local authorities gave in to VOC demands. If these concessions were not forthcoming, Barentszoon was instructed to "tell the governor that that we will attack all the Moorish ships; that we will prevent all trade to Mocha, Persia, Bassora Aden and other districts; and that we will not desist until we receive 400,000 rupees as security."[30] The campaign started badly, but in September of the next year the Dutch fleet was able to seize two rich prizes owned by Gujarati merchants with close ties to the Mughal regime. These provided the company with a strong bargaining position, and after a short negotiation the local governor acceded to most of Batavia's demands, including compensation for plundered goods, permission to construct a warehouse, and a promise to halt ships from Surat from trading freely with ports in Southeast Asia.[31] In response, the governor-general jubilantly informed his superiors that the company's position was much improved by the use of force, as the "Moors now see and have experienced . . . that we can obstruct their entire sea trade."[32]

In this way, when confronted by the Gordian knot of difficult conditions, overly effective competitors, and recalcitrant officials, Batavia readily unsheathed its sword. Indeed, so frequently was violence employed that the Heeren 17 felt compelled to intervene, instructing their subordinates to "bring some moderation into the policy of maintaining trade everywhere with power and armed force."[33] After one particularly aggressive attack on Persian shipping, they complained that the governor-general resorted too readily to such tactics: "Too promptly one argues: we can not accept such conditions, ergo one may attack somebody without looking for any reason or justification. This is a stance we cannot vindicate to ourselves or to the world."[34]

While they displayed a ready willingness to use privateering as a weapon in other parts of Asia, the Dutch never turned their guns against Japan-based shipping to force Tokugawa officials to change policies or alter trading conditions. Indeed, the Tokugawa/VOC relationship was marked by a striking lack of violence and the absence of the kind of tactics conventionally employed by the company in dealing with Asian states. This stemmed not from an absence of points of conflict—for there were numerous instances in which the company felt unfairly treated by the Bakufu—but from the enduring power of a single document, the shuinjō.

Probably originating in the 1590s, the maritime pass or shuinjō system came to full development in the first decade of the seventeenth century under Tokugawa Ieyasu.[35] It required all outgoing merchant vessels known as *shuinsen* to obtain special trading passes authorizing the holder to undertake a single voyage from Japan to a stated destination.[36] While successful applications required the support of a high-ranking Bakufu official, any Japan-based merchant could receive a pass as long as they possessed the right contacts.[37] After 1604, the first year for which records exist, a total of 356 licenses were issued to a range of recipients, including daimyo, Japanese merchants, and foreign traders, permitting them to sail to ports across East and Southeast Asia. The system remained in place for almost three decades, until it was shut down in 1635 as the Bakufu moved to restrict the flow of maritime traffic out of the country.

The pass system was created for two reasons, neither of which had anything to do with European overseas enterprises like the VOC. The first related to Japan's troubled history as an international pirate hub. In the sixteenth century the archipelago had played host to thousands of maritime marauders who launched devastating raids, primarily against the Chinese coast but extending as far as the busy shipping lanes of Southeast Asia. When Tokugawa Ieyasu came to power in 1600, he was determined to boost long-distance trade, but in order to do so required a mechanism for port authorities to distinguish between Japanese pirates and legitimate merchants. The result was the shuinjō, which offered a concrete marker that could be readily displayed when ships from Japan dropped anchor in a foreign port. To publicize the new arrangements, the shogun wrote to his counterparts across Southeast Asia informing them that all Japanese traders were now expected to possess one of these documents. If a junk arrived from Japan without a Bakufu pass, it should, Ieyasu explained, be barred from the port and refused trade.[38] Requiring Japan-based merchants to obtain passes that were issued by the central government also served an important domestic purpose. By providing a framework to conduct long-distance trade, the Bakufu was able to regulate daimyo access to the most lucrative sea routes. Indeed, the shuinjō system can be seen as one part of much broader program of daimyo control that included the sankin kōtai arrangements described in the previous chapter. It allowed the regime to first strip away the profits from maritime trade, which had previously boosted the coffers of some of the most powerful western domains and then to suppress this revenue stream altogether.[39]

If these passes served a clear purpose, they also represented a risk to the Bakufu. Despite its vast armies, the Tokugawa family ruled Japan through a combination of prestige, reputation, and, only in the last resort, actual coercion.[40] It was an arrangement that enabled the Tokugawa to maintain control over a precarious coalition of more than two hundred daimyo without prolonged recourse to force. As part of its strategy of control, the Bakufu propagated the fiction that the shogun's superior military might (*bui*) compelled respect or, more properly, subdued obedience, both inside Japan's borders but also, equally important, beyond in the realm of international politics.[41] The idea proved comparatively easy to maintain as, unlike Hideyoshi, who had launched an invasion of Korea in 1592, the Tokugawa Bakufu largely contented itself with exerting power over Japan and made little effort to show the flag outside the archipelago. Since the regime did not send its own troops or even official embassies beyond Japan, there was little occasion for the potential disruption of these military myths.

The one consistent exception to this policy was the shuinjō. Ships carrying these documents were specially authorized by the shogun's administration, and they functioned as rare outposts of Tokugawa authority in seas and ports far distant from Japan. Because the state's prestige was directly invested in such vessels, any attack on a shuinsen, regardless of where it occurred, was treated "as a direct challenge to its authority."[42] Such cases were rare—only three of the more than three hundred shuinjō were infringed upon in some way—but in each instance the regime opted for a disproportionate response.[43] The result was to inscribe these vessels with an indelible mark of Tokugawa legal authority and to convince all parties that substantial punishment would swiftly follow any violation, even if the actual incident occurred in distant seas hundreds of miles away from Japan.

The Dutch witnessed this firsthand in 1610, just months after the establishment of the Japan factory, when the Bakufu enforced a stiff penalty on the Portuguese for a perceived infraction that had taken place years earlier in Macao. In 1608 a shuinsen belonging to Arima Haranobu, a prominent lord in Kyushu, had arrived in that city on its way back to Japan from a successful voyage to Cambodia. When the Japanese crew became involved in a violent riot, Portuguese authorities responded by executing at least one of the offenders. After Tokugawa officials learned of this incident—almost certainly via a doctored version of events that emphasized Portuguese culpability—they determined to take action for what was seen as an infringement of Arima's trading license. Their chance came when the Macao carrack, the great trading vessel upon which Portuguese commerce in East Asia depended, arrived in Nagasaki. In early 1610, after the Portuguese failed to hand over the ship's captain, Japanese troops attacked and destroyed this vessel.[44] When the news of the incident reached the Japan factory, the newly installed opperhoofd wrote to his superiors that the ship's "very costly cargo [was] burnt and sunk by the efforts of the Japanese, who by the Emperor's [shogun's] order tried to seize the ship by force." Clearly stunned at the scale of the loss, he estimated that the total cargo "was valued at 8 million ducats, being the richest that has ever been in Japan till now."[45] Even more shockingly, this vast sum lay at the bottom of Nagasaki harbor because of a relatively minor episode that would have been routine in many ports of the time.

The "destruction of the costly carrack," to quote one VOC writer, had an enduring influence on Dutch thinking about what they could and, more importantly, could not do in Japan.[46] The incident and the lessons that should be learned from it became a frequent theme in documents sent from Hirado to Batavia.[47] The Bakufu's willingness to retaliate in a manner completely disproportionate to the actual offense persuaded VOC officials that they should not, under any circumstances, authorize an attack on a vessel carrying a Tokugawa trading pass. In practice, and because it was often difficult to tell whether an individual ship possessed a shuinjō, particularly when viewed from a distance across a windswept sea, this meant that all vessels identified as Japanese were exempt from attack. A typical instruction issued to VOC commanders stated that if they encountered "any Japan jouncks upon the coast of Manilla or elcewhere, you shall not endamage them butt let them pass & repass, franck & free, where they please."[48] In this way Dutch ships were ordered to show all possible friendship to Japanese mariners regardless of where they might find them.

So fearsome were the potential consequences if a shuinjō was violated that the policy was extended even to those Japanese vessels that had transgressed VOC blockades. In 1618, for example, a Dutch fleet allowed one such ship to pass through its lines and enter Manila Bay carrying supplies. According to a gleeful Spanish account: "Early in November, when the enemy was in the mouth of the bay, a Japanese ship came here. When it reached Ilocos, a port of the island of Manila, it learned that the enemy was in the passage through which it must go to reach this city. But as it carried a *chapa*, or license, from the Japanese emperor it feared nothing. For the Hollanders respect the emperor's license in so far as it concerns them, and they give free passage in every part of these seas to all Japanese ships bearing it."[49] So concerned were the Dutch with not violating the shogun's passes that they were prepared to pay out for any incidents involved Japanese merchants, even if there was only a remote possibility that the vessel in question had carried one of these documents.[50]

Beyond this immediate desire not to be seen impeding Japanese traffic, the company's concern about the shuinjō also shaped the way it responded to Bakufu policies more generally, and it turned a usually aggressive organization into a far more timorous creature. Whereas in other parts of Asia any restriction that had a negative impact on trade could supply a ready justification for maritime violence, things looked very different in Japan where the VOC accepted even the harshest regulations without recourse to force. When the second Tokugawa shogun decided to shut down the company's outposts in central Japan in 1616 and to confine its agents to just two ports, this restriction, while greatly limiting access to the Japanese market and erasing any hope of a quick profit, was accepted without violent protest.[51] Similarly, when trade was, from Batavia's perspective, unfairly suspended in 1628 and dozens of its employees thrown into prison in Japan, even the most aggressive of VOC administrators pulled back from the use of force.[52] Instead the company's strategy became, as succinctly expressed by one senior official, to "accommodate the Japanese and suffer everything so that we may freely reap the fruits of commerce."[53]

Although maritime violence was a potent and proven weapon in Asian waters, the company was never prepared to gamble with it in Japan. The shuinjō drew a bright line around Japanese ships that was never willingly crossed by VOC leadership during the three decades that the system operated. Viewed more broadly, the Bakufu's success in protecting Japan-based shipping created a system of passes and protection that effectively inverted what had happened in other parts of Asia. In the sixteenth century the Portuguese established a system of maritime control in the Indian Ocean based on the issuing of a pass called a *cartaz*. All merchants sailing through the region were compelled to obtain one of these documents and subsequently to visit a Portuguese-controlled settlement to pay customs duties there.[54] If they refused, their vessel was liable to be boarded and sunk if it encountered a Portuguese warship. This apparatus of license and toll, which was adopted by the Dutch in the seventeenth century, meant that the European pass became the most valuable document in the Indian Ocean. In maritime East Asia, by contrast, the Tokugawa-issued pass offered the most reliable protection for vulnerable shipping. The result was that such documents became especially coveted, even drawing interest from Spanish and Portuguese captains, who recognized their value in securing their own vessels from attack.[55] While VOC mariners found their hands tied by the shuinjō system, the constraining influence of Bakufu law was not confined to Japanese shipping. Instead, it extended to the company's European rivals, most notably the Portuguese, the attempted targets of an aggressive VOC privateering campaign in Japanese waters.

LAW AND VIOLENCE

Alongside the exotic commodities filling the holds of its ships, the Dutch brought with them to Asia a new kind of conflict in the form of global war that was fought simultaneously in multiple theaters across the world. While English adventurers like Francis Drake had intermittently attacked Spanish interests in the New World, the Dutch were the first to launch a systematic war that was waged without respite or concern for the geographical limits of the conflict. Although aggressive privateering campaigns quickly became a standard part of VOC operations, the first attempts by ships attached to the organization to target Portuguese vessels in Asia were highly controversial, generating a series of legal disputes that were played out in courts in the United Provinces. We know a great deal about these, in large part because they prompted some of Hugo Grotius's most famous publications, but fights over the legality of VOC actions were not restricted to the European continent.[56] Instead, Europe's first global war was fought out in a crowded Asian political and legal landscape populated by dozens of states, each of which responded in different ways to the incursion of a new, and often highly destructive, conflict into their waters and ports.[57]

When it was created in 1602, the VOC was intended, according to one prominent statesman who played midwife to the new organization, "to inflict damage on the Spaniards and the Portuguese."[58] But before the company could be turned into an instrument for carrying the war in Europe to Asia, a series of legal hurdles needed to be overcome. While all Dutch vessels that departed for Asia were authorized to defend themselves against Iberian attacks, there was no precedent for the offensive strategy envisaged by the VOC's creators and no certainty that it was lawful. The test case came in the form of a dispute over a Portuguese vessel, the *Santa Catarina*, that had been seized in 1603 by a Dutch fleet under the command of Jakob van Heemskerck. Captured in the straits of Singapore, the *Santa Catarina* was a prize of almost unbelievable value, carrying within its hold more than three million guilders of goods, but there were also serious questions about the legality of the action and whether van Heemskerck had any right to take the vessel.[59]

As the leader of a trading venture, van Heemskerck had clear authorization to defend his fleet against any party that attempted to hinder his expedition and to obtain appropriate redress for damages, but he was not legally entitled to launch an attack.[60] As a result, there was a general uncertainty as to whether his actions were justified, if he had overstepped the bounds of his authority, and what should happen to the prize.[61] The appearance of the *Santa Catarina* also prompted a debate over the legality of the offensive strategy more generally. Opponents charged that aggressive privateering was illegal, that even if not strictly outside the letter of the law it was immoral (bringing a permanent stain upon the country's reputation), and finally that such a strategy would result in long-term losses as resources better used elsewhere were misallocated.[62]

Although van Heemskerck had been dispatched by one of the precompanies, his defense was vigorously championed by the VOC, which had, after its creation in 1602, taken over the assets of these organizations. The company's representatives proceeded to exhibit "various acts, titles, attestations, and other documents" in support of their case and requested that the Admiralty Board "render a definitive verdict and impound carrack and cargo, declaring them good prize."[63] Their defense of Van Heemskerck's actions was helped by the fact that no Portuguese agents were actually present at the trial, enabling charges of Iberian perfidy to go unanswered. On 9 September 1604 the Amsterdam admiralty court determined that the "the aforesaid Admiral had a sufficient cause to capture the carrack, as belonging to the Portuguese and subjects of Philip III, enemies of these United Provinces and their Indies trade."[64]

Although the jumbled verdict, which pulled together disparate notions including natural law and the law of nations (*ius gentium*), lifted the stain of illegality from van Heemskerck's actions, it did little to codify the argument in favor of privateering.[65] That task fell to Hugo Grotius, a young Dutch jurist who emerged as one of the company's most important defenders. Grotius's great achievement was to untangle a complicated skein of arguments about privateering and to reformulate these coherently within an overarching legal framework.[66] In a lengthy manuscript entitled *Commentary on the Law of Prize and Booty*, one chapter of which was published in 1608 as *Mare Liberum*, Grotius developed the most organized, most complete defense of Dutch privateering in Asia yet produced. In so doing, he stilled any lingering doubts about the legality of the company's offensive strategy and provided the new organization with a versatile legal framework for future operations. Aiming to quash any possible objections through the deadening weight of argument, Grotius provided a series of distinct rationalizations for the attack, suggesting that van Heemskerck had been engaged in both a private and a public war, with the latter fought on behalf of two separate sovereign authorities. While each explanation could stand alone, the combination put the case, so Grotius argued, beyond any dispute.

He began by suggesting that the Portuguese, the targets of van Heemskerck's attack, had, in their quest to monopolize Asian trade for themselves, violated the principles of natural law by working to exclude the Dutch through the twin tactics of force and treachery.[67] Because there was no appropriate judge in the Indies who could take action against this breach, van Heemskerck was fully entitled to punish the Portuguese by attacking their ships, including, of course, the *Santa Catarina*.[68] The claim was remarkably bold, transforming the Dutch admiral from an unprovoked aggressor into the enforcer of natural law. Martine van Ittersum calls it a "major innovation in legal theory and practice," and it gave the company unlimited rights to act against Portuguese shipping wherever it was encountered.[69] As if this was not enough, Grotius also justified the attack on the *Santa Catarina* as part of a wider public war conducted on behalf of the United Provinces.[70] To make the point, he set out first to prove that the republic was a properly constituted state that was entitled to authorize such actions and not a rebel league in illegal revolt against its former overlord, the king of Spain. This was done by arguing that it was possible for a nation to shake off "the rule of some sovereign and set themselves free without being described as rebel peoples" (414). If the Dutch war against Spain was essentially legal, van Heemskerck, as a servant of the Dutch state, had every right to participate in it and could do so a lawful combatant.

The third and final argument centered on the rights of Asian rulers, with Grotius arguing that van Heemskerck had in fact been waging a public war on behalf of the king of Johor, the ruler of important sultanate that spread across the southern end of the Malay Peninsula and part of Sumatra. The starting point for his assertion was a recognition that Johor "has long been considered a sovereign principality" and hence could claim the same rights as European states (432). But if its ruler "possessed the authority necessary to conduct a public war," he nonetheless required a grievance, and Grotius supplied a list of affronts, including the denial of the king's right to engage in free trade as well as various Portuguese misdeeds (434). Since he was unable to wage war by himself, the king of Johor had enlisted the Dutch on his side, and they had becomes his defenders (436). Thus in Grotius's argument the Dutch were reconfigured as unlikely champions of indigenous rights, sympathetic allies willing to help local sovereigns in a campaign against a shared enemy. In typically neat fashion, he sidestepped any notion that the Dutch were required to surrender their prizes to the state on whose behalf they had supposedly fought. Although it followed logically that the *Santa Catarina*, if captured in Johor's name, should be turned over to its ruler, Grotius argued that the vessel and all its contents had been ceded to the Dutch through an unspecified grant.[71]

By combining notions of public and private war, Grotius developed a powerful language of legal rationalization that could be wrapped around almost any act of VOC maritime violence. Reading through page after page of densely argued justification, it is easy to become overwhelmed by what is unquestionably a legal tour de force and to assume that such interventions, along with a string of favorable verdicts in Dutch courts, essentially ended any controversy over the basic question of legality. In fact, variants of the same dispute played out in ports and cities across Asia, where company officials were forced to defend the legality of their employer's actions. In these cases they operated not in the controlled confines of a Dutch court but in neutral spaces where they were frequently confronted by the Portuguese representatives so notably absent in the *Santa Catarina* case while being, forced at the same time to make their arguments before judges who could not be relied upon to render a verdict favorable to the VOC. In the process, company agents discovered that a logic of legal rationalization that had proven so effective in Europe could unravel when transplanted to Asia. This was the case in Japan where the Dutch struggled to defend the legality of their assault on Portuguese seaborne traffic.

THE PORTUGUESE IN JAPAN

After they appeared in Japan in 1542, the Portuguese quickly established themselves as an important part of the archipelago's commercial networks. They did so almost by chance, moving into a fortuitous vacuum created by the collapse of official commercial links between China and Japan after the breakdown of the tally trade (*kangō*) system, which had previously permitted limited ties, in 1547. This gap was filled by Portuguese merchants, who were able to provide a reliable conduit for Chinese goods through their newly established base in Macao.[72] After experimenting with a number of domainal partners, they eventually settled on Nagasaki as their primary terminus in Japan and the town quickly emerged as a thriving commercial entrepôt. Although other goods flowed along it, the Macao-Nagasaki route, the mainstay of Portuguese trade in East Asia, hinged on a straightforward silk for silver exchange. The carracks that arrived in Nagasaki imported Chinese silk and silk goods that were subsequently traded for a cargo of Japanese silver bullion. The quantities involved were impressive. A single carrack captured in 1603 yielded over eighty thousand kilograms of silk, while one traveler estimated that the Portuguese bring out of Japan "every yeere above six hundred thousand Crusadoes: and all this Silver of Japan."[73]

Although they played a key economic role, the Portuguese were, by the early seventeenth century, a controversial presence within Japan, and their relationship with the Tokugawa Bakufu increasingly strained.

The tension stemmed in large part from their close connection with the Jesuits, who had engaged in an aggressive proselytizing campaign that had culminated in their expulsion from the archipelago in 1614.[74] As its hostility toward Christianity mounted, the Bakufu became more and more suspicious of Portuguese merchants, who were accused, often with no real basis, of aiding the Christian community in Japan and of secretly ferrying in priests to continue missionary work.[75] As much as it might have preferred simply to expel the Portuguese along with the Jesuits, the regime could not afford cut the Macao-Nagasaki route without finding a reliable alternative to access Chinese trade. As a result, it was forced to tolerate the Portuguese presence, but there was little trust on either side. Instead both parties found themselves locked together in an uneasy embrace made bearable only by their shared desire to preserve the steady flow of Chinese goods into Japan.

The strained relationship between the Bakufu and the Portuguese provided the backdrop against which the company attempted to carry its global war into Japanese waters. When the Dutch arrived in Japan in 1609, Portuguese shipping that sailed between Nagasaki and Macao was already firmly in their sights. As previously discussed, the company's factory in Japan was only established as the result of a failed privateering expedition, and, for much of its early history, maritime predation was given at least equal and often far higher priority than trade. Considering the potential prize, this was not surprising. The sheer value of the cargo carried aboard the Macao-Nagasaki carrack, a single slow-moving vessel that plied a fixed route along a predictable time line, made it an irresistible target for company administrators and one that would continue to obsess them for decades. The first actual incident of VOC maritime violence in the waters near Japan did not, however, involve the great ship from Macao. Rather it centered on a small Portuguese vessel, the *Santo Antonio*, of no great value or importance. Its capture provided the first test of VOC efforts to bring its campaign against the Portuguese into Japanese waters, and it sparked a bitter legal dispute in which both sides converged on the shogun's court determined to argue their case.

In August 1615, six years after the opening of the Japan factory, a VOC yacht, the *Jaccatra*, seized the *Santo Antonio* as it made its way from Macao to Japan. The incident took place against the backdrop of a renewed escalation in the company's war with the Portuguese brought about by the collapse of a temporary truce that had come into effect in 1609 but had quickly broken down after both sides accused the other of violating its provisions.[76] When it was seized, the *Santo Antonio* was near the island of Meshima, part of a small chain of five islands called the Danjo guntō that are located just over a hundred miles off the west coast of Kyushu.[77] Uninhabited and lacking any economic value, Meshima possessed two attributes that made it disproportionately significant to its size. The island functioned, in the first place, as a key navigational signpost marking the correct approach to the archipelago. With its distinctive shape, described by one observer as "high and ragged," it was easily recognizable, with the result that it featured prominently in contemporary sailing directions, both European and Japanese.[78] Meshima was, for example, well known to the Dutch and appeared in Jan Huygen van Linschoten's *Itinerario*, a famous 1596 manual that was an indispensable aid to the company's mariners in Asia.[79]

Alongside this role as gateway, Meshima had a second, less well-defined function. For European mariners, the island marked the outermost boundary of Japan proper.[80] Approaching the archipelago after days out of sight of land, it was eagerly sought out by sailors as a concrete marker that they had reached the archipelago; sailing past Meshima meant moving out of the open ocean and into Japanese waters. From Edo, however, the view was far less clear. While the island was a familiar landmark to Europeans, who had all at one time or another approached Japan by sea, it lay on the furthest peripheries of the Tokugawa realm. Because of this, Japanese official records from this period are—in contrast to the confident declarations that appear in European sources—far less clear about Meshima's status. Indeed, it was only after the *Santo Antonio* case that we see the first affirmation from the center about the island's place as part of Japan.[81]

After it was captured, the *Santo Antonio* was brought into Kochi harbor, a secondary port located a few miles away from the Japan factory, on 18 August.[82] The arrival of the company's prize prompted a flurry of activity both in Hirado, where the factory's governing council convened to discuss its capture, but also in Nagasaki, where Portuguese merchants and their allies sprang into action. Tellingly, their response was not a military one, to assemble warships or launch reprisal attacks on VOC shipping, but rather legal, and it took the form of a protest demanding Tokugawa action. The logic of the argument was simple: the

Dutch had no right to capture a Portuguese vessel in what were clearly Japanese waters and hence the Bakufu must intervene not only to punish the company but also to force it to provide restitution.

In making this argument, the Portuguese and their Japanese supporters could draw on crucial precedents related to the nature of the regime's juridical prerogatives. During the *sengoku* era (1467–1568), the absence of any policing from the center and the easy availability of weapons combined with a "habit of violent recourse—sanctioned by traditions of private justice and self redress of grievances"—to create endless space for conflict.[83] The result was a period of endemic conflict that pitted families, villages, and warlords against each other in a series of seemingly endless confrontations. When Toyotomi Hideyoshi came to power, he worked to establish a more general state monopoly over the use of force.[84] This process, which was subsequently continued and expanded upon by the Tokugawa Bakufu, involved the elimination of the physical means to wage war—through edicts such as the famous sword hunt order of 1588—as well as the legal basis for private redress. As they worked to first curtail and then to suppress private violence, the unifiers placed a high premium on their own role as legal arbiters over any violent clashes that took place within the archipelago. The point is well made by Elizabeth Berry who notes that the "unification regimes were politically aggressive . . . in only one arena: peace keeping."[85]

This process of pacification and the concomitant insistence on legal arbitration for any clashes was not limited to the land. As Peter Shapinsky has so clearly shown, it extended to the seas around Japan, where Hideyoshi gradually stripped away the rights of formerly autonomous "sea lords," maritime daimyo based especially in the Seto Inland Sea, to engage in non-state violence. In his words, once "Hideyoshi had largely succeeded in unifying the country, he began enforcing his position as the sole sanctioning body for violence."[86] He did so by asserting his own sovereignty over the seas around Japan via an insistence on the central regime's role as the arbiter of all violent clashes in Japanese waters.[87] Given this overarching concern with peacekeeping, and assuming one accepted the Portuguese argument that the *Santo Antonio* had been captured in Japanese waters, there was thus a strong case to be made that the incident necessitated, like any other act of nonsanctioned violence, adjudication from the center.

But if there was an obvious parallel in Japanese history, the capture of the *Santo Antonio* also represented something quite different. The episode marked the first intrusion of the company's global war, an essentially European conflict imported from a distant continent, into Japanese waters. Because of this, VOC representatives were fully prepared to defend the legality of the seizure, arguing that the incident should be seen as a properly sanctioned and lawfully pursued act of war—violence yes, but not violence that fell within the Japanese regime's legal remit. In these ways the *Santo Antonio* incident looked markedly dissimilar from past episodes of maritime violence involving pirate groups or individual warlords, and there was no certainty how the Bakufu would respond.

At stake was much more than just the vessel itself. The *Santo Antonio* was not, by any criteria, a rich prize, especially when compared to the Macao-Nagasaki carrack, and it carried an entirely unremarkable cargo consisting primarily of ebony wood and pewter.[88] Rather both sides were concerned with the question of precedent. If the Bakufu ignored the episode, opting not to assert its role as arbiter, or signed off on it, then the stage would be set for future attacks against the Macao-Nagasaki trade route, which was acutely vulnerable to VOC maritime predation. If, on the other hand, the regime ruled in favor of the Portuguese, the result could be disastrous for the company, which might be forced to halt its privateering operations in Japanese waters while paying out for Portuguese losses.

The company's case was led by the incumbent opperhoofd, Jacques Specx, the same VOC official that subsequently orchestrated a shift in the organization's diplomatic strategy toward Japan. As soon as he received word of the incident, Specx moved to prepare "letters of advice in the Japanese language" to defend the company's position.[89] One of these went to the governor in Nagasaki, the relevant local official, while a second document was dispatched to Honda Masazumi, who was described as the "president of the [shogun's] council." As the Bakufu had some knowledge of the 1609 truce with the Portuguese, which had been described in an earlier letter sent to Japan, Specx's first step was to explain the resumption of hostilities by informing Honda that the Spanish and the Portuguese had not kept their promises, "but had falsely broken their word and tried to do all possible damage to us." As a result, the Dutch in Japan had received explicit instructions from "our prince [Maurits] . . . to wage war and to do as much damage as possible."[90] If any the company's ships encountered Iberian vessels at sea, they could not, therefore, allow them to pass but were duty bound to attack.

After the letters were sent on 18 August, the factory returned to normal business, but by the time its governing council met again on 10 September it was clear that something more needed to be done to combat Portuguese pressure. The solution was to dispatch a delegation to Kyoto, where the Bakufu was temporarily based, to "argue our matters against the Portuguese" directly before the shogun.[91] As opperhoofd, Specx was tasked with leading the delegation, but the council also called in Jan Joosten, one of the original *Liefde* mariners who had been in Japan since 1600.[92] To secure a favorable decision, Specx was authorized to spend whatever it took, but, even though it was prepared to open its cashbox, the council struggled to find appropriate gifts that might lure Bakufu officials over to its side. As the warehouse in Hirado yielded little of any value, it was necessary—as it had been in 1609 when the first VOC embassy arrived in Japan—to dispatch an agent to purchase some "beautiful" goods from Portuguese merchants in Nagasaki.[93] There was of course an obvious irony, that it was necessary to secretly purchase goods from the Portuguese in order to defend their rights against the same group, and the council instructed their agents to do so in the most discreet way possible through multiple intermediaries to ensure that no word of the transaction leaked out. To make doubly sure of obtaining the right decision, the council resolved to present a cannon from one of its ships to Tokugawa Ieyasu, who had displayed a sustained interest in European military technology. Once these items were added to the gifts intended for other Bakufu officials, the final total came to 2,734 guilders, a large sum for a factory that had yet to turn a profit.[94]

On 24 September Specx and his delegation reached Fushimi, an important stronghold near Kyoto, where they discovered Portuguese agents already at work lobbying the Bakufu for a favorable decision.[95] Their presence marked a stark contrast with the *Santa Catarina* incident, the foundational moment for VOC privateering in Asia, which was resolved within the walls of an Amsterdam admiralty court before Dutch judges. In this instance, representatives from both sides, each armed with their own arguments and allies, converged on a neutral space to make their case before a set of independent adjudicators. As expected, Portuguese representatives argued that the attack had taken place in the "king's [shogun's] waters," that is firmly within the "territory of Japan."[96] Richard Cocks, the head of the English factory in Japan, who watched the dispute unfold, wrote that the Portuguese "complaine to the Emperour [shogun] because the Hollanders take them w'thin his dominions."[97]

Such claims hinged on an understanding that the assault on the *Santo Antonio* must be seen as piracy. Portuguese representatives across Asia had a great deal of experience in making this kind of argument as it was the standard proposition put to local rulers in an attempt to denounce the Dutch and in so doing deny them any foothold in the region. In China the Dutch were described as "Universal Robbers" and the "Arch-Pyrates of all Seas, whom all other Principalities did shun, as the most pernicious Danger in their Dominions."[98] In Japan Portuguese agents had made similar allegations on a number of occasions prior to the *Santo Antonio* incident. When the *Liefde* arrived in Japan in 1600, for example, its crew were loudly denounced as "thieves and robbers of all nations and were we suffered to live it should be against the profit of his Highness and of his country: for no nation should come hither without robbing them."[99] As part of this, Portuguese representatives argued that any appearance of honest commerce was nothing more than a thin veneer designed to conceal the true nature of the company's activities. Thus, according to one Portuguese letter, even when Dutch merchants "bring cargo to your country [and claim they have acquired these through trade] this is a complete lie" as all these goods were simply plunder acquired through force.[100]

Their role as pirates, stateless marauders marooned permanently outside the law, pushed the Dutch outside international orders. A later petition submitted to the Bakufu explained the "pirate ships of Holland are infesting the high seas. . . . Since they are nothing but pirates, no other country allows their ships to anchor in their ports."[101] If one accepted the attack on the *Santo Antonio* as piracy, then there could be only one conclusion. Piracy had been outlawed in the seas around Japan for decades, and there was a long-standing ban on pirate groups using the archipelago as a base. In 1588 Ieyasu's predecessor, Toyotomi Hideyoshi, had famously banned pirates from operating in the "the seas of the various provinces [of Japan]," while enforcing strict penalties on any group that sheltered or supported maritime marauders.[102] Given these facts, the company was, it seemed, doubly condemned, both for the initial attack, which had taken place in the waters around the "various provinces," but also because the *Jaccatra* had brought its prize to Japan, thereby turning the archipelago back into a pirate lair.

In response, Specx put forward his own arguments designed to uphold the company's rights to the captured ship. Pushing aside any discussion as to whether Meshima was or was not part of Japan, he insisted that the attack on the *Santo Antonio* was legal regardless of where it had actually taken place. His argument rested on one central assertion, that VOC privateering was a legitimate act of war in the service of a properly constituted state. The Dutch in Asia had, he explained, received orders from their prince, a figure still understood in this period as the "king of Holland," to "wage war in any way and to do all possible damage [to the Spanish and the Portuguese] on water as well as on land."[103] Rather than pirate chiefs, the captains of vessels like the *Jaccatra* were thus soldiers who "have been expressly charged that wherever we may encounter one of their ships not to allow it by any means to pass without fighting but to attempt to capture it even if we die in the process."[104] In this way there was no room for personal choice and certainly none for individual enrichment; the Dutch were simply at war, and any encounter with a Spanish or Portuguese vessel—even if it was with an unarmed trading ship—must be seen in its proper context as part of this wider conflict.

The presentation was a pale version of Grotius's submission, lacking the overlapping arguments that made his case so effective. In part this was because one of the key points used by Grotius to justify the offensive strategy, that the VOC was a natural ally for Asian sovereigns in a shared struggle against Iberian tyranny, had failed to make any real headway at the shogun's court. It was not for want of trying, with Dutch agents in Japan frequently repeating the charge made in Maurits's December 1610 letter to Tokugawa Ieyasu that Spanish ambitions to universal monarchy were a direct threat to the Bakufu.[105] To buttress the case, they conjured up a vast master plan for domination involving the Portuguese, the king of Spain, and the Jesuits, all of whom were working together to destabilize the Japanese realm. If Spanish tyranny could be made to seem a genuine threat, it turned the Dutch into natural allies because they had faced and overcome precisely the same danger. But although the argument was put persistently to them, Bakufu officials showed no interest in joining the fight against the Spanish, who were still seen in this early period as potential trading partners. Because of this, Specx abandoned any notion of the company as the natural champions of Asian sovereigns and any sense that the attack on the *Santo Antonio* could be read as part of a shared struggle.

Instead, he worked to divorce the conflict from the shogun, who must, he insisted, not intervene even as the company's war was brought to his shores: "We reverently seek from His Imperial Majesty [the shogun] that if we encounter the Portuguese or the Castilians somewhere around his majesty's land [to allow us] to wage war and do all possible damage or to capture their ships."[106] Although phrased in typically obsequious terms, the proposition represented a bold declaration of the company's right to wage its global war unimpeded by legal structures in Asia. Encounters such as the one off the coast of Meshima were simply a "matter between enemies at war with each other (*vianden oorloge mett malcanderen*)" and must be treated as such.[107] Put more bluntly, the shogun should stay out of a conflict that did not concern him by permitting any assault on shipping coming to Japan as a legitimate act of war. In this way the company's global conflict should, he insisted, take precedence over local legal structures.

The Dutch delegation did not have to wait long for an answer. Far more preoccupied with domestic matters including the winding down of its successful campaign against Hideyoshi's heir, the regime moved quickly, and on 26 September Bakufu officials informed the Dutch that they had awarded them the "junk, people and everything connected."[108] The decision was significant for a number of reasons. It affirmed, first of all, that Meshima and the waters around it were part of Japan. When the question as to the island's status was first raised by VOC agents after the capture of the *Santo Antonio*, there was a clear hope among the factory's staff that the Bakufu would simply declare that its authority did not extend out into the ocean to encompass this isolated chain of uninhabited islands. This is what happened, for example, in later instances of VOC privateering that had taken place on more distant sea routes, which Tokugawa officials pronounced as lying beyond their jurisdiction.[109] In 1615, however, the Bakufu did the opposite, moving to confirm that the waters around Meshima were part of Japan and hence fell under the shogun's authority. The result was to fix the island's role as the outermost boundary of Japan proper and to confirm to European mariners that it must be treated as part of the shogun's realm. There Meshima would remain for the rest of the Tokugawa period, appearing in map compilations like the *Nihon bunkeizu* as the outer marker of Japanese territory.[110]

Second, the decision confirmed the Bakufu's role as legal adjudicator. Instead of washing their hands of a European conflict involving no Tokugawa subjects, Bakufu officials accepted the petitions presented by both sides, considered their arguments, and came to a decision. In taking this action, the regime effectively marked out its right to act as an arbiter for a maritime dispute between two foreign groups that had taken place hundreds of miles away from its headquarters in central Japan. The result was a confirmation that any act of nonsanctioned violence—regardless of motivation or participant—required adjudication from the center. As was the case with Hideyoshi, this was in effect an affirmation of the central regime's maritime sovereignty over the waters around the archipelago, although it extended only to a limited set of rights related to the arbitration of violent disputes.[111]

But, if the decision affirmed a basic willingness to adjudicate any maritime dispute that had taken place in Japanese waters, it was paired with a strikingly limited definition as to the extent of Tokugawa legal protection and hence as to which plaintiffs could expect to find redress for their claims. Before issuing its verdict, the Bakufu dispatched an envoy to speak directly with the captured Portuguese mariners at the heart of the dispute. The subsequent interrogation consisted of a single question that illuminated the extent of the regime's concern: did their vessel carry the shogun's "seal," that is, a shuinjō?[112] When the captives confessed that they possessed no such pass, the interview was terminated and their request for protection dismissed. Once it became known that a shuinjō was not involved, the Bakufu showed no interest in draping its protection over the *Santo Antonio* regardless of the fact that it had been captured in the seas around Japan. The message was clear: the regime's concern extended only as far as the shuinsen, and it had no intention of either enforcing punishment or mandating compensation if the incident did not involve one of these vessels.

If there was no ambiguity in this regard, the Bakufu's view on the essential legality of Dutch privateering was less obvious. While Tokugawa officials did not denounce the incident as piracy, something they would do when faced by later instances of VOC maritime aggression, they offered no affirmation of Specx's argument that the actions of the *Jaccatra*'s captain should be seen as a legitimate act of war. What is clear, however, is that the decision to award the *Santo Antonio* to the company did not derive from an especially positive attitude toward

Dutch privateering activities but rather from an overriding concern with shuinjō vessels to the exclusion of any other shipping making its way to Japan.

For the Portuguese, the ruling represented a clear setback, but it did at least offer a slender reed of hope. Although the decision had gone against the *Santo Antonio*'s owners, the Bakufu had confirmed its role as legal arbiter over all acts of violence within Japanese waters, even those stemming from an intra-European conflict.[113] In the aftermath of the *Santo Antonio* incident, it was clear that the shogun's court could be pressed into action as an international legal node, a space for petition, investigation, and arbitration of maritime disputes. While this offered scant consolation in the short term, it was possible that the Bakufu might be persuaded over time to expand the boundaries of its protection to include ships that did not carry a shuinjō.

The company, for its part, took a very different lesson. Pushing to one side the possibility that future decisions might go against them, Specx and his superiors read the successful resolution of the *Santo Antonio* case as a clear endorsement of VOC privateering operations and a wide-ranging dispensation for further action. This was the position taken by the soon to be governor-general, Jan Pieterszoon Coen, who became increasingly convinced that the company could launch extended privateering campaigns against Portuguese ships sailing to Japan, even if it resulted in the extension of the conflict into the shogun's harbors. Coen's letters after 1615 reveal a persistent belief that the Bakufu was either clearly sympathetic or essentially indifferent to VOC privateering and that it did not necessarily hold coastal waters or even its own harbors as a special preserve. The result was a reckless pursuit of prizes that would ultimately prompt a Tokugawa backlash.

EXPANSION AND ESCALATION

Once the plunder from the *Santo Antonio* had been squared away, the company's attention turned naturally back to the Macao-Nagasaki carrack, the great prize shimmering always on its horizon. Reflecting the importance placed on the capture of this vessel, Coen wrote to the opperhoofd in Japan asking that "if you can advise us, how the carrack travelling from Macao to Nagasaki can be trapped, do not hesitate to inform us, so that the Company can receive some respite from its heavy burden."[114] Little encouragement was needed to prompt action. In Japan the factory's employees watched enviously as these ships anchored in Nagasaki, disgorging vast quantities of goods that dwarfed their own meager trade. If just one of these vessels could be seized, their fortunes would be transformed and the company's outpost in Hirado turned from a remote backwater into "one the most profitable trading posts" in the VOC empire.[115]

After years of trying, the stage seemed at last perfectly set for a successful assault on the great ship from Macao. Through the work of informants like Jan Huygen van Linschoten, the company had access to remarkably detailed information about these ships, including sailing directions and timetables.[116] In Hirado the company had, moreover, an ideal base for operations near the terminus of the Macao-Nagasaki route. With the successful resolution of the *Santo Antonio* incident, the last piece of the puzzle seemed to have fallen into place. The shogun's verdict convinced a number of VOC administrators that they could and indeed should carry their war directly into Nagasaki, where the carrack was most vulnerable. With this in mind Coen ordered the dispatch in April 1617 of two vessels, the *Swarten Leeuw* and the *Galiasse*, with instructions to assault their target if it was found anchored in Nagasaki harbor.[117]

On their way to Japan, the *Swarten Leeuw* and the *Galiasse* met up with a third VOC ship, the *Oude Sonne*, under the control of admiral Jan Dirckzoon Lam who proceeded to assume command of the expedition. Reaching Nagasaki on 3 July, the small fleet discovered that it had arrived before the carrack, which was nowhere to be seen. Faced with two choices, anchor in Nagasaki or blockade the entrance to the harbor, Lam decided to enter the port and wait there for the prize to fall into his hands.[118] Almost as soon as the fleet dropped anchored, word reached it of the imminent arrival of the carrack, which was estimated to be just eight or ten leagues away. Any hope that it could be seized without a significant Japanese backlash were, however, quickly dispelled when Nagasaki officials moved to push back against the company's aggressive tactics. Sailing out in a small boat, Hasegawa Gonroku, the Nagasaki bugyō, who like many of the city's elites had a personal stake in Portuguese trade, ordered Lam to give up his pursuit of the carrack and leave immediately for Hirado. His prize so close at hand, the admiral refused, insisting that he had clear instructions to seize Portuguese shipping even if it was within the confines of Nagasaki harbor itself. The response from the city was swift and forceful. According to Lam, he was "charged expressly by the governor of Nagasaki not to harm [the carrack] in the slightest and to depart immediately . . . or we should be prevented by armed force."[119] As proof of Hasegawa's intent, eighty barks packed with soldiers were assembled to attack the company's ships if they moved against the carrack. Although they posed little danger on the open sea, the barks were a formidable threat in the narrow channels of Nagasaki harbor and Lam opted to retreat.

The controversy over VOC privateering deepened still further when news reached Japan of Dutch attacks against neutral shipping sailing to Manila. As part of their overall plan to force the Spanish out of the Philippines, the company targeted the steady flow of junks sailing between China and Manila. In 1617, for example, VOC ships deposited the massive sum of 823,134 guilders worth of plunder as well as a number of prisoners that had been seized from at least seven Chinese junks in the Japan factory.[120] Amazed by the richness of the loot, one observer wrote enviously of the "great quantities of raw silk, tafities, satins, velvets and Chine wares which they steal from the Chinese, having of late robbed many junks."[121]

The arrival of plundered goods in such quantities and captured sailors in such numbers sent shock waves through Hirado. Uncertain of the legality of the company's campaign, concerned domainal authorities impounded its ships and warned that no goods could be sold until they had received instructions from the Bakufu. Part of the problem was that VOC attacks on Chinese shipping looked so much like the wakō raids that had been suppressed by Hideyoshi's 1588 prohibition, an event still within living memory for many inhabitants of what was after all a former pirate stronghold. Drawing the obvious connection, one domainal official told an English resident of the port that he believed the shogun would not allow the Dutch to take Chinese shipping because Hideyoshi had already banned such attacks.[122] While this was clearly a problem, there was a further obstacle for the company in the form of Hirado's substantial Chinese community, which vehemently protested attacks against their countrymen. Li Dan, the famous China captain, complained bitterly to Specx and demanded access to one of the captured junks.[123] Although refused permission, he did manage to speak to some of the prisoners, who lamented that they had been treated with "great cruelty."[124] Rather than taking captives, the Dutch had, they claimed, simply thrown most of the captured mariners overboard, leaving them to drown.

As was the case after the seizure of the *Santo Antonio*, the appearance of captured vessels and crew in Hirado triggered a series of legal protests that went straight to the shogun's court, thereby confirming its role as an active center for the arbitration of maritime disputes. Predictably, the first complaint came from Li Dan, but at roughly the same time a second petition emerged from an unexpected place. In his official report, Lam noted that one captured Chinese junk with six or seven of his men had been separated from his fleet in a typhoon.[125] Seeing their opportunity to escape, the Chinese captives, numbering about thirty or forty men, had overwhelmed the small prize crew.[126] Sailing their junk to nearby Satsuma domain, they proceeded to gather funds in order to "pursue law against them [the Dutch] at themperour's [shogun's] Court."[127] In contrast to the Portuguese, who had been at war with the Dutch for years, Chinese merchants had, the petitioners explained, no quarrel with the company, which had attacked them "w'thout law or justice, w'thout pronounsing war against them, they taking them for frendes & haveing contynewall traffick w'th them at Bantam, Molucos, Pattania, Syam, Japon & other placese."[128] While this was happening, other groups of merchants also converged on the shogun's court to prosecute their case against the Dutch. Summarizing this flood of protests, Cocks noted that the "Spaniardes, Portingales, & Chinas . . . did joyne together and went to the Japon court to complaine against the Hollanders as comune theeves or pirattes."[129]

The Bakufu, however, refused to intervene even when pressed by Chinese merchants, who had suffered the greatest losses from VOC depredations. Unlike the *Santo Antonio*, which had been captured in Japanese waters, the attacks on shipping sailing to Manila had taken place far away from the archipelago in distant seas over which Bakufu officials were adamant they had no authority.[130] If the Chinese wished to seek compensation, they should apply, therefore, either to authorities in China or to the Spanish governor in the Philippines.[131] But, ominously for the Dutch, this refusal came with a commitment to take action if subsequent attacks took place in Japanese waters. Cocks, who was in Edo at the time, wrote that the shogun promised to order compensation if acts of maritime violence occurred in his "jurisdictions" or "w'thin the presinctes of [his] dominions."[132]

The promise represented a hardening of the Bakufu's attitude toward privateering and the first sign that the regime might revisit its definition of what was acceptable in its waters. This shift was clear to the staff of the Japan factory, who were increasingly concerned about the company's deteriorating reputation. With so few trade goods coming in and so much plunder going out, it looked to many observers as if the factory had become little more than a pirate depot. Desperate to combat this impression, the opperhoofd begged his superiors to fill a hundred empty crates with any available merchandise and send them on to Japan, regardless of whether or not the contents could be sold for a profit. This would, he explained, allow the Dutch to at least present the image of "respectable merchants" and combat the growing pirate stain.[133] No goods were forthcoming, however, and by 1621 it was clear that the factory's time had run out.

THE 1621 EDICT

On 14 September 1621 Jacques Specx, then in his last days as opperhoofd, was presented with a newly issued order from Edo prohibiting the Dutch—as well as their English counterparts, who were also based in Hirado—from taking arms out of Japan, hiring mercenaries, and, most important, engaging in maritime violence. According to the description of events in Dutch sources, they were told that the "Hollanders and the English shall not pirate (rooven) on the sea around the land of Japan." This can be paired with the original Japanese edict, dated the twenty-second day, fifth month of Genna 7, or 11 July 1621, which repeated the message in almost identical terms: "The Dutch or English must not pirate (bahan) in the waters around Japan (Nihon chikaki kaijō)."[134]

It was a significant setback for the company. For the first time Tokugawa officials had unequivocally condemned VOC actions as piracy and had attached the the term bahan to Dutch privateering. The Japanese-Portuguese dictionary (Nippo Jisho), which was published in Nagasaki in 1603 and provides an invaluable resource for contemporary usage, defines this term as referring to the plundering of foreign lands.[135] It was used most commonly in Japan to refer to the wakō marauders who had launched raids against China in the sixteenth century from bases scattered across Kyushu and other parts of the archipelago. Bahan pirates were stateless predators famous only for brutal violence, and the term was a uniformly negative one. Writing to his superiors, Specx lamented that the "word pirate is shameful in Japan and is very different from the taking of enemy ships. . . . Our procedures are announced to them as piracy and understood as such."[136] Whereas Dutch representatives at the shogun's court had once talked confidently about privateering as a legitimate act underpinned by a universally recognized logic of war, by 1621 such arguments had shattered, leaving the opperhoofd to pick up the pieces.

The 1621 edict painted the Dutch with an enduring pirate stain that they would struggle for decades to erase; it left the company with no room to appeal and little to maneuver. The Bakufu did not distinguish between attacks against the Portuguese, which had once seemed broadly acceptable, and the recent spate of clashes with Chinese merchants. Instead, the 1621 order prohibited the Dutch from capturing "any vessel, be it Japanese, Chinese or Portuguese."[137] The result was to erase any possibility of nuance and to leave no room for blurring the edges of legality to permit action. Any assault by a VOC ship, however clearly justified, was to be treated as piracy and, if it took place in Japanese waters, was to be swiftly dealt with. Within the organization itself, there was no question as to the dangers represented by the label. When news of the edict reached Batavia, one high-ranking official wrote forcefully of the need to expunge the designation so that the Dutch could regain their reputation as the representatives of "a fixed and imposing nation."[138]

How to do so, however, was more difficult, and Batavia could provide little guidance on the matter. Beyond reducing the number of vessels coming to Japan for maritime operations—a step quickly taken—it was not clear how to shake the impression that the "Dutch were only pirates that come to [Japan] with empty ships."[139] Simply retreating to claims about the essential legality of VOC operations offered little help. The potent suite of arguments presented by Grotius in Europe had faltered when transferred across to Japan, where they had failed to gain any traction in a far more uncertain legal environment. The only option was, it seemed, to wait it out and hope that the association would gradually fade. In fact, the *bahan* association would continue to dog VOC agents in Japan well into the second half of the seventeenth century. Some years after the initial 1621 edict, one Bakufu official offered a reminder of this when he informed the Dutch that "it is imprinted in his

Majesty's [the shogun's] mind that you are pirates and are daily involved with piracy."[140]

But if the Dutch were labeled as pirates, they were also placed in a special category that allowed them to continue to operate in Japan. Whereas Hideyoshi had banned all pirates from using the archipelago as a base, the Bakufu, which saw the Dutch as a useful if as yet far from reliable trading partner, settled on a more pragmatic response, allowing them to remain in Japan while seeking to curtail the worse excesses of VOC violence. The result was to carve out a special exemption for the company, which was, the edict seemed to suggest, free to continue its piratical ways as long as it did so in distant waters beyond the gaze of Bakufu officials.

In legal terms the 1621 edict represented a significant expansion of Tokugawa authority to encompass the seas around Japan. In 1615 the Bakufu had confirmed its legal rights to those waters, but had done so in a decidedly limited way by insisting that its protection extended only as far as the deck of the shuinsen. Six years later, it moved to effectively guarantee the security of all shipping in the seas around the archipelago, regardless of whether or not the vessel in question carried a shuinjō. The result was to significantly expand the scope of the Bakufu's legal remit. Having previously reserved its right to act as legal arbiter, the regime now confirmed that it would punish all nonsanctioned acts of violence. In this way the Bakufu moved to, borrowing Emily Tai's evocative phrase, mark the waters around Japan and to do so in a way that could not be missed by the Dutch.[141] After 1621 it was increasingly clear to VOC officials like Jan Coen, who had authorized the dispatch of ships into Nagasaki harbor, that the shogun had no intention of ceding the maritime sphere to the Dutch to do with as they willed. Instead, faced by a steady escalation in VOC activities, the regime moved to shut down the company's privateering campaign in its waters by inscribing juridical authority on all shipping within a loosely defined band around the archipelago.

Although the 1621 edict did not stipulate what punishment would follow if the Dutch continued to "pirate in the waters near Japan," there was no doubt within the factory as to the severity of the potential penalty. As a result, the primary concern of VOC representatives in Japan was to make sure that the injunction was not simply ignored by their more aggressive superiors, who might assume that the shogun could be bullied into reversing his position. Leonard Camps, who took over from

Specx as opperhoofd in late 1621, wrote a strongly worded letter to Batavia insisting that any attempt to pursue operations against the Macao carrack in Japanese ports would prove disastrous. The regime was not, he warned, to be treated like one of the smaller polities the company had encountered in Southeast Asia. The shogun was "no king of Makassar [and] violations of his harbors or waters will not be tolerated. I believe as well that the [king of] Makassar did not wish for this as well but lacked the strength (to prevent this from happening). Japan does not lack this strength. God grant that this is never proven."[142]

Although they decided not to test the regime's resolve, VOC agents were determined to map out the boundaries of, to use their term, the shogun's "jurisdiction" (jurisdictie). The company must, Specx wrote, pay special attention to learn "how far the law and jurisdiction of the Prince [shogun] extends in the sea."[143] The goal was to find "fixed limits" that could be drawn on a chart specifying the precise extent of Japanese jurisdiction. If no such lines were drawn, the "seas around the land of Japan" might bulge outward in unpredictable ways, encompassing waters that the company believed lay far beyond the limits of shogunal authority. If they could not obtain "further explanation, then it would," Specx warned, "be dangerous for us to capture any Portuguese or Spanish cargo ships [in the waters] around Japan."[144]

But, despite pressing for it, there was no further clarification from Edo. With no way of knowing exactly how far the limits of the shogun's authority extended, the company was compelled to settle on the most cautious strategy possible. Pulling back initially from its campaigns against Portuguese shipping in Japanese waters, it later halted all attacks on the carrack as it made its way between Macao and Nagasaki. By the 1630s, Dutch representatives regularly promised Tokugawa officials that their vessels would not damage Portuguese shipping sailing to Japan "even though they are our mortal enemies."[145] The result was the effective suspension of the company's global war in a theater that had once seemed destined to produce significant returns. When a Dutch fleet encountered four richly laden Portuguese galliots, smaller vessels that had replaced the massive carrack, on their way to Nagasaki they were allowed to sail on unharmed "in order not provoke any new troubles in our Japan trade" even though it was "truly a difficult matter to see such an impressive prize pass by."[146] Unable to sever Portuguese trade links with Japan by force or to substantially damage their rival's position through sustained attacks, the Dutch were forced to compete on purely commercial terms. The result was the continued domination of Portuguese merchants who, once violence was taken out of the equation, were far better placed to exploit the vagaries of the Japanese market. James Boyajian sums it up well when he notes that so "long as the Portuguese galliots frequented Nagasaki, VOC trade in Japan was never more than a fraction of . . . [their] trade."[147] This remained the case until 1639 when the Portuguese were finally expelled from Japan after the Shimabara uprising.

In this way, the company's determination to wage its global conflict unhindered by local legal authorities collided with Tokugawa maritime sovereignty. The result was a retreat by VOC officials, who were compelled to accept the parameters of Tokugawa authority and give up their rights to deploy violence independently of Bakufu consent in Japanese waters. While the history of VOC privateering in Japan stands alone, it can be connected to a much longer process in which the ability of independent groups to deploy force in Japanese waters was gradually limited and then largely suppressed. Indeed, the regime's treatment of the Dutch shares a number of features with Hideyoshi's confrontation with the maritime lords that dominated the Seto Inland Sea. As such, the Bakufu's declawing of the company can be fitted into a multiple-decade-long process that began in the 1580s when the unifiers first began to clamp down on unsanctioned maritime violence.

But, if it fits into this longer time line, there was also an obvious and highly significant difference between semi-autonomous domestic actors like the Noshima Murakami family, which occupies a central place in Shapinsky's pioneering study, and an organization like the Dutch East India Company, which claimed its own sovereign rights to wage war. And yet, in the end, both were subjected to a similar process; just as Hideyoshi tamed the "sea lords," by eliminating their rights to autonomous violence, so did the Tokugawa Bakufu tame the Dutch East India Company, at least when it came to VOC operations in the waters around Japan. The result was the same for both groups: inclusion into a domestic order in which they were forced to give up the right to deploy maritime violence in order to find accommodation with the central regime.[148] Considering the nature of the company's maritime advantage and the scale of its ambitions, it was a significant turnaround. In 1609, when its first ships appeared in Hirado, Japan seemed to offer a rich hunting ground for VOC privateering. The Portuguese were entrenched in Kyushu, but their trade routes, dominated by the lumbering Macao-Nagasaki carrack, were clearly vulnerable to assault. In the end, however, a minor vessel of no great value, the *Santo Antonio*, formed the sum total of Portuguese prizes captured on the sea-lanes leading into Japan. The result was that the Bakufu, which never deployed a ship of it own or indeed fired a shot in anger, succeeded in taming the most formidable maritime power then active in Asia and shutting down its campaign against a declared enemy.

CHAPTER FIVE

POWER AND PETITION

If we called pirates all those who maintain their rights with weapons,
then we would find few princes and kings in the world but only pirates.

—Governor-General Antonio van Diemen, 1642

In 1663 seven half-dead Chinese sailors washed up onto the Gotō
Islands, a small chain located near the coast of Kyushu. Their ship had
departed Chaozhou in Guangdong province a few weeks earlier on its
way to Japan but had run into a fierce storm that had swept away one of
its masts. As the crew struggled to rig new sails, they sighted an unfamiliar Dutch ship on the horizon. It was not there to help, and, after
refusing to submit to an inspection, the Chinese junk came under fire,
heavy cannon shot from the Dutch ship ripping into their vessel's hull.
Forced to abandon ship, the surviving mariners, clinging desperately to
the wreckage, were tossed by the sea for days before favorable currents
washed them onto Japanese shores. The casualty list, both as a consequence of the bombardment and later in the cold waters of the East
China Sea, was high. So too were the damages from the lost vessel and
the rich cargo it had carried. Determined to extract full compensation
from the company for their lossses, the survivors moved quickly to file
a petition with the Nagasaki bugyō, the highest-ranking Bakufu official
on Japan's maritime frontiers.

The resultant document and others like it that were submitted by Chinese plaintiffs to Tokugawa authorities in protest of VOC actions form

the subject of this analysis. In contrast to chapter 4, which considered a period when the Bakufu permitted, and in some ways actively encouraged, maritime trade through the shuinjō system, this chapter examines a later period during which Tokugawa foreign policy was defined by a series of maritime restrictions, the so-called closed country or *sakoku* edicts, promulgated between 1633 and 1639, that seem to mark a determined withdrawal from the sea. Given the fact that they combined to effectively shut down Japan's merchant marine, these edicts seem to suggest an almost total abdication of responsibility over the ocean and an open pass for an organization like the Dutch East India Company to act as it saw fit on the sea lanes leading into Japan. But if we look more closely at the Dutch experience in these years a very different picture emerges. Even as it dramatically reduced the volume of maritime traffic moving in and out of the archipelago, the Tokugawa regime continued to cast a long shadow over the ocean.

To highlight this ongoing influence, this chapter shifts the focus away from the shogun's court in Edo, where debates over attacks on Portuguese shipping played out, to consider the rise of Nagasaki as its own space for petition, investigation, and arbitration. The key protagonists of this story are Chinese or *tōjin* (literally, people of Tang) merchants, a diverse community of traders that was concentrated in Nagasaki after 1635. With no access to Edo, they turned to the Nagasaki bugyō who became an active participant in maritime disputes involving the Dutch. Beginning in the 1630s, the path to the governor's office became a familiar one for Chinese merchants who, seeking to exploit Tokugawa law and carve out a space in which they could operate as plaintiffs, submitted a series of legal petitions demanding redress for episodes that had taken place as far away as modern-day Taiwan and Vietnam. The picture that emerges of Nagasaki as an international legal node casts further doubt on the traditional view of Japan in this period—already shaken to the core by the work of scholars such as Ron Toby and Arano Yasunori—as an essentially isolated state by showing that the Tokugawa regime, through officials on the water's edge, continued to intervene in distant maritime disputes long after the promulgation of the *sakoku* edicts.[1]

The corollary of a surprisingly activist Bakufu was continued Dutch frustration on the sea routes leading into Japan, and these cases provide further evidence of the company's ongoing struggle to make use of the sharpest weapon in its arsenal. For VOC officials, the rise of Nagasaki represented a profoundly unwelcome development because it meant that any violent action directed against Chinese shipping with some connection to Japan—and there were plenty of instances in which the company wished to target precisely this traffic—could prompt a petition in that city and an investigation by the bugyō. Even if no compensation was ordered, Batavia had to contend with the disturbing presence of Japanese officials constantly looking over its shoulders, demanding explanations for VOC actions, and threatening retribution if none were provided. While such supervision was far from desirable, it was not the extent of the problem, and, as was the case when the company sent vessels to target Portuguese shipping, its campaigns against Chinese maritime traffic ultimately prompted an extension of Bakufu legal markers, which pushed out in this period from the waters around the archipelago to distant corridors of the ocean. The result was a further restriction on VOC operations, the climax of which came in the 1660s when the company was compelled to abandon a vital maritime campaign.

This chapter commences by looking at private Chinese merchants in Nagasaki before shifting to consider the mercantile networks attached to two figures, Zheng Zhilong and his famous son Chenggong, who emerged at the head of impressive maritime organizations that came to dominate the seas around China. As such, it draws on the steady stream of innovative work on the Zheng family by scholars such as Xing Hang, Patrizia Carioti, Tonio Andrade, Leonard Blussé, and others that has combined to reassess the nature of maritime East Asia, while aiming at the same time to bring the Tokugawa legal dimension more fully into the picture.[2] The portrait of the early modern seas that emerges is one characterized above all else by complexity, of waters crossed and recrossed by the tangled lines of authority and law described by Benton.

THE CHINESE COMMUNITY IN NAGASAKI

The Chinese merchant community had a long history in Kyushu, the traditional maritime center of the Japanese archipelago. During the *sengoku* period, Chinese towns had sprung up across the island as new arrivals were welcomed by local strongmen eager to gain access to the potential riches represented by expanded maritime trade. By the early seventeenth century, the community was increasingly concentrated in the important hub of Nagasaki, and in 1604 the first interpreter (*tōtsūji*) was appointed to mediate between Chinese merchants and the city's authorities.[3] The key figure in this early period was Li Dan, who had been elected captain and chief commander "of all the Chinas in Japon, both at Nangasaque, Firando, & else wheare."[4] His tenure marked the high point of political influence for the Chinese community in Japan and after his death no comparable figure emerged capable of commanding the allegiances of the community as a whole. In 1635, the Bakufu moved to establish clear boundaries around Kyushu's foreign population by restricting Chinese merchants and their families to Nagasaki. The decision boosted the city's Chinese population, which increased rapidly in size while prompting a surge in junk traffic.[5]

Although Japanese sources refer uniformly to the members of this group as *tōjin*, this characterization conceals a diverse community made up of a number of clusters, each with their own dialect, organization, and trading interests.[6] Tōjin merchants had their hand in a wide range of commercial networks that extended not only to China but also to entrepôts across Southeast Asia. Of the ninety-seven Chinese vessels that arrived in Nagasaki in 1641, two were from Cambodia, three from Cochinchina and three from Tonkin, while subsequent years saw the arrival of shipping from Siam and other states across the region.[7] But for all their success, these networks were also fragile. Whereas European merchants like the Dutch claimed the protection of state-sanctioned mercantile corporations and, at times of crisis, their home governments, Chinese traders possessed no such guarantors. Since commerce was officially prohibited between Japan and China (and had been since 1547), those merchants trading directly with the Chinese mainland were effectively smugglers whose presence in Nagasaki directly flouted Ming laws. Although the limited reach of Chinese authorities meant they had little to fear, tōjin merchants had, at the same time, no access to legal structures capable of providing redress for attacks against their ships or for lost goods. They were thus acutely vulnerable to maritime predation, incidents of which increased substantially after the intrusion of Dutch ships into East Asian waters.

In the first decades after its formation in 1602, the VOC aggressively targeted Chinese merchants on a number of occasions by initiating campaigns against the China-Manila trade route in 1617 and Chinese coastal shipping in 1622. In the absence of organized campaigns, violence lurked just below the surface. Sanjay Subrahmanyam describes the "banal use of violence" that was so characteristic of the company's operations, noting its presence "whether acted out or potential—whenever the VOC appeared on the scene."[8] This proclivity for force stemmed in part from the fact that the organization was for much of its history at war with at least one of its many enemies or competitors, and its well-armed ships traversed Asian waters in a constant state of readiness. The company, moreover, aggressively enforced its rights to inspect neutral ships on the open ocean in order to determine their origins and the provenance of their cargo. When combined with the endless possibilities for conflict created by mistranslation, mutual suspicion, and the difficulties of communicating on the windswept waters of the open sea, the result was a sequence of violent episodes that occurred even in the absence of direct orders from Batavia.

Chinese merchants responded to the rise of the VOC in different ways. One favored preemptive strategy was to obtain some protection before setting out in the form of passes or flags. It was thus not uncommon to see Chinese junks flying the famous prince's flag, sometimes decorated with the additional slogan "Viva Orangie."[9] A second strategy, of more direct interest to this chapter, relied on the use of the petition to protest incidents that had already taken place. As we have seen, the first such petitions were submitted directly to the shogun's court by Li Dan and other Chinese representatives. Over time, however, these channels were shut down and Chinese merchants, private traders with no official status, denied access to Edo. The result was that petitions were redirected toward Nagasaki and particularly to the office of the bugyō, which was occupied in this period by two officials who rotated in and out of the city.[10]

It is easy to understand why Chinese merchants turned to the governor's office to prosecute their case. There were other officials in Nagasaki, but only the bugyō, the senior Bakufu representative in Kyushu, possessed sufficient clout to order an investigation, collect the facts, and issue a ruling. While the attitude of individual governors toward the Chinese community varied, none displayed any sympathy toward VOC privateering. As the key officials tasked with securing Japan's trade routes, they had no reason to tolerate attacks on constituent parts of this network, particularly if it could be proved that the Dutch had seized goods destined for the Japanese marketplace. Because of this, the governors were predisposed to consider—or at least not instinctively reject—complaints and to accept a role as conveners of an ad-hoc court of maritime arbitration. The next section examines two such documents submitted in 1635 and 1637 to the *bugyō*. Although neither elicited a favorable ruling, they confirmed Nagasaki's emerging role as an important legal center; within just a few years the route to the governor's office had become so well worn that one of these officials lamented that "Chinese complaints come daily to my ears."[11]

FAITHFUL AND DECENT PEOPLE

In September 1635 two Chinese merchants submitted a written petition to the Nagasaki bugyō, Sakakibara Hida-no-kami Motonao (in office 1634–38) and Sengoku Yamato-no-kami Hisataka (in office 1635–36), asking for restitution for an attack that had taken place near the company's colony on the island of Taiwan. Eager to know what they were dealing with, Dutch agents obtained a copy of the petition, which they included in the factory's *Dagregister*:

> We are people who come annually to trade in Japan and we were here last year. As the junk that we came in was in poor condition, we requested and received permission from you to buy a confiscated junk. We departed [Nagasaki] on the 20th day of the 9th month. On the 6th day of the 10th month we encountered the Hollanders at sea. They said to us, "Good people and friends, come into Tayouan and conduct your trade there." And as we come there every year for trade, we accepted this and went there. But they took not only our ship but also all our silver and cargo by force and they sent all our crew against our will to Jaccatra [Batavia]. We are very distressed about this. We made numerous submissions and requests about this matter to the Hollanders but were given an answer that the junk that was taken was a pirates' junk and hence a legitimate prize. We said we had purchased this junk last year from the Regents [governors] in Nagasaki and had sailed out on it. We also said that, as they well knew, we were people who traded annually in Tayouan.

With these facts established, the last section of the petition came to the point: "We have faith and hope [that you will deal with this matter] as we are people who trade every year under Japan's protection. We are known not only to the other Chinese but also to the Japanese who reside here as decent people and the whole world knows that we purchased the junk from Your Honours. We respectfully ask Your Honours to consider this matter. The loss of our money, goods and junk does not weigh on us so heavily as the 31 people [taken from us] who we fear will die."[12] The document set out to first establish the complainants' credentials as respectable merchants who were well known by all parties in Nagasaki. As regular traders with the archipelago, they operated under "Japan's protection," but this security had been ripped away by the Dutch, who had seized not simply cargo but also most of their crew. While it lamented the fate of these lost mariners, the document was, in the end, as all the petitions coming into Nagasaki, about money and was designed to secure restitution from the company for its alleged offenses.

Although the petition presented a straightforward case, the reality seems to have been far murkier. The available sources suggest that the company did in fact seize goods from some Chinese vessels near Tayouan, but when a delegation connected to these ships traveled to Batavia to plead their case, the governor-general responded with conciliatory measures, agreeing, probably in an effort to the keep the Chinese pipeline to the new colony open, to pay restitution for the confiscated goods.[13] While this process was still ongoing, a separate group of merchants, the authors of the 1635 petition to the bugyō, journeyed to Nagasaki to submit their own request for compensation. Their document seems, therefore, to have been a largely opportunistic attempt to secure a quick payout before word of the case's resolution reached Japan. Given how long it took for news to travel between Nagasaki and Batavia, there was plenty of room for such maneuvering and certainly some reason to hope that compensation could be secured in two places at once.

In response to the petition, the governors asked the incumbent opperhoofd, Nicolaes Couckebacker, to appear before the complainants. During the subsequent interview, he denied all knowledge of the incident while arguing that the allegations were completely unfounded. To further discredit the petitioners, Couckebacker ridiculed their claims to be honest merchants by suggesting that they had either traded with pirates or had used their own ships for piracy.[14] The bugyō, however, remained unconvinced and concluded that the complaint must have some basis. Part of the problem was the company's association with piracy, which had not diminished in the years since 1621. The *bahan* label, which continued to cling to the Dutch, meant that any rumor of maritime predation, however farfetched, was seized upon by Bakufu officials as further evidence of these tendencies. This was clear when Sakakibara, the more senior of the two bugyō, informed the Dutch that he believed that the bulk of the goods they brought to Japan each year had in fact been taken by piracy. In those years when their marauding yielded no prizes, the Dutch came, he concluded, "mainly with empty ships."[15]

While the bugyō seem to have been persuaded of the essential justice of the petitioners' claims, there was only so much they could actually do. The 1621 edict, the Bakufu's official policy on VOC privateering, had declared piracy, or any indeed any act of maritime violence, in the waters around Japan illegal while making it clear that no limitations were placed on activities beyond this vaguely defined band. Any incident that took place outside Japanese waters, and this particular episode had occurred near Taiwan, lay beyond the bounds of Bakufu authority, and the bugyō were in no position either to adjudicate on its legality or to force the offenders to pay out. But, if their hands were tied, the governors were far from powerless, and there was a great deal they could do to make life difficult for the company's representatives. Even if they could not enforce a penalty, they were free to range ahead of their superiors' official position by conducting an investigation (in order to ascertain what had happened) and to exert pressure (in the hope that the Dutch would choose to settle of their own accord). After the initial interview, the message coming out of the governor's office was thus for the Dutch to admit fault and offer some compensation even if they were not legally required to do so. In December 1635, for example, one of the bugyō's subordinates advised the factory to "make good . . . [the plaintiff's] damages" as his superiors wished to ensure the security of the vessels that traded with Japan.[16] The company was, however, equally dogged in its refusal to countenance such a settlement, and, after months of stubborn resistance, Couckebacker was finally able to procure evidence demonstrating that compensation had already been paid in Batavia.[17]

While the incident had produced no direct action, it confirmed that Nagasaki was an open forum for such petitions. The staff of the Japan factory did not have to wait long for a further reminder of this. In August 1637 another group of Chinese merchants presented a complaint to Sakakibara and Baba Saburōzaemon Toshishige (in office 1636–52), who had taken over from Sengoku one year earlier. They alleged that on "the 6th day of the 6th month, we sailed with our junk from Cochin-China. On the 12th of the same month, at the height [latitude] of Canton at a place named Taijchum, we encountered a vessel of the Hollanders. Most of them came onto our ship and dragged us to Tayouan where we were later released."[18] The list of goods confiscated by the Dutch in the process included 677 pieces of ray skin, a large quantity of aguila wood, and the sailors' clothes, which had, they claimed, been stripped from their very backs.[19]

Once again, the bugyō took the side of the petitioners by ordering local officials to examine the cargo holds of all VOC ships then in the port. So the searchers knew exactly what to look for, they attached the list of stolen goods that had been provided by the Chinese complainants.[20] Aware that they were walking a fine line between appropriate interrogation and overstepping the bounds of their authority, the governors emphasized that they did not intend to punish the Dutch even if the confiscated goods were found, as they did not directly concern themselves with "the piracy that the Hollanders engage in on the sea."[21] Instead, the goal of the search was simply to get to the bottom of the matter. Although the subsequent examination yielded no sign of any stolen goods, the governors made it clear to the opperhoofd that they had no doubt about what had actually happened. "We cannot," they explained, "prove the truth of the claim that the Hollanders' ships seized the junk ... [but] we do not doubt that you have done this." Going further, they berated the Dutch that, while "it is true that we cannot command or forbid what you do on the seas," they were deeply troubled by these accusations.[22]

While neither the 1635 nor the 1637 petition secured the desired result, they established an important precedent that was rapidly seized upon by tōjin merchants. For all their flaws, both petitions were accepted and some kind of investigation ordered. In the Nagasaki bugyō, therefore, Chinese merchants discovered a willing facilitator capable of intervening in maritime disputes and forcing the company to respond. The result was to open up a reliable path into Tokugawa legal structures, one that could, if the right kind of petition appeared, produce a far more advantageous result for the plaintiffs. For effectively stateless merchants operating in a dangerous maritime world, this was a valuable discovery, and it is not surprising that future petitioners were willing to travel across considerable distances to exploit Nagasaki's potential as legal center.

For the company, the precedent was far less positive. Even as they were cautious not to overstep the bounds of the Bakufu's 1621 edict, the Nagasaki governors showed a distressing willingness not only to receive petitions concerning incidents that had taken place far away from the archipelago but also to investigate them. This readiness to treat accusations from a group that the Dutch derided as natural liars, "deceitful and villainous" people who should not be trusted, had, VOC officials believed, created an overly permissive environment in which any and all complaints could be raised.[23] There were, one opperhoofd lamented, no penalties for false petitions and any accuser could simply retreat and return with a new, and equally baseless, grievance.[24]

While there were certainly spurious protests, this was not the extent of the company's concern. The far more significant problem related to the emergence of a legal node lying beyond Batavia's control and accessible to a dispersed group of merchants that traded in many of the areas in which the company was most active. While it was always possible for aggrieved shipowners or merchants to petition VOC authorities directly in Tayouan, Batavia, or, in very rare cases, the Dutch Republic for compensation, the odds were tilted entirely in favor of the company, which was able to control such environments.[25] Tayouan and Batavia were company towns in which nothing happened without the governor-general's consent, while in the republic there was no lack of support for its operations. Nagasaki was a different kind of space, a neutral forum in which local officials were predisposed to view maritime violence as piracy. There the Dutch had to answer not to a company administrator or a sympathetic judge, but to a quite different and far less reliable arbiter. Equally disturbing was the prospect (always on the horizon) that if Edo moved, as it had done once before in 1621, to redefine the nature of its authority over the ocean the governor's office would acquire new powers to punish VOC actions.

The opening of a Nagasaki channel and the appearance of an activist bugyō willing to range ahead of the regime's official policy on VOC privateering combined to make the ocean a far more uncertain place for Dutch mariners and administrators. This is evident in a planned but never implemented campaign against Zheng Zhilong, a dangerous rival to the VOC whose growing commercial empire threatened to undermine the foundations of its East Asian strategy. Rather than turning the full force of its fleets against shipping attached to the Zheng maritime network, a target that the Dutch believed they had ample justification to assault, VOC officials found themselves plunged instead into a prolonged and ultimately unsatisfying negotiation with Bakufu officials.

THE ZHENG THREAT

Born in 1604 in Fujian, Zheng Zhilong started his career in the Portuguese stronghold of Macao before moving to Hirado, where he rose to prominence through a close connection with Li Dan.[26] By the 1620s Zhilong had moved his operations to the seas around Fujian, where he emerged as one of many pirate captains who prospered in the busy shipping lanes off China's traditional maritime hub. In 1628 the Ming administration, using a well-worn tactic of charging pirates to suppress pirates, co-opted Zhilong by offering him a position as admiral.[27] Armed with this official endorsement, he soon dispensed with his rivals and emerged at the head of a powerful maritime network.

Given the area in which he operated, it was inevitable that Zheng Zhilong would come into close contact with the Dutch and their colony at Tayouan. At first Zhilong, who appears in Dutch sources as Iquan, worked with the company by providing its representatives with a share of the plunder in return for shelter, but this relationship soon began to fray. The main point of contention concerned the flow of Chinese goods from the mainland to Tayouan. In 1624, when the company had moved onto the island, Dutch agents had obtained a vague promise from Ming officials that that they would ensure that Chinese merchants regularly visited the new colony, but this agreement, which was despite VOC claims to the contrary never endorsed by the Chinese state, broke down almost from the beginning. Few Chinese traders appeared in Tayouan, and the volume of goods that the company believed it had been promised never materialized. As Zheng Zhilong's influence over the surrounding seas grew, VOC officials became increasingly convinced that he was impeding trade, and in July 1633 they decided to take action by launching a surprise attack against his fleet. Although they won an initial victory, the campaign soon turned against them when Zhilong reappeared with a formidable fleet comprised of 150 ships.[28]

After a precarious peace was established, VOC officials had no choice but to cooperate with Zheng Zhilong. Tayouan's economic fortunes depended on access to a steady flow of silk from China's maritime provinces, and only the Zheng network was in a position to properly guarantee this. At the conclusion of the conflict in 1634, Zhilong had agreed to provide the Dutch with a regular supply of Chinese goods, and, initially at least, the commitment was honored. The result was an increase in VOC silk imports into Japan, which remained the most important market for such goods. From 855,094 guilders in 1635, imports more than doubled to 2,094,375 in 1637 and then increased still further to 3,008,209 in 1638.[29] As silk poured in, the company received an unexpected fillip when their primary competitor for market share, the Portuguese, were expelled from Japan in 1639. With its most formidable rival gone, it seemed as if the company's fortunes in Japan were at last assured, and this sense of growing optimism was further buttressed when the governor of Tayouan managed to renew the contract with Zhilong in 1640.[30]

Any expectation of a golden age for Dutch trade in Japan was shattered, however, just one year later when ships belonging to Zheng Zhilong began to arrive in Nagasaki harbor, thereby displacing the company's role as middleman. In June 1641, dismayed VOC agents, recently relocated to the island of Deshima, recorded the arrival of a richly laden junk belonging to the "mandarin Iquan" in the quiet waters of Nagasaki harbor.[31] It was followed in subsequent weeks by five more "great junks," all carrying significant quantities of silk that were injected directly into the Japanese marketplace without VOC mediation.[32] The only explanation put forward for this sudden incursion was that the governor on Tayouan had lacked the necessary funds to pay for the ships' goods, causing them to proceed directly to Nagasaki, but it seems more likely that Zhilong simply saw an opportunity to dispense with an unnecessary partner and gain direct access to the region's most lucrative market.[33] The result was a dramatic drop-off in VOC trade with Japan; from more than six million guilders in 1640, imports fell to 1,022,908 guilders in 1641 and to 529,357 guilders in 1643.[34]

In Batavia the governor-general, Antonio van Diemen, was faced by a deteriorating situation that seemed destined only to get worse. In a letter sent to the Heeren 17 in 1642, he explained that "so long as the Chinese bring great quantities of silk and silk goods from China to Japan, the Company cannot survive there."[35] Of the two available options—to abandon the factory in Japan or to use the company's superior naval might to halt this incursion—van Diemen favored the second, and his letters to Japan reflected his determination to "enforce our rights by weapons" by attacking Zheng vessels on their way to the archipelago.[36] If the need to strike and strike hard was clear, there was still the tricky issue of the potential Japanese reaction to contend with. Unlike his famous predecessor Jan Pieterszoon Coen, who had felt no hesitation in dispatching a fleet directly into Nagasaki harbor to attack enemy shipping there, van Diemen was compelled to adopt a far more cautious attitude.

There were ample reasons for concern. An attack on one of Japan's most important trading partners could damage the company's standing and ruin its relationship with the Bakufu. The potential legal consequences were equally troubling. Even if a Zheng vessel was captured on the open ocean far beyond the sight of land-based officials, it could, past cases had made clear, prompt legal proceedings in Nagasaki. Above all, van Diemen wanted to avoid the specter of his representatives being dragged before Tokugawa officials determined to order compensation for VOC attacks. Confronted with this uncertain legal landscape, he resolved to seek assurances from Bakufu officials before taking any action. The result was a sustained lobbying campaign designed to convince Tokugawa officials of the essential legality of the company's planned actions. If the regime could be persuaded to accept the legitimacy of the campaign, it would, van Diemen hoped, abandon any claim to authority over Zheng ships, even if they were in Japanese waters, and stay out of the company's war.

The problem was, however, that the Bakufu had previously rejected any such arguments, choosing instead to label all VOC privateering as piracy in 1621. Because of this, van Diemen was forced to improvise by stitching together an unlikely legal rationale that received its first airing in a June 1642 letter sent to the shogun's senior councilors:

The government in China has noticed that their subjects come in greater numbers with their junks and merchandise from China to Japan, even though this is forbidden on pain of death by the king [emperor] of China. Because of this, the regents have charged us, in the name of the king of China, to go to sea to take their goods and people. Having understood this command, we wish to communicate it to Your Honors as we wish to know how the government in Japan will respond as we wish to remain in the favor of His Majesty [the shogun] and not to be considered as pirates, which we have never been. If we called pirates all those who maintain their rights with weapons, then we would find few princes and kings in the world but only pirates.[37]

The Japanese translation of the letter was even more direct: "Because the Great Ming has outlawed the trade routes with Japan, the officials of the Great Ming have charged us that wherever we encounter Chinese vessels we should seize their goods and people regardless of which country's waters they are in."[38]

The purpose of such explanations was to attach the use of force to a state, but, instead of arguing that VOC privateering should be seen as the legal extension of the Dutch government, van Diemen drew a line to a very different polity, Ming China. Considering that the VOC had gone to war with China just two decades earlier and the uncomfortable fact that Zheng Zhilong was actually a high-ranking Ming official, this was a bold claim, but it had a number of advantages. It connected VOC maritime operations not to a distant government in Europe that Bakufu officials knew very little about but rather to a familiar regional power, albeit one that was destined soon to collapse. Tokugawa officials were well aware that direct trade between China and Japan was prohibited by the Ming state, and it was at least possible to imagine the company as the unlikely instrument of this policy. Once the connection was drawn from Chinese emperor to Dutch captain, any attack on Zheng shipping could be presented as the legal enforcement of official prohibitions rather than a piratical assault. In an impassioned closing plea designed to resuscitate the logic of legitimate war and in so doing erase the pirate stain that had so dogged the company's past efforts, van Diemen offered an implicit criticism of the Bakufu's past propensities to label all maritime violence as piracy. While the regime had previously failed to distinguish between illicit predation and legitimate war waged in the service of "princes and kings," it must, he argued, now recognize the vital distinction between the two. The alternative was a disordered world in which soldiers were bandits, sailors became pirates, and legitimate policy turned into illicit act.

When his letter failed to produce any official response, van Diemen shifted his efforts to Nagasaki, which represented the front line of any potential dispute. If the city's bugyō could be persuaded to accept the company's logic of legitimate war, they would be far less likely to act upon petitions submitted by Chinese merchants, thereby giving the company its desired space to maneuver. In 1643 van Diemen dispatched two letters to Nagasaki, one to the bugyō and the second to Ebiya Shirōemon, a local merchant seen as a useful ally.[39] The letter to Ebiya provided a detailed rationalization for the company's planned actions, and when he arrived in Nagasaki the new opperhoofd, Jan van Elserack, largely parroted its arguments. It featured a familiar claim that because Chinese merchants were violating the "express orders of their king" they constituted a fair target for the Dutch, who were simply acting in accordance with the Ming emperor's orders. This was paired with additional arguments designed to convince the bugyō of the justness of the company's case.[40] In particular, van Diemen returned to the 1624 promise made by Chinese officials to supply Tayouan with goods, a commitment that enabled him to suggest that Zheng merchants were doubly condemned for breaking both the emperor's regulations and a sworn agreement with the Dutch. Just in case this was not enough, he maintained as well that Chinese merchants had violated Tokugawa prohibitions by secretly bringing Catholic paraphernalia and priests into Japan. When all these justifications were combined, the Dutch had, he insisted, an absolute right to "seize and destroy" Chinese mariners sailing to Japan.[41]

When he reached Nagasaki in late July 1643, van Elserack immediately presented the letters to Ebiya and the incumbent bugyō, Yamazaki Gonpachirō Masanobu (in office 1642–50). Before the governor could respond, however, the opperhoofd found himself unexpectedly outflanked by Nagasaki's Chinese community, which launched its own legal appeal.[42] On 28 September, van Elserack discovered that a group of tōjin merchants had submitted a petition to Yamazaki asking him to prohibit attacks on their ships as they returned from Nagasaki to their home ports.[43] The next day he was presented with a document that had been drawn up by the bugyō and which required the Dutch to pledge that no action would be taken until formal sanction had been received from Edo:

> Before this (for twenty or thirty years or more) the captain of the Hollanders promised the Japanese authorities that they would not attack or damage any junks sailing between China and Japan. . . . Your people have said that you will seize the junks of Iquan, but that you will not do so before you learn how the Japanese government will respond. As a result, I charge you not to attack or damage any Chinese junks that sail from China to Japan or from Japan to China, before you receive permission from the emperor [shogun] and the Japanese authorities. If you violate this promise, you will be punished with death.[44]

If the governor's office received reports that any junks sailing between China and Japan had gone missing, an immediate investigation would be ordered and, if necessary, torture used to procure information from the factory's staff.

VOC agents in Nagasaki and Batavia recognized the document for what it unquestionably was, a "perilous note" that, once signed, would hang like a millstone around their necks.[45] Even before one considered the wider implications, it showed that the attempt to win consent for an aggressive campaign by convincing Nagasaki officials of its essential legality had failed and that van Diemen's carefully constructed argument had gained no ground in Japan. At the same time, the document contained within it a massive expansion of the governor's authority at precisely that moment when the company sought to define and limit the extent of the office's influence over the sea. If the Dutch committed themselves to this promise, they could be held accountable for any attack on tōjin shipping on the sea routes linking China and Japan, regardless of whether or not the assault had taken place in Japanese waters. The document made it clear that any damage to Chinese maritime traffic as it moved between its home port and Nagasaki was prohibited. The result was to create a vast zone over which the governor's office could preside and to fix this to an undefined time line. There was no guarantee when the Bakufu would issue a decision as to whether the company could or could not attack Zheng shipping or even if it would respond to the request. Rather than allowing space for action, the document threatened, therefore, to trap Batavia in a perilous limbo in which it could face severe consequence with no assurances that these would lead ultimately to a favorable outcome.

Reluctant to make any such commitment, van Elserack argued that he lacked the necessary authority to sign off on the document.[46] The company was, he protested, already tormented by false complaints from Chinese merchants, inveterate liars prepared to say anything, and if given this chance they would simply fabricate incidents to harm the Dutch. Faced with this resistance, and concerned not to be seen overstepping the boundaries of his office, Yamazaki relented, informing the opperhoofd that he did not have to sign the document because it "was not the charge of the emperor [shogun]" but rather his own formulation.[47] Although this was an important concession, he demanded a guarantee nonetheless that VOC vessels in Nagasaki not attack Chinese ships on their way back from Japan. The opperhoofd must, the governor explained, "inform the governor in Tayouan and the Governor-General . . . that no Chinese traders coming to Japan should be harmed unless the high authorities [of Japan] give their permission."[48]

In Batavia, news of the governor's reaction quashed any hope that a campaign against Zheng shipping could proceed without Japanese resistance. Rather than accepting the company's legal arguments, the bugyō seemed determined to expand the boundaries of their authority to ensure the safety of Chinese maritime traffic to Japan. Batavia's initial response was to persist with the same strategy, and in 1644 van Elserack recycled the message by explaining again that the company was, despite claims to the contrary, fully entitled to enforce its legal rights by targeting Chinese ships.[49] One year later, however, van Diemen, who had consistently backed the campaign, died in office, leaving his more cautious successor to terminate such plans. Concluding that the solution did not lie with hostile action, the new governor-general, Cornelis van der Lijn, decided that the company would be better served by cultivating alternative sources for silk.[50] Soon after, Zheng Zhilong himself faded from the scene when he was placed under house arrest after defecting to the newly established Qing regime.[51]

The company's failure to launch its campaign against Chinese shipping sailing to Japan provides compelling evidence as to continued Tokugawa influence over the seas. Batavia had the ships and, as it repeatedly maintained, an unassailable logic for war, but any attempt to move onto the offensive faltered in the face of Japanese resistance and the power of the petition. In the years after this setback, Nagasaki remained an open forum for Chinese merchants seeking redress and petitions continued to filter in, creating more trouble for the factory, which was forced to defend a range of VOC operations in remote parts of Asia. In July 1653, for example, a group of Chinese mariners recently arrived from Siam submitted a written petition to the bugyō demanding compensation for 26,366 deerskins seized by the company from Chinese junks near Ayutthaya.[52] According to the factory's opperhoofd, who recorded the details in his diary, "the people of the [recently arrived] junks, making a great noise, went together with some Japanese . . . [who were included] to make the crowd seem larger, to hand over a written complaint to the governors."[53]

After questioning VOC representatives, the governor decided not to act, but cautioned the Dutch against attacking any Chinese junks coming to Japan, as these supplied the shogun and his subjects with necessary goods crucial to the functioning of the Japanese economy.[54] When he heard about the warning, the governor-general inveighed against the attitude taken by Tokugawa officials, writing that "it has become evident that they seek to protect the Chinese either with just or unjust means before us even though they are a ruin to the Company's trading [activities] everywhere. . . . Nonetheless, in order to trade peacefully in the Japanese realm we will have to obey their unlawful orders whether we like it or not."[55] The result of such petitions was to further entrench Nagasaki's role as a site for legal maneuvering and to establish patterns that would come dramatically to the fore when the company was thrust into confrontation with Zheng Zhilong's son, Chenggong, or, as he is more commonly known, Coxinga.

THE *BREUKELEN* CASE

On 12 June 1657 four VOC vessels, the *Hegersom, Wachter, Breukelen,* and *Urk,* sailed from Batavia heading north toward Tayouan.[56] On 30 June the *Breukelen* encountered a Chinese junk off the island of Pulau Condor (Côn Đao) near the coast of Vietnam. The vessel in question had sailed from Johor near modern day Singapore and was headed, its passengers would later claim, to Japan via Amoy (Xiamen) in Fujian.[57] The transit port was of particular significance as it lay in this period under the control of Zheng Chenggong, who after breaking with his father had set himself up as an important loyalist commander in the long struggle that followed the toppling of the Ming regime by Qing forces in 1644. From his base in Xiamen he waged an extended campaign against the new government, launching a series of attacks against Manchu strongholds that culminated in an ambitious but ultimately unsuccessful attempt to seize control of the former capital of Nanjing.

To support his campaign, Zheng Chenggong built up an extended maritime network stretching from his base in Fujian to ports across Asia. At its peak this network represented the largest organization of Chinese merchants active in Asia and a natural competitor for Batavia.[58] One Dutch official summed up this rivalry when he wrote that Zheng Chenggong's "strength and power is greatly enlarged and he is dominant along the seacoast. . . . He seeks in all ways to become master over the trade and to create a monopoly. To this end, he sends many trading junks to Japan, Tonkin and other profitable places." The result was to turn this network into what VOC officials described as "a terrible thorn in our side."[59] As his father before him, Chenggong made a point of targeting the Japan trade, which offered an unparalleled opportunity for profit. The first Zheng vessels appeared in 1653, and within a few years they constituted the bulk of incoming Chinese traffic into Nagasaki. In the 1657 trading season, for example, the Japan factory recorded the arrival of forty-seven Chinese junks (twenty-eight from Anhai, eleven from Cambodia, three from Siam, two from Quinam, two from Patani, and one from Tonkin), all belonging "to the great merchant Coxinga and his followers."[60]

Because the Zheng maritime network and the Dutch jostled for control of the same markets, there was ample room for friction, and violent clashes occurred even in the absence of an open conflict between the two sides, which only eventuated after Coxinga's invasion of Taiwan in 1662. This was the case in 1657 when the *Breukelen*, which carried no direct orders from Batavia to attack Zheng shipping, encountered the aforementioned junk near Vietnam. Recognizing a chance to secure an easy prize, the Dutch ship closed with the distant vessel. By the time it had come within firing range the fight was effectively over with the Chinese crew opting to surrender as soon as the first shots boomed out from the *Breukelen*'s cannon. A small prize crew was subsequently dispatched to sail the ship to the Dutch colony on Taiwan. Since it was too dangerous to allow the captured Chinese mariners, numbering around fifty men, to remain on board where they might be able to overwhelm their captors and retake the ship, they were split among the small fleet. Of most importance to subsequent events were the eleven prisoners transferred to a second vessel, the *Urk*, that would later find its way to Nagasaki.[61] Once the handover was complete, the *Breukelen* and *Urk* resumed their voyage, but were later separated after running into poor weather. Reaching its destination on 7 August, the *Breukelen* dropped anchor near Tayouan. Before the colony's governor could rule on the legitimacy of the prize, however, disaster struck. As strong waves battered the exposed anchorage, the cable securing the captured junk snapped, and it was driven ashore, eventually going down in sight of the company's primary fortress with the loss of seven lives.[62] Since there was no point in holding the remaining prisoners, they were released on the island where they immediately demanded compensation for their losses.

While this was happening, the *Urk*, still with its eleven Chinese prisoners on board, was in a desperate state. Although it had managed to come within sight of Tayouan, it failed to reach the anchorage and was driven away by strong winds and currents. Out of water and running dangerously low on other provisions, the vessel was pushed further and further north toward Japan. Given the poor state of supplies, it was not possible to ride out the weather and head for the familiar port of Nagasaki. As a result, *Urk*'s skipper, Gerbrand Bock, decided to make for the nearest land in a last-ditch effort to find fresh water.[63] Edging closer to the unfamiliar coastline, the ship became stranded in shallow water near Satsuma domain in Kyushu. As the crew struggled to free their vessel, one of the captives, seeing a chance to escape, leapt overboard and swam ashore. It was a dangerous gamble, to seek help in a domain on high alert against infiltrating Christian missionaries, but it quickly paid off when the fugitive made contact with sympathetic local officials who resolved to investigate the matter. Coming on board, they discovered the remaining ten prisoners held below deck.

With no authority over the Dutch and no desire to meddle in a complicated case, the lord of Satsuma elected to hand the ship as well as its Chinese captives over to Bakufu officials. The *Urk* was refloated, provided with supplies, and sent under guard to Nagasaki, where its arrival on 23 August during the Japanese festival of *Obon* created a stir of interest. Once there, the incumbent bugyō, Kainoshō Kiemon Masanobu (in office 1652–60) decided to confine the *Urk*'s officers and crew in an empty warehouse so he could conduct a proper investigation.[64] The factory's opperhoofd, Zacharias Wagenaer, whom we met in chapter 3, was ordered to interrogate the crew and provide a written transcript of their answers so it could be compared to the account obtained from the Chinese captives.

Clearly troubled by the affair, Wagenaer prepared twenty-two questions that were subsequently put to Gerbrand Bock, the *Urk*'s second mate and the ship's constable.[65] Recorded in full in the opperhoofd's diary, the questions dealt with each aspect of the capture, beginning with the most basic details as to the composition of the squadron and the date of its departure, but extending to far more difficult issues such as why exactly the *Breukelen* had decided to attack in the first place. This last question proved particularly tricky to answer, especially after it became apparent that none of the four ships that had left Batavia on 12 June carried instructions to assault Chinese shipping. Why then had the master of the *Breukelen*, who was of course not available to testify himself, chosen to engage with this particular junk? According to Bock and his fellow mariners, the vessel had been seized because it could not produce a pass (*zeepas*) indicating its origins and destination. Deeming this failure suspicious, the master assumed that the junk must have been trading with one of the company's enemies and was thus a legitimate prize.[66]

While it was presented as a definitive explanation, this was in fact just one of a number of possible accounts to appear in Dutch sources. The most likely explanation, and the one supported by the broadest range of materials, is simply that the master of the *Breukelen* acted on his own initiative without proper orders or any more substantial logic than a desire to secure easy plunder that could enrich him and his subordinates at little risk.[67] Indeed, it quickly became clear in the answers to the twenty-two questions that the Chinese junk encountered on 30 June had not been the only quarry. According to Bock, the *Breukelen* and its sister ships chased four other vessels, on 29 June, 6 July, 14 July, and 17 July. Three of these had evaded pursuit, while the fourth had to be released because it carried a properly authorized pass from Siam. The *Breukelen*'s actions provide evidence of what Virginia Lunsford has called the "slippery slope" of maritime predation.[68] For the VOC commander in the field, the already loose distinction between illegal pirate (*zeerover*) and legally authorized privateer (*kaper*) had a tendency to fade completely away when faced by easy prizes on the open ocean: "An 'anything goes' attitude prevailed in these far-off colonial outposts, these frontiers where the licit and illicit not only rubbed shoulders, but enjoyed a symbiotic relationship and intermingled almost seamlessly. To be a pirate in these regions meant that one could evidently wear several hats simultaneously, acting as either a *kaper* or *zeerover* in the same instance, depending on the perceptions of the audience and the exigencies of the moment."[69] If this was, as it certainly appears, simply an attempt to seize goods for personal profit, then the plunder was disappointingly meager, consisting of small quantities of *lakenen* (a kind of woolen cloth), some tin, and other inexpensive goods.[70]

Once the answers to Wagenaer's questions had been recorded, the document was translated into Japanese and submitted to the governors. As the opperhoofd waited for a decision, he recorded an angry mood in the city where the Dutch were taunted as pirates and the *Urk* labeled the "thieves' ship of the Hollanders."[71] The next day a group of laborers employed by the company to unload goods threw stones at the windows of the warehouse in which the *Urk*'s crew was confined while taunting them that they would be crucified for piracy.[72] On 2 September the situation worsened when Wagenaer discovered that the junk captured by the *Breukelen* had in fact sunk, taking with it any hope that the captured sailors could simply be repatriated to Tayouan to reclaim their vessel.[73] The news was, he confided in his diary, certain to create more problems that would further disrupt Dutch business in Japan. As he fretted about what was to come, the eleven Chinese sailors arrived in Nagasaki determined to take action. Following a well-established path, they moved on 5 September to submit a formal petition to the governor's office.[74] Rather than dealing with the matter personally, the bugyō decided that the incident was so serious that it was necessary to seek judgment from his superiors and the document was sent on to Edo.

The petition struck a nerve in the Tokugawa capital. Although the initial episode had taken place thousands of miles from Japan, the regime was clearly growing tired of the steady flow of complaints about the Dutch and decided it was time to act. On 12 October 1657 Wagenaer and his incoming replacement, Johannes Boucheljon, were summoned to the governor's residence in Nagasaki to receive a new order from Tokugawa authorities.[75] It consisted of three parts with a sting in the tail. The *Urk* was given permission to leave Nagasaki since it had not been involved in the original act of aggression, but the Bakufu ordered that some sort of compensation be paid to the owners of the junk for their losses. Finally, the Dutch were instructed to refrain from pursuing or damaging Chinese junks sailing to Japan. To both Wagenaer and Boucheljon it was obvious that the order represented something new. For the first time and without any warning, Edo had asserted its authority beyond the coastal waters around Japan to the trade routes binding the archipelago to distant ports and had directly intervened to order compensation.

But, for all the potential implications, the order also came with ample wiggle room. Lacking any real detail, it did not specify where the payment should be made, stipulate an actual sum, or mandate an acceptable time line. Unsurprisingly, VOC officials in Japan opted to play a waiting game in the hope that the Bakufu's determination to ensure that compensation was paid would eventually fade. In the meantime, the aggrieved merchants could be redirected to Batavia to seek restitution there, and, once in the company's headquarters, months or even years could be lost in its bureaucratic maze. At first the decision to do nothing seemed entirely vindicated. No further protests were raised in Nagasaki, and when Boucheljon made his annual trip to Edo he was informed that the shogun had not yet issued a formal edict concerning Chinese shipping.[76] In its current state, therefore, the admonition not to attack tōjin vessels was simply a recommendation that lacked the binding force of law.

By early 1658 it seemed as if the company was in the clear, and the opperhoofd could be forgiven for thinking that he had evaded responsibility. In fact, the legal net thrown around the factory by the first petition was beginning to tighten. In August a second group of Chinese merchants arrived in Nagasaki to protest the *Breukelen* incident.[77] Led by the captain of the junk itself, described in the *Dagregister* as Tantsinquan, this was a more formidable delegation that was determined to see the case to justice.[78] Explaining that he had already sought and failed to receive proper restitution in both Tayouan and Batavia, Tantsinquan submitted a new petition to the two bugyō, Kainoshō Masanobu and Kurokawa Yohyōe Masanao (in office 1650–65), who responded by calling in the Dutch interpreters to explain why no compensation had yet been paid. In this second petition Tantsinquan valued his lost goods at around thirty thousand taels, a figure that came very close to the eventual payout.[79]

In Nagasaki, Boucheljon continued to stall by explaining that Zheng Chenggong had submitted his own claim for one hundred thousand taels to Batavia and that this matter had to be settled before Tantsinquan's petition could even be discussed.[80] With both sides prepared to fight, the case dragged on, but it was becoming clear that some compensation would need to be paid out in either Nagasaki or Batavia. Before this could happen, however, the Bakufu moved to formalize its 1657 order. In October 1659 Zacharias Wagenaer, who had returned for a second term as opperhoofd, was issued with a Bakufu order banning all attacks on Chinese shipping. The relevant provision stated simply that the Dutch "shall not pirate [bahan] Chinese ships [tōsen] coming by sea to Japan."[81] Although typically brief, the edict represented an important next step in the Bakufu's response to VOC privateering. It was first of all a damning reminder that, despite all their attempts to distinguish between the need to "maintain their rights with weapons" and maritime predation, the Dutch remained unable to shake the pirate stain. As before, the term bahan boxed the company in, allowing no room to appeal, negotiate special exemptions, or argue for a more nuanced ruling that might permit some attacks while prohibiting others.

At the same time, the ruling significantly expanded the boundaries of Tokugawa authority. Whereas in 1621 the Bakufu had prohibited all acts of bahan in the waters near Japan, the 1659 edict focused on a single group rather than a specific maritime space. It effectively asserted legal rights over tōjin merchants, who were drawn under Bakufu protection for the first time. But, because the edict covered these individuals as they moved between their home ports and Japan, the result was a significant geographical expansion of the limits of Bakufu justice. Indeed, the order had the implicit effect of pushing legal markers out along a series of maritime corridors extending beyond the archipelago to Japan's primary trading partners. After 1659 any shipping falling within the broad category of Chinese vessel or tōsen was exempt from attack and any captain able to provide some evidence that he was on his way to Japan could expect to find redress in Nagasaki. For the company, it was a particularly difficult pill to swallow as it meant that all "Chinese ships coming by sea to Japan" had access to the Bakufu's legal structures regardless of how far away they were from Nagasaki.

The result was to hand the Nagasaki bugyō policing rights over a vast expanse of ocean.

The 1659 edict represented a new evolution in the Bakufu's ongoing response to VOC privateering, and it marked the final stage in a long process during which the regime's definition of its own legal rights had shifted from the deck of the shuinsen to a band around the archipelago before settling on entire trade routes. While the spark had been supplied by *Breukelen*'s reckless actions, the impetus for the 1659 edict had clearly been building for a number of years. Despite occasional statements about the unimportance of trade and the low status of merchants, the Tokugawa regime relied on Chinese traders to connect the archipelago to wider commercial networks and assure the flow of vital commodities required by the Japanese economy.[82] Chinese vessels consistently brought in larger quantities of goods than the Dutch, and unrestricted maritime violence threatened to cut these circuits. As illustration of this, the best account of the rationale for the new order was provided by a senior Bakufu official who explained that the Dutch "should refrain from seizing Chinese junks as they supply this realm with many necessary goods."[83] Another noted that Japan could not manage without the "silk goods, medicines, and other commodities" brought by Chinese merchants to Japan.[84] By asserting its authority over trade routes, the regime acted, therefore, to secure the supply of goods into Japan.

Back in Nagasaki and presumably buoyed by word of the new edict, Tantsinquan continued to negotiate behind the scenes to advance his petition. In October 1660 the bugyō took another step along the long road to final resolution when they attached a figure, 27,096 taels, to the basic demand for compensation.[85] As the governors' determination to extract payment hardened, so did the company's attitude. In 1657 it was still possible to contemplate some kind of compensation in the hope that it might pacify Zheng Chenggong, who was too formidable a foe to anger unnecessarily, but as relations with their rival deteriorated VOC officials became less and less willing to make even the slightest concessions. By 1660 it was increasingly clear that Chenggong had set his sights on Taiwan, which he planned to turn into an impregnable base from which to continue his campaign against the Qing.[86] As they nervously debated these plans, VOC officials in Japan were insistent that they could not consider "giving the Chinese here any restitution or in the slightest way promising to do so in the future."[87] How could they, the opperhoofd asked, contemplate paying out to a group of merchants associated with the very rival that threatened the company's key East Asian possession?

Despite this resistance, the pressure continued to ratchet up, and in October 1662, five years after the original complaint, the company's agents in Japan were backed into a corner. With no alternative in sight, they agreed to hand over the full sum to Nagasaki officials.[88] While it had taken years to produce a result, the *Breukelen* case provides tangible proof of the power of the petition and the ease with which even the strongest of European overseas enterprises could become entangled within legal nets. It was to be followed just a few years later by another legal controversy involving Dutch and Chinese merchants that further constrained the company's ability to act against its declared enemies.

THE *KLAVERSKERK* INCIDENT

In the same year that the *Breukelen* case was finally settled, the company suffered arguably its most significant setback since its establishment sixty years earlier when Fort Zeelandia, its headquarters on Tayouan, fell to Zheng forces after a long siege. Faced with such a devastating loss, but without the resources to retake the island, Batavia was determined to strike back at Zheng shipping, both to gain some compensation for its conquered colony but also to revive the company's shattered reputation.[89] To achieve these ends, the company assembled a powerful fleet of twelve ships manned by 756 sailors and 528 soldiers under the command of Balthasar Bort.[90] It was dispatched from Batavia in June 1662 with instructions to attack any shipping connected with Zheng Chenggong, including the rich trading junks sailing between China and Japan. So that there was no ambiguity, Bort was specifically authorized to take the fight into Japanese waters if prizes could be seized there.[91] Aware that such an aggressive campaign would inevitably prompt a response in Japan, VOC agents on Deshima were instructed to inform Bakufu officials of their plans, but to also make it clear that their superiors were determined to exact revenge on Zheng shipping regardless of whether or not the shogun consented.[92] The company had an absolute right, they insisted, granted to them by the law of nations to attack such targets whenever and wherever they were encountered.[93] The result was to set the stage for renewed conflict with the Bakufu over VOC privateering.

In the end it was not Bort's fleet that instigated the inevitable confrontation, but one of the company's regular trading vessels. On 29 August 1663 a VOC *fluyt*, the *Klaverskerk*, encountered a Chinese junk on its way from Chaozhou in Guangdong province.[94] When it was sighted, the junk was just seventy-five miles south of the island of Meshima on the sea routes leading into Japan.[95] There was thus, in contrast to the *Breukelen*'s earlier prize, no question that it was destined for Nagasaki. As the *Klaverskerk* closed, its captain discovered that the vessel from Chaozhou was already in distress, having been demasted in a recent storm. Although they had no means of escape, the Chinese crew refused to allow the *Klaverskerk*'s sailors to come on board to conduct an inspection, prompting the Dutch vessel to respond with force by firing on the junk until it was "shot to smithereens" and ready to sink.[96] Leaving its target foundering, *Klaverskerk* resumed its course and reached Nagasaki on 1 September where the master reported the details of the encounter to the incumbent opperhoofd, Hendrick Indijck. Although the attack had produced no actual plunder, there was also little reason to fear any repercussions as the chance of survivors was minimal at best.[97] It appeared, therefore, an easy, if clearly minor, victory in the company's war against Zheng forces.

On 11 September, however, word reached the Japan factory that seven Chinese sailors from the destroyed vessel had washed ashore on the Gotō Islands.[98] Some weeks later a second group of survivors was discovered on the barren slopes of Meshima.[99] Once they had recovered, both groups made their way to Nagasaki where they moved rapidly— and entirely predictably—to file a petition with the bugyō. As compensation, they demanded 150 cases (150,000 taels) of silver, a massive sum far in excess of the final award to Tantsinquan.[100] For officials in Edo, who received the petition via fast messenger from Nagasaki, the *Klaverskerk* case represented a difficult quandary.[101] While there could be no question that the company had broken the regime's 1659 proclamation, which applied to all Chinese ships coming to Japan, there was also, given the open war between Zheng Chenggong and the Dutch, grounds for restraint. By the time it received word of the *Klaverskerk* episode, Edo was well aware that Zheng forces had seized the Dutch settlement on Tayouan, and the prospect of repeatedly intervening in a conflict that looked set to continue for years cannot have been particularly palatable.[102]

In the end the Bakufu opted for the middle ground, issuing a decision that reached Nagasaki on 1 February 1664. For once both the original Japanese edict and the Dutch translation are extant, with the former reading as follows.

> At this time, near Meshima there was an attack on a Chinese ship. This is totally outrageous. This is certainly something that should be punished. But we believe this is intended as retaliation for Koxinga's attack on Taiwan. In the 6th month of Manji 4 (1661), a letter came to the Nagasaki magistrate that Taiwan had been attacked. This complaint reached the ears of the shogun, and so this time it has been forgiven. From now on, if Chinese vessels coming to Japan are attacked, even if they are far from Japan, then they [the Dutch] will be punished. This should be transmitted to Holland. The Dutch should also come . . . to present their greetings in Edo. In Edo, there will be further orders, which they will be told about.[103]

It was a decidedly mixed message. Encouragingly for the Dutch, it omitted the term *bahan* and the automatic designation of VOC privateering as piracy, acknowledging instead that the company was involved in an ongoing conflict that had been precipitated by Zheng Chenggong's invasion of Taiwan. At the same, however, the Bakufu condemned the *Klaverskerk* affair as an "outrageous" (*futodoki senban*) violation of past orders that clearly merited punishment. Its final conclusion was a one-off exemption for the incident paired with a requirement for the Dutch to come to Edo to discuss what had happened directly with the regime.

In March 1664, the new opperhoofd, Willem Volger, reached the Tokugawa capital to hear the promised "further orders." Subjected to a lengthy interrogation, he was asked to explain in "all sincerity, how do you think His Majesty [the shogun], who has forbidden the taking of junks coming to Japan to trade, on pain of his highest displeasure, will think of this matter."[104] Volger's response was to insist that the company's war with Coxinga had no connection with the Bakufu and hence that the *Klaverskerk* incident required no decision from Edo: "Our lord general in Jaccatra [Batavia] could not grasp and still cannot understand that the slightest misdeed has been done to the Japanese realm in carrying out a just war [*rechtveerdigen oorlogh*] against the faithless Chinese of Coxinja as revenge for their great damage and abuse they have done to us on Formosa and Tayouan."[105] But, rather than signing off on this logic, Bakufu officials continued to insist that any attack on Zheng shipping was unacceptable while offering an individual loophole for the *Klaverskerk* incident, which had, they explained, been "done by inexperienced people who have no knowledge of Japanese customs."[106] It came attached to a familiar condition that any further attacks on Chinese shipping would prompt swift punishment and Volger was cautioned that if this happened again the Dutch would learn the true "seriousness His Majesty's [the shogun] commands."[107]

The contradictory nature of the response makes it difficult to interpret. Given the fact that there was an ongoing war in the region, it is possible read this decision as a retreat from the Bakufu's prior insistence that it would punish all attacks on Chinese shipping regardless of where they took place, but this assessment seems less convincing if we examine how the company actually reacted to its apparent good fortune. VOC policy after the incident makes it clear that the *Klaverskerk* exemption had the opposite effect, further entrenching the Tokugawa regime's authority over the sea-lanes leading into the archipelago. The obvious penalty for breaking one of the shogun's laws was to expel the Dutch from Japan, and it was clear that this had been discussed as a potential punishment for the episode.[108] As satisfying as it might have been, such a decision would have been fraught with potential dangers.

Pushing the Dutch out of Japan would have put them firmly beyond the Bakufu's reach, rendering them far more menacing. With no fear of retribution on land, the company would be free to pursue its war against Zheng shipping unhindered and could cut off key trading routes to Japan. A sense of the regime's dilemma is provided by a revealing conversation between the opperhoofd and a local contact: "A merchant living in Edo told us . . . that before we came to Edo, he was called by the councilors and asked: if the Hollanders were [forced] out from Japan, would the trade of the Chinese grow and become double what it is today, as they had been informed? They answered no and if the Hollanders were expelled the Chinese trade would not increase but would decrease. There was no doubt that the Hollanders would seek to keep the Chinese out of Japan in any way possible and would hinder their voyages."[109]

Coming from a contemporary observer with a long history of contact with the company, it was a succinct summary of what might happen if the Dutch were expelled from Japan and the potential perils that could accompany this decision.

In the end, as these comments make clear, the Bakufu's hold on the company depended on keeping its agents within reach and susceptible to future penalties. What was needed then was to keep the Dutch close at hand while ensuring that they were sufficiently intimidated not to try such aggressive actions again. And this was precisely what the regime's decision achieved. While no punishment was immediately forthcoming, VOC officials were left in no doubt that another violation of the Bakufu's laws would lead to unacceptably punitive consequences. As a result, when it received word of the regime's warning, Batavia moved quickly to suspend its campaign against Zheng shipping sailing to Japan. While protesting that the company had every right to engage in lawful war, the governor-general instructed his subordinates to inform the Bakufu that he had received the shogun's command and would honor it.[110] The message was dutifully delivered in September 1665 when the opperhoofd informed the Nagaskai bugyō that all campaigns against Chinese maritime traffic coming to Japan had been abandoned because of the shogun's edict.[111] In this way the Bakufu succeeded in halting a determined maritime operation that had threatened to disrupt the flow of goods into Japan.[112]

Forced to accept an edict that they could do nothing to alter, the Dutch scrambled once again to map out more precise boundaries of Bakufu authority. Much as they had done after the promulgation of the 1621 edict, VOC officials attempted to draw lines on a map delineating the limits of the shogun's authority and hence allowing action beyond these markers. The opperhoofd in Japan was instructed to find out exactly how far the Bakufu's jurisdiction extended into the ocean.[113] If, for example, a Zheng junk was taken in the Taiwan straits or on its way from China to Manila, would this constitute a fair prize or another site for the exercise of Tokugawa legal rights?[114] The opperhoofd was to press, above all else, for precision, to discover exactly how many miles beyond Japan the company might be permitted to act freely.[115] As before, however, Tokugawa officials refused to provide any further details, with the result that the VOC was forced to adopt the most cautious attitude possible by carefully avoiding any acts of aggression against Chinese shipping.

The long-term effect was to ensure that the Dutch had little choice but to compete peacefully with merchants attached to the Zheng maritime network. With the threat of violence removed, a trade boom ensued between Taiwan and Nagasaki. Between 1663 and 1673 a total of 111 ships arrived in Nagasaki from Taiwan, then under the control of Coxinga's son Zheng Jing, bringing large quantities of goods and disrupting VOC profits.[116] Xing Hang estimates that the Zheng network brought in between 564,037 and 605,464 taels per year in trade with Nagasaki, meaning that, in his words, "Zheng Jing maintained the family's superiority over the Dutch at Nagasaki, capturing, at the very least, half of the Japanese market in terms of both revenue and income."[117]

AN OCEAN OF LAW

There can be no question that the VOC was a formidable maritime power both in terms of its ships and its potent language of legal justification. It was also an organization accustomed to violence that made use of maritime force as a fundamental tool of policy. But in the waters around Japan, and on the sea routes linking the archipelago to other Asian ports, we see very little evidence of this. By any measure, the years from 1609 onward produced a remarkably meager record of success, whether against Portuguese or Chinese shipping, for what was after all the "largest, best-capitalized privateering enterprise in the world."[118]

The history of the petitions submitted in Nagasaki or Edo by aggrieved merchants shows that maritime encounters did not always end when the weaker vessel surrendered or was destroyed and that it is not enough simply to focus on technology without considering the political context in which it operated. These documents and the Tokugawa response draw attention to the fact that the early modern seas were not the empty expanses they are sometimes imagined as, essentially lawless zones in which Europeans were able to make full and unrestricted use of their superior maritime firepower. Instead, organizations like the VOC found they could become swiftly entangled within the confining grip of legal structures that stripped away their ability to act when they were most determined to do so.

The previous chapter suggested, following Benton's work, that the ocean can be seen as an unpredictable space filled with law and characterized by the presence of "jurisdictional tangles."[119] With this in mind, it argued that a second map delineating legal markers can be productively overlaid onto the familiar charts of empty spaces to produce a more accurate image of the early modern seas. An examination of the company's privateering campaigns in Japan provides some sense of what one section of such a map might look like. Beginning with a limited scattering of dots marking individual vessels carrying shuinjō, Bakufu legal markers ballooned out in this period to a loosely defined band encircling the archipelago before expanding once again to encompass long sea corridors. The result was that Dutch administrators and captains were forced to confront a complex legal landscape whenever they sought to run out their guns, effectively limiting the company's capacity to make use of its most effective weapon.

3
Sovereignty

CHAPTER SIX

PLANTING THE FLAG IN ASIA

Tayouan is a place without a king or a lord and they [the Japanese]
have as much right as you to it.

—Matsura Takanobu, 1633

In 1625 two Japanese vessels arrived in the bay of Tayouan on the west
coast of the island of Taiwan.[1] The contours of the bay, sheltered from
the ocean by the sweeping curve of a sandy peninsula, were a familiar
sight to their captains and crew, who had been sailing to the island for a
number of years to rendezvous with Chinese traders far from the prying
eyes of Ming officials. But this year, peering out from the swaying deck
of their ship, they confronted something new. Perched on the peninsula
was a small fort facing out to the open sea and protected by the jutting
muzzles of naval cannons. Hastily erected with low walls, the makeshift
structure inspired little trepidation, particularly in comparison to the
vast citadels scattered across early modern Japan, but its construction
marked a pivotal moment in the history of Taiwan. In a few short years
the island, which despite its close proximity to China had remained
outside government control for centuries, was subject to an aggressive
transformation that turned it from a stateless space into the company's
"beautiful colony."[2]

The colonization of Tayouan represented the company's bold-
est experiment in East Asia. A direct product of article 35 of its charter, which gave the organization the right to plant fortresses and

strongholds across Asia, it sent ripples of impact flowing out through the wider region. When the company asserted its authority over incoming vessels by enforcing trading restrictions and requiring the payment of taxes, it came swiftly into conflict with Japanese traders, who had already been using the bay for a number of years. As first these merchants and then Bakufu officials in Edo pushed back against its exclusionary tactics, the company responded by deploying an aggressive legal language of sovereignty and possession that it had used with great effect in similar disputes with its European competitors.

European claims to sovereignty over territory in Asia were frequently contentious and produced a series of both rhetorical and more violent skirmishes. These disputes form a traditional topic of analysis within the broader history of European expansion and have generated a significant volume of studies. Most histories of Europeans in Asia include, for example, a section on the long struggle between the Dutch and English companies for sovereignty over the Spice Islands.[3] Such studies are unified by a focus on disputes between Europeans, and they combine to show clashes over sovereignty as a closed loop fed by a shared, if vigorously contested, vocabulary. When Asian political actors appear, they do so in most cases as unwilling participants, whose sovereignty was subject to steady erosion, or as silent allies, tossed from one side to another. But what happened when European claims to sovereignty over a peripheral zone triggered a response from an Asian state rather than another group of Europeans, or when a language of possession deployed so effectively in intra-European disputes encountered a different audience?

The conflict over the bay of Tayouan provides a rare example of a clash played out between an Asian state and a European overseas enterprise over rights to a nonaligned space. The result was yet more frustration for Batavia, which discovered—as it had when it attempted to justify aggressive maritime campaigns—that carefully constructed arguments about legal rights yielded no benefit when deployed before Bakufu officials who shared none of the same assumptions. Even worse, the gulf between Dutch and Japanese ideas about what to do with a territory like Tayouan prompted a steady escalation of the conflict as VOC agents, reading Bakufu actions against a European script that had little relevance in Japan, drove the dispute forward onto dangerous ground.

As these points suggests, the conflict over Tayouan can best be understood as a clash between two world orders. On the one side was a distinctively European model of direct sovereignty over colonial possessions justified through the invocation of a shared repertoire of practices and ceremonies. Arrayed against this was a hierarchical model of foreign relations—borrowed from China but inflected by the particular needs of the Tokugawa regime—organized around the voluntary submission of tribute and justified in those terms. Acknowledging this clash helps explain why the conflict developed in the way it did. It also permits comparison with a later period and there is an obvious parallel with the more famous nineteenth-century encounter between Western models and an East Asian international order.[4] But if it involved similar opponents, the seventeenth-century iteration had a very different outcome. In contrast to the more familiar dynamic, the Japanese government made no move to embrace an essentially European vision of international relations. Instead, it was the Western partner that was forced to concede ground and shift away from its initial assertions.

Of the three contained conflicts described in this study, the clash over sovereignty was the most compressed and the most limited. In contrast to the struggle over diplomatic rights, which saw the Dutch transformed from sovereign ambassadors into loyal vassals, or violence, which prompted the abandonment of important maritime campaigns, its long-term consequences were less obvious. It did not, for example, result in the collapse or even the temporary suspension of the company's colonial project on Taiwan, which endured until its overthrow by Zheng Chenggong's armies in 1662. Nonetheless, the conflict did have consequences. Most obviously, it provided yet another demonstration of the limited power of the company's legal vocabulary in Japan. Just as the Dutch found themselves unable to convince the Bakufu of their right to engage in privateering campaigns in Japanese waters, so too did they fail to persuade Edo that they were the legal masters of the bay of Tayouan. The result was another retreat from the company's insistence on the inviolability of its sovereign rights in favor of a more accommodating policy. At the same time, the conflict over sovereignty was directly responsible for a rupture in relations between the company and the shogun that ended in the remarkable act of surrender, the handing over of the former governor of Tayouan to Bakufu jurisdiction, described in chapter 7.

COLONIAL TAYOUAN

After its creation in 1602, the company experimented with a range of strategies designed to secure it access to the coveted prize of Chinese trade. When a series of expeditions failed to break through even the first layer of provincial officials, VOC leaders resolved in 1622 to shift to a new strategy by attempting to seize control of Macao, the one European settlement with a foothold in China proper. To achieve their aims, the Dutch assembled a powerful fleet of eight vessels with over a thousand sailors and soldiers under the command of Cornelis Reijersen. Despite the size of the force and the weakness of Macao's defenses, the attack faltered and the fleet was forced to retreat with many casualties.[5] Having failed to take the city, Reijersen proceeded to implement his secondary instructions, which called for a fortified base to be established near the coast of China.[6] Although Taiwan provided an obvious location for such a settlement, the choice settled on the far smaller Penghu or Pescadores Islands that lay in the straits between China and Taiwan.

The occupation of the Penghu Islands, combined with an aggressive privateering campaign designed to force Ming officials to open trading links, triggered a predictable backlash. Local authorities in Fujian, the closest province, demanded that the Dutch demolish their fort and retreat from the Penghus, which they viewed as Chinese territory that must be defended from foreign incursions. When the Dutch refused, the situation settled into a stalemate that lasted until 1624 when a large Chinese force of 150 war junks and 10,000 men assembled "to continue the war against us until we were driven from the Pescadores and out of Chinese jurisdiction."[7] To ward off the impending assault, the Dutch could muster just a few hundred men under the command of Martinus Sonck, who had recently replaced Reijersen.[8] Massively outnumbered, Sonck's last hope rested on negotiating a compromise with Chinese officials who might, he reasoned correctly, be interested in avoiding conflict if a suitable compromise could be reached.

It was against this backdrop that Taiwan emerged as an option acceptable to both sides. Unlike the Penghus, the island lay on the peripheries of the Chinese political order, dismissed as "beyond the seas" (*haiwai*) and having no link to the emperor.[9] It was therefore, as Dutch sources constantly repeated, "outside the jurisdiction of China" (*buyten de jurisdictie van China*) and could be freely occupied.[10] The move to Taiwan offered advantages to both sides. The Dutch could operate there without constraint, shielded by the Taiwan straits from the gaze of Ming officials, while the commanders of the Chinese fleet could claim credit for ousting a group of dangerous foreigners from the emperor's territory. In late August an agreement was reached when the Dutch were informed that if they destroyed their fort on the Penghu Islands and retreated to Taiwan trade relations would be opened and a regular supply of goods assured.[11]

While the terms of the deal were broadly acceptable, Sonck was desperate to secure a more definite promise, preferably in the form of an official contract signed by senior Ming officials. When it became clear that no such document would be forthcoming, he was forced to order the move to Taiwan based only on the vague promises he had already received. While the Dutch believed, and would later argue, that the Ming state had transferred sovereignty over Taiwan through this agreement, there is no evidence in Chinese records that it was anything more than a temporary arrangement orchestrated by relatively low-ranking officials whose sole concern was the expulsion of the Dutch from Chinese territory. It was never the binding promise or the definite cession of territory imagined in VOC documents—a point made clear in the official chronicle of the Ming dynasty, the *Mingshi*, which described the campaign in simple terms as a victory over a foreign invasion that concluded when the Dutch "fled by sea . . . removing the blight of the ocean."[12]

For the company's new base, Sonck, appointed its first governor, selected the bay of Tayouan on the west coast of the island.[13] The result of this decision was to bring the Dutch into contact with the Siraya, a subgroup within the larger Taiwanese aboriginal population that occupied the coastal plans spread across the southwest of the island.[14] Near Tayouan the VOC discovered four Siraya villages, Sinkan, Soulang, Baccluan, and Mattau, with an estimated total population of over ten thousand, that would come to play a key role in the first decades of the colony.[15] The bay of Tayouan, the site of the new settlement, formed a natural harbor that was protected from the open sea by a hooked promontory. Rather than moving directly onto the island, the Dutch elected to establish a fort on this peninsula, which offered a more readily defensible position.[16] Initially named Orangie, later rechristened Zeelandia, the stronghold became the center of the company's colonial project on Taiwan.

At first limited to the sandy banks of the peninsula, Zeelandia's authority quickly expanded onto the island proper, lapping around unclaimed areas before spilling over to submerge new lands and people beneath its authority. From their headquarters near the fort, a string of VOC governors proceeded to deploy the familiar apparatus of European colonial control, sending out expeditions to survey the coastline, laying out new towns, building forts and warehouses, bringing in settlers, binding indigenous communities to their authority, creating systems of registration and taxation, and working in a variety of other ways to reshape Tayouan by inscribing authority over land and bodies. The result was that the Dutch proceeded to exert direct control over an expanding section of the island, digging in deep roots that would not be easily dislodged.

The sudden appearance of the Dutch in Tayouan sparked a reaction from a number of groups including the Spanish in Manila, Chinese pirate groups (such as the one led by Zheng Zhilong), and Japanese merchants. Of these, it was the last that proved to be the most immediate threat to the new colony. Japan-based merchants, who had been sailing regularly to Tayouan for a number of years, had no intention of relinquishing access to their thriving and completely unregulated trading hub. The predictable result was a series of clashes that disrupted relations between the company and the shogun.

RESTRICTION AND RESISTANCE

By the time the company moved onto Tayouan, well-established commercial links already existed between Japan and the island. VOC officials noted that two or three Japanese junks arrived in Tayouan each year to purchase deer hides and to rendezvous with Chinese junks, which arrived there laden with silk.[17] The Japan-Tayouan route was initially dominated by the Chinese merchant community and particularly by its chief, Li Dan, but his death in 1625 caused it to pass into the hands of two merchant/officials, Suetsugu Heizō Masanao (hereafter Heizō) and Hirano Tōjirō.[18] Although they were well aware of this connection, the Dutch had no intention of letting Japanese merchants trade freely in Tayouan. Motivated by a concern that the Japanese would undermine their plans to claim a role as middleman between Chinese sellers and the market in Japan, it was also consistent with the company's wider commercial strategy as it was implemented across Asia. Whenever possible, the VOC, an organization with little appetite for competition, attempted to establish monopoly control over trade by excluding potential rivals so it could gain a stranglehold on the most profitable goods. Indeed, its exclusionary tactics became the primary complaint leveled at it by European competitors such as the English East India Company, which vigorously protested these tactics.

In May 1625 Batavia sent a letter to Tayouan instructing Governor Sonck to stop Japanese merchants from trading there.[19] While the letter was still in transit, however, two Japanese junks, owned almost certainly by Heizō and Hirano, arrived in the bay of Tayouan.[20] Without clear instructions as to what to do, Sonck elected to implement a tax rather than an outright ban and informed the Japanese captains that they were now required to pay a levy of 10 percent on all goods taken out of Tayouan. As justification, he explained that the revenues from the tax were intended to contribute to the construction costs of Fort Zeelandia as well as other defensive expenditures the Dutch had been required to make to facilitate trade. In response, the Japanese captains argued that they had traded in Tayouan for a number of years before the Dutch arrived. Having turned the bay into a prosperous hub through their own efforts, they saw no reason why they should be liable for the company's fortifications, of which they had no need, or why they should be required to pay a toll to access what had always been a free trading port. As these negotiations continued, Japanese merchants aboard the two junks proceeded to buy up seventy thousand taels worth of silk and other goods.[21] The size of the transaction and the fact that it was all paid for in silver quickly pushed up the price of silk, thereby disrupting the company's own trading plans. When the Japanese continued to refuse any suggestion of a tax, Sonck, in an aggressive assertion of VOC rights, switched tactics by confiscating fifteen piculs or around nine hundred kilograms of silk from their cargo holds.[22]

News of what had happened traveled quickly back to Japan where Bakufu officials reprimanded two company envoys, Isaac Brogaert and Pieter Muijser, for their employer's policy. As they prepared to leave Edo on their way back to the factory, the pair was informed that the shogun was unhappy because he had "understood that the governor of the Hollanders nation resident in Tangesau or Tayouan intended to collect tolls from Japanese merchants trading there."[23] When he received the news, the factory's opperhoofd, Cornelis van Neijenroode, gloomily predicted that the "payment of tolls will cause great trouble here" and might destabilize the company's position in Japan.[24]

A second confrontation followed close on the heels of the first. In 1626 two more junks, including one captained by Heizō's trusted lieutenant, Hamada Yahyōe (sometimes Yahei), arrived in Tayouan carrying a huge quantity of silver estimated at around three hundred thousand taels.[25] Determined to safeguard the company's market, Zeelandia's new governor, Gerritt de Witt, informed the Japanese captains that they would be allowed to trade, but insisted on a vital restriction. Although they were free to do business in Tayouan, they were prohibited from purchasing raw silk, the most valuable commodity available on the island and one that was central to their trading plans.[26] A further clash soon developed over maritime passage to China. The previous year, Hamada had negotiated a large delivery of silk goods from merchants in Fujian, but, due to a surge in pirate activity in the Taiwan straits, these remained in China and needed to be fetched.[27] The obvious solution, for Hamada and his men to sail directly to Fujian, worried the Dutch, who feared that the appearance of heavily armed Japanese vessels in Chinese waters might antagonize Ming officials and ruin their own chances of gaining access to goods from the mainland.

After much pressing, de Witt agreed to allow transit, but imposed strict conditions by requiring the Japanese to use smaller, less well-armed ships that would not be mistaken for a hostile fleet. Not surprisingly Hamada refused to brave the Taiwan straits—dangerous waters plagued by pirates and unpoliced by any authority—with such vessels and protested that the Dutch had no right to bar him from sailing to China. The negotiations over these issues dragged on for weeks, stalling trade and damaging Japanese profits. Later, Heizō, the master of Hamada's junk, would claim that he had lost some two hundred piculs (approximately twelve thousand kilograms) of silk because of these restrictions, and, while this was probably an exaggeration, his bottom line was clearly under pressure.[28]

By 1626, therefore, the terms of the conflict were clearly established. On the one side were VOC officials, who argued that their claims to sovereignty over the bay of Tayouan meant that they were within their rights to prohibit trade entirely, tax incoming vessels or implement any manner of restriction. Arrayed against them were Japanese merchants who refused to recognize Dutch assertions that they were masters of the bay or that previously free activities were somehow subject to supervision just because the company had erected a small fort. To break the impasse, Batavia, employing tactics it had used with considerable success in disputes with other European powers, launched a rhetorical campaign designed to convince Bakufu officials of its superior rights to Tayouan and the legal underpinnings of its presence on the island. The result was an attempt, arguably for the first time, to press a distinctively European language of sovereignty and possession into service in Japan.

In instructions issued to its representatives and in documents sent to Japan, the company produced a standard genealogy of its claims, all hinging on the same carefully manipulated story. In Hirado, the factory's opperhoofd received detailed instructions describing how best to present the company's rights to Tayouan, while VOC agents traveling to Japan for the first time were provided with almost identical versions of the same arguments to be deployed whenever possible in discussions with Bakufu officials.[29] When oral presentation failed to elicit the appropriate reaction, the company was also prepared to dispatch lengthy documents, including page after page of tightly reasoned arguments designed to demonstrate once and for all why the "sovereignty of the Hollanders over this land cannot be doubted."[30] Across the years, these explanations displayed a notable consistency, returning again and again to the same script and hammering home an identical message about the incontrovertible nature of the company's rights.

DEFENDING SOVEREIGNTY

In documents sent to Japan, VOC agents referred repeatedly to their "sovereignty" (*souverainiteyt*) over Tayouan and the lands around it, although they refrained from stipulating precise boundaries.[31] Such rights did not derive from an understanding of Taiwan or indeed of Asia more generally as an empty space, a *terra nullius* in which sovereignty could be claimed by the first group of Europeans that arrived. To the contrary, both company administrators on the ground and legal scholars in the United Provinces were quick to acknowledge the political rights of local rulers and people. Hugo Grotius, who wrote copiously on the subject, provided a succinct expression of this when he commented that Asian lands and territories "now have and always have had their own kings, their own government, their own laws, and their own legal systems."[32] This recognition was paired, however, with a malleable sense of sovereignty that could be readily turned to the organization's advantage.[33]

The company conceived of sovereignty as a readily transferrable commodity that could be acquired through a variety of mechanisms, some of which required only the most limited consent from local rulers or communities. This view was underpinned by, as Edward Keene has demonstrated, an understanding of sovereignty as a collection of rights—rather than a monolithic and indivisible whole—that could be split up and parceled out to more than one party according to the exigencies of the moment.[34] The result was a tripartite division of the company's area of operations, as expressed most clearly in the Heeren 17's famous 1650 instructions, according to the extent of its own claims to sovereignty.[35] At the bottom of the hierarchy were areas such as Japan, in which the company enjoyed no special privileges and where the issue of sovereignty was immaterial for it could not be claimed. One step up were territories in which the organization had, by virtue of exclusive agreement, claimed partial sovereignty, usually in terms of economic rights to certain key crops and markets. At the top of the triangle were lands or settlements, including Batavia and Tayouan, over which it exerted full sovereignty. Given the company's limited resources, such spaces were rare commodities and included just a handful of territories in which it could operate untrammeled by another political will.

The company claimed sovereignty through a range of mechanisms, all of which were subject to ready manipulation to ensure the best opportunities for profit and power. The most straightforward of these was the "right of conquest."[36] In the right conditions and assuming a just cause, something that a Grotian interpretation of natural law was usually able to provide, territory could be claimed after a violent battle in which rights to land and power were transferred from the defeated to the victor.[37] The company had taken possession of the territory on which Batavia sat, claimed by force of arms after a brief war with the local prince, in this way.[38] Such cases were, however, relatively rare, and the far more common mechanism for the transfer of sovereignty involved a cession of rights from a local authority, preferably willingly, but if necessary under duress. The usual vehicle for accomplishing this was the treaty, hundreds of which are gathered together in Heeres and Stapel's diplomatic compilation.[39] In some cases, these agreements transferred full sovereignty to the Company, but the more common practice was for a partial cession of some sovereign rights.[40]

In its earliest treaties the company often gained very limited rights, usually involving monopoly privileges to certain trade goods, but then worked over time to gradually expand the boundaries of its sovereignty by encroaching on the powers claimed by local rulers. This was the case in modern-day Sri Lanka where the company accrued, over a period of several decades, more and more rights until it was able to claim sovereignty over a large part of the island.[41] In places where it was not possible to sign a treaty, sovereignty could also be transferred through a well-timed ceremony. This occurred, for example, in Taiwan in the 1630s when a number of Siraya villages offered local products to Fort Zeelandia as a token of their submission.[42] In other cases the simple act of accepting protection could, VOC officials argued, result in an implicit cession of at least partial sovereignty to the company, which gained such rights in return for defending the local population against an often vaguely defined threat.[43]

Given this range of mechanisms, how had Tayouan been claimed, and, perhaps the more important question, in what form was this logic of possession presented to the Bakufu? The most straightforward logic, the right of conquest, could not be applied to the island as there had been no single battle or other military action in which the company had established itself by dint of arms. Instead, Batavia claimed, and defended its rights to, Tayouan by pointing to an act of cession from local authorities to the company's representatives. The issue was complicated by the fact that both the island as a whole and the bay of Tayouan in particular lacked a single sovereign figure, equivalent to a king or chief, capable of (even in theory) ceding control. As a result, when presenting their claims in Japan, the Dutch paired two lines of argument together, suggesting that they had secured both an actual contract with Chinese authorities and an implicit agreement with the local Siraya population. In the words of one VOC official, Tayouan had been "lawfully occupied . . . through a contract with China and because of the consent of the inhabitants themselves."[44]

The first argument centered on rights conferred after the conclusion of the company's war with the Ming in 1624. In explaining this logic to the Bakufu, VOC representatives were careful to emphasize the justness of the initial conflict in order that they not appear as violent aggressors. One explained that "for more than twenty years our nation has made friendly requests in the appropriate way to open Chinese trade, but our friendly overtures did not have the desired effect and so we were forced to seek the same through war."[45] The subsequent agreement was described as a binding accord, "ratified in solemn form" by senior Ming officials, giving the company permanent rights to take up residence in Tayouan and guaranteeing Chinese authorities would open trade with the Dutch.[46] The uncomfortable fact that no documentary evidence existed to back up this claim was glossed over in favor of repeated assertions that the government of China had given the Dutch permission to settle in Tayouan and to use the territory in any way they desired.

Alongside this argument, the company maintained that local villagers had willingly ceded control over the bay to its agents. In his instructions to the opperhoofd in Japan as to how best to present the case, the governor-general advised him to emphasize the "willing reception" of the indigenous inhabitants as a key plank of the company's rights.[47] Along these lines, one VOC official explained "when we came [to Tayouan] the inhabitants of this land received us in such a welcoming fashion that . . . they not only permitted us to construct a fort for our protection, and hence to take possession of this place, but willingly asked us to protect and shelter their people with our strength and authority."[48] To strengthen its case, the company took pains to emphasize Siraya backwardness by providing long descriptions of the supposed poverty, savagery, and general anarchy of the villages. This, in turn, justified the absence of a written contract or official agreement ceding territory to the Dutch. Since they were "poor and barbarous people" with no clear leaders, the act of willing reception described by the governor-general functioned in the same way as a more formal treaty, allowing Batavia to assume possession of the surrounding lands.[49] In addition to endorsing Dutch control over the bay, local villagers had, VOC officials argued, eagerly transformed themselves into colonial subjects by accepting Fort Zeelandia's protection against their enemies.[50] The result was that they had surrendered political independence in return for the shelter provided by VOC arms—a point that suddenly assumed considerable importance when an embassy made up of some of these villagers arrived in Japan in 1627.

By the time it came to defend its rights to Tayouan, the company had a great deal of experience in using sovereignty claims to ward off potential rivals, having just emerged largely triumphant from a long dispute with the English East India Company over control of the Banda Islands, a small chain in modern Indonesia that, like Tayouan, lacked a clear indigenous overlord.[51] But in Japan a similar campaign designed to assert the company's rights to Tayouan proved far less compelling. Although the Dutch tried persistently and with the occasional flash of aggression to push their case, the result was always the same, a deafening silence as Bakufu officials refused to engage with the company's carefully constructed arguments. In those rare instances in which Tokugawa officials did respond, it was only to reject Dutch assertions while adding the refrain that the company could claim no special rights over Tayouan.

In 1626, for example, three Bakufu elders cornered a VOC agent at the shogun's court and explained that the Dutch had no right to stop Japanese merchants, who had visited the island for years, from trading in the bay of Tayouan.[52] The company was, they protested, acting "unfairly against all right and reason (*recht en reeden*)" by claiming a false dominion over the island. As the shogun was unwilling to "tolerate such a great wrong any longer," the Dutch must take immediate steps to open Tayouan up to trade.[53] While some opposition to VOC claims might have been expected, it was noteworthy that even the company's allies refused to accept its logic. The daimyo of Hirado, whose prosperity depended to a large extent on the continued success of Dutch trade, informed them that any attempt to maintain Tayouan "for you alone" will fail as Bakufu officials "know and will say that Tayouan is a place without a king or a lord and they [the Japanese] have as much right as you to it."[54]

When confronted with this reaction, VOC agents responded by finding evidence of hidden motives and thinly disguised conspiracies working against them. The villain must be, some suggested, Portuguese agents, who were working relentlessly to sabotage their position in Japan.[55] Others were convinced that they were the unfortunate victims of Japanese greed. Bakufu officials must be secret investors in Heizō's ships, causing them to resist the company's legitimate claims to sovereignty.[56] While some Tokugawa officials may have been motivated by financial considerations, this cannot fully account for the regime's persistent unwillingness to accept the logic of VOC claims, and we should be wary of accepting the evidence offered up by Dutch agents of hidden conspiracies arrayed against them. Rather, to gain a complete picture of why the company's campaign of persuasion faltered, we need to look again at the substance of arguments put forward and consider the possibility that these may have failed to gain ground in Japan because they made little sense there. Although Batavia presented its claims as the product of universal ideas that should be immediately recognizable to all parties, they derived in fact from a European language of sovereignty and possession that had no equivalent in Japan.

Although there was never a consensus on the precise mechanisms for claiming authority over new territories, Europeans made use of a shared, if always contested, language for sovereignty claims.[57] The result was that they operated within the same basic framework; first by recognizing that sovereignty could be transferred via ceremony or contract and second by making use of "a common repertoire" to facilitate this transfer.[58] This was evident in the aforementioned dispute over the Banda Islands, in which English East India Company representatives took issue not with the idea that sovereignty could be transferred via treaty but rather with the way in which the Dutch had done so.[59] As a result, the clash quickly settled into a familiar, largely predictable, pattern of claim and counterclaim in which strident arguments over sovereignty were backed up by competing readings of the "Law of Nations."[60] In the case of Tayouan, however, the VOC faced an audience that shared none of its assumptions about how foreign territories could be acquired. Instead, the Tokugawa Bakufu possessed its own mechanism for the political incorporation of places like Tayouan that had little in common with European models.

A JAPAN-CENTERED CIVILIZATIONAL ORDER

Having abandoned any attempt to find a place in the wider Chinese system, the Tokugawa regime set about constructing its own international order in the early seventeenth century. Sometimes called the Japan-centered civilizational order (*Nihon-gata kai chitsujo*), the Tokugawa model was adapted from the Chinese system, but reconfigured to place Japan and the shogun at the center as the locus of civilization (*ka*) surrounded by rings of increasingly barbaric (*i*) states.[61] Unlike the Chinese state, however, which could rely on its own prestige to attract participants, the Bakufu was forced to improvise to engineer the illusion of a world order in which outside sovereigns spontaneously recognized Tokugawa supremacy. To acquire the necessary satellites, rulers willing to bring their kingdoms into the Tokugawa order as tributaries, it was prepared to take unorthodox measures, including sanctioning the use of force. Thus, in 1609, Satsuma domain received permission from the first shogun to invade the Ryukyu kingdom, an independent state located in current-day Okinawa.[62] One year later the captive monarch, Shō Nei, was dutifully paraded before the Bakufu and the kingdom he represented forced into a new position as a tributary. Yet, even as it made use of unorthodox means to gain satellites, the Bakufu operated consistently within the normative framework provided by the Chinese system, which offered an overarching language for the incorporation of such territories.

Unlike the Dutch East India Company whose involvement in foreign territories was designed to yield direct economic benefit, the Tokugawa regime was more interested in the political legitimacy that could be gained from such territories. The result was that it put a premium on display, with the arrival of embassies from states like the Ryukyu kingdom providing the regime with a powerful propaganda tool that was used to buttress the shogun's power. Ronald Toby, who has produced the pioneering study in this field, argues that the "ability of the early shoguns to produce ostentatious foreign embassies on Japanese soil, thereby demonstrating international legitimacy, was a powerful propaganda tool in the building of domestic legitimacy."[63] As a result, the Bakufu made no effort to exert direct control over a satellite like the Ryukyu kingdom or to exploit its territory, as, for example, the Dutch did in Tayouan, for more concrete benefits. Instead, relations were framed, in line with the Chinese tributary system model, in terms of the willing submission of tribute from a peripheral state to a more civilized center, or, as one Ryukyuan monarch put it, from an "isolated barbarian dependent state" to the realm of "Civilization."[64] This connection was confirmed by the regular arrival of embassies, which appeared in Edo bearing tribute for the shogun.

Whereas the European system of colonization could flourish in a political vacuum such as existed on Taiwan, the Tokugawa order required the presence of a sovereign or some kind of regime capable of dispatching an embassy to the capital. The existence of this prerequisite rendered it, as Stephen Turnbull has noted, poorly suited to the incorporation of stateless spaces, a fact that becomes immediately evident if we consider the company's and the Bakufu's contrasting relationship with Taiwan.[65] In the same year as Satsuma's troops set sail for the Ryukyu kingdom, the shogun authorized a second expedition designed to draw Taiwan into the Tokugawa order as a vassal state. Its leader, Arima Harunobu, was instructed to find suitable envoys that could be brought back to the capital to render appropriate reverence to the shogun.[66] If Arima's men were unable to secure envoys peacefully, they were authorized to seize them with force. Although the instructions allowed for considerable leeway, no amount of violence would have produced the desired outcome for, unlike the Ryukyu kingdom, Taiwan was not unified under one ruler. Once on the island, Arima's retainers, handicapped by a lack of knowledge about local conditions, encountered immediate resistance. In the end, and after a considerable struggle, they succeeded in bringing back a number of captives from nearby villages to Japan, but the shogun showed little interest in a group with no political status.[67]

In 1616 the Bakufu decided to try again, sanctioning a second expedition to Taiwan. This one was placed under the Nagasaki magistrate, Murayama Tōan, who assembled thirteen ships laden with soldiers.[68] If anything, Murayama's operation achieved even less than Arima's earlier attempt. Scattered by a powerful storm, only one vessel successfully reached Taiwan, where once again the landing of troops provoked a violent response from local villagers who fiercely resisted any incursion into their territory. In the aftermath of the debacle, the Bakufu abandoned any attempt to pull Taiwan into the Tokugawa order and turned its attention back to domestic politics. Crucially this was not because, as the Dutch would later surmise, the regime lacked the necessary resources to accomplish its goal, but rather because its template for maritime incorporation could not be fitted (however much its agents tried) over a blank political space like Taiwan, which was, to use Turnbull's words, susceptible to the "language of gunpowder and the spade," but not to the "language of the tributary system."[69]

In the clash over Tayouan, therefore, two distinct world orders, each with its own practices, language, and expectations, came into contact with each other. Once this divide is acknowledged, it becomes far easier to understand why the company's presentation failed to yield any response in Japan. No matter how frequently they repeated the same carefully rehearsed story, the Dutch, in the end, could gain no footing because their claims were fundamentally at odds with the Tokugawa schema of international relations. The result was that they were rendered (at least from the Japanese perspective) nothing more than a small group of European squatters, possessors of a minor fort and outsized rhetoric, but with no authority over the island. Taiwan was, exactly as the lord of Hirado insisted, a place without lord or sovereign over which the Dutch could claim no more rights than any Japanese merchant.[70]

The problem could not be solved by coercion. In the final analysis the company possessed no ability to force its vision onto the Bakufu, which waved off Batavia's claims to sovereignty. The dynamic was thus the reverse of that present in the nineteenth century, when the Japanese government was compelled to retreat from the parameters of the Tokugawa order in order to embrace an essentially European vision of colony and metropole. In that period a well-established political vocabulary was forced to give ground to a Western order of sovereignty and direct possession that had acquired more compelling weight.[71] In the early seventeenth century, however, it was the European side of the equation, in this case the Dutch East India Company, that was left with little choice but to retreat from its assertions.

By 1627 when it became clear that its defense of sovereignty was making no headway, Batavia, as it had in the clashes over diplomacy and violence, opted to retreat. Although he continued to insist on the company's absolute rights to Tayouan (in the hope that it might still be possible to secure a turnaround in Bakufu attitudes), the governor-general moved to offer concessions designed to draw the heat out of the conflict. Retreating from earlier assertions, de Carpentier, the current incumbent, decided that Japanese vessels arriving in Taiwan would now be allowed to engage in "free and unencumbered" trade.[72] The company's willingness to drop restrictions and any expectation of a tax would, he hoped, prevent further complaints in Japan while buttressing the VOC position there. Before this conciliatory tone could yield any benefit, however, the conflict escalated suddenly when company employees misread the Bakufu's response to a group of Siraya villagers that appeared without warning in Japan in 1627.

THE EMBASSY FROM TAIWAN

The villagers in question had been brought to Japan by Suetsugu Heizō, who, in the years since the first clash in the bay of Tayouan in 1625 had emerged as one of the company's most determined enemies. Frustrated with Batavia's policies and unaware of its planned concessions, he decided to resolve the impasse through an unorthodox but ingenious scheme that promised, if carried out successfully, to undermine the company's claims to Tayouan. In 1627 Heizō's captain, Hamada Yahyoē recruited sixteen aboriginal men from the village of Sinkan, a community of about four hundred located approximately a mile from Fort Zeelandia. Accompanied by two Chinese translators, the villagers were transported to Nagasaki, where they were housed in Heizō's own residence, clothed, equipped with appropriate gifts, and then dispatched to Edo.

Such measures raise an obvious question as to Heizō's purpose in bringing a group with no apparent status or importance all the way first to Nagasaki and later to the shogun's headquarters in central Japan. To resolve this, we need to look first at the ways in which these villagers were represented in Japan.[73] Clearly, the men from Sinkan were not presented simply as the residents of a minor settlement, only one among many in Taiwan. Rather the available sources suggest that Heizō set about transforming them into ersatz ambassadors capable of playing a role in the Tokugawa diplomatic order. The Dutch, who observed this metamorphosis from their base in Hirado, described them as "manufactured" (*gefabriceerde*) ambassadors who were "housed in his residence, clothed, disciplined, instructed and given deer skins [to be presented] as the fruits of their land."[74] In other words, everything was done to ensure that they could "pay homage to the emperor [shogun] in a solemn fashion" appropriate to diplomatic envoys. The first step was to remake their appearance. The villagers were provided with Chinese clothes and red ribbons for their hair so that it "could not be said that they were people that had been naked all their lives."[75] Embassies traditionally brought local products, usually items that could serve as a symbol of the territory from which they originated, to be presented as gifts. In keeping with this, Heizō supplied the delegation with deerskins, Taiwan's most important native product, and a collection of more exotic gifts, including tiger skins, fur rugs, and peacock feathers.[76] Particular attention was devoted to the group's leader, named in contemporary sources either as Dika or Rika, who assumed a central role in the endeavor. Once in Japan, he took on the role of "principal lord of Formosa" (*principael heer*) or the "lord of the land" (*heer van dat lant*).[77] According to the Dutch, "they give out that one of these blacks is the lord of the land Formosa and he comes in order to greet His Majesty."[78]

In arranging things in this way, Heizō sought to tap into the regime's long-standing, albeit, at that time, largely dormant interest in the island. Twice in a decade the Bakufu had authorized expeditions designed to bring the island into the shogun's orbit by securing envoys from Taiwan. Operating in the most important port city in Kyushu, Heizō must have been aware of both expeditions and certainly knew all about the latter campaign, which had been orchestrated by one of his rivals. He would also have known that they had failed in large part because Taiwan's decentralized political landscape was not capable of delivering up suitable figures. The decision to bring over a group of villagers from Sinkan seems, therefore, to have been an attempt to outmaneuver the company by providing the Japanese regime with what it had long sought, representatives capable of speaking for Taiwan as a whole. In presenting the group in this way, Heizō aimed to transform it into a viable embassy that arrived in Japan headed by the lord of the island.

The ruse offered a way to draw the Bakufu more directly into his conflict with the Dutch. If the shogun accepted the embassy's identity and pulled Taiwan into the Tokugawa diplomatic order as a tributary, then it is difficult to see how the company, which maintained a small number of troops on the island, could continue to exclude Japanese mariners and merchants from a territory in which Japan had a direct interest. The opening of a diplomatic link between Edo and Tayouan would, moreover, mean that the Bakufu would be far more likely to take an active interest in keeping the trade route open, if for no reason other than to ensure the regular arrival of subordinate embassies from the island. All of this depended, however, on the regime's willingness to accept that this was in fact an actual embassy and that Rika could speak for the island.

At first it seemed as if Tokugawa officials would do precisely this. As the group made their way from Nagasaki to Edo, it was issued with horses, servants, and a travel document—a clear sign that they were viewed as a genuine embassy meriting official support.[79] But any triumph Heizō must have felt proved to be short-lived when disaster struck in the form of smallpox, which infected most of the group.[80] Two of the villagers died immediately; the rest were quarantined until they were able to travel again. Once they had recovered enough to proceed, the ambassadors continued on to Edo, reaching the city in October 1627. Their subsequent reception is described in *Ikoku nikki*, which also includes accounts of the first Dutch embassies to Japan:

> In the 11th month, 5th day (12 December 1627), a person from Takasago called Rika came and presented his greetings to both shoguns. Accompanying him, more than ten people came to the garden. Rika presented his greetings on the small veranda. His presents were five tiger skins, twenty fur rugs and twenty peacock feathers. He presented his greetings first in the main keep and then in the western keep. The ceremony was the same and no letter was presented. This time, the people from Takasago all got smallpox and it is not known if they survived. Rika also got smallpox, and during his audience the color of his face was strange.[81]

On the surface, the reception seems favorable enough. Despite the fact that the group was clearly suffering from smallpox, it was received at both the western and main keeps, that is, at Iemitsu's and Hidetada's official residences. It is not clear if the shogun was personally present, but it seems likely that the audience did at least involve some senior officials. At its conclusion the villagers were presented with gifts of clothing and six hundred bars of silver, while the Chinese translators who had accompanied the embassy received twenty bars of silver.[82]

But there were also a number of discordant elements that jar with Heizō's carefully engineered presentation. Rather than being led into the castle, the traditional location for audiences, the villagers were received in a garden. If we assume that Tokugawa officials simply wanted to keep a distance between themselves and a dangerous disease, the decision makes sense, but it also provides the first indication that Rika was not treated as the lord of Taiwan. Far more damning was the choice of words to describe Rika, who was named simply as a person from Takasago. He was not a king, a lord, or even a notable, and *Ikoku Nikki* made no reference to a state or any sort of political structure standing behind the embassy. There was thus no recognition that this delegation consisted of anything more than a few villagers coming from a distant frontier to offer presents to the shogun. While it did not reject the group without an audience, the Bakufu was clearly unprepared to treat them as legitimate ambassadors or accord them any political status.

In itself this fact should not be surprising. For an individual, even one with Heizō's resources and connections, to create a believable embassy capable of meeting Tokugawa expectations was always going to be a challenge. The regime's willingness to sponsor the embassy as it made its way to Edo showed that the prospect of receiving the supposed "lord of Taiwan" was an attractive one, but this initial interest broke down in the face of an all-too-modest reality. Instead of mustering a grand embassy, Heizō was, in the end, only able to present a small group of villagers afflicted with smallpox and with their credibility further undermined by Dutch representatives who insisted that they were counterfeit ambassadors brought to Japan by subterfuge.

Although it must have involved considerable expense, the embassy, at least at first blush, achieved nothing. When the audience concluded, it seemed as if the members of the delegation would simply return to their village and fade quietly from view. Instead, the crisis escalated— and did so in dramatic fashion. Tellingly, this occurred not because of anything that Heizō or, indeed, the delegation from Sinkan had done but rather as a consequence of the company's reaction. At its heart the 1627 embassy represented an illusion created to appeal to the logic of the Tokugawa world order. For this reason Rika assumed the role of supplicant, arriving in Edo as the lord of a barbaric state that wished to submit to the more civilized center. The Dutch, however, read the embassy according to a different set of signifiers, with disastrous results.

ESCALATION

From the beginning, many VOC agents were convinced that Heizō wished to use the villagers to bring Tayouan under Bakufu control by transferring full sovereignty to the shogun, thereby turning their cherished colony into a Japanese possession. They saw it, in other words, as an aggressive power grab designed to wrest the island away from them through a ceremonial transfer of sovereignty from villagers to shogun. The embassy became, in this reading, a mechanism "to pull the sovereignty of Tayouan and Formosa" from Batavia to Edo, which would result, VOC officials feared, in the direct occupation of Tayouan by Japanese forces.[83] It is not difficult to understand where this suspicion originated. This was, after all, precisely what the company had done, and what had been done to it, in its competition with its European rivals over the Banda archipelago and other similar territories.[84] But it was also a flawed reading. Even if the embassy from Sinkan had succeeded in its purpose, it is highly unlikely that the Bakufu would have taken steps to exert direct political control over Tayouan. To bring the island under central control, that is, to claim sovereignty in the way imagined by the Dutch, would have required a complete reorganization of the Tokugawa order, which relied on the embassy and the language of tribute to bind overseas states to Edo.

The company's concerns were magnified when news reached the Japan factory that the delegation from Sinkan had been received in Edo. This prompted a mounting fear by some within the VOC that Bakufu troops were massing just over the horizon, ready to seize the Tayouan colony from their grasp. Reflecting this general sense of disquiet, the opperhoofd in Japan wrote to his superiors on 20 February 1628 suggesting that an expedition would be sent from Nagasaki to Tayouan in order to "take possession on behalf of the shogun."[85] As evidence, he seized on rumors circulating in Nagasaki that Heizō was preparing a fleet of many vessels "for war in order to bring about the incorporation of Tayouan."[86] A secret message was also dispatched to Fort Zeelandia warning its garrison to guard against a possible assault, while in Batavia the governor-general was equally concerned with the possibility of a looming threat from Japan: "As to the sovereignty over Tayouan or the island of Formosa, which the Japanese appear to claim out of the strength of a dedication that, some Japanese say, sixteen people from the village of Sinkan (who were secretly taken out of Tayouan) made to the emperor [shogun] of Japan. In Tayouan you should in no way cede our rights to any nation in the world, be they Japanese, Oriental or European, but maintain these inviolate as they belong to the company and we have exercised them until now."[87] In this way, by reading the Bakufu's indifferent response to the delegation from Sinkan according to their own script, Dutch agents assumed ambitions that did not exist, plans that had never been formed, and a threat that had little basis in fact. The result was to set the stage for further escalation, with VOC officials moving to make certain that no part of the company's sovereignty, however slight, was ceded to a Japanese advance.

The administrator charged with carrying out these orders was Pieter Nuyts, who, after the failure of his embassy in 1627, had become governor of Tayouan. Eager to redeem himself in his superiors' eyes, he was determined to take all necessary steps, and, when on April 1628 two Japanese junks commanded by Hamada Yahyōe arrived in Tayouan harbor, Nuyts leapt into action, ordering his men to search the vessels and strip them of all weapons.[88] In the process he discovered the villagers from Sinkan, in transit back to their homes, who were promptly thrown into jail. When Hamada went ashore to protest the action, he was also imprisoned, along with a number of his crew, and deprived of food and water.[89] All these actions were justified by Nuyts as preventive measures designed to preserve the company's sovereignty against Hamada's "evil design," but there is little evidence to support the view that any sort of invasion had in fact been planned.[90] Even if the Dutch garrison was relatively weak, two ships were hardly enough to stage an attack, and the Japanese account of the reception of the villagers from Sinkan in Edo makes it clear that the Bakufu had dismissed them without any plans for further action.[91]

Not surprisingly, Nuyts's response soon backfired. On 29 June Hamada, who had been released from prison, visited the governor in his personal quarters. Although it was clear that he was spoiling for a fight, Nuyts elected to receive the party without any guards, attended only by his son Laurens and an interpreter. When the governor refused to give the Japanese permission to depart, Hamada and his men "flew upon him like roaring lions" and took him prisoner.[92] As more and more men poured in from both sides, the confrontation seemed set to end in bloodshed. Eager to prevent this and secure his own survival, Nuyts intervened to defuse the situation. The result was an agreement that an equal number of hostages would be taken on both sides and exchanged at a later date. As part of the deal, Hamada insisted that he be fully reimbursed for past taxes as well as for the losses caused to his employer's trading profits by Zeelandia's interference. The final figure was substantial, including full compensation for the fifteen piculs of silk levied by Sonck in 1625 as well as a further two hundred for lost revenue from 1626 when Hamada was refused permission to sail directly to China.[93]

In Edo news of Nuyts's actions sparked an outraged reaction. Hamada's ships carried with them a shuinjō, one of the regime's prized maritime trading licenses. For Tokugawa officials, the governor's decision to detain Hamada's vessels, strip them of their armament, and arrest their crew constituted an unacceptable infringement of the shogun's authority. If this was not provocation enough, Edo soon learned that Nuyts and his men had confiscated the gifts presented to the villagers from Sinkan. Incensed at this twin assault on shogunal prestige, they proceeded to arrest all VOC shipping then in Japan, confiscate their cargo, and throw their crews in prison. In Hirado the Japan factory's staff were placed under house arrest, and all communication with Batavia was suspended. The result was a complete rupture in relations between the company and the shogun that would only be repaired by the striking act of surrender that will be described in the next chapter.

CHAPTER SEVEN

GIVING UP THE GOVERNOR

In Japan you cannot be too humble.

—General Letters of the Governor-General and the
Council of the Indies, 1638

By early 1632, Pieter Nuyts's once ascendant star had fallen to new depths. Recalled from his position as governor of Tayouan for gross incompetence, he had languished for months in the company's dank fortress in Batavia. While his career within the organization was clearly over, no charges had as yet been formally laid against him, and it was possible to believe that his superiors might elect simply to send him back to the republic without further punishment. In May, however, he was summoned to appear before the governor-general. To reopen relations with Japan, which had by this point remained suspended for four years, his superiors were, Nuyts discovered to his horror, prepared to contemplate the unthinkable: handing him over to the shogun to answer for his crimes.

Given a chance to respond to the proposal, Nuyts sprang into action. For all his evident failings, no one could question his intelligence; Nuyts had already established himself as a master of the written defense, producing long documents designed to browbeat his less educated superiors into submission with elegant formulations mixed liberally with classical allusions. The case in his favor seemed a strong one. It was, he argued, unwise, illegal, and, in a word, impossible to extradite such a high-ranking official—Nuyts was a former governor and a member of the Council of the Indies—to face judgment before a "heathen" monarch.[1] The company had never taken such a step before, and it could surely not contemplate doing so regardless of how much it wished to reopen ties with the shogun.

In fact, this is precisely what happened, and in September of that year Nuyts was returned to Japan as a prisoner dispatched to face Bakufu justice. Even centuries later the decision to give up the former governor still surprises as it so obviously contradicts not only the company's policy but also the position taken by other European enterprises in early modern Asia. But, if the extent of the company's surrender is clear, did it really matter? In the end, Nuyts was only one man, and, after being imprisoned for four years, he eventually left Japan unscathed, going on, in fact, to have a second far more successful career in the United Provinces.[2] In this way the surrender of the governor was an essentially symbolic act; one might view it as little more than a clever move that succeeded in resolving an impasse with the Bakufu without any particular cost to the company, which had, at this point, a very low estimation of Nuyts. This assessment seems less convincing, however, if we consider the logic behind the decision, what was at stake, and the aftermath of the handover.

On the most basic level the episode tells us something about the nature of the company's position in Japan after some of the conflicts over diplomacy and violence described earlier in this study. That it was even prepared to contemplate the extradition of a senior official provides perhaps the best evidence as to how few tools were left available to Batavia when it came to dealing with the Bakufu. In this way the transfer of the governor's body serves as a symbol of the wider Tokugawa/VOC relationship as it had begun to stabilize after a flurry of clashes. While Nuyts was prone to hyperbole, he was not mistaken when he wrote that any plan to send him to Japan violated his employer's most basic principles. The preservation of legal sovereignty had, from the beginning, been a consistent VOC priority, something to be jealously safeguarded against any and all incursions. Ever since its first ships had arrived in Asian waters, the VOC had insisted on maintaining absolute jurisdiction over its employees, who were pulled aggressively away from local legal systems. Because of this, the decision to hand over Nuyts represented not only a surrender of legal sovereignty but also a subversion of decades of the company's own practices.

With this in mind, it is revealing how deeply Nuyts's extradition troubled Dutch officials. Documents produced after the initial handover show a stark contrast between the bile spilling out from Batavia about the former governor, who was condemned in the strongest possible terms, and the company's frantic efforts to pull him back into its sovereignty. Nuyts's ongoing presence in Japan was a festering wound that could only be sutured by pulling his body back into the embrace of Dutch jurisdiction. The campaign designed to do this culminated in the presentation of another revealing symbol, a glittering brass chandelier that was handed over as a visible marker of VOC subordination and which still stands today at the shrine to Tokugawa power in Nikkō.

CRIME AND PUNISHMENT

In the aftermath of the clash between Nuyts and Hamada Yahyōe on Tayouan, the company's leadership in Batavia struggled to obtain a measure of a crisis that had materialized without warning and to determine how best to set about reopening relations with Japan. Their first move was to dispatch a special emissary to Japan to investigate the situation. The difficult task was handed to Willem Janssen, who was sent to secure the release of the company's personnel and assets by negotiating directly with the Bakufu.[3] Arriving in Japan in September 1629, he was unable to secure permission to travel to Edo and was compelled to rely on a Japanese interpreter, who was permitted to make the journey to the shogun's capital, to speak for the VOC. Although it was clear that the regime would mandate some form of punishment for what had happened on Tayouan, Janssen had no way to find out what form this might take, and he could do little more than wait for the axe to fall.

Months dragged by with no news until February 1630, when a letter finally arrived in Nagasaki informing the Dutch of the Bakufu's verdict.[4] The company's crimes were twofold. In arresting Hamada's ship, the VOC had contravened the regime's authority by violating a pass that had been issued directly by the shogun. To make matters worse, the Dutch had mistreated the villagers from Sinkan by, among other things, confiscating the gifts given to them by Tokugawa officials in Edo.[5] The penalty for these offenses was simple. If the Dutch wished to reopen trading relations, they must, the regime insisted, destroy

the company's key stronghold and the bastion of Dutch power on Tayouan, Fort Zeelandia.[6]

While the demand stunned VOC representatives, who were completely unprepared for the severity of the penalty, it was consistent
with the Bakufu's policy toward the shuinjō. From the beginning, the
regime's absolute insistence on preserving the integrity of the shuinjō
system meant that it was willing to respond to minor infractions with
outsized punishment. It was for this reason that Japanese troops had
destroyed the Macao-Nagasaki carrack in 1610 and would subsequently
contemplate an assault on Manila in retaliation for a Spanish attack on
a shuinsen. In 1630, the appropriate penalty for Nuyts's actions on Tayouan was the razing of the company's prized fortress, a suitably dramatic act of contrition that would allow for the reopening of relations.
Perhaps the best summation of Edo's logic is provided in a letter sent
to the governor-general by the daimyo of Hirado in which he explained
that "two years ago, Suetsugu Heizō's junk traveled to Taiwan with a
pass from the emperor [shogun] as always before. Because the governor
treated this junk badly in Taiwan, the Dutch ships have been imprisoned
by order of the emperor. . . . If the Dutch destroy their fort on Tayouan,
then they can conduct trade [in Japan] as before."[7]

In Batavia the new governor-general, Jacques Specx, unequivocally
rejected the suggestion. The shogun had, he maintained, no right or
authority to order the destruction of the fort, and he dispatched Janssen back to Japan to negotiate an acceptable compromise.[8] This time
the company's envoy was able to secure permission to travel to Edo,
but once there negotiations stalled and months dragged by with no dis-
cernable progress.[9] By early 1632 no resolution was in sight, and there
seemed little hope of achieving one as long as the company refused to
accept the designated punishment. The current situation was also not
sustainable. It had been almost four years since the original incident,
and the costs to the VOC's bottom line were mounting. Without access
to the Japanese market, the colony in Tayouan was not economically
viable; each month that trade remained suspended further damaged the
company's once profitable operations in East Asia.

Although things looked increasingly desperate, Specx had few options
left to resolve the crisis. When it came to relations with Japan, neither of
the company's two most consistently reliable tools, the formal diplomatic
mission, designed to settle problems through the presentation of official

letters and gifts, and the maritime campaign, used to compel a shift in policy through the application of force, were available. Edo had rejected the governor-general's status as an independent diplomatic actor, and another embassy would likely cause more problems than it would solve. The use of force was equally perilous. In other parts of Asia the VOC might have contemplated using its superior maritime force to halt all shipping until the offending government, confronting economic losses and the severing of key trade routes, agreed to reopen relations on VOC terms. This was the tactic used with great success in the aftermath of the 1648 assault on the factory in Surat, which was discussed in chapter 4. In Japan, however, the potential dangers far outweighed any chance of success, and, although it was clearly discussed, there was uniform agreement within the company that the use of force would not produce a favorable outcome. Running through the available options, Antonio van Diemen, an official well known for authorizing military campaigns in other parts of Asia, wrote that "to maintain the company's rights through reprisal and to engage in attacks against the Japanese is not advisable now or in the future." Instead, he concluded that "trade must be directed with the best manner and with the most circumspection."[10] How then to break the impasse without giving in to the shogun's demand?

It was against this backdrop that Specx and other VOC officials first began to consider the extradition of Pieter Nuyts as the best of a shrinking set of alternatives. If the company was not prepared to surrender the bricks and mortar of its stronghold in Tayouan, it could relinquish its hold over the colony's former governor and hope that that this would be enough to placate the Tokugawa regime. Conveniently for Specx, Nuyts was detained at that very moment in Batavia awaiting trial. Since 1628 the governor had written a stream of letters exonerating himself from all blame, but while his superiors showed an initial willingness to accept these explanations they gradually became convinced that Nuyts had acted recklessly by mistreating Hamada, throwing the villagers from Sinkan into jail, and confiscating the gifts with which they had been presented in Edo. Even if there was a genuine concern about a Japanese attack, he could have handled the matter more prudently, thereby defusing any potential backlash in Japan.[11] After a disastrous start, the governor had not redeemed himself in his role as the colony's chief administrator, and there were disturbing rumors about his behavior there. By late 1629 Batavia had lost all patience with Nuyts and summoned him back to explain his actions. As further revelations emerged about what he done during his tenure on Tayouan, Nuyts was placed under arrest until the company could decide what to do with him.[12]

Although the former governor had few supporters left in his camp, there were nonetheless significant obstacles standing in the way of the proposed extradition to Japan. For one thing, no trial had yet been held in Batavia and no formal charges filed. With the legality of the transfer not yet resolved, Nuyts was given the chance to respond to the suggestion that he should be sent to Japan to answer for his crimes there. The result was a long document that attacked the proposition in point after closely argued point as foolhardy, dangerous, and clearly illegal. He was, Nuyts protested, contracted to "the lord directors to do the company's service in these lands. I stand under their oath, order, and rescission, and no others."[13] Because of this, any attempt to make him answer to a separate authority could only harm the company's standing in Asia: "If a subordinate governor was forced to answer before the . . . [Japanese shogun], who cannot exercise dominion or rights over Their Honors or their servants, it would greatly offend, yes even damage, the authority and sovereignty of Their Honors."[14]

While Nuyts insisted that he wished to serve his superiors, he was also adamant that far greater issues were at stake. If he was ejected from the company's jurisdiction in order to stand trial before a foreign potentate, it would, he argued, compromise the organization's legal sovereignty with potentially disastrous consequences. The claim was of course entirely self-serving; it was also an accurate reflection of VOC policy. From the moment that the company arrived in Asia, it had worked to carve out a legal space around the bodies of its employees and to pull them from the jurisdiction of the sovereigns in whose territory they operated.[15] The result was the creation (albeit not always successfully) of a juridical cocoon capable of ensuring that although the company's men operated in Asia, they were not bound by Asian laws.[16] This is not to say of course that VOC employees were in any way exempt from the law. Rather punishment for any offense was to come only from their superiors acting within a self-contained legal structure.

This overarching concern with the creation and preservation of legal sovereignty is immediately visible in dozens of treaties concluded between the company and local rulers containing clear provisions as to the adjudication of crimes.[17] In its first years of its existence, the VOC was most concerned with maintaining jurisdiction over wayward mariners who might be tempted to seek shelter in Asian ports. A 1602 agreement with a group of elders on one of the Banda Islands specified that any Dutch sailor who attempted to escape onto land after committing an offense must be handed back. The document was also careful to shut down any possibility that religious conversion might be used as a potential loophole by stipulating that even if the runaway desired to "become a Moor" he should nonetheless be returned to his vessel to face punishment.[18] An accord concluded in 1606 with the king of Johor addressed the same problem by insisting that "if one of the Hollanders runs away to the King of Johor because of some serious crime or other offense, or should one of the King's subjects [run away to] the Dutch, then either party shall be bound to hand over the runaway to the [appropriate] authority" (1:44).

After the company moved onto land by establishing factories and trading posts, these treaties changed to reflect a new concern that its agents might get drawn into local legal orders. The result was an insistence on extraterritoriality very much in line with the legal rights demanded by Europeans in the nineteenth century. A treaty concluded with the ruler of Ternate in 1607 stipulated that "neither of the parties shall harm the other, but if any of the Hollanders harms a Ternaten, he will be condemned and punished by his own authorities, and the same shall apply with the Ternatens" (1:52). Another with the prince of Jakatra in 1611 stated simply that VOC authorities reserved the right to punish any crimes committed against the Javanese by Dutch offenders (1:91). A subsequent agreement concluded in 1623 with the shah of Persia focused on more serious offenses: "if it happens, God forbid, that that any one of the Netherlands nations murders another person, regardless of which nation he comes from, or commits another crime, that person [the offender] will not face justice in Persia, but will be punished by his president or chief" (1:189).

If the company was unable to obtain these rights in the initial raft of treaties, it was prepared to work over many years to extract its employees from local jurisdiction. This was the case in Siam, where the question of jurisdiction was tested in 1636 when two inebriated VOC merchants were arrested for attacking the servants of the king's brother. They were subsequently joined by a group of their compatriots when

they attempted a poorly planned rescue attempt.[19] When Siamese officials moved to execute the offenders, it provoked a loud protest from
the company's representatives. Eventually a compromise was reached
after both sides agreed that a symbolic affirmation of guilt would suf-
fice. In return, however, the Dutch had to pledge to obey "all the laws
and customs of the realm."[20] The agreement effectively subjected the
company's men to "local legal procedures and punishments and to the
power of the Siamese king—who promulgated Siamese law."[21] As such,
it constituted an unacceptable breach of VOC legal sovereignty, and the
organization spent the next three decades trying to extract its employees from the king's authority. This was finally achieved in 1664 when it
inserted a judicial clause in a new treaty with Siam stipulating that any
Dutch offenders could only be judged by their superiors.[22]

If this consistent concern with jurisdiction is easily documented, the
rationale behind it is more elusive. One explanation was simply that
it stemmed from a general apprehension about the barbarity of local
laws. In Siam, for example, the Dutch wrote at great length about possible penalties that included "banishments into Desarts, slavery, con-
fiscations, mutilation of hand or foot, burning in oyl, quartering . . .
ducking under water, holding their hands in boyling oyl, to go bare-foot
upon hot coales, or to eat a mess of charmed rice."[23] Such savage punishments were, they insisted, made worse by the arbitrary nature of justice
that hinged entirely on the king's whim. These overblown descriptions
should not, however, be accepted at face value as VOC agents displayed
a notable tendency to lump together different Asian sovereigns into the
single category of "oriental despot" while insisting that they presided
over systems that were fundamentally incapable of offering appropriate legal protections. Even if there was a genuine apprehension about
local law, this does not explain the company's insistence on obtaining a
blanket exemption. Instead, such arrangements—as was the case in the
nineteenth century when claims for extraterritoriality were justified by
pointing to barbarous practices either real or imagined—had more to do
with the preservation of power.[24]

Throughout its history the company treated the law as a servant to be
bent to its will, refusing for example to tolerate the presence of an independent judicial apparatus that might compromise its legal hold over
its employees. When the company was chartered in 1602, it was empowered to install judicial officers, and initially legal matters were dealt

with directly by the governor-general and his governing council (known usually as the High Government). This arrangement, which allowed no room for the separation of judicial and political power, changed, at least in theory, with the appointment in 1620 of the Council of Justice, with jurisdiction over civil and criminal cases, but this body never escaped the shadow of Castle Batavia.[25] Judges were appointed directly by the High Government, and a member of the administration served as the president of the council.[26] The predictable result was that decisions almost never went against the governor-general's wishes. Individual rights of appeal were, moreover, strictly curtailed. Unlike the employees attached to competing European overseas enterprises, VOC personnel could not make use of courts in their home country.[27] The result was to ensure an essentially subservient judicial apparatus and a tight VOC grip over its employees.

This reluctance to accept legal meddling extended to the company's dealings with foreign states. The organization resisted any notion that an external power should have the right to adjudicate the actions of its employees. The issues at stake were clear. To yield to the jurisdiction of a local official or ruler meant to submit to control and hence to restrictions on what its employees could and could not do. In contrast, the preservation of legal sovereignty allowed VOC agents to negotiate trade deals according to their own terms and exempted them from prosecution if they violated contractual practices. It also ensured that the company, an organization with a propensity for violence, could continue to make use of force as a basic tool of policy without fear that it would spark a litany of legal cases. Batavia wanted above all else to avoid the situation that had developed in Nagasaki where its agents were forced to explain their actions before a foreign judge and to pay up if the decision went against them. In contrast, extraterritorial arrangements ensured, as they did in the nineteenth century, "every possible advantage to maximize profits and power."[28]

The company's persistent attempts to draw bright lines around its employees and to pull them outside the ambit of local law should have ensured absolute protection for Nuyts. Even if he had committed his offense in Japan proper, the VOC would normally have insisted on its right to adjudicate the case without outside interference. To paraphrase its many treaties, crimes committed by Hollanders could only judged by Hollanders, and there was no room for the extradition of offenders to stand trial before a foreign potentate. But, of course, the governor had not detained Hamada's vessel in a Japanese port or even in the waters surrounding the archipelago. To the contrary, the offense had taken place in a territory which the company claimed as its own, a place where, to use Grotius's definition of sovereignty, "acts are not subject to another's Power, so that they cannot be made void by any other human Will."[29] Nuyts's decision to order Hamada's imprisonment may have been reckless, but it was entirely within his rights as the designated governor of a VOC territory. To admit otherwise and to accept that the shogun's judicial reach extended to offenses in Tayouan was thus to undercut Dutch claims to sovereignty over the island. Because of this, the former governor was, it seemed, protected on two fronts: the shogun could not claim authority over VOC bodies or lands in Asia and any attempt to sacrifice either one would irrevocably damage "the authority and sovereignty" of the company.[30]

To strengthen his case, Nuyts pointed to a concrete example that seemed to confirm everything that he had been saying.[31] When he left the United Provinces in 1626, he would have been well aware of a bitter legal dispute that was brewing with the English government over the actions of another VOC governor on the small Indonesian island of Amboina (also known as Ambon or Amboyna). Not only did the Amboina incident resemble Nuyts's case, but, more importantly for his defense, it offered a reassuring story centered on the absolute commitment to the preservation of legal sovereignty. It is not surprising then that in 1632, when Nuyts came to prepare his answer for the governor-general, the case came immediately to the forefront of his argument.

THE AMBOINA PARALLEL

The incident began in February 1623 when a Japanese mercenary was arrested for making persistent inquiries into the defenses and garrison of one of the company's castles on the island of Amboina.[32] After torture, he confessed that he was part of a conspiracy that had been orchestrated by a group of merchants attached to the English East India Company, which maintained a nearby trading post, to seize control of the fortification. Armed with this information, the VOC governor, Harman van Speult, arrested and began torturing these merchants until he had extracted confessions from the majority of them. The ringleader of the plot was identified as Gabriel Towerson, the chief agent of the English company in Amboina, who confessed that he had plotted with the Japanese to make himself master of the castle. Armed with multiple confessions, van Speult convened a council of local VOC employees, later known as the Amboina judges, to pronounce sentence on the conspirators. The result was a predictable verdict, and on 9 March ten English merchants as well as a group of Japanese mercenaries were put to death.

There were obvious similarities with Nuyts's actions on Tayouan. Both men were governors over recently acquired territories, but were forced to contend with the presence of competing groups of merchants who threatened to disrupt well-laid plans to dominate the local market. Seeing a conspiracy—that may well not have existed—to launch a surprise assault, the pair had responded with aggressive measures. Whereas Nuyts had simply detained Hamada's vessel, van Speult had tortured and executed ten English merchants. The seriousness of his actions was further amplified by the fact that England was one of the United Provinces' most important supporters in Europe and the two companies were, at the time of the incident, actually in alliance with each other.

When news of the Amboina case reached London at the beginning of June 1624, it sparked an outraged reaction. The governors of the English company protested the irregular nature of the judicial proceedings, which hinged entirely on confessions extracted by torture, argued that a Dutch court had no right to try the king's subjects, and ridiculed the notion that a small group of poorly armed merchants would plot to seize a well-defended castle. Determined to gain legal redress, they moved quickly to enlist the support of the king, James I. The result was three clearly articulated demands: the Dutch must punish van Speult and the remainder of the Amboina judges, compensate the English company for its losses, and make "reparations to his [the king's] subjects whose honour he considers seriously impugned."[33] If the Dutch government refused to act, the king was prepared to take appropriate measures by impounding Dutch ships passing through English ports and if necessary threatening war.[34]

In Batavia the administration recognized immediately that van Speult's actions left much to be desired, with the governor-general writing to his superiors that "we wish well that in these proceedings the proper style of justice had been followed."[35] Despite these misgivings, the company sprang immediately and vigorously to the defense of its employees. A pamphlet, published anonymously in 1624, but rumored to be the work of a senior VOC official, defended the legality of the proceedings in the strongest possible terms. Since the island of Amboina had been acquired through "just and lawful title," the company was, the author of the pamphlet maintained, fully entitled to administer justice "according to the laws of the Netherlands" and did not need to provide any explanation to the English government for what its officials had done.[36] Any suggestion that the Amboina judges should be sent back to Europe to face further investigation (and possible punishment) was met with sustained resistance. While it was prepared to organize an investigation to obtain further details, the Heeren 17 insisted that the matter could only be dealt with in-house and that its legal rights over its employees should not be encroached upon.

Over time, however, English pressure began to tell, and in November 1624 the States-General overruled the Heeren 17 by agreeing to summon the Amboina judges to Europe for questioning.[37] After more threats from across the Channel and the seizure of three VOC ships at Plymouth, Dutch leaders eventually consented in September 1627 to appoint a panel of seven judges to determine if the execution of Towerson and his countrymen had been legal.[38] Although it represented a chance to pick through what had happened on Amboina, it was clear from the beginning that the proceedings were nothing more than a show trial intended to placate English sentiment.[39] The court case dragged on for years during which time the English government repeatedly demanded access to the Amboina judges or some say in deciding the matter. The States-General could not, it insisted, claim full authority over the case, which "equally belongs to his Majesty and the States."[40] These requests were ignored, however, and in January 1632 the seven judges returned a verdict of not guilty, thereby ending any possibility of judicial retribution.[41]

The story of the Amboina incident hinged on the defense of legal sovereignty. When pressed, the company did agree to surrender the Amboina judges to the States-General, the one body that could exercise authority over the organization, but there was never any chance that the offenders would be dragged beyond the boundaries of Dutch jurisdiction. Although it was required to make the occasional conciliatory gesture to its English ally, the States-General was insistent that certain lines could not be crossed. When the English government made good on its threats to seize Dutch vessels, it responded with minor concessions while keeping the Amboina judges inside its legal system. In this way there was never any question that the offenders would be called to account before a foreign judge. Instead, as one English official lamented, the Dutch consistently claimed "entire jurisdiction" by refusing to countenance the possibility that an external body might claim judicial rights in the matter.[42]

For Nuyts, the Amboina case seemed to perfectly buttress his own claims about the impossibility of sending a high-ranking official to Japan to face trial there. As he explained it, Dutch authorities had persistently resisted the English government's "frequent requests, yes even mingled with threats, [and had] never allowed the extradition of the Dutch judges from Amboina, nor consented to having them tried by a stranger outside of their territory."[43] If the company had stood by van Speult and the other judges even at the risk of open war with one of its oldest allies in Europe, then it surely could not, Nuyts insisted, contemplate handing him over to the Japanese shogun.

GIVING UP THE GOVERNOR

While Nuyts's written answer to the governor-general's proposal survives, we know very little about the subsequent discussion that eventually resulted in the decision to extradite the former governor to Japan. This stems in large part from the decidedly irregular nature of the proceedings as the formal trial against Nuyts only commenced in September 1633, more than a year after he had arrived in Japan. What is clear, however, is that the decision was prompted by a sense of increasing desperation and a belief that—however unpalatable it might be—this was the only option available to break the Bakufu's embargo on trade. With this in mind, Nuyts was loaded onto an outgoing ship, the *Warmond*, on 15 July 1632 to answer for his offenses in Japan.[44]

Not surprisingly, Nuyts's appearance in Japan seems to have caught everyone by surprise, and initially the former governor, always the opportunist, was able to turn this to his advantage by insisting that he be treated in accordance with his prior rank. When it became clear that he had in fact been sent as a prisoner rather than a special envoy, the illusion was shattered and any privileges revoked.[45] In Edo Willem Janssen, who had been negotiating fruitlessly for months, seized on the news and moved quickly to file a petition with the Bakufu in which he explained that Nuyts had been handed over to the shogun's jurisdiction without qualification or restriction to be dealt with in any way Tokugawa authorities deemed appropriate.[46]

From the beginning, it was clear that Bakufu officials recognized the scale of the company's concession. Without even being asked, Batavia had elected to voluntarily transfer the primary perpetrator to Bakufu justice while making it clear that the regime could do as it wished with Nuyts. Although not the mandated punishment, it was an acceptable penalty that demonstrated the company's willingness to submit unconditionally to the shogun's authority. As a result, the regime's primary concern was not whether to approve the transfer but rather to check that this was really the former governor and not an imposter sent by the Dutch to trick it into lifting the embargo.[47]

When confirmation was received from a Japanese mariner with first-hand experience of Nuyts, Janssen was summoned to a meeting with the shogun's senior councilors and informed that their master was satisfied with the governor-general's decision to hand over the chief offender.[48] With Nuyts's identity confirmed, the regime was now prepared to reopen relations and to allow trade to continue as before. Having agreed to this, the Bakufu did not, much to the company's relief, stage a prolonged trial in which Nuyts was forced to explain himself and VOC policy on Tayouan before Japanese judges.[49] Instead, it accepted that Nuyts was to blame for the incident and placed him under indefinite house arrest in Hirado, where he was separated from his countrymen and confined in a private residence under constant guard.

The decision to hand over the former governor thus achieved the company's stated goal, and by 1633 trade with Japan was back in full swing. But while sending Nuyts to Japan as the shogun's prisoner succeeded in reopening relations, it also represented an unprecedented surrender of legal sovereignty that had no equivalent in the organization's broader history. Before Nuyts, the company had never transferred one of its employees to the jurisdiction of an Asian state, and it would never do so again. He was, in Blussé's words, the only VOC official that was ever "put at the mercy of an Asian monarch and forced to ask forgiveness for his past actions."[50] Any success came, therefore, at a steep cost. Nuyts's extradition displaced well established expectations about the relationship between VOC employees and local legal structures, while stripping away any notion that the company's bright lines could be preserved in its dealings with Tokugawa Japan. At the same time, the handover effectively inserted the Tokugawa shogun into a space above the governor-general as the ultimate legal arbiter for an offense that had taken place in VOC territory and which involved a high-ranking official. In that moment the company was, therefore, forced into an unfamiliar role as legal subject—even if the effect was only felt by a single employee—of the Tokugawa shogun.

As unexpected as it seems, the decision to hand over Pieter Nuyts was consistent with other developments in the company's wider relationship with the shogun. His extradition represented yet another retreat in a sequence of retreats from the organization's stated conception of its sovereign rights. Having surrendered its claims to conduct diplomacy and to wage war against its enemies in Japanese waters, the company was by 1632 prepared to forfeit its jurisdiction over its employees in order to find accommodation with the shogun. The handover was further recognition of the capacity of Bakufu interests to trump Batavia's wishes. By surrendering the governor, the Dutch effectively acknowledged that they were not just the shogun's loyal vassals but also, at least as it pertained to this offense, his legal subjects and that the regime's reach could extend into the heart of VOC territory to pluck one of its employees from within the walls of Batavia Castle. And yet, if it was part of a larger pattern, this was a particularly difficult concession to accept. While VOC officials were prepared to authorize the extradition, they were deeply troubled by it, and an examination of the aftermath of Nuyts's arrival in Japan reveals just how much his presence marooned outside the company's jurisdiction unsettled his superiors, who were determined to set things right by regaining control over the former governor's body.

GETTING THE GOVERNOR BACK

In September 1633 the Council of Justice in Batavia at last convened to try Nuyts. The charge sheet was lengthy, extending for page after damning page and spanning his time in both Japan and Tayouan. The transgressions had commenced during his ill-fated embassy, which had been fatally undermined by his arrogant behavior.[51] During his time as the governor of Tayouan, he led an "ungodly life," in which he had given full reign to his "filthy and indecent desires." Although "tied to his lawfully wedded wife," he had slept with and later married a "heathen woman" called Polcke.[52] In addition to these charges, he was condemned for engaging in private trade, employing irregular accounting practices, disrupting the company's shipping, lying to his superiors, and in numerous other ways violating the terms of his service. Given all these charges, there could be no doubt as to the verdict. All in all, the defendant had, the members of the Council of Justice concluded, caused a remarkable amount of harm in a very short space of time, bringing "great disadvantage to the company and disrepute to the Dutch nation." Their outrage was reflected in the tone of the charges, which repeatedly castigated Nuyts for his "rashness" (onbedachtsaemheyt), "carelessness" (sorgelosheyt), "inflated arrogance" (opgeblasen hoochmoet), and "cowardice" (cleynherticheyt).[53]

Considering both the diversity and the gravity of Nuyts's crimes, it would have been easy to understand if the company had simply washed its hands of the former governor and abandoned him to his fate. Instead, the reverse occurred. Beginning in 1633, VOC officials engaged in a determined lobbying campaign to repatriate Nuyts. His release became an unlikely priority for the organization, one to which it was prepared to devote time, energy, and resources. So glaring was the contrast between the bitter tone of the charges leveled against the former governor and this campaign that it requires some explanation. Although Nuyts did have allies, particularly within the Zeeland chamber, there is no indication that significant pressure was coming out of Europe. At the same time, the conditions of his imprisonment in a private house in Hirado were not particularly unpleasant. As much as Nuyts might lament his confinement in his letters, there were no stories of brutal treatment at the hands of callous jailers capable of inflaming the imagination in Batavia.

The repeated attempts to free Nuyts can only be explained by acknowledging the deep unease created within the VOC by his presence in Japan. In handing him over to face Bakufu justice, the company had, just as Nuyts insisted, violated one of its most basic principles and by doing so had crossed over to new and uncertain ground. Although confined a few hundred feet away from the Japan factory's walls, the former governor inhabited a different world beyond the comforting embrace of VOC jurisdiction. His presence in that space rankled company administrators; it was a nagging reminder of what they had done and of Batavia's inability to preserve the borders of its legal sovereignty. By regaining the governor's body, the company could not erase the original handover, but it could at least hope to paper over the concession. The result was that VOC officials began to submit a steady drumbeat of petitions, all pleading for Nuyts's release.

In 1633, when Nicolaes Couckebacker traveled to Japan to take up his position as opperhoofd, he carried with him instructions to use all possible measures to reclaim the former governor by "imploring and interceding" with Tokugawa officials.[54] To help achieve this goal, he was told to assure the Japanese that if Nuyts was released he would be relieved of all office and title before being sent back to the United Provinces in disgrace. Once there, the governor would never be allowed to return to Asia or to serve in any capacity in "any place of the Indies."[55] The message was reinforced in a letter sent from Batavia to Edo asking the Bakufu to hand back Nuyts so that the governor-general could strip him of all office and send him back to the Netherlands to answer for his crimes there.[56] When he reached Edo, Couckebacker submitted the first of a series of petitions, augmented in this case by an improvised and essentially baseless guarantee that if Nuyts was set free in Japan he would be held permanently in confinement once he arrived back in Europe.[57]

When this produced no result, the company shifted from a promise of further punishment to a plea for release on compassionate grounds. While Couckebacker had already suggested that Nuyts was losing his mind, later documents painted him as a pathetic figure worthy of sympathy. A petition submitted in September 1634 requested his release on the grounds that he would soon die if he was forced to remain in Japan for much longer.[58] Another request handed over in April 1635 brought in the fate of his young son, Laurens, who had been imprisoned by Bakufu officials in 1628 and later died in captivity: "We ask Your Honors to release the Governor this trip. The child of this person was imprisoned on your orders and died there. Your Honors have held him [Nuyts] for so many years that we fear he will die from misery. We feel compassion for him and ask Your Honors to give him his life and allow him to depart for his land while he still lives."[59]

Yet another petition submitted in the same year added in the loss of the former governor's family, noting that "out of sorrow and longing his wife and children came from Holland to Jacatra to seek him, but, seeing that he was imprisoned in a distant land, the mother and the children died of torment."[60] Clearly believing this exaggerated plea, which significantly magnified the actual death toll, was not enough, VOC officials produced a new document in January 1636 that brought everything together in a final, but once again fruitless, appeal for the shogun's charity: "This governor has now been imprisoned for four years through the command of the High Authorities. His son was held . . . and died there. The rest of his family, namely his wife and children, came to Jaccatra for him and have now died. There is almost no-one of his family left . . . and therefore all the captains implore Your Honors to forgive his misdeed and allow him to depart for his land. We ask Your Honors to be charitable and forgiving by allowing him to depart before he dies."[61] The frequency and urgency of these pleas, filled with melodramatic exaggerations and spread out over a period of years, make it clear that Nuyts's presence in Japan was not simply a topic of academic interest to VOC officials. As despised as he was, the company wanted him back and was prepared to press the issue again and again. The problem was, however, that it was far from clear how its representatives could persuade the Bakufu, which showed little interest in relinquishing its hold over the former governor, to shift position on Nuyts.

As his imprisonment stretched into its fourth year, the company opted for a change in tactics. As was the case in 1632, when it had decided to surrender the governor in the first place, there were few available options. Unable to rely either on the formal embassy, which might secure Nuyts release through direct negotiation, or to an ultimatum backed up by the force of its ships' guns, VOC agents turned to a gift, an outsized brass chandelier that was presented to the shogun in 1636. It proved highly effective and within just a few months of the chandelier's appearance in Edo Nuyts was on his way back to Batavia. That the Bakufu would opt to give up its prisoner in such short order, particularly when so many petitions had failed to secure any response, suggests that the chandelier was not just a run-of-the-mill gift, comparable to the objects that were offered annually at the conclusion of the hofreis. Rather this was a particularly charged object that was quickly seized upon by the regime and transported to its most important sacred site where it remains on display today.

THE GIFT

The first clear reference to the company's gift appears in a list of offerings prepared by the Japan factory's opperhoofd on 21 March 1636.[62] The entry describes the item simply as a brass chandelier with thirty arms, but this designation gives no sense of its massive dimensions or its splendor.[63] It was (and remains) a huge object, weighing almost eight hundred pounds and suspended when it was first displayed on a special nine-foot wooden frame.[64] So large was it that it had to be broken down for transport with each individual piece marked with Japanese characters so that they could be put together correctly in the shogun's castle.[65] Its intricate design was equally impressive with a large sphere hanging at its base supporting a long stem. The arms are arranged in three groups of ten moving upwards with the overall effect resembling a kind of tropical plant, its lush branches spilling gracefully outward in extravagant S shapes from the central trunk.[66]

When it was commissioned, probably by the Amsterdam chamber in 1634, the chandelier was intended as a general-purpose gift designed to improve the company's standing in Japan, but as it transited between the United Provinces and the archipelago its objective gradually narrowed. By the time it arrived in Edo, it had been tied to a series of far more specific goals, foremost of which was the release of Pieter Nuyts.[67] The logic of the exchange was clear—the gift for the governor—and it was hoped that the its presentation would be enough to secure his release after years of petition. Although VOC agents had given hundreds of gifts to the shogun prior to 1636, the chandelier was a very different kind of object. Prior to this point, the company had usually offered up utilitarian objects, most notably cannon, when it wanted to make a special appeal. In 1615, for example, Dutch representatives had presented a ship's gun to the shogun in the hope of assuring a favorable verdict in the *Santo Antonio* case, while in 1627 Nuyts himself had transported four cannon as part of his embassy to Edo. In both cases these gifts, which were presented with powder and shot, were essentially utilitarian,

Figure 7.1. Chandelier presented by the Dutch in 1636. Author's photograph

designed to be pressed into service against the regime's opponents. The chandelier, by contrast, was a display item that was designed to be seen—and indeed seen by as many people as possible—rather than used.

Massive brass light hangings of this kind were a common sight in the United Provinces where they were frequently presented by wealthy guilds to decorate reformed churches.[68] Examining the style of the chandelier, Lunsingh Scheurleer concludes that it was probably made by Joost Gerritszoon, who rose to prominence in the 1640s when he produced a number of similar items for Dutch churches, including a series for the Oude Kerk in Amsterdam. Although these particular chandeliers have not survived, they can be clearly seen in contemporary paintings and appear almost identical to the shogun's gift.[69] The use of objects with clear religious associations to placate foreign potentates was not lost on contemporary observers, and the practice prompted a critical verse from the poet Jan Vos: "J.G. [Joost Gerritszoon] would cast no copper crucifix, so he made a copper lamp, which will burn before the idol of the Emperor of Japan. In olden times no copper crucifix would be made sanctimoniously. Now he makes something that shall blaze before a devil's image; But this promises more money than the crucifix in my reckoning; Is that not the work of the devil, to light a candle for profit?"[70] In the shogun's court, a political center periodically convulsed by anti-Christian paroxysms, any mention of a church context was clearly taboo. As a result, the chandelier functioned here not because of its Christian association but because it was a conspicuous display item that could be pressed into service in a variety of spaces. In the paintings of the Oude Kerk, it is striking how dominant the chandeliers are. Suspended high above the floor of the church, their brass work gleams brilliantly against the whitewashed walls and the dark wood of the pews. When fully illuminated with all their candles blazing in place, they would have been even more impressive, the light flickering off their brilliant metal. In Japan, where such objects had an added exoticism, the effect would have been particularly imposing, and by all accounts contemporary observers were transfixed by the company's spectacular gift.

In Edo the arrival of a massive brass chandelier created an immediate stir of interest. Assembled in the daimyo of Hirado's residence, it drew a steady stream of curious onlookers eager to see the celebrated item firsthand. Indeed, it proved so irresistible that the daimyo was forced, according to Dutch reports, to expend a huge sum providing appropriate hospitality for his swarm of unexpected visitors.[71] When it came time for the audience with the shogun, the chandelier was disassembled and brought to the castle where it was laboriously put back together in sight of the audience chamber so the opperhoofd could perform his annual declaration of loyalty with the gift looming in the background.[72] From the beginning, it was clear that Tokugawa officials were delighted with the unexpected gift and on 5 July the Dutch received formal notification that Nuyts had been released from Bakufu custody and was free to depart Japan. As a further symbol of the shogun's pleasure, they were presented with two hundred bars of silver.[73]

No gift that the company had ever presented before—and no future offering—elicited such an unambiguously favorable response. To understand why the Bakufu reacted with quite this much enthusiasm requires some consideration of the gift's intended recipient, the third Tokugawa shogun, Iemitsu, who had came to power four years earlier. This was, to put it simply, just the right gift for just the right shogun at just the right time. While his two predecessors had used spectacle as a mechanism to entrench their power, Iemitsu carried the use of lavish display to new levels. This reliance on spectacle was directly linked to the distance that lay between him and the foundational moments of the government he had inherited. Born in 1604, Iemitsu missed the battle of Sekigahara, which had brought the Tokugawa to power, entirely and was too young to have participated in the siege of Osaka. This meant that he was the first Tokugawa ruler fortunate enough to inherit a pacified realm, but an added—and less desirable—consequence was that he lacked any connection with the great military victories associated with his grandfather and father.[74] When he came to power in 1632, the new shogun moved quickly to secure his position through a massive display of authority, and two years later he led a procession of more than three hundred thousand soldiers to Kyoto in an awesome demonstration of power that was further augmented by the appearance of an embassy from the Ryukyu kingdom.[75] A year later, Iemitsu made the alternate attendance system a formal requirement, thereby placing the daimyo in a constant and highly visible orbit around the Tokugawa sun.

While these policies produced impressive spectacles, they were essentially transient, and the shogun's greatest energies focused on the construction of the massive religious complex at Nikkō that was built to honor the twentieth anniversary of the death of Tokugawa Ieyasu, who had been deified as *Tōshō daigongen* or the Great Avatar Illuminating the East.[76] It was a vast undertaking, involving close to eight hundred thousand men, who labored at a cost over half a million gold *ryō*, and consuming almost one fifth of the vast inheritance that Iemitsu had received from his father.[77] While it had, of course, a religious function, the Nikkō complex, which became the key sacred space for the regime, was always as much about domestic politics as religious worship. As such it was designed to entrench Iemitsu's place at the apex of power in Japan.

It did so in at least three important ways. For previous projects such as the construction of Osaka castle, the regime forced the daimyo to contribute the bulk of materials and labor.[78] In 1634, however, when Iemitsu ordered building at Nikkō to commence, he deliberately excluded the domains from the project, with the result that it became a site financed, built, and controlled absolutely by the shogun. It thus served as a monumental demonstration of the power of the Tokugawa family as hegemon over Japan and a signal that it was now capable of orchestrating massive projects without assistance. By ordering the reconstruction of Nikkō on such a vast scale, Iemitsu, just twelve when his celebrated grandfather died, succeeded, moreover, in creating a direct, highly visible link to the regime's founding figure. Although their actual connection was relatively slender, the decision established Iemitsu as the personal guardian of his grandfather's memory and the inheritor of his legitimacy. Finally, the project provided a center for a growing Tokugawa cult. Once completed, the new site became a required stop for daimyo, an alternative sources of authority in early modern Japan, who were required to make periodic trips to Nikkō to worship at what was effectively a shrine to Tokugawa power.[79]

The company's gift arrived in Edo in March 1636, just two months before the twentieth anniversary of Ieyasu's death, that is, just in time to feature in the opening celebrations for the new complex.[80] The timing was so perfect that it is easy to imagine that the Dutch had deliberately planned it that way, although there is no conclusive evidence of this.[81] As soon as it was unveiled, however, it was clear to all observers that the chandelier was destined for Nikkō. Just a few days after it appeared in Edo, the lord of Hirado informed the Dutch that the object "would serve to hang in the great church Nikkō, which was the grave or sepulcher of the old deceased empeor [shogun]."[82]

It was an obvious assumption. To buttress its legitimacy, the Bakufu had long sought to propagate the notion that the shogun's power extended beyond the shores of the archipelago to distant states, and Iemitsu was determined to secure international recognition of Nikkō as a sacred site. This was accomplished, first of all, by making the complex a required stop on the road for visiting embassies, and in 1637 a Korean embassy was paraded through it with great fanfare. Alongside such one-off events, the Bakufu was also interested in securing items for permanent display, but obtaining these presented a problem as few neighboring monarchs showed any interest in gifting valuable objects to a domestic cult. In the case of Korea, for example, it was only in 1642 that the regime finally succeeded in obtaining a large bronze bell from its ruler. That it was able to do so was, in part, because Tokugawa officials went so far as to provide the bronze from which the bell was eventually cast, but, even with this concession, final consent was only obtained when Korea's precarious situation, menaced from the north by Manchu forces, made its government reluctant to refuse an appeal that they might otherwise have dismissed. When it arrived in Japan, however, these long years of negotiation were concealed so that the bell could be

Figure 7.2. The Dutch chandelier in Nikkō. The bell from Korea can be seen in the background. Author's photograph

presented as a spontaneous gesture made by the Korean king when he had, according to its inscription, first learned of Iemitsu's "filial piety."[83]

A year before the Korean embassy made its pilgrimage to Nikkō, and seven before the arrival of the bronze bell, the Dutch chandelier appeared in Edo.[84] It is not surprising, therefore, that it was seized upon by the regime and swiftly relocated to the complex where it remains today. The chosen site tells us something about the value placed on Joost Gerritszoon's creation in Japan. Rather than being marooned in a distant corner where it might go unnoticed, the chandelier was deliberately positioned close to the Yōmeimon, the famous "sun-bright gatehouse" that marked the entrance to the sacred inner precinct.[85] If, as Karen Gerhart has argued, we should see "each part of Nikkō [as] a carefully planned component of a powerful program of political iconography," then the company's gift clearly played a starring role, particularly in the early years of the complex.[86]

Today, as in the seventeenth century, the approach to Ieyasu's mausoleum begins at a torii gate at the bottom of a long slope and rises up through eleven separate stone stairways before reaching the Yōmeimon, where generations of pilgrims, including the daimyo who were not allowed to proceed past this point, paid homage to the founder of the regime.[87] As they moved upward, closer and closer to the center of Tokugawa power, visitors would have passed directly by the chandelier, which was housed in a special eight-sided structure on the side of the last flight of stairs before the Yōmeimon itself. For any pilgrim, the meaning of the Dutch chandelier would have been obvious. Transported across great distances from a remote land, it provided tangible evidence of the regime's capacity to exert influence outside Japan and offered unmistakable proof of the shogun's might. Dutch writers had little doubt about the powerful propaganda value of the company's gift, writing that the "Lustre" of "the Emperors Tomb in *Niko* . . . was made the greater, by the Branch'd Candlestick given by the *East India* Company, to the *Japan* emperor, as being Cast of Copper, and brought from *Holland*."[88]

The chandelier functioned, at the same time, as a signifier of the wider relationship between the company and the shogun. By 1636 conspicuous displays of devotion represented one of the last tools available to the company when it wanted to secure a shift in Tokugawa policy. The presentation of this object served as another symbol of the company's compliance with the *omote* illusion of perfect subservience demanded of it by the regime. In this case it took the form of a concrete and readily visible marker of devotion that could be displayed in the Bakufu's key sacred space. Thus the presentation of the chandelier functioned in the same way as the hofreis by placing the Dutch in a central role in an ongoing theater of submission.

While it is possible to dismiss the chandelier as an appendix to the business of trade, an essentially meaningless object that hardy Dutch merchants were happy to offer up in order to secure profit, symbols must surely matter. Commenting on the famous scene described by Kaempfer of VOC representatives performing before the shogun, Robert Markley notes how rarely the apparatus of postcolonial scholarship is brought to bear on moments in which Europeans were rendered strikingly powerless. "If the situation were reversed—if a European monarch were ordering representatives from a small, far-off country to 'speak broken' English or Dutch and to endure the indignity of performing 'apish tricks'—postcolonial critics would have little trouble analyzing (and deploring) this spectacle."[89] If the chandelier had, to paraphrase Markley, gone the other way, presented from a subordinate group of Japanese representatives to a European king and placed in a towering cathedral, we would have little difficulty in recognizing its potency.

Objects, whether presented voluntarily or taken by force, provided important symbols of political, cultural, and military hegemony. A single item, when acquired and pressed into service in a public space, could stand in for the wider subordination of lands and people. It is for this reason that historians working on European empire have turned their attention to palaces, museums, and exhibitions, arguing that they were part of the wider fabric of dominance and hence worthy of the same analysis as conventional instruments of power.[90] Such sites served as imperial pageants in which visitors were paraded past items drawn from the colonies and presented as concrete evidence of the glory of the imperial sovereign and the enduring reverence of the colonial subject. Although it incorporated the opposite dynamic of Asian dominance and European subservience, we should, following Markley, be careful to give the same weight to symbols like the company's chandelier. Like the gifts presented to European rulers, it meant something and it functions as an emblem of the company's wider relationship with the shogun, which has been the focus of this study.

CONCLUSION

THE DUTCH EXPERIENCE IN JAPAN

Perhaps the best way to sum up the nature of the Dutch experience in Japan is by briefly expanding the picture to consider how the company's relationship with the shogun compared with the situation in other parts of Asia. In their important study of VOC activity, George Winius and Markus Vink divide the company's development into three periods: an aggressive phase of expansion from 1600 to 1680, a competitive period from 1680 to 1748, and a period of "disengagement and decline" from 1748 to 1795.[1] During the first period, which has been the focus for this study, the VOC expanded very rapidly, establishing a string of factories and colonies across Asia while, in the process, engaging with a wide array of states ranging from tiny port polities to vast empires. Given this diversity, it is not surprising that the subsequent relationships were extremely varied, and, as we would expect, the outcome was very different depending on whether the VOC confronted a small city state in Southeast Asia or a regional superpower like Mughal India.

On one side of the scale were relationships in which the company came to occupy a more dominant position, gradually accruing power until it was able to dictate the terms of engagement. This category was populated primarily by Indonesian states such as Mataram, Banten, and

Makassar, all of which started off the seventeenth century as formidable rivals but were eventually subsumed into the company's empire in a subordinate role. While there were frequent (and sometimes devastating) setbacks along the way, the VOC succeeded in all three cases in maneuvering itself, across the long period of aggressive expansion laid out by Winius and Vink, into a ascendant position. The company's relationship with the sultanate of Mataram in central Java, briefly discussed in an earlier chapter, provides one example of the slow growth of VOC power. Over time, Mataram, which under Sultan Agung (r. 1613–46) had come close to conquering Batavia, was forced into an increasingly subordinate role, becoming by 1677 reliant on VOC military support to suppress internal dissent.[2] In the same period the company gained increasing influence over another former rival, the port polity of Banten, which was eventually compelled in 1684 to sign a one-sided treaty acknowledging the governor-general's authority.

Batavia's dealings with the Sultanate of Gowa or Makassar in South Sulawesi followed a similar trajectory. Emerging as a commercial and military power in the late sixteenth century, the sultanate became one of company's most persistent opponents during the first half of the seventeenth century, an enemy capable of mustering ten of thousands of troops and boasting in the city of Makassar a thriving center that was as large as many European capitals.[3] The company opened a factory in Makassar in 1607, but relations soon deteriorated, and the Dutch withdrew in 1615. The subsequent clash, which lasted on and off for over five decades, centered primarily on control over trade. Makassar flourished in the face of the company's determined attempts to establish a monopoly over precious spices by providing a haven for foreign traders, including the Portuguese, seeking to evade VOC restrictions.[4] Indeed it was the ruler of Makassar who famously protested that "Allah created the earth and sea. The earth he divided among the people and the sea became common to all. It has never been heard that anyone prohibited navigation."[5]

Batavia responded to the challenge represented by the sultanate by making full use of the weapons at its disposal and particularly by the aggressive deployment of both its diplomatic as well as its military apparatus. In an effort to gain control over trade, the company exchanged a series of letters and embassies with successive sultans who addressed the governor-general as an independent political actor in his own right as the ruler of "all the land and forts, ships great and small and all the subjects of the Hollanders below the winds."[6] When persuasion failed, the company was quick to resort to force, sending ships, as it had done in Japan, to assault Portuguese shipping in Makassar's waters and later engaging in a string of wars with the sultanate itself in 1653, 1660, and again in 1666.[7] The last of these proved decisive, and in 1667 Sultan Hasanuddin (r. 1653–69) was forced to sign the treaty of Bungaya, which effectively turned Makassar into a VOC vassal.

In all three cases the company came, over time, to control the terms of the relationship, gradually increasing the pressure until it was able to exert significant influence over its former rivals. This dynamic was, however, far from standard, and there are numerous examples of other relationships in which the company was forced onto the back foot and where it came to occupy a far more precarious position. This broad category, in which VOC power proved far more elusive, included some of the most important states in early modern Asia such as Ming and then Qing China, Mughal India, Safavid Persia, and the Ayutthaya kingdom of Siam, all of which wielded military resources far in excess of what the company could muster. The relations that developed between Batavia and these states were predictably varied. In some cases, to cite the most obvious difference, the company succeeded in establishing enduring ties while other interactions proved far more sporadic.

The VOC engaged intermittently with China, for example, during the seventeenth century, but it never succeeded in establishing a durable relationship. Indeed, its two attempts to entrench itself on the peripheries of the Chinese realm both ended in military repulse, in 1624 when the Dutch were forced from the Penghu Islands by a Ming fleet and in 1662 when the VOC banner was hauled down from Taiwan by Zheng Chenggong's armies. Given China's size and potency, the company was, even in a period characterized by considerable domestic turbulence and the collapse of one domestic regime, never in a position to dictate terms, but it behaved nonetheless with a surprising degree of aggression by making full use of the powers granted to it in article 35 of its charter. Thus in 1622, the VOC, as previously discussed, effectively declared war on China in a determined attempt to use the power of its ships' guns to pressure Ming officials into opening trade with the Penghu Islands, which the company had recently colonized.[8] But while such tactics had been used to great effect in Southeast Asia, they proved far less successful in bullying Chinese officials who, the Dutch discovered, were prepared to respond with an overwhelming display of military strength. Indeed, one result of Batavia's campaign was to draw the full attention of Chinese coastal officials, who proceeded to assemble troops to eject the Dutch from the Penghu Islands. In this way the company's first protracted engagement with Ming China ended not in a settlement but with a VOC retreat to Taiwan, a territory that lay beyond the boundaries of the Chinese state.

After the collapse of the Ming, the company was faced with a more complex political environment in which it was compelled to manage relations with two rival Chinese polities, the Qing regime, which had control over most of mainland China, and a de facto maritime state under Zheng Chenggong. Its preferred tool for dealing with the former was the official embassy, a number of which were dispatched to Beijing equipped with letters and gifts from the governor-general in an attempt to secure a military alliance in return for commercial concessions.[9] While this was happening, the company faced a growing threat from Zheng Chenggong, who was increasingly interested in using Taiwan as a base from which to wage his campaign against the Qing. The tipping point came, as it had in 1624, when Chinese authorities, in this case Zheng Chenggong, decided that the Dutch presence was no longer tolerable and assembled a large force to expel them from their stronghold on Tayouan. The result was another repulse for the company, which was never in a position to fend off a concerted assault from Chinese forces, and the effective end of the VOC presence on the Chinese coast.

In Siam, by contrast, the company succeeded in establishing an enduring relationship with the Ayutthayan kingdom (1351–1767). The VOC opened a factory in Siam in 1608 and operated there with sporadic breaks for over 150 years until 1765. The longevity of this connection hinged in large part on a generally favorable relationship with the Ayutthayan court, which engaged enthusiastically with the Dutch. Bhawan Ruangsilp, who has provided one of the best studies of the Dutch presence in Siam, argues that a partnership developed between Batavia and the kings of Siam, although she is careful to point out that it was always conditional.[10] At the heart of the relationship was a flourishing diplomatic engagement first between the princes of Orange and the Siamese monarchs, but later with Batavia as regular embassies transited between

VOC headquarters and the capital city of Ayutthaya.[11] The company's ability to make use of diplomacy in this way was strengthened by the fact that it was seen not only as a commercial and diplomatic partner but also as a valuable military ally. Indeed, the kings of Siam repeatedly pleaded with Dutch officials for naval assistance in various campaigns against enemies and recalcitrant vassals.[12]

As was the case in China, the company was never in a position to dictate to Siam, which its employees described as a "famous and potent Kingdom," but it was prepared to act aggressively and possessed the necessary tools to force a shift in Ayutthayan policy on key issues.[13] This is most clearly evident in 1663 when Batavia decided that, to quote Ruangsilp, a series of "accumulated problems between the VOC and the Siamese crown had to be solved on its terms."[14] Its chosen mechanism to do this was to make use of a well-worn tactic, the naval blockade. From November 1663 to February 1664, the company's ships sealed off the Chao Phraya River, seizing Siamese junks until the crown gave in to Batavia's demands. The result was a treaty concluded, according to one contemporary Dutch report, "out of fear and awe of the Company's might and weapons" that secured for the VOC a series of important concessions.[15] The overall effect of this short but highly effective campaign was thus to reset the company's relations with Siam on far more advantageous terms for Batavia.

This brief discussion brings us back to the question of Japan and the company's experience there. There is, of course, an obvious difference between the enduring ties that Batavia developed with Tokugawa Japan, which lasted for over two centuries, and the intermittent interaction that took place in China. But the Japanese example also has surprisingly little in common with the relationship that developed with the Ayutthaya kingdom in Siam, where the VOC did succeed in establishing a durable presence. Most noticeably, we see in Japan very little evidence of the conditional partnership that Ruangsilp has described. Instead this was a decidedly unequal relationship in which the VOC found itself forced into a consistently subordinate role. While this was certainly due in part to the relative strength of the Tokugawa Bakufu, one of the more formidable regimes in early modern Asia, simply pointing to this fact does not account for why things developed in the way they did. This study has attempted to offer some explanation for this by focusing on a series of contained conflicts involving the company and the Tokugawa regime that took place in the seventeenth century during a period of aggressive VOC expansion.

When it arrived in Japan in 1609, the VOC, a hybrid organization that combined the attributes of both corporation and state, came equipped not simply with ships and merchandize but with a set of sovereign powers derived from its charter that it was determined to exercise. The company's subsequent assertion of its rights over diplomacy, violence, and sovereignty triggered a series of clashes with the Bakufu. Within the confines of these conflicts—over whether the company could engage in high-level diplomacy with the shogun, over its rights to deploy maritime violence either in Japanese waters or against Japan's trading partners, and over its claims to full sovereignty in Tayouan—the terms of the relationship between the company and the shogun were, I have suggested, largely determined. In each case it was the VOC rather than the Tokugawa regime that was compelled to give ground, albeit always in different ways, and to retreat from its insistence on its proper rights and sovereign privileges. By the time this process was complete, the company found that it had lost access to tools that it took for granted in other parts of Asia.

Whereas in Siam a lavish embassy or carefully planned maritime campaign, such as the one that took place on the Chao Phraya River in 1663, offered the chance to swing the balance back toward the company, no such weapons of leverage were available in Japan. That this was the case was apparent by 1632 when the VOC, faced with no other alternative, elected to take the extraordinary step of handing over a high-ranking official, Pieter Nuyts, to reopen relations with Japan. It can also be seen in a range of comments made by Dutch officials in this period. In December 1638, for example, the governor-general clearly explained the company's strategy in Japan: "The Japanese must not be troubled. You must wait for the right time and opportunity and with the greatest patience to obtain something. They will not suffer being spoken back to. Therefore the smaller we make ourselves, pretending to be small, humble and modest merchants that live because of their wishes, the more favor and respect we can enjoy in their land. This we have learned from long experience. . . . In Japan you cannot be too humble."[16]

In the United Provinces the company's directors embraced a similar message. When they turned to the topic of Japan in their famous general instructions, which were issued in 1650, the Heeren 17 observed that "we can give our officers no other instructions than to satisfy this arrogant, grand and punctilious nation in everything."[17] VOC officials should, the directors insisted, "go armed with modesty, humility, courteousness and friendship," seeking never to dictate to the regime but always to bend to its wishes.

But it was not simply that the company lost access to effective tools that it relied on in other parts of Asia. Rather it was also the case that the Dutch in Japan were incorporated into the domestic system in a way that was quite distinct from the Ayutthayan example. Some sense of this divide can be obtained by looking at two separate military campaigns in which Batavia offered its support first to the king of Siam and later to the Tokugawa shogun. Beginning in 1633, King Prasatthong of Siam (r. 1629–56) attempted to lure the Dutch into participating in a war against his former vassal state of Patani by promising lucrative trade concessions in return for naval support.[18] These pleas eventually bore fruit and in 1634 the company dispatched a small fleet to take part in military operations. Although the actual impact of VOC involvement was negligible, Batavia's willingness to provide aid earned the Dutch a raft of new privileges that significantly improved their position in Siam.[19] The Shimabara campaign, which took place three years later, played out very differently. Rather than being drawn into participating by the promise of rewards, the Dutch, trapped by their own rhetoric and past promises, were compelled to volunteer alongside the shogun's domestic subordinates for service against the rebels.

The difference between these two campaigns speaks to the distinctive nature of the company's relationship with the shogun. In Japan the company was domesticated, confined within a self-designated role as vassal, and saddled with a raft of attached responsibilities. Abandoning their claims to represent a powerful external figure, whether the Stadhouder or the governor-general, the Dutch were, for all their obvious foreignness, transformed into domestic subordinates. As part of this, VOC representatives were subjected to a tailored version of the sankin kōtai system; required to render military service (either directly or in the form of intelligence reports); forced to give up key rights (most notably related to the deployment of maritime violence) while accepting the shogun's legal authority (as least as it related to certain offenses); and compelled, like other vassals, to play their part in theatrical displays of submission. It was a role they would become intimately familiar with, acting it out year after year until the boundaries between performance and reality became irrevocably blurred. Whether the Dutch were real vassals or were simply playing the part became largely irrelevant; they behaved, to all intents and purposes, like the shogun's loyal servants and, as the inclusion of a separate section, *hōkō,* or service, in *Tsūkō ichiran* makes clear, were recognized as the sole occupants of a unique category in the Tokugawa order.

This study has not attempted to document the history of the Dutch in Japan. Rather, by focusing on a series of contained conflicts, its goal has been to chart a process of socialization, in which the Dutch were forced to adapt to find a place in a Tokugawa order. Given that these clashes were almost uniformly resolved in the Asian partner's favor, it should be clear that company's relationship with the Tokugawa shogun was not entirely typical, but nor was it so far removed from the more general experience of Europeans in Asia that it should be seen as a historical outlier with no relevance beyond Japan. While there has been an understandable tendency to focus on places where direct colonization occurred or on relations—like those between the company and Mataram, Banten, or Makassar—where the European impact was greatest, these were not the norm, and the more common scenario was one in which Europeans struggled to manage the terms of their engagement with Asia. Arguably no other encounter better illustrates this point than the one that took place between the Dutch and Tokugawa Japan.

If, following the work of Pomeranz, Bin Wong, and others, we accept the enduring power of Asian states in the early modern period as a fact, then it is surely incumbent on historians to better chart the long process of integration in which Europeans were assimilated into Asian orders. The Dutch experience in Japan shows that European footholds in Asia did not invariably morph from isolated trading posts into fortified bases before finally becoming full colonies. Rather the presence of formidable Asian states meant that even the most forceful of European organizations could be confined to enclaves from which they never escaped. Japan provides the emblematic dead end for Europeans enterprises in Asia, a site of total containment, and thus serves as a valuable counterpoint to those studies that assume that the "rise of Europe" began with the voyages of exploration in 1492 or 1497 and continued, marching according to the relentless beat of some great drum, in subsequent centuries.

NOTES

INTRODUCTION: TAMING THE DUTCH

1. 7 November 1627, Daghregister van de reijse gedaen bij Pieter Nuijts ende Pieter Muijser, oppercoopman, als ambassadeurs aen den keijser ende rijcxraden van Japan van 24 Julij 1627 tot 18 Februarij 1628, VOC 1095:491v.

2. Major, *Select Letters of Christopher Columbus*, 2.

3. Scholarship on these ceremonies has been shaped by Patricia Seed's pioneering work. Seed, *Ceremonies of Possession*.

4. Markham, *The Journal of Christopher Columbus*, 35–36.

5. Elliott, "The Spanish Conquest and Settlement of America," 175.

6. Parker, *The Military Revolution*, 119.

7. De Certeau, *The Writing of History*, xxv–xxvi.

8. Greenblatt sums up this image when he writes that the "Europeans who ventured to the New World in the first decades after Columbus's discovery shared a complex, well-developed, and, above all, mobile technology of power: writing, navigational instruments, ships, warhorses, attack dogs, effective armor, and highly lethal weapons, including gunpowder. Their culture was characterized by immense confidence in its own centrality, by a political organization based on practices of command and submission, by a willingness to use coercive violence on both strangers and fellow countrymen, and by a religious ideology centered on the endlessly proliferated representation of a tortured and murdered god of love." Greenblatt, *Marvelous Possessions*, 9.

9. The distorting influence of the Columbian experience on world history has been examined by a number of scholars. My own thinking on this issue has been most influenced by Tonio Andrade and Robert Markley. Andrade, "Beyond Guns, Germs and Steel"; Markley, *The Far East and the English Imagination* and "Gulliver and the Japanese."

10. In his famous study, Carlo Cipolla suggested that military technology was the key factor enabling the "rise of Europe." Cipolla, *Guns, Sails, and Empire*. A similar argument sits at the heart of the military revolution thesis, which argues for the centrality of military technology in both European and world history. Parker, *The Military Revolution*, 83.

11. Said, *Orientalism*.

12. Singh, *Colonial Narratives/Cultural Dialogues*, 2.

13. Landes has made a similar argument in the 2006 article "Why Europe and the West?"

14. Landes, *The Wealth and Poverty of Nations*, 96.

15. Andrade, "Beyond Guns, Germs and Steel," 167.

16. Due to space constraints, I have only been able to reference a small selection of this scholarship.

17. Swope, "Crouching Tigers, Secret Weapons"; Lorge, *The Asian Military Revolution;* Sun, "Military Technology Transfers from Ming China."

18. Blussé, *Visible Cities* and *Strange Company;* Andrade, *How Taiwan Became Chinese;* Thompson, "The Military Superiority Thesis"; Scammell, "The Pillars of Empire."

19. Pomeranz, *The Great Divergence;* Wong, *China Transformed;* Frank, *ReOrient.*

20. Ravenstein, *The Journal of the First Voyage of Vasco da Gama*, 51–63.

21. Quoted in Boxer, *South China in the Sixteenth Century*, 56–57.

22. Swift, *Gulliver's Travels.*

23. I am by no means the first to make a connection along these lines. Linda Colley starts off her superb book *Captives* by using the twin figures of Gulliver and Crusoe to compare different visions of European expansion. Colley, *Captives*, 1–3.

24. Swift, *Gulliver's Travels*, 39.

25. Ibid., 104.

26. Ibid., 313.

27. Smail, "On the Possibility of an Autonomous History of Modern Southeast Asia."

28. This notion of a Vasco da Gama era was put forward by Panikkar, *Asia and Western Dominance.* For a discussion of the "age of partnership," see Kling and Pearson, *The Age of Partnership.*

29. Furber, "Asia and the West as Partners Before Empire and After."

30. Ruangsilp, *Dutch East India Company Merchants at the Court of Ayutthaya.*

31. Some years later, Ashin das Gupta offered a more cautious reframing of Furber's framework by suggesting that "the partnership was probably never one of unreserved human acceptance of each other but for much of the time the acceptance of a structure of trade and politics within which everybody functioned." Das Gupta, "The Indian Ocean in the Eighteenth Century," 132.

32. Subrahmanyam, *The Political Economy of Commerce*, 297.

33. For a summary of related scholarship, see Vink, "Indian Ocean Studies and the New Thalassology," 56.

34. Felipe Fernández-Armesto sums up the wider point in typically memorable fashion: "When those creatures of my imagination, the Galactic Museum-Keepers, look back on our past, with the objectivity of a vantage point near the edge of the universe, ten thousand years in the future, they will center their display on China, and cram Western civilization into a corner of some small vitrine." Fernández-Armesto, *Civilizations*, 22–33.

35. In an important study, Mark Ravina has labeled the Tokugawa Bakufu a "compound state" and has emphasized the relative independence of the domains. Ravina, *Land and Lordship in Early Modern Japan*, 27.

36. Although the VOC itself collapsed, the Dutch trading outpost in Japan endured into the second half of the nineteenth century.

37. Boxer, *The Christian Century in Japan*. This work has been reprinted in 1967, 1974, and 1993.

38. Arano, *Kinsei Nihon to Higashi Ajia*; and Toby, *State and Diplomacy in Early Modern Japan*.

39. The most directly relevant of these is Reinier Hesselink's pioneering study, which directly addresses the relationship between the company and the Bakufu through a focus on the 1643 Breskens incident. It will be discussed in more detail in chapter 3. Hesselink, *Prisoners from Nambu*. Matsukata has analyzed Dutch intelligence reports submitted to the Bakufu. Matsukata, *Oranda fūsetsugaki to kinsei Nihon*. Mention should also be made of Michael Laver's important work, which, although it does not focus exclusively on the Dutch, includes significant sections on the VOC. Laver, *Japan's Economy by Proxy* and *The Sakoku Edicts and the Politics of Tokugawa Hegemony*.

40. Nagazumi and Takeda, *Hirado Oranda shōkan Igirisu shōkan nikki*. The first half of this book, which focuses on the Dutch factory, has been written by Nagazumi, who has also produced a number of other important works on the VOC connection with Japan.

41. Scholars differ as to whether to label these powers sovereign or quasi-sovereign. Janice Thomson argues that the VOC was "endowed with nearly all the powers of sovereignty," while M. C. Ricklefs calls these powers "quasi-sovereign." Thomson, *Mercenaries, Pirates, and Sovereigns*, 32; Ricklefs, *A History of Modern Indonesia*, 30. To my mind, there seems, given the extent of the company's hybrid nature, no compelling reason not to make use of the term *sovereign*.

42. Van Goor calls the company a "hybrid state: run as a business concern but acting like a kingdom." Van Goor, "A Hybrid State." Barendse states it particularly well when he notes that "in Europe the Companies were merchants; in Asia they were states." Barendse, *The Arabian Seas*, 299.

43. Van der Chijs, *Geschiedenis der stichting van de Vereenigde O.I. Compagnie*, 130. The clauses of the original document are not numbered, but it has become standard practice to refer to this as article 35.

44. Blussé, "Amongst Feigned Friends and Declared Enemies," 154. For a study of the constant interplay between these two tactics, see Borschberg, *The Singapore and Melaka Straits*.

45. Gaastra, *The Dutch East India Company*, 60.

46. In thinking about the VOC in this way, I have been influenced by Philip Stern's pioneering work on the English East India Company. Arguing against the standard "trade to empire" narrative, he suggests an "alternative vision of the pre-Plassey East India Company, not as a commercial body or an arm of the Anglo-British state but as an independent form of polity and political community." Stern, "'A Politie of Civill & Military Power,'" 257. See also his *The Company-State*.

47. Quoted in Winius and Vink, *The Merchant-Warrior Pacified*, 30–31.

48. As an example of a different view, Els Jacobs has argued that historians have given the "smoke of battle and the roar of cannon" too much attention and suggests that the focus should be brought back to the company's commercial activities. Jacobs, *Merchant in Asia*, 10.

49. Temple, *The Works of Sir William Temple*, 173–74.

50. Martine van Ittersum has demonstrated that Grotius, formerly the subject of hagiographic studies that framed him as the father of a cosmopolitan system of international law, should be understood as the key legal collaborator to Dutch expansion in Asia. Van Ittersum, *Profit and Principle*.

51. Most recently by Laver, *Japan's Economy by Proxy in the Seventeenth Century*.

52. Goodman, *Japan and the Dutch*, 16.

53. Swift, *Gulliver's Travels*, 223.

54. Kaempfer, *Kaempfer's Japan*.

55. Ibid., 359.

56. Tokyo daigaku shiryō hensanjo, *Dagregisters gehouden door de Opperhoofden van de Nederlandse Faktorij in Japan*, 6:204. The Historiographical Institute at the University at Tokyo is engaged in an ongoing project to publish the diaries of the Dutch *opperhoofden* in Japan. The series commences with the 1633 diary of Nicolaes Couckebacker. Hereafter *Dagregisters Japan*.

57. Sen, *Distant Sovereignty*, xii–xiii.

58. In an important but seldom cited article, George Winius and Markus Vink have clearly documented the failure of VOC aspirations in East Asia. Winius and Vink, "South India and the China Seas: How the V.O.C. Shifted Its Weight from China and Japan to India."

59. Markley, *The Far East and the English Imagination*, 246–47.

60. Craig, *Civilization and Enlightenment*, 149.

61. Suzuki, "Japan's Socialization."

1. ROYAL LETTERS FROM THE REPUBLIC

1. Goodman, *Japan and the Dutch*, 10; Mulder, *Hollanders in Hirado*, 53.

2. Goodman, *Japan and the Dutch*, 10.

3. Wills, *Embassies and Illusions*. The past decade has seen a renewed interest in diplomacy. Zoltan Biedermann and Stefan Halikowski-Smith have analyzed Portuguese diplomacy in Asia. Biedermann, "Portuguese Diplomacy in Asia"; Halikowski-Smith, "The Friendship of Kings Was in the Ambassadors." Richmond Barbour's work will be discussed later in the chapter. Markus Vink's recent study of VOC diplomacy in India came out after the completion of this manuscript. Vink, *Mission to Madurai*.

4. Barbour, *Before Orientalism*, 146–91, and "Power and Distant Display."

5. Quoted in Barbour, "Power and Distant Display," 357.

6. Radwan, *The Dutch in Western India*, 130. Wills has made a similar point. Wills, *Embassies and Illusions*, 52.

7. Typically, Tokugawa foreign relations are divided into two groups: diplomatic (*tsūshin*) and commercial (*tsūshō*). Bruce Batten sums up the conventional categorization as follows: "Korea and Ryukyu were considered 'diplomatic partner states' (*tsūshin no kuni*), while China and Holland were 'trade partner states' (*tsūshō no kuni*) without formal diplomatic ties." Batten, *To the Ends of Japan*, 44. Since the VOC was indeed a commercial organization that had been formed for the business of trade, it appears self-evident that its representatives would fit into the second, subsovereign category from the moment they arrived in Japan in 1609. In fact, the opposite was true.

8. Ravenstein, *The Journal of the First Voyage of Vasco da Gama*, 50.

9. Boxer, *Four Centuries of Portuguese Expansion*, 18.

10. In later periods the Portuguese colonial government in Goa gained possession of a royal seal, which enabled it to speed up the process of diplomatic exchange. Wills, *Embassies and Illusions*, 103.

11. Ravenstein, *The Journal of the First Voyage of Vasco da Gama*, 59.

12. Disney, *A History of Portugal and the Portuguese Empire*, 2:138.

13. Ibid.

14. Ravenstein, *The Journal of the First Voyage of Vasco da Gama*, 62.

15. Masselman, *The Cradle of Colonialism*, 463

16. These were the governor, deputy, treasurer and 24 members of the board. Masselman, *The Cradle of Colonialism*, 281.

17. Bruce, *Annals of the Honourable East-India Company*, 132.

18. Ogborn, *Indian Ink*, 42.

19. Markham, *The Voyages of Sir James Lancaster*, 76.

20. Ibid., 78–80.

21. For an analysis of this letter, see Markley, "Riches, power, trade and religion." Markley notes that Elizabeth requires "the king of Aceh to decree, with his absolute power, favourable trading conditions for her subjects."

22. Ogborn, *Indian Ink*, 40–4.

23. Barbour, "Power and Distant Display."

24. Foster, *Early Travels in India*, 229–30.

25. Ibid.

26. For a comprehensive introduction to the Dutch Republic, see Israel, *The Dutch Republic*.

27. Rowen, *The Princes of Orange*, 38.

28. Temple, *The Works of Sir William Temple*, 94.

29. Van Gelderen, *The Political Thought of the Dutch Revolt*, 59.

30. In diplomatic terms the Dutch republic was, as Frijhoff and Spies note, "the odd man out in Europe." Frijhoff and Spies, *Dutch Culture in a European Perspective*, 93.

31. The United Provinces was not of course the only republic in Europe, with Venice as the obvious point of comparison.

32. This only changed after the conclusion of the twelve-year truce with Spain, which effectively recognized the republic as an independent state. After this a number of states in Europe including France and England agreed to receive the republic's envoys as full ambassadors. Israel, *The Dutch Republic*, 405.

33. Gaastra, *The Dutch East India Company*, 17.

34. De Jonge and van Deventer, *De opkomst van het Nederlandsch gezag in Oost Indië*, 2:372.

35. Frijhoff and Spies, *Dutch Culture in a European Perspective*, 94.

36. Although the Princes of Orange played a vital role in the history of the United Provinces and its successor states, their title and position as sovereign princes were derived from the tiny principality of Orange, which lay within the borders of France.

37. Troost, *William III the Stadholder-king*, 2.

38. Groenveld, "The King-Stadholder," 19–20.

39. Between 1650 and 1672, the States-General was able to dispense with the *Stadhouder* entirely.

40. The appearance of the Stadhouder in diplomatic negotiations has been noted by a number of scholars. In his classic examination of the legal aspects of European expansion into Asia, which was first published in 1967, C. H. Alexandrowicz argued that the "formal introduction of the Sovereign of the Netherlands [that is the 'king of Holland'] as a transacting party in negotiations and agreements was another way of satisfying the demands and aspirations of the major powers in the East Indies." Alexandrowicz, *An Introduction to the History of the Law of Nations*, 33. See also: Borschberg, *The Singapore and Melaka Straits*, 110–11. Ruangsilp, *Dutch East India Company Merchants*, 31–32.

41. Frijhoff, "The Princely Court at The Hague," 71.

42. Ibid. It took, for example, until 1639 for the States-General to publish a set of guidelines involving the role of the Stadhouder in diplomatic ceremonies in Europe. Frijhoff notes that "the function given the stadholder in the code of 1639 . . . [was] to receive the emissaries in the name of the States."

43. This was not always the case, and the States-General did feature in certain diplomatic negotiations.

44. As in the epigraph at the beginning of this chapter. Groeneveldt, *De Nederlanders in China*, 34. The comment comes from a letter sent by a Dutch admiral to a Chinese official in 1607. Wassing-visser writes that for "even for the most Republican of merchants . . . it was more opportune for trade and for commercial contracts, expressly and only on paper, [to refer] to their stadholder as Maurice, Prince or Orange, Sovereign or, if it were more convenient, even 'Coninck' or 'King.'" My reading of the

sources suggests that such references were not confined simply to paper. Wassing-visser, *Royal Gifts from Indonesia*, 22–36.

45. De Jonge and van Deventer, *De opkomst van het Nederlandsch gezag in Oost Indië*, 2:372.

46. Keblusek and Zijlmans, *Princely Display: The Court of Frederik Hendrik of Orange and Amalia van Solms*. Frijhoff and Spies note that "this minuscule state [the principality of Orange] was spread over a few small towns and a dozen or so villages." Frijhoff and Spies, *Dutch Culture in a European Perspective*, 95.

47. Michiel Jansz. van Mierevelt, *Maurice, Prince of Orange*, Rijksmuseum Amsterdam, object number SK-A-255.

48. This explanation appears in a number of compilations of VOC materials. W. Ph. Coolhaas suggests "it was not possible for the Dutch to make it clear how their state was governed" to Asian officials. Coolhaas, *Generale Missiven*, 1:13. In a different publication, he maintains that "the constitutional arrangements of the Republic were incomprehensible to Asians." Coolhaas, *Pieter van den Broecke in Azie*, 30.

49. Rouffaer and Ijzerman, *De eerste schipvaart der Nederlanders naar Oost-Indië*, 1:80.

50. Unger, *De oudste reizen van de Zeeuwen naar Oost-Indië*,15.

51. As expressed in Zhang, *Mingshi*, juan 134.

52. While in some instances, this reference to Maurits as monarch may have been the result of a misunderstanding, it was clearly also the case that Asian rulers were simply responding to the presentation of Maurits directly as the "king of Holland."

53. Wassing-visser, *Royal Gifts from Indonesia*, 27–8.

54. De Jonge and van Deventer, *De opkomst van het Nederlandsch gezag in Oost Indië*, 3:305; Borschberg, *The Singapore and Melaka Straits*, 110.

55. Ibid., 3:291–92.

56. Van der Cruysse, *Siam and the West*, 47; see also Duyvendak, "The First Siamese Embassy to Holland."

57. Ruangsilp, *Dutch East India Company Merchants*, 57–70.

58. Purchas, *Hakluytus posthumus*, 2:486.

59. Edmundson, *Anglo-Dutch Rivalry During the First Half of the Seventeenth Century*, 78.

60. We know as well that Dutch representatives were prone to exaggeration when it came to describing Maurits and the United Provinces. One emissary explained that the boundaries of the republic encompassed most of western Europe. Vlekke, *Nusantara*, 115.

61. Farrington, *The English Factory in Japan*, 1:778–79.

62. Purchas, *Hakluytus posthumus*, 2:457.

63. Arasaratnam, *Francois Valentijn's Description of Ceylon*, 299.

64. The sources for this expedition can be found in Weider, *De Reis van Mahu en De Cordes*. For a recent study, see De Lange, *Pars Japonica*.

65. Farrington, *The English Factory in Japan*, 1:54.

66. For details of William Adams, see Massarella, *A World Elsewhere*. For Joosten, see Iwao, *Jan Joosten*.

67. For an account of this connection, see Toyama, *Matsura-shi to Hirado bōeki.*

68. Weider, *De Reis van Mahu en De Cordes*, 3:85–86.

69. Sūden, *Ikoku nikki shō*, 77–8. Katō, "Unification and Adaptation," 215.

70. Weider, *De Reis van Mahu en De Cordes*, 3:42.

71. The letter can be found in Weider, *De Reis van Mahu en De Cordes*, 3:81–84.

72. Ibid., 83–84.

73. Opstall, *De Reis van de Vloot*, 2:328.

74. Tokyo daigaku shiryō hensanjo, *Dai Nihon shiryō*, series 12, 6:457.

75. De Jonge and van Deventer, *De Opkomst van het Nederlandsch gezag in Oost Indië*, 3:296. Although the Dutch knew of the existence of an actual emperor in Kyoto, they consistently referred to the shogun as either emperor or imperial majesty.

76. One Korean ambassador, who serves as a typical example, was the third minister of the board of taxation and later rose to become chief state councilor. Although clearly qualified for the job, he was assisted by a deputy ambassador, who held the position of first tutor of the Crown Prince Tutorial Office. Lee, "Cultural Expressions of Tokugawa Japan and Choson Korea," 136.

77. Van den Broek and Puyck are generally described in VOC sources as merchants but the former at least held the rank of senior merchant (*opperkoopman*). Originally a merchant in Matelieff's fleet, van den Broek rose to become head of the factory in Johor in 1607. In 1612, he was condemned for murder, but was later reprieved.

78. McCune, "The Exchange of Envoys"; see also Toby, "Carnival of the Aliens."

79. Van Goor, *Prelude to Colonialism*, 27.

80. Ferguson, *The Earliest Dutch Visits to Ceylon*, 381.

81. Focusing on just one extremely valuable commodity, James Lewis has shown that delegations from Korea gifted a large share of all the ginseng sold in Japan in any one year to the shogun. Lewis, *Frontier Contact Between Choson Korea and Tokugawa Japan*, 136.

82. Wap, *Het Gezantschap van den Sultan van Achin*, 16.

83. Van der Chijs, Colenbrander, and de Hullu, *Dagh-register gehouden int Casteel Batavia*, 188. Hereafter *Batavia Dagregisters.*

84. Van Spilbergen, *De reis van Joris van Spilbergen naar Ceylon*, 49.

85. Tokyo daigaku shiryō hensanjo, *Dai Nihon shiryō*, series 12, 6:465.

86. Ibid.

87. Ibid., 464.

88. De Jonge and van Deventer, *De opkomst van het Nederlandsch gezag in Oost Indië*, 3:294–99.

89. Ogborn, *Indian Ink*, 43.

90. Van Foreest and de Booy, *De Vierde schipvaart der Nederlanders*, 142.

91. Wassing-visser, *Royal Gifts from Indonesia*, 29.

92. Letter from Jacques Specx, November 1610, VOC 1054:1–5.

93. My discussion is based on a 1601 patent issued by Maurits to Jacob van Neck. Van Foreest and de Booy, *De Vierde schipvaart der Nederlanders*, 141–44.

94. Miles Ogborn, who has examined similar letters sent by English monarchs, argues that these documents "attempted to use personal relationships between

powerful individuals who were unlikely to meet to establish trading relations between 'nations.'" Ogborn, *Indian Ink*, 45.

95. Van Foreest and de Booy, *De Vierde schipvaart der Nederlanders*, 141.

96. Ibid., 145.

97. Ibid., 143.

98. One observer writing in 1612 described it as "a body by themselves, power-full and mighty in this State, and will not acknowledge the authority of the States [-General] generally more than shall be for their private profits." Quoted in Adams, *The Familial State*, 54.

99. This quote comes from a subsequent letter sent to Japan. Sūden, *Ikoku nikki shō*, 108–25.

100. The most important source for reconstructing the events of the embassy is Puyck's diary. While it provides a basic sense of what happened, the diary is also frustratingly short and bears little resemblance to the lengthy accounts kept by later ambassadors. Opstall, *De Reis van de Vloot*, 2:345–63.

101. Ibid., 2:352.

102. Gotō Shōzaburō (1571–1625) ran the Bakufu's gold mint (*kinza*). Honda Masa-zumi (1565–1637) and his father Masanobu (1538–1616) were both key Bakufu advis-ers. When Hidetada became shogun in 1605, Masanobu was attached to him as a sec-retary while Masazumi remained with Ieyasu at Sunpu.

103. Opstall, *De Reis van de Vloot*, 2:352.

104. Sūden, *Ikoku nikki shō*, 17.

105. Ravenstein *The Journal of the First Voyage of Vasco da Gama*, 62.

106. Arano, *Edo Bakufu to higashi Ajia*, 26.

107. Table adapted from Fujii, "Jūnana seiki no Nihon: buke no kokka no keisei."

108. The surge of Japanese diplomatic correspondence is dealt with in Clulow, "Like lambs in Japan and devils outside their land."

109. As evidenced in the multiple embassies from Siam which were rejected by Bakufu officials. Iwao, "Reopening of the Diplomatic and Commercial Relations."

110. This translation comes from the original Japanese letter. Sūden, *Ikoku nikki shō*, 17–20. The original Dutch translation can also be found in the same source.

111. Toby, *State and Diplomacy in Early Modern Japan*, 178.

112. Sūden, *Ikoku nikki shō*, 17–20.

113. For a similar letter to the king of England, see Satow, *The Voyage of Captain John Saris to Japan*, lxxviii.

114. Kondō, *Gaiban tsūsho*, in *Kaitei shiseki shūran*, 21:140–41.

115. Ibid.

116. De Jonge and van Deventer, *De opkomst van het Nederlandsch gezag in Oost Indië*, 3: 294–99.

117. The Dutch were not alone in thinking this. English East India Company merchants who arrived in Japan in 1613 also congratulated themselves on securing unprecedented favors and privileges from the shogun.

118. Satow, "Notes on the Intercourse Between Japan and Siam in the Seven-teenth Century," 146.

119. Kuno, *Japanese Expansion on the Asiatic Continent*, 2:305.

120. Jacques Specx, letter, 3 November 1610, VOC 1054:5.

121. Both the Japanese original and the Dutch translation can be found in Sūden, *Ikoku nikki shō*, 108–25.

122. Markley has analyzed a similar trope in English letters to Asia. Markley, "Riches, Power, Trade, and Religion," 499.

123. See, for example, St. Aldegonde, *A pithie, and most earnest exhortation.*

124. Sūden, *Ikoku nikki shō*, 113.

125. Ibid., 131–32.

126. Tokyo daigaku shiryō hensanjo, *Dai Nihon shiryō*, series 12, 9:189.

2. THE LORD OF BATAVIA

1. *Batavia Dagregisters, Anno 1625–1629*, 1.

2. Multiple variations of Nuyts's name appear in VOC materials. I have chosen the most common spelling.

3. Each of these potential culprits is pushed forward in the Daghregister van de reijse gedaen bij Pieter Nuijts ende Pieter Muijser, oppercoopman, als ambassadeurs aen den keijser ende rijcxraden van Japan van 24 Julij 1627 tot 18 Februarij 1628, VOC 1095:449–509, quote at 462v. Hereafter Nuijts/Muijser *Dagregister*.

4. Much of the scholarship on 1627 embassy mission has followed Batavia's findings by emphasizing Nuyts's personal failings. Leonard Blussé writes that "Nuyts upon his arrival in Japan . . . succeeded in antagonizing his hosts so much by his haughty demeanor and the antics of his travel companions that he was refused an audience with the Shogun." Blussé, "Bull in a China Shop," 103. Nagazumi Yōko notes that "due to his complete ignorance of Japanese affairs, his mission ended in failure." Nagazumi, "The Japanese Go-shuinjo (Vermilion Seal) Maritime Trade in Taiwan," 33. While I agree with both assertions, the goal of this chapter is to address some the larger issues faced by Nuyts that made it unlikely that any ambassador, however skillful, could have succeeded.

5. Roe, *The Embassy of Sir Thomas Roe to India.*

6. 10 October 1627, Nuijts/Muijser *Dagregister*, 468v. Roe, *The Embassy of Sir Thomas Roe to India*, 2:497.

7. Gaastra, *The Dutch East India Company*, 39–40.

8. Van Dam, *Beschrijvinge van de Oostindishe Compagnie*, 1:517–31.

9. May 30, the anniversary of the "the conquest of the kingdom of Jakatra" became an annual celebration for VOC officials in Asia. For one such celebration, see *Batavia Dagregisters, Anno 1625–1629*, 257.

10. De Jonge and van Deventer, *De Opkomst van het Nederlandsch Gezag in Oost-Indie*, 5:248–49.

11. Quoted in Gaastra, *The Dutch East India Company*, 68.

12. This process was accelerated after the Heeren 17 lost control of the right to appoint new governors-general. The directors had directly appointed Pieter Both and his immediate successors, but in 1629, after an incumbent died in office, the governing

council in Batavia selected his replacement without waiting for a decision from Europe. The result was a crucial precedent that quickly settled into custom. After this, the decision as to the next governor-general was made in Batavia and then sent to the republic to be rubber-stamped there. This is not to say, however, that the Heeren 17 retreated into the background. Each governor-general was required to provide exhaustive reports explaining their decisions and detailing developments within the company's trading sphere. Even more important, the directors retained control over the supply of personnel, vessels, and funds.

13. The Heeren 17 were quick to condemn what they saw as an excessive focus on prestige. On one occasion the directors wrote that "no great attention should be paid to the question of reputation and honour, which is often taken too heavily; in our opinion (for we are merchants) he has the honour who without doing unright or violence has the profit." Quoted in Steensgaard, "The Dutch East India Company as an Institutional Innovation," 255.

14. Blussé, "Amongst Feigned Friends and Declared Enemies," 154.

15. *Batavia Dagregisters, Anno 1641–1642*, 75.

16. Israel, *The Dutch Republic*, 323

17. *Batavia Dagregisters, Anno 1625–1629*, 80.

18. For a history of the city, see Abeyasekere, *Jakarta*.

19. Valentijn, *François Valentijn's oud en nieuw Oost-Indien*, 3:510.

20. *Batavia Dagregisters, Anno 1625–1629*, 80.

21. Tavernier, *A collection of several relations & treatises singular and curious of John Baptista Tavernier*, 65.

22. Valentijn, *François Valentijn's oud en nieuw Oost-Indien*, 3:548.

23. Nieuhof, *An Embassy from the East India Company*, 27.

24. Bolling, "Friderici Bollingii Oost-Indisch reisboek," 331.

25. De Haan, *Oud Batavia*, 178.

26. *Batavia Dagregisters, Anno 1631–1634*, 97.

27. Frick and Schweitzer, *A Relation of Two Several Voyages Made into the East-Indies*, 203.

28. Zandvliet, *The Dutch Encounter with Asia*, 41.

29. Carel Reyniersz (in office, 1650–1653), Joan Maetsuyker (in office, 1653–1678), and Cornelis Speelman (in office, 1681–1684) all received such funerals. For Speelman's remarkably lavish funeral, see Stapel, *Cornelis Janszoon Speelman*. The account is also published in *Bijdragen tot de taal-, land- en volkenkunde* 94 (1936): 1–121.

30. In Goa Portuguese viceroys also cultivated "a quasi-regal image." They did so through the use of a flagship, a personal bodyguard, and regular processions through the city under "a symbolic canopy or pallium of brocade" accompanied by trumpeters and drummers. Disney, *A History of the Portugal and the Portuguese Empire*, 2:161–62.

31. Tavernier, *A collection of several relations & treatises singular and curious of John Baptista Tavernier*, 65.

32. For an important analysis of VOC diplomatic protocol, see Blussé, "Queen Among Kings."

33. Tachard, *A Relation of the Voyage to Siam*, 110.

34. *Batavia Dagregisters*, 1679, 620.

35. Tachard, *A Relation of the Voyage to Siam*, 121.

36. *Batavia Dagregisters, Anno 1679*, 621.

37. *Batavia Dagregisters, Anno 1647–1648*, 94.

38. *Batavia Dagregisters, Anno 1664*, 10.

39. De Haan, *Oud Batavia*, 212. Valentijn, *Oud en Nieuw Oost-Indiën*, 3:31.

40. Van Goor, "A Hybrid State," 212.

41. For a description of an ostentatious 1689 embassy to Persia, see Valentijn, *Oud en Nieuw Oost-Indie*, 5.2: 250–69.

42. For one example see the 1655 letter from the governor-general to the emperor of China. Van Dam, *Beschrijvinge van de Oostindische Compagnie*, 2.1:767–68.

43. Over time, Batavia gained its own satellite states in the form of kingdoms such as Ternate that paid homage directly to the governor-general and supplied troops to serve in his army. For one example, see Widjojo, *The Revolt of Prince Nuku*, 30.

44. Ruangsilp, *Dutch East India Company Merchants*, 70

45. Missive aen den coningh uyt den name van sijn hoogheit den heere prince van Orangien, VOC 865: 392–93.

46. Cornelis van Neijenrood (Hirado) to Batavia, letter, 17 November 1625, VOC 1087: 237–41.

47. Further details on this important figure will be provided in chapter 6.

48. Memorie voor de E. Pieter Nuyts, raet van India, gaende voor commandeur over de vlote naer Tayouan gedestineert, ende van daer voorts in ambassade aen den Keijser van Japan, 10 May 1627, VOC 854: 51–60.

49. Blussé, "Bull in a China Shop," 102; see also Blussé, "Pieter Nuyts."

50. Quoted in Boxer, *The Dutch Seaborne Empire*, 52.

51. Coolhaas, "Een lastig heerschap tegenover een lastig volk." 27.

52. The valediction included here in brackets does not appear in the copy of the letter preserved in the VOC archives, but a range of other sources make it clear that it was in the original document handed over to Tokugawa officials.

53. Prouisionele Memorie van de die geprojecteert sijn met gesanten de heer Pieter Nuijts, VOC 854:76.

54. Provisionele raminge van schenckagien voor haere keyserlijcke Mayesteit rijcxraden ende andere grooten in Japan VOC 854:72–75.

55. Letter from Cornelis van Neijenroode to Governor-General Jacques Specx in Batavia, letter, 31 October 1630, VOC 1103:114–17.

56. After the embassy failed, Batavia condemned the "excessive and extraordinary expenses" caused by its great "pomp" and ordered Nuyts to personally reimburse all the costs he had incurred in Japan. Leupe, "Stukken betrekkelijk Pieter Nuyts."

57. Barbour, *Before Orientalism*, 166.

58. Roe, *The Embassy of Sir Thomas Roe to India*, 552.

59. Ibid., 44

60. Colenbrander, *Jan Pietersz. Coen*, 7.2:1155.

61. As clearly documented by Ogborn, *Indian Ink*, 57–64.

62. Roe, *The Embassy of Sir Thomas Roe to India*, 46.

63. Ibid., 47.

64. Colenbrander, *Jan Pietersz. Coen*, 7.2:1154.

65. Cornelis van Neijenroode to Governor-General Jacques Specx in Batavia, letter, 31 October 1630, VOC 1103:114–17.

66. Tokyo daigaku shiryō hensanjo, *Dai Nihon shiryō*, series 12, 8:646.

67. Colenbrander, *Jan Pietersz. Coen*, 7.2:1154.

68. By 1627 the company had access to a small group of Japanese translators, but while their abilities seem to have been adequate for the day-to-day business of commerce, they were clearly less adept at preparing official documents for Bakufu consumption. To make the job of translation more difficult, all documents had to pass through Portuguese, which served as a lingua franca in maritime East Asia, on their way from Dutch to Japanese. For a discussion of these translators, see Katō, *Bakuhansei kokka no keisei to gaikoku bōeki*.

69. Cornelis van Neijenroode to Governor-General Jacques Specx in Batavia, letter, 31 October 1630, VOC 1103:114–17.

70. Colenbrander, *Jan Pietersz. Coen*, 7.2:1170.

71. 19 September 1627, Nuijts/Muijser *Dagregister*, 453.

72. 1 October 1627, Nuijts/Muijser *Dagregister*, 455v.

73. 1 October 1627, Nuijts/Muijser *Dagregister*, 455v–455.

74. Colenbrander, *Jan Pietersz. Coen*, 7.2:1171. Although the temple in question is not named, it may have been Honseiji, a temple in Bakoruchō that was used to lodge ambassadors from Korea.

75. 1 October 1627, Nuijts/Muijser *Dagregister*, 455.

76. Hirado domain's reliance on foreign merchants is detailed in Clulow, "From Global Entrepôt to Early Modern Domain."

77. 3 October 1627, Nuijts/Muijser *Dagregister*. 456v.

78. Ibid. Itami Yasukatsu, the lord of Harima, held the position of *kanjō bugyō* or governor of finance in the Bakufu.

79. 4 October, Nuijts/Muijser *Dagregister*, 456. One of these monks was almost certainly Konchiin Sūden, the compiler of *Ikoku nikki*.

80. 4 October 1627, Nuijts/Muijser *Dagregister*, 456.

81. Purchas, *Hakluytus posthumus*, 1:486.

82. Ibid. Greenblatt, *Marvelous Possessions*, 10.

83. 4 October 1627, Nuijts/Muijser *Dagregister*, 458v.

84. The questions with their complete answers can be found in 4 October 1627, Nuijts/Muijser *Dagregister*, 456–58v.

85. 4 October 1627, Nuijts/Muijser *Dagregister*, 458v.

86. 12 October 1627, Nuijts/Muijser *Dagregister*, 470.

87. In reading the diary entries for the subsequent weeks, it is sometimes difficult to pinpoint who exactly is speaking or which statements originated with whom. Since Nuyts was unquestionably the dominant voice within the embassy, I have assumed that key statements came from him and that he controlled the ways in which the members of the mission explained themselves to Bakufu officials.

88. Hayashi, *Tsūkō ichiran*, 4:495. In 1621 the Bakufu had rejected a letter from China in part because it addressed the shogun in an inappropriate manner. Toby, "Reopening the Question of *Sakoku*."

89. Iwao, "Reopening of the Diplomatic and Commercial Relations."

90. Ibid., 15.

91. 10 October 1627, Nuijts/Muijser *Dagregister*, 467v.

92. 7 October 1627, Nuijts/Muijser *Dagregister*, 462v.

93. 6 October 1627, Nuijts/Muijser *Dagregister*, 459.

94. 6 October 1627, Nuijts/Muijser *Dagregister*, 460v.

95. Ibid.

96. Jan Baptist Weenix, Johan van Twist as ambassador to the sultan of Visiapoer, Rijksmuseum, SK-A-3879.

97. 24 October 1627, Nuijts/Muijser *Dagregister*, 479v.

98. Roe, *The Embassy of Sir Thomas Roe to India*, 553.

99. Barbour, *Before Orientalism*, 155.

100. 14 October 1627, Nuijts/Muijser *Dagregister*, 472v.

101. Ogborn, *Indian Ink*, 62.

102. 7 October 1627, Nuijts/Muijser *Dagregister*, 461 and 462v.

103. Colenbrander, *Jan Pietersz. Coen*, 7.2:1226–27.

104. 7 October 1627, Nuijts/Muijser *Dagregister*, 460.

105. 7 October 1627, Nuijts/Muijser *Dagregister*, 462v.

106. 6 November 1627, Nuijts/Muijser *Dagregister*, 487v.

107. Roe, *The embassy of Sir Thomas Roe to India*, 140.

108. For details of the first embassies, see Wills, *Pepper, Guns, and Parleys*.

109. 6 October 1627, Nuijts/Muijser *Dagregister*, 459.

110. Toby, *State and Diplomacy*, 234.

111. W. J. Boot suggests that "diplomatic exchanges were seen as ritual confirmation of existing ties. Embassies were not intended to go and discuss things; they were intended to confirm the existing ties in a ritually appropriate manner." Boot, "Maxims of Foreign Policy," 11.

112. 6 October 1627, Nuijts/Muijser *Dagregister*, 459.

113. In the case of embassies from Korea, for example, much of the negotiations were done through the Sō family.

114. 6 October 1627, Nuijts/Muijser *Dagregister*, 459.

115. 9 October 1627, Nuijts/Muijser *Dagregister*, 465.

116. 3 November 1627, Nuijts/Muijser *Dagregister*, 483.

117. 10 October 1627, Nuijts/Muijser *Dagregister*, 469v.

118. 30 October 1627, Nuijts/Muijser *Dagregister*, 481.

119. 10 October 1627, Nuijts/Muijser *Dagregister*, 468.

120. 5 November 1627, Nuijts/Muijser *Dagregister*, 484. Doi Toshikatsu (1573–1644) was the most consistently influential of Hidetada's advisers. He served as an elder (*toshiyori*) and was later promoted to the rank of *rōjū* or senior councilor by Iemitsu.

121. *Ikoku nikki shō*, 189–90.

122. For details, see Leupe, "Stukken betrekkelijk Pieter Nuyts, 1631–1634."

123. 6 November 1627, Nuijts/Muijser *Dagregister*, 489.

124. 5 November 1627, Nuijts/Muijser *Dagregister*, 484.

3. THE SHOGUN'S LOYAL VASSALS

1. Kaempfer, *Kaempfer's Japan*, 187.

2. I do not include the 1649 Frisius embassy, which is discussed in Hesselink, *Prisoners from Nambu*.

3. Very little has been written concerning the idea of the Dutch as vassals with the best analysis in the form of a short article by Nagazumi. Nagazumi, "Orandajin no uketa goon to hōkō."

4. Colenbrander, *Jan Pietersz. Coen*, 5:163.

5. Pieter Nuyts (Tayouan) to Governor-General Pieter de Carpentier in Batavia, letter, 28 February 1628, VOC 1094:135–40.

6. Remonstrantie aen de heeren rijcxraden van Sijne Keyserlijcke Mayesteyt in Japan pr. den E. Willem Janssen derwaerts gesonden, 24 July 1630, VOC 855, unfolioed. Antwoorde op de ontfangene missive van Phesodonne, VOC 855, unfolioed.

7. Remonstrantie aen de heeren rijcxraden van Sijne Keyserlijcke Mayesteyt in Japan pr. den E. Willem Janssen derwaerts gesonden, 24 July 1630, VOC 855, unfolioed.

8. *Dagregisters Japan*, 3:302, 4:262, 4:295.

9. Ibid., 6:204.

10. Governor-General Hendrik Brouwer to the emperor of Japan, letter, 31 May 1633, VOC 856:234–35v.

11. *Dagregisters Japan*, 1:43.

12. The translation of Specx's 1630 letter can be found in Nagazumi, *Hirado Oranda shōkan no nikki*, 1:425–38. The 1642 letter can be found in Kanai, *Nichiran kōshōshi no kenkyū*, 368–78.

13. Such a broad overview does no justice to the range of *fudai* daimyo. The classic study of this group is by Harold Bolitho, who notes that "there is a general tendency amongst historians to treat them [the *fudai*] as an undifferentiated company. But it must not obscure the fact that the lines between the groups were not very clearly defined. At their outer extremities, fudai and tozama shaded into each other." Bolitho, *Treasures Among Men*, 47.

14. Najita, *Japan*, 20.

15. Remonstrantie aen de heeren rijcxraden van Sijne Keyserlijcke Mayesteyt in Japan pr. den E. Willem Janssen derwaerts gesonden, 24 July 1630, VOC 855, unfolioed.

16. The Dutch initially described Hideyori as "the son of the deceased emperor [Hideyoshi] . . . who is by blood the rightful emperor over Japan but through different circumstances does not rule." Tokyo daigaku shiryō hensanjo, *Dai Nihon shiryō*, series 12, 8:606.

17. Colenbrander, *Jan Pietersz. Coen*, 7.1:6–30.

18. Resolutions, 26 September 1615, Japan factory, VOC 1061:252.

19. Macleod, *De Oost Indische Compagnie als Zeemogendheid in Azie*, 1:307.

20. *Dagregisters Japan*, 6:198.

21. *Dagregisters Japan*, 4:128.

22. *Dagregisters Japan*, 6:201–2.

23. *Dagregisters Japan*, 1:43–44.

24. *Dagregisters Japan*, 4:295.

25. 7 October 1627, Nuijts/Muijser *Dagregister*, 462.

26. For one example see Vogel, *Journaal van J. J. Ketelaar's hofreis naar den Groot Mogol te Lahore*. For a visual representation of this enormously expensive embassy, see Zandvliet, *The Dutch Encounter with Asia*, 124–26.

27. *Dagregisters Japan*, 4:60.

28. Hesselink, *Prisoners from Nanbu*, 133.

29. *Dagregisters Japan*, 1:155.

30. Goodman argues, for example, that the hofreis stemmed from rights granted to the Dutch in 1609. Goodman, *Japan and the Dutch*, 25.

31. Kanai, *Nichiran kōshōshi no kenkyū*, 172. While the Dutch had visited the court before 1634, it was only in this year that it became a formal requirement.

32. Toby, *State and Diplomacy*, 36–37 and 48–49.

33. According to one much cited figure, the total cost for a single embassy from Korea came to the vast sum of one million *ryō*. Lee, "Cultural Expressions of Tokugawa Japan and Chosŏn Korea," 214.

34. For a description of the central role of the diplomatic letter in Korean embassies to Japan, see ibid., 163.

35. Toby, *State and Diplomacy*, 185.

36. The daimyo of Hirado domain, for example, regularly visited the shogun's headquarters prior to the advent of the alternate attendance system. Between 1615 and 1619 he made four such trips staying for a few months each time.

37. Lu, *Japan: A Documentary History*, 2:208.

38. For the most recent study of the system, see Vaporis, *Tour of Duty*.

39. Ikegami, *The Taming of the Samurai*, 158.

40. Kaempfer, *Kaempfer's Japan*, 280.

41. Dagregister Zacharias Wagenaer, 2 November 1656 to 26 October 1657, NFJ 70, unfolioed. Hereafter Wagenaer *Dagregister*. An excellent English summary of the diary is provided in: Viallé and Blussé, *The Deshima Dagregisters*, 12:272–328. Wagenaer was an experienced VOC employee who would end his career as governor of the company's colony in South Africa.

42. The company was, for example, permitted to skip the 1637 hofreis because of the Shimabara uprising.

43. *Dagregister Japan*, 1:155. To give some sense of how the calendars compare, the Japanese year started on 9 February in 1633, 29 January in 1634 and 18 February in 1635.

44. Wagenaer's audience took place on 27 February 1657 or the fifteenth day, first month, Meireki 3. In the subsequent year the audience took place on 17 February 1658 or the fifteenth day, first month, Manji 1. In 1659, however, the audience occurred on

9 March or the twenty-eighth day, first month, Manji 2. A list of these dates is provided in Kanai, *Nichiran kōshōshi no kenkyū*, 172–92.

45. The Dutch did not always follow this timeline precisely. In 1661 for example, the first year after the new requirement, the main group only departed on the second day, second month, although the barge carrying their goods was scheduled to depart on the correct day.

46. Kaempfer, *Kaempfer's Japan*, 280. The initial sankin kōtai edict required all participating daimyo to make the trip to Edo in the fourth month, but, as more and more lords were brought into the system, the time table had to be split to avoid congestion and confrontation on the roads. Over time, the daimyo were divided into groups and, exactly as the Dutch, provided with specific dates to depart and arrive.

47. Two years later the Bakufu intervened with a new regulation, requiring the Dutch to take the overland route across Kyushu from Nagasaki to Shimonoseki, before proceeding by boat to Osaka.

48. Viallé and Blussé, *The Deshima Dagregisters*, 12:284.

49. Kaempfer, *Kaempfer's Japan*, 285.

50. Nachod, *Jūshichiseiki nichiran kōshōshi*, 452.

51. Vaporis suggests that the requirement could consume as much as 75 percent of the domain's available revenue. Vaporis, *Tour of Duty*, 2.

52. Viallé and Blussé, *The Deshima Dagregisters* 12:286.

53. Such audiences, known as standing or *ritsurei* audiences, were given to daimyo in the lower fifth rank (*jugoi-ge*) and below. During these ceremonies the shogun stood at the lower part of the great hall concealed behind a screen with the daimyo arrayed before him in neat rows. The screen was then opened by two councilors and the daimyo bowed deeply before the shogun. Takeuchi, *Tokugawa Bakufu jiten*, 79–80.

54. 27 February 1657, Wagenaer *Dagregister*.

55. 16 March 1654, Dagregister Gabriel Happart, NFJ 67, unfolioed.

56. 27 February 1657, Wagenaer *Dagregister*.

57. For a diagram of one such audience, see Takeuchi, *Tokugawa Bakufu jiten*, 80.

58. Hayashi, *Tsūkō ichiran*, 6:212.

59. 16 March 1654, Dagregister Gabriel Happart, NFJ 67, unfolioed.

60. The verandah running around the *ōhiroma* was used for certain important ceremonies involving large numbers of participants such as the imperial investiture of the shogun (*shogun senge*). However, the hofreis seems to be distinct in that the Dutch performed their obeisance on the verandah in front of a largely empty hall.

61. Hayashi, *Tsūkō ichiran*, 6:212. The opperhoofd was not always confined to the verandah, and in some years the audience was clearly performed on the mats of the great hall itself. On 16 April 1665, for example, Jacob Gruijs, bowed "with my head on the mats (*op de matten*)." 16 April 1665, Dagregister Jacob Grujs, NFJ 131, unfolioed. In contrast, the audience one year earlier was performed on the "planks (*plancken*) of the verandah." 24 April 1664, Dagregister Wilhelm Volger, NFJ 77, unfolioed.

62. Toby, *State and Diplomacy*, 190.

63. Katagiri, *Edo no Orandajin: Kapitan no Edo sanpu*, 69. Katagiri notes that gifts to the shogun were called *kenjōbutsu* while offerings to Bakufu offcials were known

as *shinmotsu*. *Tokugawa Jikki* consistently describes Dutch gifts as *nyūkō*. Narushima, *Tokugawa Jikki*, 3:38.

64. Tsukahira, *Feudal Control in Tokugawa Japan*, 65.

65. 2 May 1664, Dagregister Wilhem Volger, NFJ 77, unfolioed. Another record of this ceremony can be found in Hayashi, *Tsūkō ichiran*, 6:225.

66. Takeuchi, *Tokugawa Bakufu jiten*, 91.

67. Hayashi, *Tsūkō ichiran*, 6:223.

68. For the complete order see Hayashi, *Tsūkō ichiran*, 6:225. For a full translation of an order issued in 1677, see Kaempfer, *Kaempfer's Japan*, 231.

69. Meijlan, *Geschiedkundig overzigt van den handel der Europezen op Japan*, 355–356. For the definitive study of these reports see Matsukata, *Oranda fūsetsugaki to kinsei Nihon*.

70. Matsukata, *Oranda fūsetsugaki to kinsei Nihon*, 4.

71. Viallé and Blussé, *The Deshima Dagregisters*, 13:186.

72. *Dagregisters Japan* 9:127, 1 May 1664, Dagregister Wilhem Volger, NFJ 77, unfolioed.

73. For a discussion between Dutch representatives and Tokugawa officials of these two figures, see Viallé and Blussé, *The Deshima Dagregisters*, 11:189.

74. Reischauer, "Japanese Feudalism."

75. Roberts, *Performing the Great Peace*.

76. Ibid., 15.

77. Ibid., 3.

78. Ibid., 15.

79. For a good description of the ongoing debate over the identity of domains, see Toby's review of Luke Roberts and Mark Ravina's work. Toby, "Rescuing the Nation from History."

80. Roberts, *Performing the Great Peace*, 8.

81. Numerous descriptions of Dutch visits to court appear in Narushima, *Tokugawa Jikki*. This work, which includes a range of officials records, was compiled in the first half of the nineteenth century by the Hayashi scholars.

82. For some representative entries, see ibid., 3:38, 3:69, 3:299.

83. 16 March 1654, Dagregister Gabriel Happart, NFJ 67, unfolioed.

84. Kanai, *Nichiran kōshōshi no kenkyū*, 172–92.

85. Doeff, *Recollections of Japan*, 82.

86. Ibid., 81.

87. Kaempfer, *Kaempfer's Japan*, 188; Hawks, *Narrative of the Expedition of an American Squadron*, 38.

88. Doeff, *Recollections of Japan*, 24.

89. Goodman writes that the Bakufu "decided to test the loyalty which these foreigners had been so loudly professing." Goodman, *Japan and the Dutch*, 14.

90. Nicolaes Couckebacker to Antonio van Diemen, letter, 9 November 1638, NFJ 483: 382–404, esp. 383.

91. I am particularly grateful to the reviewers of my manuscript for their astute comments in regard to this section.

92. The company did occasionally consent to help Asian sovereigns in campaigns against their enemies, but only if it was promised significant rewards. The difference between such campaigns and VOC involvement in Shimabara is briefly discussed in the conclusion.

93. I agree with Yamamoto Hirofumi, who has argued persuasively that the 1637 proposal to attack Manila did not originate with the shogun in Edo. Rather it seems to have been the pet project of Nagasaki officials. Yamamoto, *Kanei jidai*, 54–55.

94. Blair and Robertson, *The Philippine Islands*, 27:229–30.

95. Iwao, "Matsukura Shigemasa no Ruzonto ensei keikaku."

96. *Dagregisters Japan*, 3:55. In this period, the office of Nagasaki bugyō was occupied by two officials. As Nagasaki was controlled by the Bakufu, they reported directly to Edo.

97. Ibid., 3:57.

98. For a contemporary description of Manila's defenses, see *Dagregisters Japan*, 3:155.

99. Ibid., 3:64.

100. Ibid., 3:64–65.

101. Ibid.

102. Resolutions, 3 November 1637, Japan factory, VOC 1124:30–31.

103. Commelin, *Begin en Voortgangh*, 4:126.

104. *Dagegisters Japan*, 3:84–85.

105. Geerts, "The Arima Rebellion and the Conduct of Koeckebacker," 61. Geerts has compiled a number of important documents related to the company's involvement in the uprising.

106. For analysis of the Tokugawa response, see Keith, "The Logistics of Power."

107. Nicolaes Couckebacker to Mouraasame Sabroseijmondonno, letter, 17 January 1638, VOC 483:372.

108. *Dagregisters Japan*, 3:98.

109. Ibid., 3:102–3.

110. Nicolaes Couckebacker to Phesodoenno, letter, 15 February 1638, VOC 483:373.

111. *Dagregisters Japan*, 3:110.

112. *Dagregisters Japan*, 3:114.

113. *Dagregisters Japan*, 3:125

114. *Dagregisters Japan*, 3:115–25.

115. *Dagregisters Japan*, 3:126.

116. *Dagregisters Japan*, 3:123.

117. Nicolaes Couckebacker to Antonio van Diemen, letter, 9 November 1638, NFJ 483:382–404, esp. 382–83.

118. The Dutch were instructed, for example, to attack any Iberian shipping they encountered on their way to Japan, thereby removing the Catholic threat to Japan. *Dagregisters Japan*, 5:46–47.

119. Alexandrowicz, *An Introduction to the History of the Law of Nations*, 33.

120. Heeres and Stapel, *Corpus Diplomaticum*, 483–85.

121. Van Goor, *Prelude to Colonialism*, 44–45.

122. Wilson, *The Early Annals of the English in Bengal*, 2:65

123. Sen, *Distant Sovereignty*, xv.

124. Aitchison, *A Collection of Treaties, Engagements, and Sunnuds*, 60 and iv.

125. For the final end of any notion that the English were somehow Mughal vassals, see Edwards, *Reminiscences of Bengal Civilian*, 55.

126. Hayashi, *Tsūkō ichiran*. 6: 264–305. The full title for the section is *gohōkosuji*.

4. THE VIOLENT SEA

1. I am grateful to the editors of *Itinerario* for giving permission to reprint parts of the following article: Clulow, "European Maritime Violence and Territorial States."

2. Barendse, *The Arabian Seas*, 493–94.

3. One much cited example is da Gama's defeat of a much larger Muslim fleet off Calicut in 1502.

4. Cipolla, *Guns, Sails, and Empires*; Parker, *The Military Revolution*. Parker focuses on changes in military technology in the sixteenth and seventeenth centuries and their impact on wider historical developments. He argues that the spread of gunpowder-based weapons and changes in the design of fortresses led to huge increases in the size of armies. Together these changes amounted to a revolution that transformed Europe by prompting the rise of centralized states that were capable of waging this new kind of war. His thesis is not, however, limited to the European continent, and, as the book's subtitle suggests, Parker looks toward military technology, and especially the gunned vessel, to account for the "rise of the West" after 1500.

5. Parker, *The Military Revolution*, 83.

6. Casale, *The Ottoman Age of Exploration*.

7. Subrahmanyam, "Of Imârat and Tijârat"; Andrade, "Beyond Guns, Germs, and Steel." In his most recent book, Andrade has modified his position somewhat by reassessing the importance of the "broadside sailing ship" in the conflict between Zheng Chenggong and the Dutch over Taiwan. Andrade, *Lost Colony*, 13. The tremendous power of the Zheng maritime empire is detailed in Xing Hang's dissertation. Hang, "Between Trade and Legitimacy, Maritime and Continent."

8. Philip Steinberg has argued for a seventeenth century shift from cartographic representations of the sea "as a terrifying wild wherein societies and nature interact to . . . an empty space to be crossed by atomistic ships." Steinberg, *The Social Construction of the Ocean*, 105.

9. Grotius, *Commentary on the Law of Prize and Booty*.

10. Grotius, *Hugo Grotius Mari libero et P. Merula De maribus*.

11. Benton, *A Search for Sovereignty*, 34.

12. Ibid., 160.

13. Ibid., 105. Benton's discussion does extend to Asian states and she includes a discussion of the ways in which Mughal officials ensured the safety of key maritime routes.

14. The quote is generally ascribed to Bahadur Shah of Gujarat. Pearson, "Merchants and states.," 97. Pearson argues that the "whole mind-set of the Mughal emperors and their nobles was land-based . . . the sea was a marvel, a curiosity, a freak." Pearson, *The Indian Ocean*, 116.

15. In an important recent article, Sebastian Prange has argued against the long-held notion that the Portuguese were the first to introduce politics into the Indian Ocean by demonstrating that Indian states displayed a sustained interest in the maritime realm. Prange, "A Trade of No Dishonor."

16. Das Gupta, "Indian Merchants and the Western Indian Ocean," 494. Other scholars have described the same dynamic as a "balance of terror" (Farhat Hasan), a "fragile equilibrium" (Sanjay Subrahmanyam), or a "finely tuned balance" (Om Prakash). Hasan, "Conflict and Co-operation in Anglo-Mughal Trade Relations," 352; Subrahmanyam, "Forcing the Doors of Heathendom, 137; Prakash, "The Mughal Empire and the Dutch East India Company," 192.

17. Subrahmanyam, *The Political Economy of Commerce*, 276.

18. According to one regularly cited estimate, VOC privateers captured between 150 and 200 prizes in the first two decades of the seventeenth century. Enthoven, *Zeeland en de opkomst van Republiek*, 212–13.

19. Andrade, "The Company's Chinese Pirates," 417. Borschberg notes that the "taking of prizes became a cornerstone not only of the economic fortunes of the company, but the establishment of the Dutch colonial empire in Asia." Borschberg, "From Self-Defence to an Instrument of War," 35, and *The Singapore and Melaka Straits*.

20. Van Santen, "Trade Between Mughal India and the Middle East, and Mughal Monetary Policy," 93. Subrahmanyam has made an almost identical point. Subrahmanyam, *The Political Economy of Commerce*, 282.

21. Boot, "Maxims of Foreign Policy," 15.

22. Although the Tokugawa regime displayed some interest in assembling a fleet in this period, it possessed no effective ocean-going force. The key figure in early Bakufu maritime development was Mukai Shōgen, whom Richard Cocks described as the "Amerall of the sea." Farrington, *The English Factory in Japan*, 1:556.

23. One of the more famous nineteenth-century examples took place in 1850 when British ships blockaded the Greek coast and threatened to seize shipping equal to the damages suffered by the British subject at the center of the affair, Don Pacifico.

24. Quoted in van Ittersum, *Profit and Principle*, 86.

25. Subrahmanyam has criticized the tendency of some scholars to assume that Dutch violence was always rational and that it was deployed in pursuit of clearly defined goals. Subrahmanyam, "Forcing the Doors of Heathendom," 135.

26. Groeneveldt, *De Nederlanders in China*, 319.

27. Prakash, "The Mughal Empire and the Dutch East India Company," 192–95.

28. Van Dam, *Beschrijvinge van de Oostindische Compagnie*, 2.3:19.

29. Ibid., 2.3:20.

30. Ibid., 2.3:22. Four hundred thousand rupees totaled about eighty thousand guilders.

31. Heeres and Stapel, *Corpus Diplomaticum*, 1:521–28.

32. Coolhaas, *Generale Missiven*, 2:375.

33. Quoted in Steensgard, "The Dutch East India Company as an Institutional Innovation," 255.

34. Quoted in Barendse, *The Arabian Seas,* 131.

35. The most important work on these vessels is Iwao Seiichi's revised edition of his classic monograph. Iwao, *Shuinsen bōekishi no kenkyū.* For a more recent work, see Nagazumi, *Shuinsen.*

36. Foreign vessels that visited Japan and then departed did not require such a pass.

37. Recipients included one Ryukyuan, eleven Chinese, and twelve European merchants. Iwao, *Shuinsen bōekishi no kenkyū,* 224.

38. These letters are collected in Kondō, *Gaiban tsūsho.*

39. Innes suggest a third reason for the creation of the shuinjō system: to divide available trading destinations between Japan-based merchants. Innes, "The Door Ajar," 117–18.

40. Philip Brown has described the Tokugawa polity as a flamboyant state in which the "divergence between nominal authority and capability [was] substantial." Brown, *Central Authority and Local Autonomy, 232–33.*

41. For a discussion of *bui,* see Asao Naohiro, "Sakokusei no seiritsu." Arano notes that "fictional military supremacy . . . became the norm in Tokugawa foreign policy." Arano, "The Formation of a Japanocentric World Order," 207.

42. Arano, "The Formation of a Japanocentric World Order," 212.

43. The Portuguese executed sailors belonging to a shuinsen in 1608, the Spanish destroyed one of these vessels near Siam in 1628, and the Dutch briefly detained a shuinsen in the same year. The last incident will be explored in chapter 6.

44. For the most detailed account of this incident, see Boxer, *Portuguese Merchants and Missionaries,* 1–90.

45. Quoted in ibid., 87. For a useful explanation from a Bakufu official of what happened, see Boxer, *The Christian Century in Japan,* 430–31.

46. Colenbrander, *Jan Pietersz. Coen,* 7.2:802.

47. Ibid.

48. Farrington, *The English Factory in Japan,* 2:1187. This instruction was issued to a joint fleet formed of vessels belonging to both the Dutch and English East India Companies.

49. Blair and Robertson, *The Philippine Islands,* 18:229.

50. In 1625 a Dutch ship encountered an unknown junk off the coast of Vietnam. The vessel had been chartered by two merchants, Itami Shirōbei and Asari Sukeuemon, who had split off from a legally authorized shuinsen voyage once they reached Cochinchina. In keeping with standard procedure, the company's vessel dispatched a small craft to investigate the junk. When interrogated, its captain explained that they were Japanese sailors on their way from Cochinchina, but the ship and the makeup of its crew told a very different story. Clearly chartered in a separate port in Southeast Asia, the junk was crewed primarily by Chinese and Portuguese mariners who seemed to have little connection with Japan. Even more tellingly, its cap-

tain could not produce a shuinjō, the key document that all Japanese vessels were required to carry. Already aroused, VOC suspicions deepened still further when a number of the junk's crew fled suddenly on a small boat. As a result, the Dutch captain confiscated the junk's cargo. When Itami and Asari returned to Japan, they immediately submitted a petition demanding full compensation for their losses, and, although the company disputed the case, it agreed to pay out for the incident. *Provisioneel concept om te dienen tot antwoorde op seeckere remonstratie bij eenige Japanse cooplieden aen de heeren van Nangasackij ende Firando overleveert,* VOC 852:80–82.

51. Cocks, *Diary Kept by the Head of the English Factory,* 1:318.

52. Coolhaas, "Een Indisch Verslag uit 1631," 90.

53. Quoted in Viallé, "In Aid of Trade," 59.

54. Pearson, *The Indian Ocean,* 121.

55. This was according to rumors received by Dutch and English merchants in Japan. Coolhaas, *Generale Missiven,* 1:149; Cocks, *Diary Kept by the Head of the English Factory,* 3:60.

56. Van Ittersum, *Profit and Principle;* Borschberg, "The Seizure of the *Sta. Catarina* Revisited"; Wilson, *The Savage Republic.*

57. In an important article, Subrahmanyam notes a "tendency to discuss the conflict without reference to the arenas themselves, as well as to ignore the political and social context within Asia, American or Africa." Subrahmanyam, "The 'Pulicat Enterprise,'" 17.

58. Quoted in Masselman, *The Cradle of Colonialism,* 150.

59. Borschberg, "The Seizure of the *Sta. Catarina* Revisited," 35.

60. Ibid., 50.

61. Van Ittersum notes that "it was by no means a foregone conclusion that the *Santa Catarina* would be declared good prize." Van Ittersum, *Profit and Principle,* 113.

62. Grotius, *Commentary on the Law of Prize and Booty,* 15.

63. Ibid., 514.

64. Ibid.

65. Van Ittersum, *Profit and Principle,* 24.

66. Ibid., 54.

67. Benton, *A Search for Sovereignty,* 131.

68. Grotius, *Commentary on the Law of Prize and Booty,* 380.

69. Van Ittersum, *Profit and Principle,* 29.

70. Grotius, *Commentary on the Law of Prize and Booty,* 392.

71. Borschberg, "The Seizure of the *Sta. Catarina* Revisited," 56.

72. Disney, *A History of Portugal and the Portuguese Empire,* 2:184.

73. Boxer, *Portuguese Merchants and Missionaries,* 10–16. The exact figure was fourteen hundred piculs with one picul equaling roughly sixty kilograms.

74. For a detailed examination of Christian activity in Tokugawa Japan, see Boxer, *The Christian Century in Japan.*

75. Portuguese merchants were well aware of the dangers of this connection. Boxer, "The Swan-Song of the Portuguese in Japan."

76. The truce, which marked a key turning point in the eighty-years war, lasted in Europe from 1609 to 1621.

77. Lenardt Camps to the Amsterdam chamber, letter, October 10 1616, VOC 1063:102–3.

78. Farrington, *The English Factory in Japan*, 2: 1189. See the sailing directions to the Philippines in Iwao, *Early Japanese Settlers in the Philippines*.

79. Linschoten, *Itinerario*.

80. Kaempfer, *Kaempfer's Japan*, 36.

81. Chinese records documenting the sixteenth century *wakō* surge show Meshima as part of Japan. It also appears in the Japanese navigational guide *Genna kōkaisho*, which was published in 1618. My thanks to Peter Shapinsky for pointing this out.

82. Resolutions, 18 August 1615, Japan factory, VOC 1061:247. The resolutions passed by the council of the Japan factory between 18 August 1615 and 2 March 1616 form the most important source for the *Santo Antonio* incident.

83. Berry, "Public Peace and Private Attachment," 242.

84. Ikegami, *The Taming of the Samurai*, 153.

85. Berry, "Public Peace and Private Attachment," 242.

86. Shapinsky, "Lords of the Sea," 442.

87. Fujiki, *Toyotomi heiwarei to sengoku shakai*, 228.

88. Resolutions, 7 November 1615, Japan factory, VOC 1061:253v.

89. Resolutions, 18 August 1615, Japan factory, VOC 1061:247.

90. Ibid.

91. Resolutions, 10 September 1615, Japan factory, VOC 1061:249v.

92. While Joosten has not received the same attention as William Adams, he functioned in a similar role as an informal adviser to the shogun. Like Adams, he vastly inflated his own influence. For details on this neglected figure, see Iwao, *Jan Joosten*.

93. Resolutions, 10 September 1615, Japan factory, VOC 1061:249v.

94. Resolutions, 28 October 1615, Japan factory, VOC 1061:250v–250. This total comes from rounding off individual figures.

95. Ibid., 250v.

96. Colenbrander, *Jan Pieterz. Coen*, 1:203. Elbert Woutersen, letter, 6 September 1615, NFJ 276.

97. Cocks, *Diary Kept by the Head of the English Factory*, 1:55.

98. Nieuhof, *An Embassy from the East India Company*, 303.

99. Danvers and Foster, *Letters Received by the East India Company*, 1:147.

100. Hayashi, *Tsūkō ichiran*, 5:7.

101. Boxer, *The Christian Century in Japan*, 435.

102. Fujiki, *Toyotomi heiwarei to sengoku shakai,* 218.

103. Resolutions, 28 October 1615, Japan factory, VOC 1061:251v.

104. Ibid.

105. Sūden, *Ikoku nikki shō*, 112.

106. Resolutions, 28 October 1615, Japan factory, VOC 1061:251v.

107. Ibid.

108. Resolutions, 26 September 1615, Japan factory, VOC 1061:251.

109. Cocks, *Diary Kept by the Head of the English Factory*, 2:163.

110. Takeda, *Sakoku to kokkyō no seiritsu*, 167.

111. It was, therefore, quite different from the situation in Europe where intense rivalry between states meant that claims to authority over coastal waters were becoming increasingly expansive. In this period, for example, the Dutch and English governments claimed a suite of maritime rights, including most controversially the right to restrict access to foreign fishermen entering coastal waters.

112. Matthijs ten Broeke and Lenardt Camps, letter, 19 September 1615, NFJ 276.

113. Not all Asian states were as interventionist. The Mughal emperors, for example, showed no interest in inserting themselves in such conflicts, ignoring the battle of Swally, a maritime clash between the Portuguese and the English, that took place in Indian waters in 1612.

114. Colenbrander, *Jan Pietersz. Coen*, 2:7.

115. Lenardt Camps to the Amsterdam chamber, letter, 10 October 1616, VOC 1063:102–3.

116. Van Linschoten, *Itinerario*.

117. Colenbrander, *Jan Pietersz. Coen*, 2:238. While he was confident that this was the right course of action, Coen did acknowledge the possibility of a Bakufu backlash (if the carrack was captured in Nagasaki) and was prepared to accept the closure of the Japan factory if this eventuated. However, he clearly believed that Specx would be able to resolve any such difficulties by appeasing Bakufu officials.

118. Colenbrander, *Jan Pietersz. Coen*, 1:293.

119. Jan Dirckz. Lam to the Amsterdam chamber, letter, 11 October 1617, VOC 1066, 286v.

120. Copie van de veroverde goederen in de Manilhas door Jacques Specx in Firando ontfangen, 12 October 1617, VOC 1066:127–31. Kato, *Bakuhansei kokka no keisei to gaikoku bōeki*, 72.

121. Danvers and Foster, *Letters Received by the East India Company*, 3:291.

122. Cocks, *Diary Kept by the Head of the English Factory*, 2:119.

123. For details of Li Dan, see Iwao, "Li Tan."

124. Cocks, *Diary Kept by the Head of the English Factory*, 2:88.

125. Jan Dirckz. Lam to the Amsterdam chamber, letter, 11 October 1617, VOC 1066, 289v–89.

126. For a Spanish account of these events, see Blair and Robertson, *The Philippine Islands*, 67–68.

127. Cocks, *Diary Kept by the Head of the English Factory*, 2:95.

128. Farrington, *The English Factory in Japan*, 1:666.

129. Ibid.

130. Jan Dirckz. Lam to the Amsterdam chamber, letter, 11 October 1617, VOC 1066, 289v.

131. Cocks, *Diary Kept by the Head of the English Factory*, 2:163.

132. Ibid, 2:163; Farrington, *The English Factory in Japan*, 1:666.

133. Colenbrander, *Jan Pietersz. Coen*, 7.1:308.

134. Copie remonstrantie van Jacques Specx overgegeven op 't comptoir Firando, 20 September 1621, VOC 1075: 89–92, esp. 92v. Extracts from this report are printed in Tokyo daigaku shiryō hensanjo, *Dai Nihon Shiryō*, series 12, 38:6–10. The complete Japanese edict can be found in Nagazumi, "Hirado ni dentatsu sareta Nihonjin baibai buki yushutsu kinshirei."

135. See the entry in Doi, *Nippo jisho*. The etymology of the term *bahan* remains unclear. The simplest explanation is that it stems from a Chinese reading of banners referring to Hachiman, one of the more popular Shinto deities, but it may also derive from the Chinese characters for *pofan* or tattered sails.

136. Copie remonstrantie van Jacques Specx overgegeven op 't comptoir Firando, 20 September 1621, VOC 1075:92v.

137. Colenbrander, *Jan Pietersz. Coen*, 7.2:801.

138. Pieter de Carpentier to Lenardt Camps, letter, 9 April 1622, VOC 849:73–74.

139. Ibid.

140. *Dagregisters Japan*, 3:56.

141. Tai, "Marking Water."

142. Colenbrander, *Jan Pietersz. Coen*, 7.2:802.

143. Tokyo daigaku shiryō hensanjo, *Dai Nihon Shiryō*, series 12, 38:8.

144. Ibid.

145. *Dagregisters Japan*, 2:164.

146. Coolhaas, *Generale Missiven*, 1:585.

147. Boyajian, *Portuguese Trade in Asia Under the Hapsburgs*, 234.

148. Shapinsky notes that "under the new regime, many sea lords, including the Noshima Murakami, parlayed their high status into positions within the retinues of larger daimyo." Shapinsky, "Predators, Protectors, and Purveyors," 305. As such, they were able to find a productive accommodation with the center.

5. POWER AND PETITION

1. Arano, *Kinsei Nihon to Higashi Ajia*; Toby, *State and Diplomacy in Early Modern Japan*.

2. Hang, "Between Trade and Legitimacy, Maritime and Continent"; Carioti, "Hirado During the First Half of the Seventeenth Century"; Blussé, "Minnan-jen or Cosmopolitan?" Andrade, *Lost Colony*.

3. Innes, "The Door Ajar," 168.

4. Cocks, *Diary Kept by the Head of the English Factory*, 3:286.

5. Iwao, "Kinsei nisshi bōeki ni kansuru sūryōteki kōsatsu."

6. This diversity can be seen in the three Chinese temples constructed in Nagasaki, each of which served a separate constituency. The first temple, Kōfuku-ji, was constructed in 1623 and was patronized by traders from northern provinces such as Jiangsu and Zhejiang. Five years later, merchants from southern Fujian responded by constructing their own temple, Fukusai-ji. Finally, Sōfuku-ji, which was built in 1632, served migrants from Northern Fujian. Berger, "The Overseas Chinese Community in Seventeenth Century Nagasaki," 36.

7. *Dagregisters Japan*, 5:184–87.

8. Subrahmanyam, "Forcing the Doors of Heathendom," 135.

9. Viallé and Blussé, *Deshima Dagregisters*, 12:79 and 13:174.

10. Earns, "The Development of Bureaucratic Rule in Early Modern Japan."

11. *Dagregisters Japan*, 2:95.

12. *Dagregisters Japan*, 1:302–4.

13. *Dagregisters Japan*, 2:111, Nicolaes Couckebacker to Governor-General Henricq Brouwer, letter, 31 December 1635, VOC 1120:193–94.

14. *Dagregisters Japan*, 1:265.

15. *Dagregisters Japan*, 1:287.

16. *Dagregisters Japan*, 1:294.

17. *Dagregisters Japan*, 2:111.

18. *Dagregisters Japan*, 3:22.

19. *Dagregisters Japan*, 3:26–27.

20. *Dagregisters Japan*, 3:25.

21. *Dagregisters Japan*.

22. *Dagregisters Japan*, 3:26.

23. *Dagregisters Japan*, 7:156.

24. Viallé and Blussé, *The Deshima Dagregisters*, 11:321.

25. In 1602, the Florentine merchant Francisco Carletti filed a lawsuit with Dutch authorities designed to win restitution for cargo lost when a Portuguese ship, *St. Jago*, was captured. Van Ittersum, *Profit and Principle*, 139–51.

26. Blussé, "Minnan-jen or Cosmopolitan?"

27. Andrade, *How Taiwan Became Chinese*, 46.

28. Andrade, "The Company's Chinese Pirates," 438–39.

29. Blussé, "No Boats to China," 65.

30. Viallé and Blussé, *The Deshima Dagregisters*, 11:iv.

31. *Dagregisters Japan*, 5:88.

32. *Dagregisters Japan*, 5:187.

33. *Dagregisters Japan*, 5:88.

34. Blussé, "No Boats to China," 67.

35. Coolhaas, *Generale Missiven*, 2:179.

36. *Dagregisters Japan*, 8:212.

37. *Dagregisters Japan*, 6:208.

38. Kanai, *Nichiran kōshōshi no kenkyū*, 375.

39. *Dagregisters Japan*, 7:217–26.

40. *Dagregisters Japan*, 7:225.

41. *Dagregisters Japan*, 7:225.

42. Any historian interested in VOC activities in Japan over this period owes a great debt to Cynthia Viallé and Leonard Blussé, who have published three superb translations of large parts of the Japan *Dagregister* from 1640 to 1670. While this section has been greatly aided by these, the translations from original sources are my own.

43. *Dagregisters Japan*, 7:150.

44. *Dagregisters Japan*, 7:153–54.

45. Coolhaas, *Generale Missiven*, 2:211.

46. *Dagregisters Japan*, 7:155.

47. *Dagregisters Japan*, 7:157.

48. *Dagregisters Japan*, 7:157–58.

49. *Dagregisters Japan*, 8:212.

50. *Dagregisters Japan*, 9:178. The subsequent shift from Taiwan to Tonkin as a new source for silk is explored in Tuán, *Silk for Silver*.

51. Andrade, *How Taiwan Became Chinese*, 210.

52. Viallé and Blussé, *Deshima Dagregisters,* 12:105–8. The king of Siam had granted a monopoly on the export of deerskins to the VOC, allowing the Dutch to claim that they were simply enforcing their legal rights.

53. 27 July 1652, Dagregister Frederik Coyett, NFJ 66, unfolioed.

54. Viallé and Blussé, *Deshima Dagregisters,* 12:121.

55. Coolhaas, *Generale Missiven*, 2:710.

56. 24 August 1657, Wagenaer *Dagregister*.

57. Viallé and Blussé, *Deshima Dagregisters* 12:321. While company agents refused to acknowledge that the ship was heading anywhere other than China, Bakufu officials clearly believed its ultimate destination was in fact Japan.

58. Mazumdar, *Sugar and Society in China*, 91.

59. Coolhaas, *Generale Missiven*, 3:55.

60. Ibid, 3:194.

61. 24 August 1657, Wagenaer *Dagregister*.

62. 3 September 1657, Wagenaer *Dagregister*. Some sources suggest that a group of Chinese mariners left onboard the junk purposefully cut the anchor cable.

63. 24 August 1657, Wagenaer *Dagregister*.

64. 23 August 1657, Wagenaer *Dagregister*.

65. 24 August 1657, Wagenaer *Dagregister*.

66. Ibid.

67. We know for example that the *Breukelen*'s master was subsequently arrested and thrown into prison when he arrived in Taiwan. 3 September 1657, Wagenaer *Dagregister*. Both the officers and crew were entitled to their own share of the loot, making easy prizes uniformly attractive. Borschberg, "From Self-Defence to an Instrument of War."

68. Lunsford, *Piracy and Privateering in the Golden Age Netherlands*, 192.

69. Ibid, 169.

70. 18 October 1657, Wagenaer *Dagregister*.

71. 24 August 1657, Wagenaer *Dagregister*

72. 26 August 1657, Wagenaer *Dagregister*.

73. 2 September 1657, Wagenaer *Dagregister*.

74. 5 September 1657, Wagenaer *Dagregister*.

75. 12 October 1657, Wagenaer *Dagregister*.

76. Vialle and Blussé, *Deshima Dagregisters*, 12:343.

77. 22 August 1658, Dagregister Johannes Boucheljon, NFJ 71, unfolioed. Hereafter Boucheljon *Dagregister*.

78. 14 October 1658, Boucheljon *Dagregister*. The available sources suggest that Tantsinquan may have been a merchant called Chen Jing Guan (陳軫官).

79. 9 October 1658, Boucheljon *Dagregister*.

80. 14 October 1658, Boucheljon *Dagregister*.

81. Hayashi, *Tsūkō ichiran*, 6:223.

82. For a statement of the shogun's supposed indifference to overseas trade, see *Japan Dagregisters* 5:42.

83. 14 March 1660, Dagregister Zacharias Wagenaer, NFJ 73, unfolioed.

84. Vialle and Blussé, *Deshima Dagregisters*, 13:43.

85. Vialle and Blussé, *Deshima Dagregisters*, 12:438.

86. As early as 1653, the opperhoofd of the Japan factory reported rumors within the Chinese community that Chenggong was planning to seize Taiwan.

87. 22 October 1660, Dagregister Johannes Boucheljon, NFJ 73, unfolioed.

88. Vialle and Blussé, *Deshima Dagregisters*, 13:61.

89. Wills, "Ch'ing Relations with the Dutch, 1662–1690," 228. See also Wills's study of VOC policy in the aftermath of the loss of Taiwan. Wills, *Pepper, Guns, and Parleys*.

90. Van Dam, *Beschrijvinge van de Oostindische Compagnie*, 2.1:721. A *fluyt* was a specialized cargo vessel much used by the VOC.

91. Ibid. Wills, *Pepper, Guns, and Parleys*, 62. Instructie voor den commandeur Balthasar Bort ende den Raedt, VOC 886:348–66, esp. 351.

92. Van Dam, *Beschrijvinge van de Oostindische Compagnie*, 2.1:722.

93. Coolhaas, *Generale Missiven*, 3:373.

94. For a summary of the incident, see Viallé and Blussé, *Deshima Dagregisters*, 13:vi–vii.

95. 28 March 1664, Dagregister Wilhelm Volger, NFJ 77, unfolioed. See also Vialle and Blussé, *Deshima Dagregisters*, 13:104. There is some confusion concerning the exact distance with some sources suggesting that the junk was closer to Meshima at the time of encounter. The most precise reference is in the *Japan Dagregister*, which describes the distance as "75 [English] miles or 25 Holland miles (*mijlen hollandts*)." One Dutch mile was roughly equivalent to between 3 and 4 English miles.

96. *Batavia Dagregister, Anno 1664*, 503.

97. Hendrick Indijck to Governor-General Joan Maatsuyker, letter, 21 October 1663, VOC 1243:1941–64.

98. Viallé and Blussé, *Deshima Dagregisters*, 13:81.

99. This brought the total number of survivors to twenty-nine. According to the records kept by the Chinese translators, there were originally forty-five sailors in the junk, which would mean a total of sixteen fatalities. Tokyo daigaku shiryō hensanjo, *Dai nihon kinsei shiryō. Tōtsūji kaisho nichiroku*, 1:175.

100. Viallé and Blussé, *Deshima Dagregisters*, 13:96; Kimura, *Bakuhansei kokka to Higashi Ajia sekai*, 95.

101. Tokyo daigaku shiryō hensanjo, *Dai nihon kinsei shiryō*, 1:175.

102. News had filtered into Japan about the fall of Fort Zeelandia in May 1662. Viallé and Blussé, *Deshima Dagregisters*, 13:43.

103. Kanai, *Nichiran kōshōshi no kenkyū*, 380.

104. *Batavia Dagregister, Anno 1664*, 504.

105. Ibid.

106. 18 April 1664, Dagregister Wilhelm Volger, NFJ 77, unfolioed.

107. 2 May 1664, Dagregister Wilhelm Volger, NFJ 77, unfolioed.

108. Viallé and Blussé, *Deshima Dagregisters*, 13:108.

109. *Batavia Dagregister, Anno 1664*, 505. 24 April 1664, Dagregister Wilhelm Volger, NFJ 77, unfolioed.

110. Batavia to Jacob Gruijs and the council in Nagasaki, letter, 27 May 1665, VOC 889.

111. Viallé and Blussé, *Deshima Dagregisters*, 13:162.

112. Wills, *Pepper, Guns, and Parleys*, 62.

113. Viallé and Blussé, *Deshima Dagregisters*, 13:162.

114. Batavia to Jacob Gruijs and the council in Nagasaki, letter, 27 May 1665, VOC 889.

115. Viallé and Blussé, *Deshima Dagregisters*, 13:167.

116. Hang, "Between Trade and Legitimacy, Maritime and Continent," 215.

117. Ibid., 224.

118. Andrade, "The Company's Chinese Pirates," 417.

119. Benton, *A Search for Sovereignty*, 160.

6. PLANTING THE FLAG IN ASIA

1. The island of Taiwan had many names in this period. It appears in Japanese sources as Takasago and in Dutch accounts as Formosa. To further confuse matters, the VOC established its colony at Tayouan, now the city of Anping, on the southwestern corner of the island.

2. Blussé, "The VOC as Sorceror's Apprentice," 90.

3. For a detailed study of this dispute, see Loth, "Armed Incidents and Unpaid Bills."

4. As recently explored in Suzuki, *Civilization and Empire*.

5. Blussé, "The Dutch Occupation of the Pescadores."

6. Groeneveldt, *De Nederlanders in China*, 61.

7. Ibid., 283.

8. Ibid., 278.

9. Teng, *Taiwan's Imagined Geography*, 36.

10. Groeneveldt, *De Nederlanders in China*, 283.

11. Ibid., 287–90. The Dutch commenced pulling down their fort on the Penghu Islands on 26 August.

12. Zhang, *Mingshi*, juan 264.

13. Andrade, *How Taiwan Became Chinese*.

14. The total Siraya population is estimated at around twenty thousand in this period. For an analysis of the island's indigenous population, see Ferrell, *Taiwan Aboriginal Groups*.

15. For the interaction between the Dutch and the Siraya population, see Chiu, *The Colonial "Civilizing Process" in Dutch Formosa*.

16. Blussé, Everts, and Frech, *The Formosan Encounter*, 1:31.

17. Nagazumi, "The Japanese *Go-shuinjo*," 29.

18. Although Hirano held the position of Kyoto magistrate (*daikan*), he engaged actively in international trade. The Suetsugu family dominated commerce in Nagasaki for over a century. Heizō's father, Suetsugu Kōzen Cosme, had moved to the port in 1571 and prospered as it began to boom as the terminus of Portuguese trade. Heizō emerged as an important merchant in his own right in the late sixteenth century when he received a number of shuinjō to send ships to Southeast Asia. His political career took off in 1619 after he seized control of the important office of Nagasaki *daikan* by accusing the incumbent, Murayama Tōan, of a range of offenses.

19. Andrade, *How Taiwan Became Chinese*, 48.

20. Schouten, "Memorabel verhael," 82–83. For details of this clash, we rely on Justus Schouten's report, which has, as is the case with so many important sources on Taiwan, been edited by Leonard Blussé.

21. Coolhaas, *Generale Missiven*, 1:187.

22. Schouten, "Memorabel verhael," 83. As the price of silk fluctuated constantly in this period, it is difficult to provide an exact estimate of the value of the confiscated goods, but even at the very low figure of two hundred taels per picul, this was a significant sum equal to three thousand taels.

23. Pieter Muijser to Governor-General Pieter de Carpentier, letter, 14 November 1626, VOC 1092:392–93.

24. Cornelis van Neijenroode, letter, 3 March 1626, NFJ 482:143.

25. Schouten, "Memorabel verhael," 84.

26. Andrade, *How Taiwan Became Chinese*, 49 and 61. As Andrade notes, the exact limits of the prohibition are not entirely clear, but the ban seems to have extended only to raw silk.

27. Schouten, "Memorabel verhael," 84.

28. This was the amount confiscated from the Dutch by Hamada in 1628 in compensation for lost profits. Valentijn, *Oud en Nieuw Oost-Indien*, 4.2:58.

29. Pieter de Carpenter to Cornelis van Neijenroode, letter, 13 May 1625, VOC 852:76–79v. Memorie voor de E. Pieter Nuyts, raet van India, gaende voor commandeur over de vlote naer Tayouan gedestineert, ende van daer voorts in ambassade aen den Keijser van Japan, 10 May 1627, VOC 854:51–60. In the latter document the governor-general referenced his earlier letter to van Neijenroode, providing a clear sense of how the same argument was consistently recycled.

30. Remonstrantie aen de heeren rijcxraden van Sijne Keyserlijcke Mayesteyt in Japan pr. den E. Willem Janssen derwaerts gesonden, 24 July 1630, VOC 855; Antwoorde op de ontfangene missive van Phesodonne, VOC 855. The quote comes from Nuyts's embassy diary. 4 October 1627, Nuijts/Muijser *Dagregister*, 458v.

31. Colenbrander, *Jan Pietersz. Coen*, 5:494.

32. Grotius, *The Freedom of the Seas*, 11.

33. The deployment of European sovereignty claims in the early modern period was intimately bound up with the development of international law. Indeed, when viewed in the most critical light, international law can be seen as little more than the

handmaiden of imperial expansion or, in Antony Anghie's words, as a tool "devised specifically to ensure their [the indigenous population's] disempowerment and disenfranchisement." Anghie, *Imperialism, Sovereignty, and the Making of International Law*, 31.

34. Keene, *Beyond the Anarchical Society*, 3.

35. Mijer, *Verzameling van Instructiën, Ordonnanciën en Reglementen*, 76.

36. The right to conquest is discussed in book 3, chapter 6 of Grotius, *The Rights of War and Peace, Including the Law of Nature and of Nations* (1901).

37. Richard Tuck argues that "many practices of non-European peoples, in Grotius's view, could count as grounds for intervention in order to punish breaches of the natural law." Grotius, *The Rights of War and Peace*, xxviii.

38. The first resolution in Batavia records the company's rights to the "whole land of Jacatra which has the previous year been conquered by us with weapons." De Jonge and van Deventer, *De opkomst van het Nederlandsch gezag in Oost Indië*, 1:221.

39. Heeres and Stapel, *Corpus Diplomaticum Neerlando-Indicum*.

40. The famous Palmas sovereignty case, in which the United States and the Netherlands fought over rights to a small island near the Philippines, rested on a 1677 grant by local chiefs to the VOC. The Dutch argued that this act resulted in the immediate and complete cession of sovereignty to the company.

41. Keene, *Beyond the Anarchical Society*, 82.

42. Campbell, *Formosa Under the Dutch*, 119. For an analysis of such ceremonies, see Andrade, "Political Spectacle and Colonial Rule."

43. Van Ittersum, "The Long Goodbye," 393. Van Ittersum describes the case of Ternate, which Grotius presented as an example of the cession of partial sovereignty in return for protection.

44. Schouten, "Memorabel verhael," 79.

45. 4 October 1627, Nuijts/Muijser *Dagregister*, 457.

46. Memorie voor de E. Pieter Nuyts, raet van India, gaende voor commandeur over de vlote naer Tayouan gedestineert, ende van daer voorts in ambassade aen den Keijser van Japan, 10 May 1627, VOC 854:55.

47. Pieter de Carpenter to Cornelis van Neijenroode, letter, 13 May 1625, VOC 852:77.

48. 4 October 1627, Nuijts/Muijser *Dagregister*, 457.

49. Antwoorde op de ontfangene missive van Phesodonne, VOC 855, unfolioed.

50. For a particularly clear expression of this point, see 5 June 1631, Dagregister gehouden te Edo door Willem Jansz. van Amersfoort, NFJ 271.

51. A good overview of this dispute can be found in Clark and Eysinga, *The Colonial Conferences Between England and the Netherlands in 1613 and 1615*.

52. Nagazumi suggests the three were Matsudaira Masatsuna, Nagai Naomasa and Inoue Masanari. Nagazumi, "The Japanese *Go-shuinjo*," 32.

53. Copie van het journaal, gehouden door Coenraedt Cramer, gecommiteerd van wege de Oostindische Compagnie uit Firando naar Miacco aan de Keizerlijke Majesteit en Raden van Japan., Stukken van Sweers, van Vliet, Nationaal Archief, Den Haag, 5:212v.

54. *Dagregisters Japan* 1:40.

55. For paranoia about the Portuguese conspiracy lurking just below the surface, see Colenbrander, *Jan Pietersz. Coen*, 5:494.

56. This view is supported by Nagazumi Yōko, who has argued for the existence of a web of concealed investments in the Tayouan trade route. Nagazumi, "The Japanese *Go-shuinjo*," 32. See also Nagazumi, "Japan's Isolationist Policy as Seen through Dutch Source Materials." Her evidence comes, however, from just a handful of speculative quotes from VOC observers who frequently detected the presence of such conspiracies and is, I would suggest, far from conclusive.

57. This view stands in opposition to Patricia Seed's important work, in which she argued that each group of Europeans employed their own, nationally rooted ceremonies. For her, it was not simply that individual ceremonies incorporated distinct elements, but that these acts "turned on mutually exclusive concepts of the legitimate means of establishing a political empire." Seed, "Taking Possession and Reading Texts,"183. While there were clear variations, I would suggest, following Benton and Straumann, that vital commonalities were also present. Benton and Straumann. "Acquiring Empire by Law."

58. Benton and Straumann. "Acquiring Empire by Law," 31.

59. For two clashing pamphlets that clearly reveal this common ground, see *The Hollanders Declaration of the affaires of the East Indies* (Amsterdam, 1622); *An Answere to the Hollanders Declaration, concerning the Occurrents of the East-India* (London, 1622).

60. *The Hollanders Declaration of the affaires of the East Indies*, 11.

61. Arano, "Nihongata kai chitsujo no keisei." The term *Nihon-gata kai chitsujo* can be translated in a number of ways. The most literal translation is probably "Japan-style civilization/barbarian order."

62. Toby, *State and Diplomacy*, 57.

63. Ibid., 76.

64. Ibid., 181.

65. Turnbull, "Onward, Christian Samurai!" In this important article Turnbull argues that the nature of the political scene in Taiwan meant that it was "open to a more western-style form of development involving the establishment of a military base and colonization."

66. Tokyo daigaku shiryō hensanjo, *Dai Nihon shiryō*, series 12, 6:132–35.

67. Ibid., 138–39.

68. Cocks, *Diary Kept by the Head of the English Factory*, 1:223.

69. Turnbull, "Onward, Christian Samurai!" 17–18. For the idea that Japan lacked the necessary resources to take effective possession of Taiwan, see Coolhaas, *Generale Missiven*, 1:252.

70. *Dagregisters Japan*, 1:40.

71. Suzuki, *Civilization and Empire*, 140–76.

72. Memorie voor de E. Pieter Nuyts, raet van India, gaende voor commandeur over de vlote naer Tayouan gedestineert, ende van daer voorts in ambassade aen den Keijser van Japan, 10 May 1627, VOC 854:56v.

73. For a detailed account of this delegation, see Clulow, "A Fake Embassy." I am grateful to the editors of *Japanese Studies* for giving permission to reprint parts of this article.

74. Schouten, "Memorabel verhael," 87.

75. Colenbrander, *Jan Pietersz. Coen*, 7.2:1191.

76. Ibid., 7.2:1156; Sūden, *Ikoku nikki shō*, 195.

77. Colenbrander, *Jan Pietersz. Coen*, 7.2:1156, 1164.

78. Cornelis van Neijenroode to Pieter Nuyts, letter, 28 August 1627, NFJ 482:252–54.

79. Colenbrander, *Jan Pieterz. Coen*, 7.2:1173.

80. 22 November 1627, Nuijts/Muijser *Dagregister*, 495.

81. Sūden, *Ikoku nikki shō*, 195. Dutch sources make it clear that the group fell ill before they arrived in Edo.

82. Colenbrander, *Jan Pietersz. Coen*, 7.2:1233.

83. Ibid., 5:69.

84. In 1616, for example, an English East India Company agent, Nathaniel Courthope, persuaded the residents of the island of Run to hand over sovereignty to the English monarch in return for a promise to protect the islanders. After a short ceremony involving the handing over of a small nutmeg tree to Courthope, he proclaimed the island English territory and its residents "true and lawful subjects" of James I, who was forthwith to be titled king of England, Scotland, France, Ireland, and Run. Armed with these documents, the English proceeded to entrench themselves on the island and to defy any attempt to displace them. Danvers and Foster, *Letters Received by the East India Company from Its Servants in the East*, 5:345.

85. Colenbrander, *Jan Pietersz. Coen*, 7.2:1233.

86. Ibid. 18 February 1628, *Dagregister* Nuijts/Muijser, 507v.

87. Valentijn, *Oud en Nieuw Oost-Indien*, 4.2:53; Colenbrander, *Jan Pietersz. Coen*, 5:265.

88. Some scholars have argued that Nuyts was acting largely out of malice toward the Japanese rather than because there was any real fear of an attack. Boxer writes, for example, that Nuyts was looking for "an opportunity to gratify his spite." While he may have been eager to take revenge on the Japanese for the failure of his embassy, my reading of the sources suggests a genuine concern (shared among a number of different VOC officials) about an imminent assault. Boxer, *A True Description of the Mighty Kingdoms of Japan & Siam*, xvii.

89. Valentijn, *Oud en Nieuw Oost-Indien*, 4.2:53.

90. Schouten, "Memorabel verhael," 89.

91. VOC sources produced in the years after 1628 reflect a more mixed view concerning the possibility of a Japanese attack on Tayouan. In his report on the Taiwan crisis prepared in 1633, Schouten suggested that Hamada's vessels sailed with an express charge from senior Bakufu officials in Edo to seize the fort, which they believed contained a small, badly equipped garrison. Schouten, "Memorabel verhael," 88–89. However, it should also be noted that some company administrators became, as the years wore on, far less convinced that any sort of assault had in fact been planned.

92. Campbell, *Formosa Under the Dutch*, 42.

93. Valentijn, *Oud en Nieuw Oost-Indien*, 4.2:58.

7. GIVING UP THE GOVERNOR

1. Leupe, "Stukken betrekkelijk Pieter Nuyts," 188.

2. Blusse, "Pieter Nuyts (1598–1655)."

3. At the time of his appointment, Janssen was serving as Batavia's *equipage-meester*, an important position that placed him in charge of the busy port.

4. 25 February 1630, Copie van het journal van de zending van Willem Jansz. naar Nagasaki, Stukken van Sweers, van Vliet, Nationaal Archief, Den Haag, 5:240v–241v. The letter was signed by Suetsugu Heizō, but we know from other sources that its contents had been approved by the Bakufu.

5. Ibid, 241.

6. Translaet missive van Feso aen den Gouverneur Generael tot Batavia, 7th year Quanie. 1st month, VOC 1101. At times, Heizō's agents suggested that the Dutch could simply hand over the fort to Japanese authorities, but the precise nature of the Bakufu's demand, that the fort should be destroyed, is confirmed in multiple documents. The idea that a simple transfer would be enough seems to have been introduced by Heizō who stood to benefit from this distortion.

7. Nagazumi, *Hirado Oranda shōkan no nikki*, 1:414–5. The document provides further confirmation of the precise nature of the Bakufu's demand.

8. Schouten, "Memorabel verhael," 98.

9. For a detailed record of these negotiations, see Dagregisters gehouden te Edo door Willem Jansz. Van Amersfoort, NFJ 271–4. The diary has been translated in Nagazumi, *Hirado Oranda shōkan no nikki*, 2:11–503. The progress of these negotiations was delayed by the illness and subsequently the death of Tokugawa Hidetada.

10. Coolhaas, "Een Indisch verslag uit 1631," 90.

11. Cheng, *De VOC en Formosa 1624–1662*, 88.

12. Blussé, "Bull in a China Shop," 105.

13. Leupe, "Stukken betrekkelijk Pieter Nuyts," 186.

14. Ibid., 187.

15. Stapel, "Bijdragen tot de geschiedenis der rechtspraak bij de Vereenigde Oost-indische Compagnie."

16. Extraterritoriality was a well-established principle in both Europe and Asia. Medieval Italian city states famously negotiated such rights for merchants operating in the Middle East, while many diasporic trading communities in Asia retained their own legal arrangements. What set the VOC apart was the extent of its operations and its systematic pursuit of extraterritorial arrangements.

17. As collected in Heeres and Stapel, *Corpus Diplomaticum Neerlando-Indicum*. For a discussion of these jurisdictional arrangements, see Alexandrowicz, *An Introduction to the History of the Law of Nations in the East Indies*, 97–128.

18. Heeres and Stapel, *Corpus Diplomaticum Neerlando-Indicum*, 1:26.

19. Ruangsilp, *Dutch East India Company Merchants*, 38–41.

20. Heeres and Stapel, *Corpus Diplomaticum Neerlando-Indicum*, 1:285.

21. Ruangsilp, *Dutch East India Company Merchants*, 39.

22. Ibid., 40.

23. Caron and Schouten, *A True description of the Mighty Kingdoms of Japan and Siam*, 133.

24. Leue, "Legal Expansion in the Age of Companies," 138.

25. Ball, *Indonesian Legal History*, 17–18.

26. Ward, *Networks of Empire*, 69.

27. Barendse, *The Arabian Seas*, 383.

28. Botsman, *Punishment and Power in the Making of Modern Japan*, 139.

29. Grotius, *The Rights of War and Peace*, 1:259.

30. Leupe, "Stukken betrekkelijk Pieter Nuyts, " 187.

31. Ibid.

32. Clulow, "Unjust, Cruel and Barbarous Proceedings."

33. Chancey, "The Amboyna Massacre in English Politics," 592–93.

34. Sainsbury, *Calendar of State Papers Colonial, East Indies, China and Japan*, 4:320–28.

35. De Jonge and van Deventer, *De opkomst van het Nederlandsch gezag in Oost Indië*, 5:xxviii.

36. Skinner, *A true Relation of the Uniust, Cruell, and Barbarous Proceedings*. This pamphlet includes a copy of *A true declaration of the newes that came out of the East-Indies, with the pinace called the Hare* from which these quotes come.

37. Coolhaas, "Ambonschen Moord," 64.

38. Chancey, "The Amboyna Massacre in English Politics," 595.

39. Hunter, *A History of British India*, 414

40. Sainsbury, *Calendar of State Papers, Colonial, East Indies and Persia*, 8:43.

41. Coolhaas, "Ambonschen Moord," 70–71.

42. Sainsbury, *Calendar of State Papers, Colonial, East Indies and Persia*, 8:43.

43. Leupe, "Stukken betrekkelijk Pieter Nuyts," 187.

44. *Batavia Dagregisters, Anno 1631–1634*, 90.

45. *Hirado Oranda shōkan no nikki*, 2:439.

46. Ibid., 2:413.

47. Ibid., 2:430–32.

48. Ibid., 2:464.

49. It is clear that Specx and other members of the High Government were genuinely concerned that this would in fact happen. Schouten, "Memorabel verhael," 105–6. If a trial was ordered, VOC representatives in Japan were ordered to do their best to limit any damages to the company, the United Provinces, and Nuyts himself.

50. Blussé, "Bull in a China Shop," 95.

51. Leupe, "Stukken betrekkelijk Pieter Nuyts," 197.

52. Ibid., 155.

53. Ibid., 190, 197, and 191.

54. *Dagregisters Japan*, 1:314.

55. Ibid.

56. Governor General Hendrik Brouwer aen de raetsheeren van de Japanse key-serlijcke Mayesteit, letter, 31 May 1633, VOC 856:235.

57. *Dagregisters Japan*, 1:38.

58. Matsura Fisennocammijsama to Nicolaes Couckebacker, 3 September 1634, VOC 1114:68. This letter was subsequently presented to the Bakufu on behalf of the Dutch.

59. *Dagregisters Japan*, 1:219.

60. Ibid., 1:248. Nuyts's wife, Cornelia, had traveled to Asia, arriving in Batavia while her husband was still imprisoned in the castle there. She had subsequently died after learning that her son, Laurens, had passed away in captivity, but she was sur-vived by three children who were placed under the care of a relative.

61. *Dagregisters Japan*, 2:8.

62. *Dagregisters Japan*, 2:18. The chandelier was initially valued at 796 guilders, but was clearly worth much more in Japan.

63. For the most detailed account of this object, see Lunsingh Scheurleer, "Koperen kronen en waskaarsen voor Japan." Mia Mochizuki has produced two important arti-cles that reference the chandelier. Mochizuki, "Deciphering the Dutch in Deshima" and "Idolatry and Western-Inspired Painting in Japan."

64. *Dagregisters Japan*, 2:48; Mochizuki, "Deciphering the Dutch in Deshima," 80.

65. *Dagregisters Japan*, 2:58.

66. Lunsingh Scheurleer, "Koperen kronen," 73.

67. As was usually the case, the company had a number of secondary objectives centering on the improvement of VOC trade in Japan.

68. Mochizuki, "Deciphering the Dutch in Deshima," 82.

69. Emanuel de Witte, *The Interior of the Oude Kerk, Amsterdam, During a Sermon*, Inventory number NG1053, National Gallery, London.

70. Quoted in Mochizuki, "Deciphering the Dutch in Deshima," 84. As far as we can make out, this verse refers not to the original 1636 gift but to a large brass lantern, also crafted by Gerritszoon, that was presented by the Dutch to the shogun in Decem-ber 1643. However, it applies more generally to a broader category of gifts, all made by Gerritszoon and shipped to Japan, that includes the 1636 chandelier.

71. *Dagregisters Japan*, 2:48.

72. *Dagregisters Japan*, 2:66–67.

73. Ibid., 2:81.

74. Gerhart, *The Eyes of Power*, 136.

75. Totman, *Early Modern Japan*, 110; Toby, *State and Diplomacy*, 71–72.

76. Coaldrake, *Architecture and Authority in Japan*, 180.

77. Ibid., 181–82.

78. Hauser, "Osaka Castle and Tokugawa Authority in Western Japan."

79. Coaldrake, *Architecture and Authority in Japan*, 191–92.

80. The anniversary fell on the seventeenth day of the fourth month or 21 May 1636.

81. Lunsingh Scheurleer, "Koperen kronen," 72–73.

82. *Dagregisters Japan*, 2:23.

83. Toby, *State and Diplomacy*, 100–1.

84. The Korean bell only reached Nikkō in 1643.

85. Coaldrake, *Architecture and Authority in Japan*, 186. Gerhart, who has analyzed the iconography of this structure, describes the Yōmeimon as the "focal point of Tokugawa efforts to create divine authority." Gerhart, *The Eyes of Power*, 74.

86. Gerhart, *The Eyes of Power*, 75

87. Coaldrake, *Architecture and Authority in Japan*, 187.

88. Montanus, *Atlas Japanensis*, 152.

89. Markley, "Gulliver and the Japanese," 475.

90. Breckenridge, "The Aesthetics and Politics."

CONCLUSION: THE DUTCH EXPERIENCE IN JAPAN

1. Winius and Vink, *The Merchant Warrior Pacified*.

2. Ricklefs, *A History of Modern Indonesia*, 92.

3. Reid, "Pluralism and Progress in Seventeenth-Century Makassar," 436.

4. Sainsbury, *Calendar of State Papers Colonial, East Indies, China and Japan*, 3:108.

5. Quoted in Masselman, *The Cradle of Colonialism*, 327.

6. *Batavia Dagregister, Anno 1656–7*, 294.

7. Ricklefs, *A History of Modern Indonesia*, 74.

8. Kops, "Not Such an 'Unpromising Beginning,'" 539.

9. For examples of two letters sent from the governor-general to the Chinese emperor, see van Dam, *Beschrijvinge van de Oostindishe Compagnie*, 2.1:767–68. These embassies are documented in Wills, *Embassies and Illusions*.

10. Ruangsilp, *Dutch East India Company Merchants*, 1.

11. Ibid., 130.

12. Ibid., 27.

13. Caron and Schouten, *A True description of the Mighty Kingdoms of Japan and Siam*, 122.

14. Ruangsilp, *Dutch East India Company Merchants*, 21.

15. Quoted in Pombejra, "The Dutch-Siamese Conflict of 1663–1664," 299.

16. Coolhaas, *Generale Missiven*, 1:704.

17. Mijer, *Verzameling van Instructiën, Ordonnanciën en Reglementen*, 99.

18. Wyatt, *Thailand*, 97.

19. Ruangsilp, *Dutch East India Company Merchants*, 27.

BIBLIOGRAPHY

Abeyasekere, Susan. *Jakarta: A History*. New York: Oxford University Press, 1987.

Adams, Julia. *The Familial State: Ruling Families and Merchant Capitalism in Early Modern Europe*. Ithaca, NY: Cornell University Press, 2005.

Aitchison, C. U. *A Collection of Treaties, Engagements and Sunnuds Relating to India and Neighbouring Countries*. 7 vols. Calcutta: Savielle and Cranenburgh, 1862–1864.

Alexandrowicz, C. H. *An Introduction to the History of the Law of Nations in the East Indies*. London: Oxford University Press, 1967.

Anand, Ram Prakash. "Maritime Practice in Southeast Asia Until 1600 A.D. and the Modern Law of the Sea." *International and Comparative Law Quarterly* 30, no. 2 (1981): 440–54.

———. *Origin and Development of the Law of the Sea: History of International Law*. The Hague: Martinus Nijhoff, 1983.

Anderson, M. S. *The Rise of Modern Diplomacy, 1450–1919*. London: Longman, 1993.

Andrade, Tonio. "Political Spectacle and Colonial Rule: The *Landdag* on Dutch Taiwan, 1629–1648." *Itinerario* 21, no. 3 (1997): 57–93.

———. "The Company's Chinese Pirates: How the Dutch East India Company Tried to Lead a Coalition of Pirates to War against China, 1621–1662." *Journal of World History* 15, no. 4 (2004): 415–44.

———. "Pirates, Pelts, and Promises: The Sino-Dutch Colony of Seventeenth-century Taiwan and the Aboriginal Village of Favorolang." *Journal of Asian Studies* 64, no. 2 (2005): 295–320.

———. "The Rise and Fall of Dutch Taiwan, 1624–1662: Cooperative Colonization and the Statist Model of European Expansion." *Journal of World History* 17, no. 4 (2006): 429–50.

———. *How Taiwan Became Chinese: Dutch, Spanish, and Han Colonization in the Seventeenth Century*. New York: Columbia University Press. 2008.

———. "Beyond Guns, Germs and Steel: European Expansion and Maritime Asia, 1400–1750," *Journal of Early Modern History* 14 (2010): 165–86.

———. *Lost Colony: The Untold Story of China's First Great Victory Over the West*. Princeton: Princeton University Press, 2011.

Anghie, Antony. "Francisco de Vitoria and the Colonial Origins of International Law." *Social and Legal Studies* 5, no. 3 (1996): 321–36.

———. *Imperialism, Sovereignty, and the Making of International Law*. Cambridge: Cambridge University Press, 2005.

Anthonisz, Richard. *The Dutch in Ceylon*. New Delhi: Asian Educational Services, 2003.

Arano, Yasunori. "Nihongata kai chitsujo no keisei." In *Nihon no shakaishi 1: Rettō naigai no kōtsu to kokka*. Ed. Asao Naohiro, Amino Yoshihiko, Yamaguchi Keiji and Yoshida Takashi. Tokyo: Iwanami Shoten, 1987.

———. *Kinsei Nihon to Higashi Ajia*. Tokyo: Tokyo Daigaku Shuppankai, 1988.

———. "Nagasaki guchi no keisei." In *Bakuhansei kokka to iiki, ikoku*. Ed. Katō Eiichi, Katajima Manji, Fukaya Katsumi. Tokyo: Azekura Shobō, 1989.

———, ed. *Edo Bakufu to higashi Ajia*. Tokyo: Yoshikawa Kōbunkan, 2003.

———. "The Formation of a Japanocentric World Order." *International Journal of Asian Studies* 2, no. 2 (2005): 185–216.

Arasaratnam, Sinnapah. *Dutch Power in Ceylon, 1658–1687*. Amsterdam: Djambatan, 1958.

———, ed. *Francois Valentijn's Description of Ceylon*. London: Hakluyt Society, 1978.

Asao, Naohiro. "Sakokusei no seiritsu." In *Kōza Nihon shi, 4: Bakuhansei Shakai*, 59–94. Ed. Arano Yasunori. Tokyo: Tokyo Daigaku Shuppankai, 1973.

Barbour, Richmond. "Power and Distant Display: Early English 'Ambassadors' in Moghul India." *Huntington Library Quarterly* 61, nos. 3/4 (1998): 343–68.

———. *Before Orientalism: London's Theatre of the East, 1576–1626*. Cambridge: Cambridge University Press, 2003.

Barendse, Rene. *The Arabian Seas, 1640–1700*. Leiden: CNWS, 1998.

Bassett, D. K. "The 'Amboyna massacre' of 1623." *Journal of Southeast Asia* 1, no. 2 (1960): 1–19.

Bataviaasch Genootschap van Kunsten en Wetenschappen, ed. *Realia: Register op de Generale Resolutiën van het Kasteel Batavia, 1632–1805*. 3 vols. Leiden: G. Kolff, 1882–1886.

Batten, Bruce. "Frontiers and Boundaries of PreModern Japan." *Journal of Historical Geography* 25, no. 2 (1999): 166–82.

——— *To the Ends of Japan: Premodern Frontiers, Boundaries, and Interactions*. Honolulu: University of Hawai'i Press, 2003.

Beekman, E. M. *Troubled Pleasures: Dutch Colonial Literature from the East Indies 1600–1950*. Oxford: Clarendon, 1996.

Benton, Lauren. *Law and Colonial Cultures: Legal Regimes in World History, 1400–1900*. Cambridge: Cambridge University Press, 2000.

———. "The Legal Regime of the South Atlantic World: Jurisdictional Politics as Institutional Order." *Journal of World History* 11, no. 1 (2000): 27–56.

———. "Legal Spaces of Empire: Piracy and the Origins of Ocean Regionalism." *Comparative Studies in Society and History* 47, no. 4 (2005): 700–24.

———. *The Search for Sovereignty: Law and Geography in European Empires, 1400–1900*. Cambridge: Cambridge University Press, 2010.

Benton, Lauren, and Benjamin Straumann. "Acquiring Empire by Law: From Roman Doctrine to Early Modern European Practice." *Law and History Review* 28, no. 1 (2010): 1–38.

Berger, Louis. "The Overseas Chinese Community in Seventeenth Century Nagasaki." Ph.D. dissertation, Harvard University, 2003.

Berry, Elizabeth. *Hideyoshi*. Cambridge: Harvard University Press, 1982.

———. "Public Peace and Private Attachment: The Goals and Conduct of Power in Early Modern Japan." *Journal of Japanese Studies* 12, no. 2 (1986): 237–71.

———. "Was Early Modern Japan Culturally Integrated?" *Modern Asian Studies* 31, no. 3 (1997): 547–81.

———. *Japan in Print: Information and Nation in the Early Modern Period*. Berkeley: University of California Press, 2006.

Biedermann, Zoltán. "Portuguese Diplomacy in Asia in the Sixteenth Century. A Preliminary Overview." *Itinerario* 29, no. 2 (2005): 13–37.

Blair, Emma, and James Robertson, eds. *The Philippine Islands, 1493–1803*. 55 vols. Cleveland: A. H. Clark, 1902–9.

Blussé, Leonard. "The Dutch Occupation of the Pescadores (1622–1624)," *Transactions of the International Conference of Orientalists in Japan* 18 (1973): 28–43.

———. "Japanese Historiography and European Sources." In *Reappraisals in Overseas History*. Ed. P.C. Emmer and H.L. Wesseling. Leiden: Leiden University Press, 1979.

———. "The VOC as Sorceror's Apprentice: Stereotypes and Social Engineering on the China Coast." In *Leyden Studies in Sinology*. Ed. W. L. Idema. Leiden: E. J. Brill, 1981.

———. "Dutch Protestant Missionaries as Protagonists of the Territorial Expansion of the VOC on Formosa." In *Conversion, Competition, and Conflict: Essays on the Role of Religion in Asia*. Ed. Dick Kooiman, Otto van den Muizenberg and Peter van der Veer. Amsterdam: Free University Press, 1984.

———. *Strange Company: Chinese Settlers, Mestizo Women and the Dutch in VOC Batavia*. Dordrecht, Holland and Riverton, NJ: Foris Publications, 1986.

———. "Minnan-jen or Cosmopolitan? The Rise of Cheng Chih-lung alias Nicolas Iquan." In *Development and Decline of Fukien Province in the 17th and 18th Centuries*. Ed. E.B. Vermeer. Leiden: Brill, 1990.

———. "No Boats to China: The Dutch East India Company and the Changing Pattern of the China Sea Trade, 1635–1690," *Modern Asian Studies* 30, no. 1. (Feb 1996): 51–76.

———. "Queen among kings: Diplomatic Ritual at Batavia." In *Jakarta-Batavia*. Ed. Kees Grijns and Peter Nas. Leiden: KITLV Press, 2000.

————. "Amongst Feigned Friends and Declared Enemies." In *Making Sense of Global History: The Nineteenth International Congress of the Historical Sciences Oslo 2000 Commemorative Volume*. Ed. Sølvi Sogner. Oslo: Universitetsforlaget, 2001.

————. "Bull in a China Shop: Pieter Nuyts in China and Japan (1627–1636)." In *Around and About Formosa, Essays in honor of Professor Ts'ao Yung-ho*. Ed. Leonard Blussé. Taipei: SMC, 2003.

————. "The Grand Inquisitor Inoue Chikugono Kami Masashige, Spin Doctor of the Tokugawa Bakufu." *Bulletin of Portuguese/Japanese Studies* 7 (2003): 22–43.

————. *Visible Cities: Canton, Nagasaki, and Batavia and the Coming of the Americans*. Cambridge: Harvard University Press, 2008.

Blussé, Leonard, Natalie Everts, and Evelien Frech, eds. *The Formosan Encounter: Notes on Formosa's Aboriginal Society: A Selection of Documents from Dutch Archival Sources*. 4 vols. Taipei: Shung Ye Museum of Formosan Aborigines, 1998–.

Blussé, Leonard, Nathalie Everts, W. E. Milde, and Yung-ho Ts'ao, eds. *De Dagregisters van het Kasteel Zeelandia, Taiwan, 1629–1662*. 4 vols. The Hague: Instituut voor Nederlandse Geschiedenis, 1986–2001.

Blussé, Leonard, Willem Remmelink, and Ivo Smits, eds. *Bridging the Divide: 1600–2000. Four Hundred Years, the Netherlands–Japan*. Leiden: Hotei, 2000.

Bolitho, Harold. *Treasures Among Men: The Fudai Daimyo in Tokugawa Japan*. New Haven: Yale University Press, 1974.

Bolling, Frederik. "Friderici Bollingii Oost-Indisch reisboek." Trans. J. Visscher. *Bijdragen tot de Taal-, Land- en Volkenkunde van Nederlandsch Indië* 68 (1913): 289–382.

Boot, W. J. "Maxims of Foreign Policy." In *Shifting Communities and Identity Formation in Early Modern Asia*, 7–23. Ed. Leonard Blussé and Felipe Fernández-Armesto. Leiden: CNWS, 2003.

Borao Mateo, José Eugenio, ed. *Spaniards in Taiwan: Documents*. 2 vols. Taipei: SMC, 2001–2.

Borschberg, Peter. "The Seizure of the *Sta. Catarina* Revisited: The Portuguese Empire in Asia, VOC Politics, and the Origins of the Dutch-Johor Alliance (1602–ca. 1616)." *Journal of Southeast Asian Studies* 33, no. 1 (2002): 31–62.

————. *The Singapore and Melaka Straits: Violence, Security, and Diplomacy in the Seventeenth Century*. Singapore : NUS, 2010.

————. "From Self-Defence to an Instrument of War: Dutch Privateering Around the Malay Peninsula in the Early Seventeenth Century." *Journal of Early Modern History* 17 (2013): 35–52.

Botsman, Dani. *Punishment and Power in the Making of Modern Japan*. Princeton: Princeton University Press, 2005.

Boxer, C. R. "The Swan-Song of the Portuguese in Japan, 1635–39." *Transactions and Proceedings of the Japan Society of London* 27 (1930): 3–11.

————, ed. *A True Description of the Mighty Kingdoms of Japan & Siam*. London: Argonaut, 1935.

————. *The Christian Century in Japan, 1549–1650*. Berkeley: University of California Press, 1951.

————. *South China in the Sixteenth Century*. London: Hakluyt Society, 1953.

———. *The Great Ship from Amacon: Annals of Macao and the Old Japan Trade, 1555–1640.* Lisbon: CEHU, 1959.

———. *Four Centuries of Portuguese Expansion, 1415–1825: A Succinct Survey.* Johannesburg: Witwatersrand University Press, 1961.

———. *The Dutch Seaborne Empire, 1600–1800.* London: Hutchinson, 1965.

———. *Jan Compagnie in War and Peace, 1602–1799.* Hong Kong: Heinemann Asia, 1980.

———. "When the Twain First Met: European Conceptions and Misconceptions of Japan, Sixteenth-Eighteenth Centuries." *Modern Asian Studies* 18, no. 4 (1984): 531–40.

———. *Portuguese Merchants and Missionaries in Feudal Japan, 1543–1640.* London: Variorum Reprints, 1986.

Boyajian, James. *Portuguese Trade in Asia Under the Hapsburgs.* Baltimore: Johns Hopkins University Press, 1993.

Breckenridge, Carol. "The Aesthetics and Politics of Colonial Collecting: India at World Fairs." *Comparative Studies in Society and History* 31, no. 2 (2011): 195–216.

Brown, Philip. *Central Authority and Local Autonomy in the Formation of Early Modern Japan: The Case of Kaga Domain.* Stanford: Stanford University Press, 1993.

Bruce, John. *Annals of the Honourable East-India Company, from their Establishment by the Charter of Queen Elizabeth, 1600, to the Union of the London and English East India Companies, 1707–08.* London: Black, Parry and Kingsbury, 1810.

Bugge, Henriette. "Silk to Japan: Sino-Dutch Competition in the Silk Trade to Japan, 1633–1685." *Itinerario* 13, no. 2 (1989): 25–44.

Campbell, William, ed. *Formosa Under the Dutch: Described from Contemporary Sources.* London: Kegan Paul, Trench, Trubner, 1903.

Carioti, Patrizia. "Hirado During the First Half of the Seventeenth Century: From a Commercial Outpost for Sino-Japanese Maritime Activities to an International Crossroads of Far Eastern Routes." In *A Passion for China: Essays in Honour of Paolo Santangelo, for His Sixtieth Birthday.* Ed. Ling-Yeong Chiu and Donatella Guida. Leiden: Brill, 2006.

Caron, Francois, and Justus Schouten. *A True description of the Mighty Kingdoms of Japan and Siam.* Trans. Roger Manley. London, 1663.

Casale, Giancarlo. *The Ottoman Age of Exploration.* Oxford: Oxford University Press, 2010.

Chaiklin, Martha. *Cultural Commerce and Dutch Commercial Culture. The Influence of European Material Culture on Japan, 1700–1850.* Leiden: Research School CNWS, 2005

Chancey, Karen. "The Amboyna Massacre in English Politics, 1624–1632." *Albion* 30, no. 4 (1998): 583–98.

Chaudhuri, K. N. *The Trading World of Asia and the English East India Company: 1660–1760.* London: Cambridge University Press, 1978.

Cheng, Shaogang. *De VOC en Formosa 1624–1662: Een vergeten geschiedenis.* Amsterdam: Bataafsche Leeuw, 1997.

Chiu, Hsin-hui. *The colonial "civilizing process" in Dutch Formosa, 1624–1662.* Leiden and Boston: Brill, 2008.

Chung, Sungil. "The Volume of Early Modern Korea-Japan Trade: A Comparison with the Japan-Holland Trade." *Acta Koreana* 7, no. 1 (January 2004): 69–85.

Cieslik, Hubert. "The Great Martyrdom in Edo 1623. Its Causes, Course, Consequences." *Monumenta Nipponica* 10, no. 1/2 (1954): 1–44.

Cipolla, Carlo. *Guns, Sails, and Empire: Technological Innovation and the Early Phases of European Expansion, 1400–1700.* New York: Minerva, 1965.

Clark, M. N., and W. J. M. Eysinga. *The Colonial Conferences Between England and the Netherlands in 1613 and 1615.* 2 vols. Leiden: Brill, 1940–1951.

Clulow, Adam. "Unjust, Cruel, and Barbarous Proceedings: Japanese Mercenaries and the Amboyna Incident of 1623." *Itinerario* 31, no. 1 (2007): 15–34.

———. "European Maritime Violence and Territorial States in Early Modern Asia, 1600–1650." *Itinerario* 33, no. 3 (2009): 72–94.

———. "A Fake Embassy, the Lord of Taiwan and Tokugawa Japan." *Japanese Studies* 30, no. 1 (May 2010): 23–41.

———. "From Global Entrepôt to Early Modern Domain: Hirado, 1609–1641." *Monumenta Nipponica* 61, no. 1 (Spring 2010): 1–35.

———. "Like Lambs in Japan and Devils Outside Their Land: Diplomacy, Violence, and Japanese Merchants in Southeast Asia." *Journal of World History* 24, no. 2 (2013): 335–58.

Coaldrake, William. *Architecture and Authority in Japan.* London: RoutledgeCurzon, 1996.

Cocks, Richard. *Diary Kept by the Head of the English Factory in Japan: Diary of Richard Cocks, 1615–1622.* Ed. University of Tokyo Historiographical Institute. 3 vols. Tokyo: University of Tokyo, 1978–1980.

Cohn, Bernard. *Colonialism and Its Forms of Knowledge: The British in India.* Princeton: Princeton University Press, 1996.

Colenbrander, H. T., ed. *Jan Pietersz. Coen, bescheiden omtrent zijn bedrijf in Indie.* 7 vols. The Hague: Martinus Nijhoff, 1919–23.

Colley, Linda. *Captives: Britain, Empire and the World, 1600–1850.* New York: Pantheon, 2002.

Coolhaas, W. Ph. "Aanteekeningen en Opmerkingen over den zoogenaamdem Ambonschen Moord." *Bijdragen tot de Taal-, Land- en Volkenkunde van Nederlandsch-Indie* 101 (1942): 49–93.

———. "Een Indisch verslag uit 1631, van de hand van Antonio van Diemen." *Bijdragen en Mededelingen van het Historisch Genootschap* 65 (1947): 1–237.

———. "Een lastig heerschap tegenover een lastig volk." *Bijdragen en Mededelingen van het Historisch Genootschap* 69 (1955): 17–42.

———, ed. *Generale Missiven van Gouverneurs-generaal en Raden aan heren XVII der Verenigde Oostindische Compagnie.* 9 vols. The Hague: Martinus Nijhoff, 1960– .

———. *Pieter van den Broecke in Azie.* The Hague: Martinus Nijhoff, 1962–63.

Cooper, Michael, ed., *They Came to Japan: An Anthology of European Reports on Japan, 1543–1640.* Berkeley: University of California Press, 1965.

Commelin, Isaac. *Begin ende Voortgangh van de Vereenighde Nederlantsche Geoctroyeerde Oost-Indische Compagnie.* 4 vols. Amsterdam: Facsimile Uitgaven Nederland, 1969.

Costa, João Paulo Oliveira. "A Route Under Pressure. Communication Between Nagasaki and Macao (1597–1617)." *Bulletin of Portuguese-Japanese Studies* 1 (2000): 75–95.

Craig, Albert. *Civilization and Enlightenment: The Early Thought of Fukuzawa Yukichi.* Cambridge: Harvard University Press, 2009.

Curvelo, Alexandra. "Nagasaki/Deshima after the Portuguese in Dutch Accounts of the Seventeenth Century." *Bulletin of Portuguese/Japanese Studies* 6 (2003): 147–157.

Danvers, F. C., and W. Foster, *Letters Received by the East India Company from Its Servants in the East.* 6 vols. London: S. Low, Marston, 1896–1902.

Das Gupta, Ashin. "Indian Merchants and the Western Indian Ocean: The Early Seventeenth Century." *Modern Asian Studies* 19, no. 3. (1985): 481–99.

———. "The Indian Ocean in the Eighteenth Century." In *India and the Indian Ocean*, 131–61. Ed. Ashin das Gupta and M. N. Pearson. Calcutta: Oxford University Press, 1987.

De Certeau, Michel. *The Writing of History.* Trans. T. Conley. New York: Columbia University Press, 1988.

De Jonge, J. K., and M. L. van Deventer, eds. *De opkomst van het Nederlandsch gezag in Oost Indië.* 13 vols. The Hague: Martinus Nijhoff, 1862–1909.

De Lange, William. *Pars Japonica: The First Dutch Expedition to Reach the Shores of Japan.* Warren, CT: Floating World, 2006.

De Vries, Jan, and Ad van der Woude. *The First Modern Economy: Success, Failure, and Perseverance of the Dutch Economy, 1500–1815.* New York: Cambridge University Press, 1997.

Disney, A. R. *A History of Portugal and the Portuguese Empire: From Beginnings to 1807.* 2 vols. New York: Cambridge University Press, 2009.

Doeff, Hendrik. *Recollections of Japan.* Trans. Annick Doeff. Victoria: Trafford, 2003.

Doi, Tadao, ed. *Nippo jisho. Vocabvlario da lingoa de Iapam.* Tokyo: Iwanami Shoten, 1960.

Earns, Lane. "The Development of Bureaucratic Rule in Early Modern Japan: The Nagasaki Bugyô in the Seventeenth Century." Ph.D. dissertation, University of Hawai'i, 1987.

———. "The Nagasaki Bugyō and the Development of Bureaucratic Rule in Seventeenth-Century Japan." *Asian Culture Quarterly* 22, no. 2 (1994): 63–73.

Edmundson, George. "Frederick Henry, Prince of Orange." *The English Historical Review* 5, no. 17 (1890): 41–64.

———. *Anglo-Dutch rivalry during the first half of the seventeenth century, being the Ford lectures delivered at Oxford in 1910.* Oxford: Clarendon, 1911.

Edwards, William. *Reminiscences of Bengal Civilian.* London: S. Elder, 1866.

Elliott, J. H. "The Spanish Conquest and settlement of America." In *Colonial Latin America*, 149–206. Ed. Leslie Bethell. Cambridge: Cambridge University Press, 1984.

Elison, George. *Deus Destroyed: The Image of Christianity in Early Modern Japan.* Cambridge: Harvard University Press, 1973.

Elisonas, Jurgis. "The Inseparable Trinity: Japan's Relations with China and Korea." In *Early Modern Japan*, vol. 4: *The Cambridge History of Japan*. Ed. John W. Hall and James McClain. Cambridge: Cambridge University Press, 1991.

Enthoven, Victor. *Zeeland en de opkomst van Republiek. Handel en strijd in de Scheld-edelta c. 1550–1621.* Leiden: Proefschrift, 1996.

Eskildsen, Robert. "Of Civilization and Savages: The Mimetic Imperialism of Japan's 1874 Expedition to Taiwan." *American Historical Review* 107, no. 2 (2002): 388–418.

Fairbank, John. *The Chinese World Order: Traditional China's Foreign Relations.* Cambridge: Harvard University Press, 1968.

Farrington, Anthony. *The English Factory in Japan, 1613–1623.* 2 vols. London: British Library, 1991.

Ferguson, Donald. *The Earliest Dutch Visits to Ceylon.* New Delhi: Asian Educational Services, 1998.

Fernández-Armesto, Felipe. *Civilizations : Culture, Ambition, and the Transformation of Nature.* New York: Free Press, 2001.

Ferrell, Raleigh. *Taiwan Aboriginal Groups: Problems in Cultural and Linguistic Classification.* Taipei: Institute of Ethnology, Academia Sinica, 1969.

Flynn, Dennis O., and Arturo Giraldez. "Silk for Silver: Manila-Macao Trade in the Seventeenth Century." *Philippine Studies* 44 (1996): 52–68.

——. "Cycles of Silver: Global Economic Unity through the Mid-Eighteenth Century." *Journal of World History* 13, no. 2 (2002): 391–427.

Foster, William. *Early Travels in India.* London: Oxford University Press, 1921.

Frank, Andre Gunder. *ReOrient: Global Economy in the Asian Age.* Berkeley: University of California Press, 1998.

Frick, Christoph. *A relation of two several voyages made into the East-Indies by Christopher Fryke and Christopher Schewitzer.* London, 1700.

Frijhoff, Willem. "The Princely Court at The Hague: A National and European Perspective." In *Dutch Culture in a European Perspective: 1650, Hard-won Unity.* Ed. Willem Frijhoff and Marijke Spies. New York: Palgrave Macmillan, 2004.

Frijhoff, Willem, and Marijke Spies. *Dutch Culture in a European Perspective: 1650, Hard-won Unity.* New York: Palgrave Macmillan, 2004.

Fryer, John. *A New Account of East-India and Persia, in eight letters.* London, 1698.

Fujii, Jōji. "Junana seiki no Nihon: buke no kokka no keisei." In *Iwanami kōza Nihon tsūshi* 12. Ed. Asao Naohiro, et al. Tokyo: Iwanami Shoten, 1993–.

Fujiki, Hisashi. *Toyotomi heiwarei to sengoku shakai.* Tokyo: Tokyo daigaku shuppankai, 1985.

Fulton, Thomas Wemyss. *The Sovereignty of the Sea.* Edinburgh: Blackwood, 1911.

Furber, Holden. "Asia and the West as Partners Before Empire and After." *Journal of Asian Studies* 28, no. 4 (1969): 711–21.

——. *Rival empires of trade in the Orient, 1600–1800.* Minneapolis: University of Minnesota Press, 1976.

Gaastra, Femme. *The Dutch East India Company: Expansion and Decline.* Zutpen: Walburg Pers, 2003.

Geerts, A.J.C. "The Arima Rebellion and the Conduct of Koeckebacker." *Transactions of the Asiatic Society of Japan* 11 (1883): 51–117.

Gerhart, Karen. *The Eyes of Power: Art and Early Tokugawa Authority.* Honolulu: University of Hawai'i Press, 1999.

Glete, Jan. *War and the State in Early Modern Europe: Spain, the Dutch Republic, and Sweden as Fiscal-Military States, 1500–1660*. London: Routledge, 2002.

Gokhale, B. G. *Surat in the Seventeenth Century*. Malmo: Scandinavian Institute of Asian Studies, 1979.

Goodman, Grant. *The Dutch Impact on Japan, 1640–1853*. Leiden: Brill, 1967.

———. *Japan: the Dutch Experience*. London: Athlone, 1986.

———. *Japan and the Dutch, 1600–1853*. Surrey: Curzon, 2000.

Goonewardena, K. W. *The Foundation of Dutch Power in Ceylon, 1638–1658*. Amsterdam: Djambatan, 1958.

Greenblatt, Stephen, *Marvelous Possessions: The Wonder of the New World*. Chicago: University of Chicago Press, 1991.

Groeneveldt, W. P. *De Nederlanders in China, 1601–1624*. The Hague: Martinus Nijhoff, 1898.

Groenveld, Simon. "The King-Stadholder: William III as Stadholder: Prince or Minister?" In *Redefining William III: The Impact of the King-Stadholder in International Context* 17–37. Ed. Esther Mijers and David Onnekink. Aldershot: Ashgate, 2007.

Grotius, Hugo. *Hugo Grotius Mari libero et P. Merula De maribus*. Leiden, 1633.

———. *The Rights of War and Peace, Including the Law of Nature and of Nations*. Trans. A. C. Campbell. New York: M. W. Dunne, 1901.

———. *The Freedom of the Seas; or, the Right Which Belongs to the Dutch to Take Part in the East Indian Trade*. Trans. Ralph Van Deman Magoffin. New York: Oxford University Press, 1916.

———. *The Rights of War and Peace*. Ed. Richard Tuck. Indianapolis: Liberty Fund, 2005.

———. *Commentary on the Law of Prize and Booty*. Ed. Martine Julia van Ittersum. Indianapolis: Liberty Fund, 2006.

Haan, F. de. *Oud Batavia*. Bandoeng: A. C. Nix, 1935.

Halikowski-Smith, Stefan. "'The Friendship of Kings was in the Ambassadors': Portuguese Diplomatic Embassies in Asia and Africa During the Sixteenth and Seventeenth Centuries," *Portuguese Studies* 22, no. 1 (2006): 101–34.

Hall, John, ed. *The Cambridge History of Japan: Early Modern Japan*. Cambridge: Cambridge University Press, 1991.

Hang, Xing. "Between Trade and Legitimacy, Maritime and Continent: The Zheng Organization in Seventeenth-Century East Asia." PhD dissertation, University of California, Berkeley, 2010.

Hanna, William. *Indonesian Banda: Colonialism and Its Aftermath in the Nutmeg Islands*. Philadelphia: Institute for the Study of Human Issues, 1978.

Hasan, Farhat. "Conflict and Co-operation in Anglo-Mughal Trade Relations During the Reign of Aurangzeb." *Journal of the Economic and Social History of the Orient* 34, no. 4 (1991): 351–60.

Hauser, William. "Osaka Castle and Tokugawa Authority in Western Japan." In *The Bakufu In Japanese History*, 153–72. Ed. Jeffrey P. Mass and William B. Hauser. Stanford: Stanford University Press, 1985.

Hawks, Francis. *Narrative of the Expedition of an American Squadron to the China Seas and Japan*. New York: Appleton, 1856.

Hayashi, Fukusai, ed. *Tsūkō ichiran*. 8 vols. Tokyo: Kokusho Kankōkai, 1912–1913.

Heeres, J. E., and F. W. Stapel, eds. *Corpus Diplomaticum Neerlando-Indicum*, 6 vols. The Hague: Martinus Nijhoff, 1907–1955.

Hellyer, Robert. *Defining Engagement: Japan and Global Contexts, 1640–1868*. Cambridge: Harvard University Asia Center, 2009.

Hesselink, Reinier. *Prisoners from Nambu: Reality and Make-Believe in Seventeenth-Century Japanese Diplomacy*. Honolulu: University of Hawai'i Press, 2002.

Howell, David. "Ainu Ethnicity and the Boundaries of the Early Modern Japanese State." *Past & Present* 142 (1994): 64–93.

———. "The Prehistory of the Japanese Nation State: Status, Ethnicity and Boundaries." *Early Modern Japan* 5, no. 2 (1995): 19–24.

———. *Geographies of Identity in Nineteenth-century Japan*. Berkeley: University of California Press, 2005.

Hunter, William Wilson. *A History of British India*. New York: AMS, 1966.

Ikegami, Eiko. *The Taming of the Samurai: Honorific Individualism and the Making of Modern Japan*. Cambridge: Harvard University Press, 1995.

Ijzerman, J. W. ed. *Cornelis Buijsero te Bantam, 1616–1618*. The Hague: Martinus Nijhoff, 1923.

Innes, Robert Leroy. "The Door Ajar: Japan's Foreign Trade in the Seventeenth Century." Ph.D. dissertation, University of Michigan, 1980.

Israel, Jonathan. *Dutch Primacy in World Trade, 1585–1740*. Oxford: Clarendon Press, 1989.

———. *The Dutch Republic: Its Rise, Greatness, and Fall, 1477–1806*. Oxford: Clarendon Press, 1995.

Iwao, Seiichi. "Matsukura Shigemasa no Ruzonto ensei keikaku." *Shigaku zasshi* 45, no. 9 (1934): 9081–9109.

———. *Nanyō Nihon machi no kenkyū*. Tokyo: Minami Ajiya Bunka Kenkyūjo, 1941.

———. *Early Japanese Settlers in the Philippines*. Tokyo: Foreign Affairs Association of Japan, 1943.

———. "Kinsei nisshi bōeki ni kansuru sūryōteki kōsatsu." *Shigaku zasshi* 62, no. 11 (1953): 1–40.

———. *Jan Joosten: The Forerunner of the Dutch-Japanese Relation*. Tokyo: Tokyo News Service, 1958.

———. "Li Tan, Chief of the Chinese Residents at Hirado, Japan, in the Last Days of the Ming Dynasty." *Memoirs of the Research Department of the Toyo Bunko* 17 (1958): 27–83.

———. *Shuinsen to Nihon-machi*. Tokyo: Shibundō, 1962.

———. "Reopening the Diplomatic and Commercial Relations Between Japan and Siam During the Tokugawa Period." *Acta Asiatica* 4 (1963): 1–31.

———. *Sakoku*. Tokyo: Chuō Kōronsha, 1966.

———. "Japanese Emigrants in Batavia During the Seventeenth Century." *Acta Asiatica* 18 (1970): 1–25.

———. "Japanese Foreign Trade in the Sixteenth and Seventeenth Centuries." *Acta Asiatica* 30 (1976): 1–18.

——. *Shuinsen bōekishi no kenkyū*. Rev. ed. Tokyo: Yoshikawa kōbunkan, 1985.

——. *Zoku nanyō Nihon machi no kenkyū*. Tokyo: Iwanami Shoten, 1987.

Jacobs, Els M. *Merchant in Asia: The Trade of the Dutch East India Company During the Eighteenth Century*. Leiden: CNWS, 2006.

Jansen, Marius, and Gilbert Rozman, eds. *Japan in Transition: From Tokugawa to Meiji*. Princeton: Princeton University Press, 1986.

Kaempfer, Engelbert. *The History of Japan*. Trans. J. G. Scheucher. London, 1727.

——. *Kaempfer's Japan: Tokugawa Culture Observed*. Ed. and trans. Beatrice Bodart-Bailey. Honolulu: University of Hawai'i Press, 1999.

Kanai, Madoka. *Nichiran kōshōshi no kenkyū*. Kyoto: Shibunkaku, 1986.

Kang, Etsuko Hae-Jin. *Diplomacy and Ideology in Japanese-Korean Relations: From the Fifteenth to the Eighteenth Century*. London: Macmillan, 1997.

Katagiri, Kazuo. *Edo no Orandajin: Kapitan no Edo sanpu*. Tokyo: Chūō Kōron Shinsha, 2000.

Katō, Eiichi. "Development of Japanese Studies on Sakoku (Closing the Country): A Survey." *Acta Asiatica* 22 (1972): 84–107.

——. "The Japanese-Dutch Trade in the Formative Period of the Seclusion Policy: Particularly on the Raw Silk Trade by the Dutch Factory at Hirado, 1620–1640." *Acta Asiatica* 30 (1976): 34–84.

——. "Unification and Adaptation, the Early Shogunate and Dutch Trade Policies." In *Companies and Trade: Comparative Studies in Overseas History*, 3:207–29. Ed. Leonard Blussé and Femme Gaastra. The Hague: Martinus Nijhoff, for Leiden University Press, 1981.

——. "Hirado Oranda Shokan no Nihonjin koyōsha ni tsuite." In *Nihon Kinseishi Ronsō*. Ed. Bitō Masahide Sensei Kanreki-kinenkai. Tokyo: Yoshikawa Kōbunkan, 1984.

——. "Rengō Oranda Higashi-Indo Kaisha no senryaku kyoten toshite no Hirado shōkan." In *Nihon zenkindai no kokka to taigai kankei*. Ed. Tanaka Takeo. Tokyo: Yoshikawa Kōbunkan, 1987.

——. *Bakuhansei kokka no keisei to gaikoku bōeki*. Tokyo: Azekura Shobō, 1993.

——. "Research Trends in the Study of the History of Japanese Foreign Relations at the Start of the Early Modern Period: On the Reexamination of 'National Seclusionism,' from the 1970s and 1990s." *Acta Asiatica* 67 (1994): 1–29.

——. *Bakuhansei kokka no seiritsu to taigai kankei*. Kyoto: Shibunkaku Shuppan, 1998.

Katō, Hidetoshi. "The Significance of the Period of National Seclusion Reconsidered." *Journal of Japanese Studies* 7, no. 1 (Winter 1981): 85–109.

Keblusek, Marika, and Jori Zijlmans, eds. *Princely Display: The Court of Frederik Hendrik of Orange and Amalia van Solms*. Zwolle: Waanders, 1997.

Keene, Donald. *The Japanese Discovery of Europe, 1720–1820*. Stanford: Stanford University Press, 1969.

Keene, Edward. *Beyond the Anarchical Society: Grotius, Colonialism, and Order in World Politics*. Cambridge: Cambridge University Press, 2002.

Keith, Matthew. "The Logistics of Power: The Tokugawa Response to the Shimabara Rebellion and Power Projection in Seventeenth-Century Japan." Ph.D. dissertation, Ohio State University, 2006.

Kim, Key-Hiuk. *The Last Phase of the East Asian World Order: Korea, Japan, and the Chinese Empire, 1860–1882*. Berkeley: University of California Press, 1979.

Kimura, Naoki. *Bakuhansei kokka to Higashi Ajia sekai*. Tokyo: Yoshikawa Kōbunkan, 2009.

Klekar, Cynthia. "Prisoners in Silken Bonds: Obligation, Trade and Diplomacy in English Voyages to Japan and China." *Journal for Early Modern Cultural Studies* 6, no. 1 (2006): 84–105.

Kling, Blair, and M. N. Pearson, eds. *The Age of Partnership: Europeans in Asia Before Domination*. Honolulu: University Press of Hawai'i, 1979.

Kōda, Shigetomo. "Taiwan ni okeru Nichiran shōtotsu: Suetsugu Heizō to Pieter Nuyts." In *Kōda Shigetomo chosaku shu 4*. Tokyo: Chūō Kōronsha, 1971–1974.

Komiya, Kiyora. "Kaizoku no ekken—Iemitsu seiken ni ni okeru Makao to shisetsu to Oranda shisetsu no shogun omemie." In *Hachi-jūnana seiki no higashi ajia chiiki ni okeru hito mono jōhō no kōryū: kaiiki to kōshi no keisei, minzoku, chiikikan no sōgo ninshiki o chūshin ni*. Ed. Murai Shōsuke. Tokyo: Tokyo daigaku daigakuin jinbun shakai-kei kenkyūka, 2004.

——. *Edo Bakufu no nikki to girei shiryō*. Tokyo: Yoshikawa Kōbunkan, 2006.

Konchiin, Sūden. *Ikoku nikki shō*. Ed. Murakami Naojirō. Tokyo: Sankūsha, 1911.

Kondō, Morishige. *Gaiban tsūsho*. In *Kaitei shiseki shūran*. Kyoto: Rinsen Shoten, 1983–1984.

Kops, Henriette Rahusen-De Bruyn. "Not Such an 'Unpromising Beginning': The First Dutch Trade Embassy to China, 1655–1657." *Modern Asian Studies* 36, no. 3 (August 2002): 535–78.

Kuno, Yoshi. *Japanese Expansion on the Asiatic Continent: A Study in the History of Japan with Special Reference to Her International Relations with China, Korea and Russia*. 3 vols. Berkeley: University of California Press, 1937–1940.

Kuroita, Katsumi, ed. "Tokugawa Jikki." In *Shintei zōho Kokushi taikei*. Tokyo: Yoshikawa Kōbunkan, 1998–1999.

Lach, Donald, and Edwin van Kley. *Asia in the Making of Europe*. 3 vols. Chicago: University of Chicago Press, 1965–93.

Landes, David. *The Wealth and Poverty of Nations: Why Are Some So Rich and Others So Poor?* New York: Norton, 1998.

——. "Why Europe and the West? Why Not China?" *Journal of Economic Perspectives* 20, no. 2 (2006): 3–22.

Landwehr, John. *VOC: A Bibliography of Publications Relating to the Dutch East India Company, 1602–1800*. Utrecht: HES, 1991.

Laver, Michael. *Japan's Economy by Proxy in the Seventeenth Century: China the Netherlands, and the Bakufu*. Amherst, NY: Cambria, 2008.

——. *The Sakoku Edicts and the Politics of Tokugawa Hegemony*. Amherst, NY: Cambria, 2011.

Lee, Jeong Mi. "Cultural Expressions of Tokugawa Japan and Chosŏn Korea: An Analysis of the Korean Embassies in the Eighteenth Century." Ph.D. dissertation, University of Toronto, 2008.

Lee, John. "Trade and Economy in Preindustrial East Asia, ca. 1500–ca. 1800: East Asia in the Age of Global Integration." *Journal of Asian Studies* 58, no. 1 (1999): 2–26.

Leue, H. J. "Legal Expansion in the Age of Companies: Aspects of the Administration of Justice in the English and Dutch Settlements of Maritime Asia, ca. 1600–1750." In *European Expansion and Law: The Encounter of European and Indigenous Law in Nineteenth and Twentieth-Century Africa and Asia*, 129–58. Ed. W. J. Mommsen and J. A. de Moor. Oxford: Berg, 1992.

Leupe, P. A. "Stukken betrekkelijk Pieter Nuyts, gouverneur van Taqueran, 1631–1634." *Kroniek van het Historisch Genootschap gevestigd te Utrecht* (1853): 184–216.

Lewis, James. *Frontier Contact between Choson Korea and Tokugawa Japan*. London: RoutledgeCurzon, 2003.

Lidin, Olof. *Tanegashima: The Arrival of Europe in Japan*. Copenhagen: NIAS, 2002.

Lieberman, Victor. "An Age of Commerce in Southeast Asia? Problems of Regional Coherence. A Review Article." *Journal of Asian Studies* 54, no. 3 (1995): 796–807.

———. "Transcending East-West Dichotomies: State and Culture Formation in Six Ostensibly Disparate Areas." *Modern Asian Studies* 31, no. 3 (1997): 463–546.

Linschoten, Jan Huygen van. *Iohn Huighen van Linschoten. his discours of voyages into ye Easte & West Indies*. Trans. John Wolfe. London: 1598.

———. *Itinerario. Voyage ofte schipvaert van Jan Huygen van Linschoten naer Oost ofte Portugaels Indien, 1579–1592*. The Hague: Martinus Nijhoff, 1939.

Liu, Lydia. *Tokens of Exchange: The Problem of Translation in Global Circulations*. Durham, NC: Duke University Press, 1999.

Lorge, Peter. *The Asian Military Revolution: From Gunpowder to the Bomb*. New York: Cambridge University Press, 2008.

Loth, Vincent. "Armed Incidents and Unpaid Bills: Anglo-Dutch rivalry in the Banda Islands in the Seventeenth Century." *Modern Asian Studies* 29, no. 4 (1995): 705–40.

Lu, David. *Japan: A Documentary History*, 2 vols. Armonk, NY: Sharpe, 1996.

Lucassen, Jan. "A Multinational and its Labor Force: The Dutch East India Company, 1595–1795." *International Labor and Working-Class History* 66 (2004): 12–39.

Lunsford, Virginia West. *Piracy and Privateering in the Golden Age Netherlands*. New York: Palgrave Macmillan. 2005.

Lunsingh Scheurleer, Th. H. "Koperen kronen en waskaarsen voor Japan." *Oud Holland* 93 (1979): 69–74.

Macleod, N. *De Oost Indische Compagnie als Zeemogendheid in Azie*. 2 vols. Rijswijk: Blankwaardt & Schoonhoven, 1927.

Macmillan, Ken. *Sovereignty and Possession in the English New World: The Legal Foundations of Empire, 1576–1640*. Cambridge: Cambridge University Press, 2006.

Major, Richard. *Select Letters of Christopher Columbus by Christopher Columbus*. London: Hakluyt Society, 1847.

Mancke, Elizabeth. "Early Modern Expansion and the Politicization of Oceanic Space." *Geographical Review* 89, no. 2 (1999): 225–36

Markham, Albert, ed. *The Voyages and Works of John Davis*. London: Hakluyt Society, 1880.

Markham, Clements, ed. *The Voyages of Sir James Lancaster, Kt., to the East Indies: With Abstracts of Journals of Voyages to the East Indies During the Seventeenth Century, Preserved in the India Office*. London: Printed for the Hakluyt Society, 1877.

———. *The Journal of Christopher Columbus (During His First Voyage, 1492–93)*. London: Hakluyt Society, 1893.

Markley, Robert. "Riches, Power, Trade, and Religion: the Far East and the English Imagination, 1600–1720." *Renaissance Studies* 17, no. 3 (2003): 494–516.

———. "Gulliver and the Japanese: The Limits of the Postcolonial Past." *Modern Language Quarterly* 65, no. 3 (2004): 457–79.

———.*The Far East and the English Imagination, 1600–1730*. Cambridge: Cambridge University Press, 2006.

Massarella, Derek. "The Early Career of Richard Cocks (1566–1624), Head of the English East India Company's Factory in Japan (1613–1623). *Transactions of the Asiatic Society of Japan* 3, no. 20 (1985): 1–46.

———. *A World Elsewhere: Europe's Encounter with Japan in the Sixteenth and Seventeenth Centuries*. New Haven: Yale University Press, 1990.

Masselman, George. *The Cradle of Colonialism*. New Haven: Yale University Press, 1963.

Mathes, Michael. "A Quarter Century of trans-Pacific Diplomacy: New Spain and Japan, 1592–1617." In *Japan and the Pacific, 1540–1920, Threat and Opportunity*, 57–86. Ed. Mark Caprio and Matsuda Koichiro. Aldershot and Burlington: Ashgate/Variorum, 2006.

Matsukata, Fuyuko. *Oranda fūsetsugaki to kinsei Nihon*. Tokyo: Tokyo Daigaku Shuppankai, 2007.

Matthee, Rudi, " Negotiating Across Cultures: The Dutch Van Leene Mission to the Iranian Court of Shah Sulayman, 1689–1692." *Eurasian Studies* 3, no. 1 (2004): 35–63.

Mazumdar, Sucheta. *Sugar and Society in China: Peasants, Technology, and the World Market*. Cambridge: Harvard University Asia Center, 1998.

McCune, George M. "The Exchange of Envoys Between Korea and Japan During the Tokugawa Period." *Far Eastern Quarterly* 5, no. 3 (May 1946): 308–25.

Meijlan, G. F. *Geschiedkundig overzigt van den handel der Europezen op Japan*. Batavia: Bataviaasch Genootschap van Kunsten en Wetenschappen, 1833.

Meilink-Roelofsz, M. A. P. *Asian Trade and European Influence in the Indonesian Archipelago Between 1500 and About 1630*. The Hague: Martinus Nijhoff, 1962.

Mijer, P. *Verzameling van Instructiën, Ordonnanciën en Reglementen voor de Regering van Nederlandsch Indië*. Batavia, 1848.

Mizuno, Norihito. "China in Tokugawa Foreign Relations: The Tokugawa Bakufu's Perception of and Attitudes Toward Ming-Qing China." *Sino-Japanese Studies* 15 (2003): 108–44.

———. "Japan and Its East Asian Neighbors: Japan's Perception of China and Korea and the Making of Foreign Policy from the Seventeenth to the Nineteenth Century." Ph.D. dissertation, Ohio State University, 2004.

Mochizuki, Mia. "Deciphering the Dutch in Deshima." In *The Boundaries of the Netherlands. Real and Imagined*, 63–94. Ed. Marybeth Carlson, Laura Cruz, and Benjamin J. Kaplan. Leiden: Brill, 2009.

————. "Idolatry and Western-Inspired Painting in Japan." In *Idols in the Age of Art. Objects, Devotions and the Early Modern World*, 239–66. Ed. Michael Cole and Rebecca Zorach. Aldershot: Ashgate, 2009.

Montanus, Arnoldus. *Atlas Japanensis: Being Remarkable Addresses by Way of Embassy from the East-India Company of the United Provinces to the Emperor of Japan*. Trans. John Ogilby. London, 1670.

Morris-Suzuki, Tessa. *Re-inventing Japan: Time, Space, Nation*. New York: Sharpe, 1998.

Morrison, Samuel, ed. *Journals and Other Documents on the Life and Voyages of Christopher Columbus*. Boston: Heritage, 1964.

Mulder, W. Z. *Hollanders in Hirado, 1597–1641*. Haarlem: Fibula-Van Dishoeck, 1984.

Murai, Shōsuke. *Chūsei wajin den*. Tokyo: Iwanami Shoten, 1993.

————. *Kokkyō o koete: Higashi Ajia kaiiki sekai no chūsei*. Tokyo: Azekura Shobō, 1997.

Murdoch, James. *A History of Japan with Maps By Isoh Yamagata*. 3 vols. London: K. Paul, Trench, Trubner, 1925–1926.

Murakami, Naojiro. "The Japanese at Batavia in the Seventeenth Century." *Monumenta Nipponica* 2, no. 2 (July 1939): 355–73.

Nachod, Oskar. *Die Beziehungen der Niederlaendischen Ost-Indischen Compagnie zu Japan im 17en Jahrhundert*. Leipzig: R. Friese, 1897.

————. *Jūshichiseiki nichiran kōshōshi*. Trans. Tominaga Mikata. Tenri: Yōtokusha, 1956.

Nagazumi, Akira. "Japan en de Nederlanden rond 1632: Terugblik op een keerpunt." *De Gids* 145, no. 1 (1982): 26–38.

Nagazumi, Yōko. "Hirado-han to Oranda boeki." *Nihon Rekishi* 286, no. 3 (1972): 1–19.

————. "Japan's Isolationist Policy as Seen Through Dutch Source Materials." *Acta Asiatica* 22 (1972): 18–35.

————. "Orandajin no hogosha to shite no Inoue Chikugo no kami Masashige." *Nihon Rekishi* 327 (1975): 1–17.

————. *Kinsei shoki no gaikō*. Tokyo: Sōbunsha, 1990.

————. "Hirado ni dentatsu sareta Nihonjin baibai buki yushutsu kinshirei." *Nihon rekishi* 611 (1999): 67–81.

————. "Ayutthaya and Japan: Embassies and Trade in the Seventeenth Century." In *From Japan to Arabia: Ayutthaya's Maritime Relations with Asia*, 79–103. Ed. Kennon Breazeale. Bangkok: Printing House of Thammasat University, 1999.

————. "Orandajin no uketa goon to hōkō." In *"Sakoku" o hiraku*, 24–34. Ed. Kawakatsu Heita. Tokyo: Dōbunkan, 2000.

————. *Shuinsen*. Tokyo: Yoshikawa Kōbunkan, 2001.

————. "The Japanese *Go-shuinjo* (Vermilion Seal) Maritime Trade in Taiwan." In *Around and About Formosa: Essays in Honor of Professor Ts'ao Yung-ho*. Ed. Leonard Blussé. Taipei: SMC, 2003.

Nagazumi, Yōko, and Mariko Takeda. *Hirado Oranda shōkan, Igirisu shōkan nikki: hekigan no mita kinsei no Nihon to sakoku e no michi*. Tokyo: Soshiete, 1981.

Nagtegaal, Luc. *Riding the Dutch Tiger: The Dutch East Indies Company and the Northeast Coast of Java, 1680–1743*. Leiden: KITLV, 1996.

Najita, Tetsuo. *Japan: The Intellectual Foundations of Modern Japanese Politics*. Chicago: University of Chicago Press, 1980.

Nakada, Yasunao, ed. *Kinsei Nihon taigai kankei bunken mokuroku*. Tokyo: Tosui Shobō, 1999.

Narushima, Motonao, *Tokugawa Jikki*, 7 vols. Tokyo: Keizai Zasshisha, 1904–1907.

Nieuhof, Johannes. *An Embassy from the East India Company of the United Provinces to the Grand Tartar Cham Emperor of China deliver'd by their excellencies, Peter de Goyer and Jacob de Keyzer, at his imperial city of Peking*. London, 1673.

Ogborn, Miles. *Indian Ink: Script and Print in the Making of the English East India Company*. Chicago: University of Chicago Press, 2007.

Oka, Mihoko, "A Great Merchant in Nagasaki in the Seventeenth Century: Suetsugu Heizo II and the System of *Respondência*," *Bulletin of Portuguese/Japanese Studies* 2 (2001): 37–56.

Onuma, Yasuaki. "When Was the Law of International Society Born: An Inquiry of the History of International Law from an Intercivilizational Perspective." *Journal of the History of International Law* 2 (2000): 1–66.

Ooms, Herman. *Tokugawa Ideology: Early Constructs, 1570–1680*. Princeton: Princeton University Press, 1985.

Oosterhoff, J.L. "Zeelandia: A Dutch Colonial City on Formosa (1624–1662)." In *Colonial Cities: Essays on Urbanism in a Colonial Context*. Ed. Robert Ross and Gerard J. Telkamp. Dordrecht: Martinus Nijhoff, 1985.

Opstall, M.E. van, ed. *De Reis van de Vloot van Pieter Willemsz Verhoeff naar Azië, 1607–1612*. 2 vols. The Hague: Martinus Nijhoff, 1972.

Pagden, Anthony. *Lords of all the World: Ideologies of Empire in Spain, Britain, and France c. 1500–c. 1800*. New Haven: Yale University Press, 1995.

Panikkar, K.M. *Asia and Western Dominance: A Survey of the Vasco Da Gama Epoch of Asian History, 1498–1945*. London: George Allen & Unwin, 1953.

Parker, Charles, and Jerry Bentley, eds. *Between the Middle Ages and Modernity*. Lanham, MD: Rowman & Littefield, 2007.

Parker, Geoffrey. *The Military Revolution: Military Innovation and the Rise of the West, 1500–1800*. Cambridge: Cambridge University Press, 1988.

Pearson, Michael. "Merchants and States." In *The Political Economy of Merchant Empires: State Power and World Trade, 1350–1750*. Ed. James Tracy. Cambridge: Cambridge University Press, 1991.

———. *The Indian Ocean*. London: Routledge, 2003.

Pombejra, Dhiravat Na. "The Dutch-Siamese Conflict of 1663–1664: A Reassessment." In *Around and About Formosa, Essays in Honor of Professor Ts'ao Yung-ho*, 291–306. Ed. Leonard Blussé. Taipei: SMC, 2003.

Pomeranz, Kenneth. *The Great Divergence*. Princeton: Princeton University Press, 2000.

Pompe van Meerdervoort, J.L.C. *Doctor on Desima: Selected Chapters from J. L. C. Pompe van Meerdervoort's Vijf jaren in Japan*, Trans. Elizabeth Wittermans and John Bowers. Tokyo: Sophia University, 1970.

Prakash, Om. *European Commercial Enterprise in Pre-Colonial India*. New York: Cambridge University Press, 1998.

———. "European Corporate Enterprises and the Politics of Trade in India, 1600–1800." In *Politics and Trade in the Indian Ocean World: Essays in Honour of Ashin Das Gupta*. Ed. Rudrangshu Mukherjee and Lakshmi Subramanian. Delhi: Oxford University Press, 1998.

———. "The Mughal Empire and the Dutch East India Company in the Seventeenth Century." In *Hof en Handel, Aziatische Vorsten en de VOC, 1620–1720*, 183–200. Ed. E. Locher-Scholten and P. Rietbergen. Leiden: KITLV, 2004.

Prange, Sebastian. "A Trade of No Dishonor: Piracy, Commerce, and Community in the Western Indian Ocean, Twelfth to Sixteenth Century." *American Historical Review* 116, no. 5 (2011): 1269–93.

Purchas, Samuel, *Purchas his Pilgrimes*. 5 vols. London: William Stansby, 1625.

———. *Hakluytus posthumus, or, Purchas his Pilgrimes: contayning a history of the world in sea voyages and lande travells by Englishmen and others*. 20 vols. Glasgow: J. MacLehose, 1905–1907.

Raben, Remco. "Het Aziatisch Legion: Huurlingen, bondgenoten en reservisten in het geweer voor de Verenigde Oost-Indische Compagnie," In *De Verenigde Oost-Indische Compagnie tussen Oorlog and diplomatie*. Ed. Gerrit Knaap and Ger Teitler. Leiden: KITLV, 2002.

Radwan, Ann. *The Dutch in Western India, 1601–1632: A Study of Mutual Accommodation*. Columbia, MO: South Asia, 1978.

Ravenstein, E. G., ed. *The Journal of the First Voyage of Vasco da Gama, 1497–99*. London: Hakluyt Society, 1898.

Ravina, Mark. "State-building and Political Economy in Early-modern Japan." *Journal of Asian Studies* 54, no. 4 (1995): 997–1022.

———. *Land and Lordship in Early Modern Japan*. Stanford: Stanford University Press, 1999.

Reid, Anthony. *Southeast Asia in the Age of Commerce 1450–1680*: vol. 2: *Expansion and Crisis*. New Haven: Yale University Press. 1993.

———. "Pluralism and Progress in Seventeenth-Century Makassar," *Bijdragen tot de Taal-, Land- en Volkenkunde* 156, no. 3 (2000): 433–49.

Reischauer, Edwin. "Japanese Feudalism." In *Feudalism in History*, 26–48. Ed. Rushton Coulborn. Princeton: Princeton University Press, 1956.

———. *The Japanese*. Cambridge: Harvard University Press, 1977.

Ribeiro, Madalena. "The Japanese Diaspora in the Seventeenth century according to Jesuit sources." *Bulletin of Portuguese-Japanese Studies* 3 (2001): 53–83.

Ricklefs, M.C. *A History of Modern Indonesia Since c. 1200*. Stanford: Stanford University Press, 2001.

Rietbergen, Pieter. *Japan verwoord: Nihon door Nederlandse ogen, 1600–1799*. Amsterdam: KIT, 2003.

Roberts, Luke. *Performing the Great Peace: Political Space and Open Secrets in Tokugawa Japan*. Honolulu: University of Hawai'i Press, 2012.

Robinson, Kenneth R. "Centering the King of Choson: Aspects of Korean Maritime Diplomacy, 1392–1592." *Journal of Asian Studies* 59, no. 1 (February 2000): 109–25.

Roe, Thomas. *The Embassy of Sir Thomas Roe to India, 1615–19*. Ed. W. Foster. London: Hakluyt Society, 1899.

Rouffaer, G. P., and J. W. Ijzerman. *De eerste schipvaart der Nederlanders naar Oost-Indië onder Cornelis de Houtman, 1595–1597*. The Hague: Martinus Nijhoff, 1915.

Rowen, Herbert. *The Princes of Orange: The Stadholders in the Dutch Republic*. Cambridge: Cambridge University Press, 1988.

Ruangsilp, Bhawan. *Dutch East India Company Merchants at the Court of Ayutthaya: Dutch Perceptions of the Thai Kingdom, c. 1604–1765*. Leiden: Brill, 2007.

———. "Dutch Interaction with Siamese law and the City Rules of Ayutthaya in the Seventeenth and Eighteenth Centuries." In *Asian Port Cities, 1600–1800: Local and Foreign Cultural Interactions*, 139–61. Ed. Haneda Masashi. Singapore: NUS Press, 2009.

Said, Edward. *Orientalism*. New York: Vintage, 1979.

Sainsbury, W. N., ed. *Calendar of State Papers Colonial, East Indies, China and Japan*, vol. 3: *1617–1621*. London: HMSO, 1870.

———. *Calendar of State Papers, Colonial, East Indies, China and Persia*, vol. 6: *1625–1629*. London: HMSO, 1884.

———, ed. *Calendar of State Papers Colonial, East Indies and Persia*, vol. 8: *1630–1634*. London: HMSO, 1892.

Satow, Ernest. "Notes on the Intercourse Between Japan and Siam in the Seventeenth Century." *Transactions of the Asiatic Society of Japan* 13 (1884): 189–210.

———, ed. *The Voyage of Captain John Saris to Japan*. London: Hakluyt Society, 1900.

Scammell, G. V. "The Pillars of Empire: Indigenous Assistance and the Survival of the 'Estado da India' c. 1600–1700," *Modern Asian Studies* 22, no. 3 (1988): 473–89.

Schmidt, Benjamin. *Innocence Abroad: The Dutch Imagination and the New World, 1570–1670*. Cambridge: Cambridge University Press, 2001.

Schnurmann, Claudia. "'Wherever profit leads us, to every sea and shore . . .': The VOC, the WIC, and Dutch Methods of Globalization in the Seventeenth Century." *Renaissance Studies* 17, no. 3 (September 2003): 474–93.

Schouten, Justus. "Justus Schouten en de Japanse Gijzeling." In *Nederlands Historische Bronnen*. Ed. Leonard Blussé. The Hague: Martinus Nijhoff, 1985.

Schouwenburg, K. L. van. "Het personeel op de schepen van de Kamer Delft van de VOC in de eerste helft van de achttiende eeuw." *Tijdschrift voor Zeegeschiedenis* 7 (1988): 76–93.

———. "Het personeel op de schepen van de Kamer Delft van de VOC in de tweede helft van de achttiende eeuw." *Tijdschrift voor Zeegeschiedenis* 8 (1989): 179–186.

Schurz, William. *The Manila Galleon*. New York: Dutton, 1939.

Seed, Patricia. "Taking Possession and Reading Texts: Establishing the Authority of Overseas Empires." *William and Mary Quarterly* 49, no. 2 (1992): 183–209.

———. *Ceremonies of Possession: Europe's Conquest of the New World, 1492–1640*. Cambridge: Cambridge University Press, 1995.

———. "Caliban and Native Title: 'This Island's Mine.'" In *The Tempest and Its Travels*, 201–11. Ed. Peter Hulme and William H. Sherman. Philadelphia: University of Pennsylvania Press, 2002.

Sen, Sudipta. *Distant Sovereignty: National Imperialism and the Origins of British India*. New York: Routledge, 2002.

Shapinsky, Peter. "With the Sea as Their Domain: Pirates and Maritime Lordship in Medieval Japan." Paper presented at the Seascapes, Littoral Cultures, and Trans-Oceanic Exchanges Conference, Library of Congress, Washington, DC, 12–15 February 2003.

———. "Lords of the Sea: Pirates, Violence, and Exchange in Medieval Japan." Ph.D dissertation, University of Michigan, 2005.

———. "Predators, Protectors, and Purveyors: Pirates and Commerce in Late Medieval Japan." *Monumenta Nipponica* 64, no. 2 (2009): 273–313.

Shepherd, John. *Statecraft and Political Economy on the Taiwan Frontier, 1600–1800*. Stanford: Stanford University Press, 1993.

Shimada, Ryuto. *The Intra-Asian Trade in Japanese Copper by the Dutch East India Company During the Eighteenth Century*. Leiden: Brill, 2006.

Singh, Jyotsna. *Colonial Narratives/Cultural Dialogues: "Discoveries" of India in the Language of Colonialism*. London: Routledge, 1996.

Skinner, John. *A true Relation of the Uniust, Cruell, and Barbarous Proceedings against the English at Amboyna in the East-Indies, by the Neatherlandish Gouernour and Councel There*. London: H. Lownes for Nathanael Newberry, 1624.

Smail, John. "On the Possibility of an Autonomous History of Modern Southeast Asia," *Journal of Southeast Asian History* 2, no. 12 (1961): 72–102.

Smits, Gregory. *Visions of Ryukyu: Identity and Ideology in Early-Modern Thought and Politics*. Honolulu: University of Hawai'i Press, 1999.

So, Kwan-wai. *Japanese Piracy in Ming China During the Sixteenth Century*. East Lansing: Michigan State University Press, 1975.

Somers, Jan A. *De VOC als Volkenrechtelijke Actor*. Deventer: Kluwer, 2001.

St. Aldegonde, Marnix van. *A pithie, and most earnest exhortation, concerning the estate of Christiandome together with the meanes to preserue and defend the same; dedicated to al christian kings princes and potentates, with all other the estates of Christiandome: by a Germaine gentleman, a louer of his countrey*. London, 1583.

Stapel, F. W. "De Ambonsche 'Moord' (9 Maart 1623)." *Tijdschrift voor Indische Taal-Land- en Volkenkunde* 62 (1923): 209–26.

———. "Bijdragen tot de geschiedenis der rechtspraak bij de Vereenigde Oostindische Compagnie." *Bijdragen tot de taal-, land- en volkenkunde van Nederlandsch-Indië* 89 (1932): 41–70.

———. *Cornelis Janszoon Speelman*. The Hague: Martinus Nijhoff, 1936.

Steensgard, Niels. *The Asian Trade Revolution of the 17th Century: The East India Companies and the Decline of the Caravan Trade*. Chicago: University of Chicago Press, 1974.

———. "The Dutch East India Company as an Institutional Innovation." In *Dutch Capitalism and World Capitalism*, 235–57. Ed. M. Aymard. Cambridge: Cambridge University Press, 1982.

Steinberg, Philip. *The Social Construction of the Ocean*. Cambridge: Cambridge University Press, 2001.

Stern, Philip. "'A Politie of Civill & Military Power': Political Thought and the Late Seventeenth-Century Foundations of the East India Company-State." *Journal of British Studies* 47, no. 2 (April 2008): 253–83.

———. *The Company-State: Corporate Sovereignty and the Early Modern Foundation of the British Empire in India.* New York: Oxford University Press, 2011.

Subrahmanyam, Sanjay. "The 'Pulicat Enterprise': Luso-Dutch Conflict in South-Eastern India, 1610–1640." *South Asia: Journal of South Asian Studies* 9, no. 2 (1986): 17–36.

———. *The Political Economy of Commerce: Southern India, 1500–1650.* New York: Cambridge University Press, 1990.

———. "Of Imârat and Tijârat: Asian Merchants and State Power in the Western Indian Ocean, 1400 to 1750." *Comparative Studies in Society and History,* 37, no. 4 (1995): 750–80.

———. "Dutch Tribulations in Seventeenth-Century Mrauk-U." *Journal of Early Modern History* 1, no. 3 (1997): 201–53.

———. "Frank Submissions: The Company and the Mughals Between Sir Thomas Roe and Sir William Norris." In *The Worlds of the East Indian Company,* 69–96. Ed. H. V. Bowen, Margarette Lincoln, and Nigel Rigby. Woodbridge, Suffolk: Boydell, 2002.

———. "Forcing the Doors of Heathendom: Ethnography, Violence, and the Dutch East India Company." In *Between the Middle Ages and Modernity,* 131–53. Ed. Charles Parker and Jerry Bentley. Lanham, MD: Rowman & Littlefield, 2007.

Suganuma, Teifū. *Dai Nihon shōgyōshi: tsuketari Hirado bōekishi.* Tokyo: Yatsuo shoten, 1902.

Sun, Laichen. "Military Technology Transfers from Ming China and the Emergence of Northern Mainland Southeast Asia (c. 1390–1527)." *Journal of Southeast Asia Studies* 34, no. 3 (2003): 495–517.

Suzuki, Shogo. "Japan's Socialization Into Janus-Faced European International Society." *European Journal of International Relations* 11, no. 1 (2005): 137–64.

———. *Civilization and Empire: China and Japan's Encounter with European International Society.* New York: Routledge, 2009.

Suzuki, Yasuko. *Nagasaki bugyō no kenkyū.* Tokyo: Shibunkaku Shuppan, 2007.

Swift, Jonathan. *Gulliver's Travels.* New York: Penguin, 2010.

Swope, Kenneth. "Crouching Tigers, Secret Weapons: Military Technology Employed During the SinoJapaneseKorean War, 1592–1598." *Journal of Military History* 69, no. 1 (2005): 11–41.

Tai, Emily Sohmer Tai, "Marking Water: Piracy and Property in the Pre-Modern West." Paper presented at Seascapes, Littoral Cultures, and Trans-Oceanic Exchanges, Library of Congress, Washington DC, 12–15 February 2003. http://www.history cooperative.org/proceedings/ seascapes/tai.html (accessed 10 September 2012).

Takeda, Mariko. *Sakoku to kokkyō no seiritsu.* Tokyo: Doseisha, 2005.

Takeuchi, Makoto. *Tokugawa Bakufu jiten.* Tokyo: Tokyodō Shuppan, 2003.

Tashiro, Kazui, "Foreign Relations During the Tokugawa Period: *Sakoku* Reexamined." *Journal of Japanese Studies* 8, no. 2 (1982): 283–306.

Tavernier, John Baptista. *A collection of several relations & treatises singular and curious of John Baptista Tavernier*. London, 1680.

Telscher, Kate. *India Inscribed: European and British Writing on India, 1600–1800*. New Delhi: Oxford University Press, 1995.

Temple, William. *The Works of Sir William Temple*. London: F. C. and J. Rivington, 1814.

Teng, Emma. *Taiwan's Imagined Geography: Chinese Colonial Travel Writing and Pictures*. Cambridge: Harvard University Press, 2004.

Theeravit, Khien. "Japanese-Siamese Relations 1606–1629." In *Thai-Japanese Relations in Historical Perspective*, 17–44. Ed. Chaiwat Khamchoo and E. Bruce Reynolds. Bangkok: Innomedia, 1988.

Thompson, Laurence. "The Earliest Chinese Eyewitness Accounts of the Formosan Aborigines." *Monumenta Serica: Journal of Oriental Studies* 23 (1964): 163–204.

Thompson, William. "The Military Superiority Thesis and the Ascendancy of Western Eurasia in the World System." *Journal of World History* 10, no. 1 (1999): 143–78.

Thomson, Janice. *Mercenaries, Pirates, and Sovereigns: State Building and Extraterritorial Violence in Early Modern Europe*. Princeton: Princeton University Press, 1994.

Tiele, P. A. and J. E. Heeres, eds. *Bouwstoffen voor de geschiedenis der Nederlanders in den Maleischen Archipel*, 3 vols. The Hague: Martinus Nijhoff, 1886–1895.

Titsingh, Isaac. *Illustrations of Japan*. London: R. Ackermann, 1822.

Toby, Ronald. "Reopening the Question of *Sakoku*: Diplomacy in the Legitimization of the Tokugawa Bakufu." *Journal of Japanese Studies* 3, no. 2 (1977): 323–63.

———. "Carnival of the Aliens: Korean Embassies in Edo-Period Art and Popular Culture." *Monumenta Nipponica* 41, no. 4 (1986): 415–56.

———. *State and Diplomacy in Early Modern Japan: Asia in the Development of the Tokugawa Bakufu*. Stanford: Stanford University Press, 1991.

———. "The 'Indianness' of Iberia and Changing Japanese Iconographies of Other." In *Implicit Understandings: Observing, Reporting, and Reflecting on the Encounters Between Europeans and Other Peoples in the Early Modern Era*, 323–51. Ed. Stuart B. Schwartz. Cambridge: Cambridge University Press, 1994.

———. "Kinsei-ki no 'Nihon zu' to 'Nihon' no kyōkai." In *Chizu to ezu no seiji bunkashi*, 79–102. Ed. Kuroda Hideo, Mary Elizabeth Berry, and Sugimoto Fumiko. Tokyo: Tokyo Daigaku Shuppankai, 2001.

———. "Rescuing the Nation from History: The State of the State in Early Modern Japan." *Monumenta Nipponica* 56, no. 2. (2001): 197–237.

Tojo, Natalia. "The Anxiety of the Silent Traders: Dutch Perception on the Portuguese Banishment from Japan." *Bulletin of Portuguese Japanese Studies* 1 (2000): 111–28.

Tokyo daigaku shiryō hensanjo, ed. *Dagregisters gehouden door de Opperhoofden van de Nederlandse Faktorij in Japan*. Tokyo: University of Tokyo Press, 1974–.

———. *Dai Nihon kinsei shiryō. Tōtsūji kaisho nichiroku*. Tokyo: University of Tokyo Press, 1984.

———. *Dai Nihon shiryō*. Tokyo Daigaku Shuppankai, 1901–.

Totman, Conrad. *Politics in the Tokugawa Bakufu, 1600–1843*. Cambridge: Harvard University Press, 1967.

———. *Early Modern Japan*. Berkeley: University of California Press, 1995.

Toyama, Mikio, *Matsura-shi to Hirado bōeki*. Tokyo: Kokusho Kankōkai, 1987.

Tracy, James, ed. *The Political Economy of Merchant Empires*. New York: Cambridge University Press, 1991.

———. "Asian Despotism? Mughal Government as seen from the Dutch East India Company Factory in Surat." *Journal of Early Modern History* 3, no. 3 (1999): 256–80.

Troost, Wouter. *William III the Stadholder-king: A Political Biography*. Burlington, VT: Ashgate, 2005.

Tsukahira, Toshio. *Feudal Control in Tokugawa Japan: The Sankin Kotai System*. Cambridge: Harvard University Press, 1966.

Tuán, Hoang Anh. *Silk for Silver: Dutch-Vietnamese Relations, 1637–1700*. Leiden: Brill, 2007.

Turnbull, Stephen. "Onward, Christian Samurai! The Japanese Expeditions to Taiwan in 1609 and 1616." *Japanese Studies* 30, no. 1 (2010): 3–21.

Unger, W. S., ed. *De oudste reizen van de Zeeuwen naar Oost-Indië, 1598–1604*. The Hague: Martinus Nijhoff, 1948.

Valentijn, François. *François Valentijn's oud en nieuw Oost-Indien*. The Hague: H. C. Susan, 1856–1858.

Valentijn, François. *Oud en Nieuw Oost-Indien*. Dordrecht: Joannes van Braam and Gerard onder de Linden, 1724–1726.

Van Dam, Pieter. *Beschrijvinge van de Oostindische Compagnie*. Edited by F. W. Stapel. 7 vols. The Hague: Martinus Nijhoff, 1927–1954.

Van der Chijs, J. A. *Geschiedenis der stichting van de Vereenigde O.I. Compagnie*. Leiden: P. Engels, 1857.

Van der Chijs, J. A., H. T. Colenbrander, and J. de Hullu, eds. *Dagh-register gehouden int Casteel Batavia vant passerende daer ter plaetse als over geheel Nederlandts-India*. 31 vols. Batavia, The Hague: Landsdrukkerij/Martinus Nijhoff, 1887–1931.

———. *Nederlandsch Indisch plakaatboek, 1602–1811*. Batavia; The Hague: Landsdrukkerij/Martinus Nijhoff, 1885–1900.

Van der Cruysse, Dirk. *Siam and the West: 1500–1700*. Chiang Mai: Silkworm, 2002.

Van Foreest, H. A., and A. de Booy, eds. *De Vierde schipvaart der Nederlanders naar Oost-Indië onder Jacob Wilkens en Jacob van Neck, 1599–1604*. The Hague: Martinus Nijhoff, 1981.

Van Gelderen, Martin. *The Political Thought of the Dutch Revolt, 1555–1590*. New York: Cambridge University Press, 1992.

Van Goor, Jurrien. "A Hybrid State: The Dutch Economic and Political Network in Asia." In *From the Mediterranean to the China Sea*. Ed. Claude Guillot, Denys Lombard and Roderich Ptak. Wiesbaden: Harrassowitz, 1998.

———. *Prelude to Colonialism: the Dutch in Asia*. Hilversum: Verloren, 2004.

Van Ittersum, Martine Julia. *Profit and Principle: Hugo Grotius, Natural Rights Theories and the Rise of Dutch Power in the East Indies, 1595–1615*. Leiden: Brill, 2006.

———. "The Long Goodbye : Hugo Grotius' Justification of Dutch Expansion Overseas, 1615–1645." *History of European Ideas* 36, no. 4 (2010): 386–411.

Van Santen, H. W. "Trade Between Mughal India and the Middle East, and Mughal Monetary Policy, c. 1600–1660." In *Asian Trade Routes*. Ed. Karl Haellquist. London: Curzon Press, 1991.

Vaporis, Constantine. "Lordly Pageantry: The Daimyo Procession and Political Authority." *Japan Review* (2005): 3–54.

———. *Tour of Duty : Samurai, Military Service in Edo, and the Culture of Early Modern Japan*. Honolulu: University of Hawai'i Press, 2008

Viallé, Cynthia. "In Aid of Trade: Dutch Gift-Giving in Tokugawa Japan." *Tokyo Daigaku Shiryō Hensanjo kenkyū Kiyō* 16 (2006): 57–78.

Viallé, Cynthia, and Leonard Blussé, eds. *The Deshima Dagregisters, Volume 11, 1641–1650*. Leiden: Intercontinenta No. 23, Universiteit Leiden, 2001.

———. *The Deshima Dagregisters, Volume 12, 1650–1660*. Leiden: Intercontinenta No. 25, Universiteit Leiden, 2005.

———. *The Deshima Dagregisters, Volume 13, 1660–1670*. Leiden: Intercontinenta No. 27, Universiteit Leiden, 2010.

Vink, M. P. M. "Mare Liberum and Dominium Maris: Legal Arguments and Implications of the Luso-Dutch Struggle for Control Over Asian Waters, ca. 1600–1663." In *Studies in Maritime History*. Ed. K. S. Mathew, 35–68. Pondicherry: Mission, 1990.

———. "Between Profit and Power: The Dutch East India Company and Institutional Early Modernities in the 'Age of Mercantilism.'" In *Between the Middle Ages and Modernity*, 285–306. Ed. Charles Parker and Jerry Bentley. Lanham, MD: Rowman & Littlefield, 2007.

———. "Indian Ocean Studies and the New Thalassology." *Journal of Global History* 2 (2007): 41–62.

———. *Mission to Madurai: Dutch Embassies to the Nayaka Court of Madurai in the Seventeenth Century*. New Delhi: Manohar, 2012.

Vlekke. Bernard. *Nusantara: A History of Indonesia*. Chicago: Quadrangle, 1960.

Vogel, J. Ph. *Journaal van J. J. Ketelaar's hofreis naar den Groot Mogol te Lahore: 1711–1713*. The Hague: Martinus Nijhoff, 1937.

Vos, Reinout. *Gentle Janus, Merchant Prince: The VOC and the Tightrope of Diplomacy in the Malay World, 1740–1800*. Leiden: KITLV, 1993.

Wap, Jan J.F. *Het Gezantschap van den Sultan van Achin*. Rotterdam: H. Nijgh, 1862.

Ward, Kerry. *Networks of Empire: Forced Migration in the Dutch East India Company*. Cambridge: Cambridge University Press, 2008.

Wassing-visser, Rita. *Royal Gifts from Indonesia: Historical Bonds with the House of Orange-Nassau (1600–1938)*. Zwolle: Waanders, 1995.

Watson, Bruce. "Fortifications and the 'Idea' of Force in Early English East India Company Relations with India." *Past and Present* 88 (1980): 70–87.

Weider, F. C. *De Reis van Mahu en De Cordes door de Straat van Magalhães naar Zuid-America en Japan, 1598–1600*. 3 vols. The Hague: Martinus Nijhoff, 1923.

White, James. "State Growth and Popular Protest in Tokugawa Japan," *Journal of Japanese Studies* 14, no. 1 (Winter 1988): 1–25.

Widjojo, Muridan Satrio. *The revolt of Prince Nuku: Cross-cultural Alliance-Making in Maluku, c. 1780–1810*. Leiden: Brill, 2009.

Wigen, Kären. "Mapping Early Modernity: Geographical Meditations on a Comparative Concept." *Early Modern Japan: An Interdisciplinary Journal* 5, no. 2 (December 1995): 1–13.

———. "Japanese Perspectives on the Time/Space of 'Early Modernity.'" Paper presented at the XIX International Congress of Historical Sciences, Oslo, August 2007.

Wills, John E. Jr. "Ch'ing Relations with the Dutch, 1662–1690." In *The Chinese World Order*. Ed. John. K. Fairbank. Cambridge: Harvard University Press, 1968.

———. *Pepper, Guns, and Parleys: The Dutch East India Company and China, 1622–1681*. Cambridge: Harvard University Press, 1974.

———. *Embassies and Illusions: Dutch and Portuguese Envoys to K'ang-hsi, 1666–1687*. Cambridge: Harvard University Press, 1984.

Wilson, Charles. *The Early Annals of the English in Bengal, Being the Bengal Public Consultations for the First Half of the Eighteenth Century*. London: W. Thacker. 1895.

Wilson, Eric. *The Savage Republic: 'De Indis' of Hugo Grotius, Republicanism, and Dutch Hegemony Within the Early Modern World-System (c. 1600 -1619)*. Leiden: Martinus Nijhoff, 2008.

Winichakul, Thongchai. *Siam Mapped: A History of the Geo-body of a Nation*. Honolulu: University of Hawai'i Press, 1994.

Winius, George, and Markus Vink. *The Merchant-Warrior Pacified: The VOC and its Changing Political Economy in India*. Delhi: Oxford University Press, 1991.

———. "South India and the China Seas: How the V.O.C. Shifted Its Weight from China and Japan to India Around A.D. 1636." In *Studies on Portuguese Asia, 1495–1689*, 125–40. Ed. George D. Winius. Aldershot, VT: Ashgate, 2001.

Wong, R. Bin. *China Transformed: Historical Change and the Limits of European Experience*. Ithaca, NY: Cornell University Press.

Wyatt, David. *Thailand: A Short History*. New Haven: Yale University Press, 2003.

Yamamoto, Hirofumi. *Kanei jidai*. Tokyo: Yoshikawa Kōbunkan, 1989.

———. *Sakoku to kaikin no jidai*. Tokyo: Yoshikawa Kōbunkan, 1996.

Yonemoto, Marcia. "Maps and Metaphors of Japan's 'Small Eastern Sea' in Tokugawa Japan (1603–1868)." *Geographical Review* 89, no. 2 (April 1999): 169–87.

———. "The 'Spatial Vernacular' in Tokugawa Maps." *Journal of Asian Studies* 53, no. 3 (August 2000): 647–66.

———. *Mapping Early Modern Japan: Space, Place, and Culture in the Tokugawa Period, 1603–1868*. Berkeley: University of California Press, 2003.

———. "Silence Without Secrecy? What is Left Unsaid in Early Modern Japanese Maps." *Early Modern Japan: An Interdisciplinary Journal* 14 (2006): 27–39.

Zandvliet, Kees, ed. *The Dutch Encounter with Asia, 1600–1950*. Zwolle: Waanders, 2002.

Zhang, Tingyu, ed. *Mingshi*. Beijing: Zhonghua shuju, 1974.

INDEX

CPSIA information can be obtained
at www.ICGtesting.com
Printed in the USA
JSHW041712120521
14656JS00001B/86